HANDBOOK OF MULTI-LEVEL CLIMATE ACTIONS

T0314960

Handbook of Multi-level Climate Actions

Sparking and Sustaining Transformative Approaches

Edited by

Mark Starik

Senior Lecturer, Sustainability Management (Program), the University of Wisconsin Extended Campus, USA

Gordon P. Rands

Professor of Management, School of Management and Marketing, Western Illinois University, USA

Jonathan P. Deason

Professor, School of Engineering and Applied Science and Director, Environmental and Energy Management Institute, The George Washington University, USA

Patricia Kanashiro

Adjunct Associate Professor, University of Southern California, USA

EE Edward **Elgar**
PUBLISHING

Cheltenham, UK • Northampton, MA, USA

Published by
Edward Elgar Publishing Limited
The Lypiatts
15 Lansdown Road
Cheltenham
Glos GL50 2JA
UK

Edward Elgar Publishing, Inc.
William Pratt House
9 Dewey Court
Northampton
Massachusetts 01060
USA

Paperback edition 2024

A catalogue record for this book
is available from the British Library

Library of Congress Control Number: 2023930162

This book is available electronically in the **Elgar**online
Business subject collection
http://dx.doi.org/10.4337/9781802202458

ISBN 978 1 80220 244 1 (cased)
ISBN 978 1 80220 245 8 (eBook)
ISBN 978 1 0353 4448 2 (paperback)

Printed and bound by CPI Group (UK) Ltd, Croydon, CR0 4YY

Contents

List of co-editors

Mark Starik (PhD, University of Georgia) is Senior Lecturer for the University of Wisconsin Extended Campus, teaching graduate courses in its Sustainability Management program, is a Contributing Faculty member of the Walden University School of Public Policy and Administration doctoral program, and is the Editor of the *Journal of Social Change*. He has published dozens of academic and practitioner articles, books, cases, editorials, curated volumes and journal special issues, and other works on the topics of sustainability, CSR, and climate action, and was a founding organizer and a Chair of the Academy of Management Organizations and the Natural Environment (ONE) Division. Mark has directed several university sustainability-related institutes, centers, and programs and has advised multiple sustainability-oriented student groups. In addition, he has served in management and energy researcher capacities for a half-dozen US business, government, and non-profit organizations, has been an active volunteer in several sustainability-oriented organizations, and has provided financial support to numerous international sustainability causes.

Gordon P. Rands, Professor of Management at Western Illinois University, teaches classes in business ethics and social responsibility, and managing organizations for environmental sustainability. He has promoted sustainability in management education since the late 1980s, has numerous articles, book chapters and presentations on the subject, was a co-editor of two journal special issues on the topic, and is the co-author of the 1995 *Academy of Management Review* article "Weaving an Integrated Web: Multilevel and Multisystem Perspectives of Ecologically Sustainable Organizations." Gordon is a co-founder and past chairperson of the Organizations and the Natural Environment (ONE) Interest Group (now Division) of the Academy, and is a past president of the International Association for Business and Society (IABS). He previously taught at Penn State University and has degrees from the University of Michigan (BS, Natural Resources), Brigham Young University (Master of Organizational Behavior) and the University of Minnesota (PhD, Business Administration).

Jonathan P. Deason, PhD, PE, is a professor and Co-Director of the Environmental and Energy Management Institute at the George Washington University. Prior to joining GW, Deason was Director of the Office of Environmental Policy and Compliance at the US Department of the Interior, where he managed nine regional offices across the nation and seven staff divisions in Washington, DC. He has served as a member of the national Boards of Directors of the American Water Resources Association and the Renewable Natural Resources Foundation, and as President of the National Capital Section, American Society of Civil Engineers. He has received a number of awards including the Founder's Medal of the National Society of Professional Engineers as the Federal Engineer of the Year, the Arthur S. Flemming Award for work related to improving the nation's water resources, an Engineering Achievement Award from the Virginia Engineering Foundation, an Executive Rank Award from the President of the United States, and designation as a Research Policy Scholar by the George Washington Institute for Public Policy.

Patricia Kanashiro (PhD, The George Washington University) is a Visiting Scholar at Loyola University Maryland. She was a tenured Associate Professor in the same institution and served in sustainability-related roles at ABN AMRO Bank, Institutional Shareholder Services (ISS), and the United Nations – International Labour Organization (ILO). Dr. Kanashiro is an engaged member of her professional association: she received an Outstanding Service Award from the Academy of Management – Organization and the Natural Environment (ONE) division and is an editorial board member of the *Organization & Environment* journal. She received a two-year Fulbright scholarship to pursue graduate education in the US and remains committed to promoting her Latinx heritage through board volunteering service. She is a sansei (third generation from Japan) born in Sao Paulo, Brazil, and lives in Bethesda, MD, with her husband and two boys.

Contributors

Gabrielle J. Evans is a Vice President at Three Twenty-One Capital Partners, a middle market investment bank. Prior to investment banking, she worked at the public accounting firm Ellin & Tucker in the Forensic and Valuation Services department. Gabrielle holds a Bachelor of Business Administration, with a concentration in Finance, and a minor in Chinese, from Loyola University Maryland. She also studied at the University of International Business and Economics in Beijing, China as a part of her undergraduate studies.

James (Jim) Fox has over 40 years of experience in helping people understand and make decisions in a complex and changing world. Jim is the past Director of UNC Asheville's National Environmental Modeling & Analysis Center, where he led the group from 2005 to 2020. He is now a Senior Resilience Associate with Fernleaf. The NEMAC+FernLeaf team is known for its development and ongoing management of the US Climate Resilience Toolkit in collaboration with NOAA's Climate Program Office.

Lea Fuenfschilling is a senior lecturer in innovation studies at CIRCLE, Lund University. Her research interests are interdisciplinary, located at the intersection of sociology and science and technology studies. In particular, she has contributed to the development of a distinctly institutional perspective on sustainability transitions. She is the coordinator of the Swedish Transformative Innovation Policy Platform (STIPP) and a board member of the Sustainability Transition Research Network (STRN).

Megan Havrda, Masters, The George Washington University; Megan is an Entrepreneur and International development leader, who has worked for the last 22 years at the helm of both the social enterprise and sustainability movements. As Senior Vice President, Megan helped build Be Green Packaging from the ground up with its founders. In 2012 she co-founded The Adventure Capitalists. In 2014, she became a founding Board Member and Executive of Ellipz Lighting USA.

Erin Rae Hoffer is an Academic Program Director and Professor with National University, chairing dissertations, developing curricula, and teaching courses in public administration and business. Her research focuses on climate, health policy, and the dynamics of regulation and business. She has taught and served in administrations with Northeastern University, Framingham State, Massachusetts Institute of Technology, Tufts, Harvard, and the Boston Architectural College. She earned a PhD in Law and Public Policy from Northeastern, an MBA from MIT, and an MArch from UCLA.

Jimmy Jia is a Research Associate at Oxford Net Zero, University of Oxford, where he studies carbon accounting systems. He is also a board member of the Center for Sustainable Energy Visiting Scholar at the George Washington University's Environmental and Energy Management Institute. He works in climate finance, corporate environmental strategy, helping investors reduce climate risk exposures. He received his BS and MS from the Massachusetts Institute of Technology and MBA from Oxford University.

Michelaina Johnson, PhD Candidate; Michelaina is a PhD Candidate in the Environmental Studies Department at the University of California, Santa Cruz. She studies natural resource management and governance, with a focus on equitable distribution and access. Michelaina has worked in environmental consulting, science communication, and for environmental non-profits. She also wrote on a range of environmental topics, including groundwater management and climate change adaptation, for ten years as a freelance reporter. She holds a BA in History and a double minor in Conservation and Resource Studies and Spanish from the University of California, Berkeley.

Mukes Kapilashrami is Director of Operations at the George Washington University Environmental and Energy Management Institute, obtained his PhD degree at the Royal Institute of Technology in 2009 and is a recognized scientist in the field of nanotechnology focusing on advancing next generation zero carbon energy innovations. His research interests encompass carbon neutral energy innovations, international environmental affairs, and global climate and energy security. Dr. Kapilashrami's previous tenures include Lawrence Berkeley National Laboratory, and United Nations' field operations in Africa.

Sakib Mahmud is an Associate Professor in Sustainable Management and Economics at the School of Business and Economics (SBE) of the University of Wisconsin-Superior. He also serves as the Academic Director of the Sustainable Management Undergraduate Program. Dr. Mahmud's research specializations include applied economics with applications on issues related to sustainable and environmental management, climate change adaptation, and community resilience. He is a recipient of Wisconsin Teaching Fellows and Scholarship (WTFS) and other numerous teaching and research scholarship awards.

Osiris Mancera is a graduate of Johns Hopkins University and Loyola University Maryland. Their activism within the Latinx, LGBTQIA+ and environmental communities has shown through various projects ranging from workshops to direct community involvement and even film projects. Currently, they champion sustainability within e-commerce and plan to continue their education through a doctorate program in sustainability management. They currently reside in Colorado with their fiancé, Jim, and dog, Betty.

Andrea Neal, PhD, explorer, scientist, technology innovator, and entrepreneur. Dr. Neal has been at the development forefront of blue circular economy models for the monetization of non-recyclable plastic, blue-energy production, and financing clean-up of marine litter from the open ocean for the last 20 years. Dr. Neal has been a senior executive and founder of five companies, and received a Bachelor of Science from Purdue University, and a PhD from The Swedish University of Agricultural Sciences.

To start a new stage of his life, **L. Stagg Newman** earned his Master of Liberal Arts and Sciences degree and completed the post-graduate certificate programs in Climate Change and Society, and Environmental & Cultural Sustainability with Gerard Voos as his advisor. Prior to this program, Stagg had a 40-year career as telecommunications/internet technologist and senior manager of research programs. He also served as Chief Technologist at the US Federal Communications Commission and co-authored *Connecting America: The National Broadband Plan* created for the US Congress and Obama Administration.

Bruce Paton is Professor Emeritus at Menlo College in Atherton, California. He teaches courses on design thinking and sustainable business. Bruce has served as a Dean, as an MBA Director, and as a co-founder of San Francisco State University's program in Sustainable Business. He also chaired the Sustainability Commission for Sunnyvale, California. Bruce earned a BA from Wesleyan University, an MBA from Stanford University, and a PhD from the University of California, Santa Cruz.

Georg Reischauer studies digital strategy, digital organization, and digital sustainability at WU Vienna University of Economics and Business as well as at Johannes Kepler University Linz.

Cathy A. Rusinko is Professor of Management in the Business School at Thomas Jefferson University. Her research focuses on competitiveness, the business case for sustainability, and models of education for sustainability. She has published numerous articles in leading journals, co-edited a special issue of *Journal of Management Education* on sustainability in the management curriculum, and is an Assistant Editor of *International Journal of Sustainability in Higher Education*. She earned a PhD in Management and Organization at Penn State University and worked in industry and government prior to her academic career.

Robert Sroufe is the Murrin Chair of Global Competitiveness and Professor of Sustainability and Management at Duquesne University's Palumbo Donahue School of Business, where he translates the value proposition of sustainability and its integration with business practices. He develops project-based pedagogy within the #1 in the USA, and globally top-ranked, MBA Sustainable Business Practices program, winner of numerous teaching awards with journal articles and multiple books on sustainable business practices. His research involves Integrated Management and Integrated Bottom Line (IBL) performance, change management, high-performance buildings, Building Based Learning (BBL), and strategic sustainable development.

Markéta Svobodová is a PhD Graduate from the University of Economics in Prague, Czech Republic, and has been a lecturer within the Academy of Sustainability Management. Her dissertation research was focused on achieving and maintaining sustainability in organizations. Markéta also is a Sustainability Auditor at IKEA, conducting external and internal audits in central, southeastern, and eastern Europe, and leading sustainability global projects. In 2015, she founded a volunteer group (now NGO) RespON, which focuses on sustainability consulting for individuals and organizations and creating awareness about environmental sustainability.

John N. Telesford is a Lecturer and Associate Dean in the School of Continuing Education, T. A. Marryshow Community College (TAMCC), Grenada and a Research Associate, Institute of Island Studies, UPEI, Canada. His current research focuses on the implementation of the SDGs and climate change mitigation in small islands. His most recent book chapters appear in *Small Island Developing States: Vulnerability and Resilience under Climate Change* (eds, Moncada et al., 2021) and *Pandemics, Disasters, Sustainability, Tourism*, Emerald Publishing Limited, Bingley (eds, Bethell-Bennett et al., 2022).

Emily Thiem is a sustainability advocate and recent graduate of Duquesne University, where she obtained her specialized master's degree in Business Administration and Sustainable Business Practices. Prior to Duquesne University, she attended Brandeis University where she studied health sciences and environmental studies. She is also the founder of Eco-Friendly with Emmy, a sustainable lifestyle blog created to help young adults pursue an eco-friendly lifestyle. In her free time, Emily enjoys hiking, gardening, and reading.

Amy K. Townsend, PhD, was founder and past president of Sustainable Development International Corporation. She has written books on corporate environmental sustainability and biofuels and currently works in the banking industry.

Madhavi Venkatesan is a faculty member in the Department of Economics at Northeastern University, Boston, Massachusetts. She is the editor-in-chief of *Sustainability and Climate Change* and the executive director of Sustainable Practices, a non-profit she founded on Cape Cod. An author of multiple articles, chapters, and books related to the relationship between economics and sustainability, her most recent text is *SDG 8: Sustainable Economic Growth and Decent Work for All*.

Gerard Voos is an environmental soil scientist who conducted research on the degradation of organic pollutants in soils and waste materials. He is former director of a master of liberal arts & sciences program and co-created post-graduate certificate programs in climate change and society, and environmental & cultural sustainability. He developed and taught many masters-level courses including: *World Wastes: Issues and Solutions, Climate and Society, Sustainability through History: Colonialism to Consumerism, Environmental Literature & Media*, and *Communicating Science*.

Dennis West is a Research Associate at the Oxford University Skoll Centre for Social Entrepreneurship, where he works at the intersection of sustainable finance and governance. His PhD at Oxford University focused on how organizations across different sectors lead, innovate, and collaborate for positive social-environmental impact. He holds an MSc in Accounting, Organizations and Institutions from the London School of Economics, and a BA/MA in Law with Economics from the Universities of Basel, Freiburg and Strasbourg.

Acknowledgments

We, the co-editors, acknowledge all of our family members, friends, colleagues, acquaintances, and anyone else in our respective networks who have incorporated significant climate actions into their lives and who will be stepping up their efforts, at every level, to ensure our descendants and their co-inhabitants can experience and thrive in a livable climate on our home planet Earth.

1. Introduction to the *Handbook of multi-level climate action: Sparking and sustaining transformative approaches*

Mark Starik, Gordon P. Rands and Jonathan P. Deason

Welcome to our *Handbook of Multi-Level Climate Action: Sparking and Sustaining Transformative Approaches*! We are excited about this topic because the complexity and urgency of this issue make multi-level climate action both challenging and chockful of opportunity. As our volume's title suggests, we four co-editors, who have collaborated with one another on numerous previous sustainability projects, are interested in promoting human climate-related actions at multiple levels of human organization (from micro to macro) in the hope of *sparking* our readers' imaginations, sense of responsibility, and enjoyment regarding the long-term benefits of evolving a more *sustainable* relationship with our planet's (and our only) climate. Nearly two dozen of our author colleagues, hailing from multiple countries and disciplines, have contributed chapters that address our topic from many different and informed perspectives. Their research includes numerous suggestions for each one of us on this planet to put into action, as soon and as much as possible, to respond to our collective climate emergency.

THE PROBLEM

That the climate and we humans and all other entities on Earth are in a state of emergency is in little doubt. The United Nations Secretary General's most recent of six reports of the Intergovernmental Panel on Climate Change (IPCC) announced that the report was

> ... nothing less than a code red for humanity. The alarm bells are deafening and the evidence is irrefutable. We are at imminent risk of hitting the internationally agreed-upon threshold of 1.5 degrees (Celsius) in the near term. The only way to prevent exceeding this threshold is by urgently stepping up our efforts and pursuing the most ambitious path. (Intergovernmental Panel on Climate Change, 2022)

Exceeding that level of climate warming will likely trigger a whole host of climate catastrophes in all world regions, including heat waves with droughts and wildfires, extreme sea level increases, melting glaciers and ice sheets, thawing permafrost, and ocean acidification, among other disastrous climate events, endangering the health of both humans and ecosystems, planet-wide, for generations. Even more recently (May, 2022), the World Meteorological Organization (WMO) indicated its estimate that a 50% likelihood exists that in one of the next five years the average annual global temperature will at least temporarily exceed 1.5 degrees Celsius above pre-industrial levels, the point at which global impacts from climate change are projected to become increasingly harmful for people and for life on the entire planet (World Meteorological Organization, 2022). *Given the scope of this monumental challenge, we co-editors are pleading for all readers and everyone in their networks to treat this colossal threat as seriously as they can and to adopt a whole-species action response at every level at which those responses are possible.*

As we indicated to our authors in our Call for Proposals for this volume, we are offering our readers an opportunity for academics, practitioners, and other thought-and-action leaders to develop and share their vision, knowledge, experience, and recommendations on what has become one of the most pressing issues of our time – the planet's climate emergency.

Governments, businesses, nonprofits, networks, professions, communities, households, and individuals around the world are increasingly recognizing the vastness, complexity, and urgency of the climate crisis. Ever-increasing and human-induced concentrations of carbon dioxide and other greenhouse gases in the Earth's atmosphere are now resulting in record global temperatures (both extremes and averages) and a full range of first-order calamities (which we are repeating for emphasis), including rising sea levels, shrinking glaciers, heat waves, increasingly frequent natural disasters such as floods, droughts, wildfires, and wind-related storms, and ocean acidification, desertification, widespread destruction and degradation of ecosystems, and decimation of biodiversity. Such environmental chaos also can trigger second- and third-order socio-economic disastrous effects, including armed conflicts, political chaos, massive increases in climate refugees, life-threatening and worsening poverty and malnourishment and other human health crises, such as pandemics and the spread of tropical diseases, and a wide range of general social and economic severe damage. The collection of evidence from researchers worldwide appears to point in directions that, unless as many members of our species as possible work together seriously, effectively, and immediately, future generations of humans, especially the most disadvantaged among us, and the millions of other species with which we share this planet, are fated to disastrous and tragic consequences, including extinction.

THE NEED

In addition, as we also suggested in the Call (Starik, Kanashiro, Rands, & Deason, 2021), although a number of well-intentioned global agreements and actions at multiple levels [including the United Nations Sustainable Development Goals (SDGs), the Paris Climate Agreement, regional compacts and emission taxes and trading schemes, national, state and local government commitments, business, nonprofit, and community programs, and household and individual efforts] have attempted to move our human civilization in the direction of climate sanity, their collective impact so far has fallen far short of achieving the results necessary to prevent our persistent climate catastrophe from worsening, let alone halting or reversing it. What appears to be needed is a whole-species multi-level approach to this cataclysm that requires the involvement of as many of the entities listed above as possible, both to enlist all others at each of those levels and to collaborate and connect with as many of those levels as possible in taking all necessary preventive actions.

Similarly, multiple professions and academic disciplines need to contribute to this multi-level climate action campaign to research, identify, and promote effective systems, technologies, policies, innovations, incentives, regulations, plans, structures, agreements, programs, and actions that can address head-on and hopefully blunt and eventually resolve the climate crisis. Our intent is for this handbook to provide a collection of informed and inspirational climate-renewing writings, thoughts, strategies, and practices that highlight what has been done, is being done, and still needs to be done on the many levels or scopes of human activity. In addition, we intend for these contributions to powerfully illustrate how actions at each of these levels can be harmonized with those at other levels, so that synergies are created, gaps are filled, and resources are shared and leveraged, all aimed at sustainably halting and reversing the global climate crisis (see Starik & Rands, 1995; Starik & Kanashiro, 2020).

The four main areas of multi-level climate action featured in this volume are: the Multi-level Climate Action Mindset; Multi-level Climate Action Education and Information Systems; Multi-level Climate Action Place and Pace; and finally, Multi-level Climate Action Economics and Finance. We thank all of our authors for their excellent research, provocative writing, and timeliness throughout the process of developing these excellent, thought-and-action-inspiring submissions. We also thank the staff of our publisher, Edward Elgar Publishing, for their dedication and efficiency in producing and delivering this volume. As you will see at the end of this chapter, we are inviting all of our readers (and anyone in their networks) to contribute their own ideas about what they themselves are doing now and will do in the near future to implement multi-level climate actions in their own lives and those of their stakeholders.

THE SOLUTIONS: EACH AND EVERY ONE OF US (SEPARATELY AND TOGETHER)

Numerous entry points into resolving Earth's climate crises are available to (and need attention from) everyone on the planet (UNEP, 2022a, 2022b), which is more than 8 billion of us and counting. Each of us who is physically and mentally able can start with one action – whether behavioral, educational, research, advocacy or otherwise – to help now and very soon look for an additional entry point (and then another). Each of us can do everything we can, at each point continuously increasing those actions which appear to be the most effective. Then, each of us can add another action and promote our actions and successes. Each of us can try to connect and synergize the different actions and levels and never give up looking for, starting, blending, and leveraging both new and ongoing actions. Each of us can try to make connections between/among levels and actions, both to assist others and to ask for assistance for maximum impact (Schlossbergaug, 2016). Each of us can use policy analysis criteria (such as administrative reality, political feasibility, effectiveness, and efficiency) and probabilities in selecting and leveraging each action for ourselves and for our multi-level network(s). Each of us needs to activate as many people and levels as we can as soon as possible. Each of us needs to research "emergency response," "disaster prevention and preparedness" and nudge, persuade, market (especially raising and retaining attention), and continuously scan for good practical climate action ideas. Each of us needs to tailor messages to/interact with different groups, such as children of various ages, cultures, and life situations. Each of us needs to learn from different spiritual and/or religious traditions, deal with the mass and social media, politicians, academics, doubters, and naysayers. Each of us needs to track climate-related actions and impacts as much as possible and publicize these as widely and frequently as possible, emphasizing primary, secondary, and tertiary benefits. Each of us needs to highlight our most visible/motivating successes and welcome/encourage others to follow our paths.

One of the most salient questions each of us can (and probably needs to) ask is, while we all can downplay our respective roles in contributing to the global climate crisis and in our restricted abilities to take action to effectively address that crisis, as several of us asked in a previous sustainability book chapter (Starik et al., 2021), *if not us, who, and, if not now, when?* We all can try to hide from our own climate complicity, but at least those of us who are adults and who say we care about the future (near and far) and about other humans (as well as other species) know that hiding from the Frankenstein monster we helped create will not "make it go away." We recommend that each of us ask ourselves (as we co-editors have done), how much we ourselves have contributed and are continuing to contribute to the global climate crisis and what more each of us can and needs to do to help resolve it. No hiding, no excuses, no more games of finger-pointing, just climate action, and in the case of this *Handbook*, multi-level climate action. If you, the reader, don't think you are part of the problem, we challenge you to use any legitimate carbon calculator, such as the Carbon Footprint Calculator at carbonfootprint.com, the Cool Climate calculator at CoolClimate Calculator (berkeley.edu), the myclimate calculator at myclimate.org or any of a dozen others, and honestly say it's not your problem. And, if you already know you are at least partially responsible for the global climate crisis and think there is nothing you can do about it, keep reading this *Handbook* for a plethora of suggestions on what you and others are doing or could be doing to join the effort to resolve our collective climate nightmare rather than ignoring it and excusing yourself of culpability. *Let's agree that our and your answer to the "who and when question" above is "us and now!"*

Why is this Volume Focusing on Multiple Levels of the Human Experience?

As several of us have advocated in our previous works (Starik & Rands, 1995; Starik & Kanashiro, 2020), focusing on multiple levels of human activity (from micro to macro and back again) has a number of advantages when compared to limiting human action to just one or two levels. One obvious advantage of a multi-level approach is potentially greater comprehensiveness in human problem-solving. Quite simply, more and higher quality information can be collected, analyzed, and utilized if more than one level of consideration is employed in any given task, such as when addressing the issue of human tobacco smoking. As a couple of us argued in a previous book's chapter,

> [A]nti-tobacco smoking campaigns often include attention to strategies that seek to influence: individual smoking behaviors (at the micro level) via personal care physician advice; retail organizations (at the meso level) which sell (or refuse to sell) tobacco cigarettes; and public policies (at the macro level) which promote anti-smoking public information and legislative campaigns (Liss, 2013). In this example, each level shares the science-based message that tobacco smoking is harmful to human health, helping to reinforce the overall anti-smoking message and behavior among and at all these levels. (Starik & Kanashiro, 2020, p. 19)

Multi-level perspectives can provide more panoramic views of human decision problems and potential solutions, including accessing and assessing the resources required and access points in applying those solutions. However, we also acknowledge that multi-level approaches can also have their disadvantages, including the potential of overwhelming human decision-making at any particular level; that is, complexity can increase when considering more than one level of a problem-solution set, which may require increased attention and management. In proposing an even more expansive perspective of "multi-level" than is typical in "governance" research, to include not only multiple levels of public organizations, but also individuals, households, groups, networks, and the whole of the human species, we are willing to risk the complexity problem in exchange for the development of a whole-species perspective on climate action.

To state the obvious, we live our lives on multiple levels and perceive multiple scopes (from panoramic or cosmic to microscopic) throughout our lives. We are simultaneously individuals, consumers, employees, investors, members of families, members of friends' networks, members of various organizations, and citizens of multiple jurisdictions, and we can take action in each and every one of these roles. One fortunate aspect (if there is one) of the global climate crisis is that the set of catastrophes can also be perceived and acted upon on at those same levels, roles or scopes. Even more obviously, our "global climate crisis" term embeds one of these – the global level. However, most levels, including that one, share a common feature – they are an accumulation of phenomena at lower levels. Global climate crises are accumulations over time and space of climate-contributing factors at the regional, national, sub-national, sector, industrial, organizational, community, household, and individual levels and at the levels of networks of each of these entities. Granted, sometimes phenomena at different levels can be offsetting, but, for our purposes here, we recommend viewing global climate crises as accumulations of all factors and of all sub-global levels. If we are correct in our analysis, it means that any positive actions each of us humans take at any level can contribute, at least a bit, to resolving those crises. For instance, the installations of solar photovoltaic energy systems on the family residences of two of our *Handbook*'s co-editors are helping to address the global climate crisis. Several of us co-editors have been involved in similar efforts to increase the energy efficiency both of our respective homes and campuses and of our transportation activities, again helping, in part, to address the global climate issue. And, we all have been involved in promoting climate solutions in our academic professions, both in and beyond our classrooms. Yet, as long as our Earth is experiencing a climate catastrophe, there is more we all can and need to do, and we expect and invite you to join us in that recognition and resolution. To begin, as readers of this volume, you might jot down a few ideas of your own multi-level climate actions, either present or near-future, focusing first on your own household's fossil fuel energy use, then that same type of usage as part of either your employer's organization or your local community (or both), and, finally the fossil fuel energy use of your profession (as a member of that profession) or of your local political jurisdiction (or both). Paying attention to one's own fossil fuel energy bills is one source of information and asking related questions of others at other levels is an additional possible starting point.

While each and every one of us has the ability to engage in actions that have significant impacts at multiple levels, we particularly invite and urge those who hold positions of leadership in private and public sector organizations to use their power (including to set examples) to do all they can to reduce their organization's and their supply chains' carbon footprint, and to work with leaders of other organizations to magnify their efforts by fostering systemic changes that facilitate rather than blunt pro-climate behaviors at all levels (Starik & Rands, 1995).

What Climate Actions have been Recommended in Research and Practice at Different Levels?

Given the ubiquity of climate change causes, including fossil fuel extraction, processing, and usage, deforestation, landfill waste, over-consumption, over-population, livestock farming and processing, industrial pollution, and ocean deterioration and destruction, it follows that addressing these causes requires a plethora of solutions, and since the causes exist on many levels, the solutions likely do, as well. Although several of us have argued that levels of human organization can be described in many ways, depending on culture and tradition (Starik & Kanashiro, 2020), for the purposes of this introductory chapter, we will limit these to micro (including individual, household, and family), meso (organizational, tribal, state, national, and local community), and macro (global, regional, culture, and network). However, we do recognize that the UN Sustainable Development Goals and their targets and indicators include mentions of the following levels:

> global (macroeconomics), "people everywhere," international (South-South), developing/least developed countries, national (expressed in number or percentages of countries), intergovernmental (cooperation), international development agencies, supply chains, transnational companies, cities and human settlements, local governments, local communities, social protection systems, farming/pastoral/forestry/fishery sectors, families, households, schools (and teachers/students), financial institutions, and populations (by multiple demographics). (Starik & Kanashiro, 2020, p. 26)

We also recognize that at least 10 of the 17 UN Sustainable Development Goals are closely associated with climate action, including those related to gender and the poor (UNEP, 2022a). Readers should therefore feel free to name levels (and classify climate actions) according to their own preferences and purposes, but, of course, however these are labelled, the most important aspect is that climate action be addressed at these levels.

Before we identify the special challenges and opportunities at each of three levels of human organization, we commend our readers to consider one approach that might be applicable to all three of those levels, called Community-Based Social Marketing or CBSM. Developed by author, consultant, and behavioral psychologist, Doug McKenzie-Mohr, this approach features some easy-to-understand-and-practice approaches in moving toward more sustainable human behaviors of many different types. CBSM especially focuses on those behaviors that can be changed, identifying barriers and benefits of such behavioral changes, and developing strategies that use social norms and diffusion, prompts, commitments, pilot plans, and evaluation (McKenzie-Mohr, 2011). One of this volume's co-editors uses this approach in modifying his own climate behaviors as often as possible with positive effect. For instance, as one very small micro example, this co-editor is prompted every morning to think about the impacts of climate change when he uses a "global warming mug" for his warm breakfast drink, since the mug, produced by the Unemployed Philosopher's Guild in Brooklyn, NY, USA, when heated, roughly displays a global map and how much land area around the world (a visibly significant amount), will be lost due to just a moderate degree of climate change. That simple prompt is often enough to nudge the co-editor to move one of his several climate projects forward that day. More information, including hundreds of examples, of CBSM can be found at cbsm.com.

Beginning with the micro level of individuals, households, families, small cities and towns, one set of researchers asserts that four climate actions that would be the most effective in reducing individual carbon emissions are to reduce airline flights, go car-free, switch to a plant-based diet, and have and encourage others to have smaller families (Wynes & Nicholas, 2017). Of course, many other individual or household climate actions are possible, including measuring and tracking energy use and expenditures, reducing waste of various kinds, investing in efficiency and renewable energy at home, reducing home energy use, investing in and otherwise supporting sustainable businesses, talking to family and friends about climate actions, biking, walking, and using EVs or mass transit and refraining from car engine idling, practicing the several "R"s, developing habits and practicing them consistently and visibly in turning off unused lights and appliances, and taking numerous other steps at the micro level (UNEP, 2022a, 2022b). One emerging popular climate action approach for individuals and small groups is voluntarily participating with non-profit organizations, such as Earthwatch, in conducting climate science studies at different global locations (Earthwatch, 2022). Yet another household climate approach is to plant "Climate Victory Gardens" which can help restore soil health by drawing down (absorbing) carbon (Green America, 2021).

In somewhat of a blend of micro and meso climate action approaches are the several thousand small-to-medium-sized businesses around the world known as benefit corporations or certified B Corps (B Lab, 2022). These for-profit businesses were established (and/or are now considered) to benefit both society and the environment and include a wide-ranging set of climate action-related criteria, including those related to energy efficiency, waste management, and the use of renewable energy. A number of such organizations have collaborated with one another within nearly two dozen regional groups (especially in the US and Canada) in order to promote similar organizations and values in those regions (see B Local Wisconsin, 2022 for one such group, which one of the co-editors helped form). In 2019, over 1100 B Corps organized themselves into the B Corp Climate Collective, each pledging to achieve carbon Net Zero by 2030, well ahead of most other business and public organizations (B Corp Climate Collective, 2022).

At the meso level of organizations and communities, including metropolitan areas, states, provinces, sub-national regions, and nations, many technological solutions have been forwarded to significantly reduce carbon emissions, including increasing electrification throughout economies, energy efficiency of buildings, transportation systems, and production and distribution facilities, advancing materials science, and developing and using more renewable energy, including many forms of solar, wind, hydro, geothermal, ocean, wave, biomass, and "green" hydrogen, relative to fossil fuels, as well as sustainable storage systems (USEPA, 2022). Two prominent examples of meso level climate action are, first, the Wisconsin Governor's Task Force on Climate Change which involved dozens of community and business representatives who developed 55 climate solutions, big and small, to help achieve the state's carbon-free goals by 2050 (Barnes, 2020) and, second, the Midwest Renewable Energy Association's "Rise Up Midwest" Call to Action for a Midwest (US) clean energy transition (MREA, 2020). The challenges at this level are that multiple stakeholders are involved in decisions such as these, and those decisions impact many more stakeholders than do individual decisions. In addition, entities at different levels often have different concerns and political power resources (Di Gregorio et al., 2019). Therefore, many more decision and resource inputs are involved in climate actions at the meso level, both of which can be time-consuming, which is a major challenge in addressing our current and near-term climate emergency. Time is certainly "of the essence" in this case, if it ever was in other situations. One global organization that recognizes the challenges and opportunities of multi-level climate action is the Global Covenant of Mayors for Climate and Energy, in which more than 11,000 cities and local governments in 142 countries participate, and which has developed and distributed *The Multilevel Climate Action Playbook*. This cost-free resource identifies, highlights, and shares hundreds of case studies and other resources to help all levels of government collaborate with one another on climate action (Global Covenant of Mayors for Climate and Energy, 2022)

Finally, at the macro level of global, regional, international, and cultural societal climate decisions and actions, supra-national organizations, such as the United Nations (especially its Environmental Programme in UNEP), the Intergovernmental Panel on Climate Change (IPCC), the Secretariat of the United Nations Framework Convention on Climate Change (UNFCCC), the International Carbon Action Partnership (ICAP), the European Commission Directorate-General for Climate Action, the Climate and Clean Air Coalition, the World Meteorological Organization, the Global Environment Facility (GEF), and the Small Island Developing States (SIDS) can and do play agenda-setting, issue-raising, action-planning, and implementation-coordinating roles in addressing climate issues. Specialists in multiple fields could assist in helping with those roles and the general public could both support their actions and communicate their successes throughout their respective networks. Many national governments can and do make climate-related policy decisions, especially regarding government-investment, regulatory, and subsidization decisions for both fossil fuel and non-fossil fuel development, efficiency, and emissions, so climate actions can be and are influenced by those policymakers and their organizational and individual supporters (and opponents). Combinations of actors at both the meso and macro levels are apparently engaged in exploring investment-intensive, ultra-technological approaches to resolving climate crises, sometimes grouped under the moniker of "geoengineering", several focusing on either carbon removal and sequestration or solar heat absorption dampening. Similar to the development and use of nuclear fission and fusion, these high-tech approaches may be double-edged swords, with potentially high levels of both opportunities and risks.

While readers of this *Handbook* are encouraged to play climate-positive roles regarding supra-national and national organizations, we want to emphasize here the possibilities of also interacting with non-governmental organizations locally, nationally, and globally. In the past decade, multiple such organizations have attracted millions of members around the world in an effort to energize those specialists and/or members of the general public who want to engage in climate action. In addition to many of the large well-known environmental organizations, some of the more prominent "macro" non-profit organizations that focus on climate action include the Citizens' Climate Lobby, 350.org, World War Zero, Climate Reality, the Global Footprint Network, Project Drawdown, Fairventures Worldwide, and Climate Action Network Europe, among many others. Once again, while these organizations also benefit from specialists in various professions, their respective "secret sauce" is a combination of energetic activists of all ages, races, genders, nationalities, ethnicities, and political persuasions and a highly motivated donor base, so readers of this volume (and their network members) are encouraged to seek out one or more organizations at any or all of these levels for potential "micro/meso/macro-level" support and energized climate engagement.

WHAT OUR AUTHORS HAVE OFFERED: THIS VOLUME'S THEMES

As we indicated earlier, we have identified four major themes among our authors' submissions, and in this section we briefly describe each of the themes and the authors, chapters, and contents within them. The four main areas of multi-level climate action featured in this volume are: Climate action and the multi-level mindset; Multi-level education and information systems; Multi-level climate action place and pace; and, finally Multi-level climate action economics and finance. In combination with and immediately following our volume's introductory Chapter 1, in Part I, Climate action and the multi-level mindset, we collectively re-emphasize the multi-level climate action theme of this volume to stress the critical need for everyone at every level of human organization to play an instrumental role in helping to address the existential climate threat we all face now and into the future. Since many individuals play multiple roles in society, such as citizen, consumer, family member, employee, and volunteer, we want to encourage each of us to take positive climate actions in each of our roles at each level (micro-to-macro) of our lived experience. In Chapter 2, "Public–private climate actions for the built environment", Robert Sroufe and Emily Thiem examine the 2030 Challenge, a public–private collaboration that has spurred numerous cities and districts to advance decarbonization of infrastructure and systems both in the US and globally. The authors also forward a multi-level climate action plan for cities of any size to collectively improve building sustainability performance.

In Chapter 3, "Goal-based development: driving climate actions and SDG implementation within a holarchic world", John Telesford identifies five holonic (whole-and-its-parts) levels, focusing on inter-holonic interactions and on goal (SDG)-based development toward a holistic approach for achieving both climate action and other sustainable development goals. In Chapter 4, "Motivations toward sustainability in manufacturing at multiple levels," Markéta Svobodová draws on the results of an extensive interview process to examine sources of motivation of employees for sustainability at multiple organizational levels in the manufacturing sector. Svobodová delves into the details of her findings that motivational levels do not depend on individuals' positions in organizations but rather on individual levels of personal conviction. In Chapter 5, "Content analysis of nationally determined contributions (NDCs)", Erin Rae Hoffer investigates the critical aspects of the Paris Agreement and identifies two overall goals – transforming behavior and providing resources – and two strategic multi-level governance factors – vertical coherence and horizontal cooperation. And, finally, in this Part, in Chapter 6, "Climate action: from multilateral negotiations to implementation," Mukes Kapilashrami reflects on the core objectives of multilateral approaches to climate change mitigation and examines the importance of multi-stakeholder partnerships, not only in terms of defining actionable targets and goals, but also in delivering actual results.

In Part II, Multi-level Climate Action Education and Information Systems, our authors forward multiple examples of the kinds of climate action that need to be ramped up and implemented as much and as soon as possible, again following the lead of this very volume. Each of the latter's co-editors has dedicated major portions of their respective careers to sustainability education and information, as have many of the volume's authors. Our hope is that our readers follow the advice of our authors and continue to develop and disseminate climate action information for the balance of their careers. In Chapter 7, "Multi-level carbon literacy in management education," Cathy Rusinko presents a multi-level educational approach that she labels carbon literacy, which includes a classroom assignment and relevant teaching resources and tools. In Chapter 8, "Non-formal sustainability, resilience, and climate-change education for professionals and life-long learners", Gerard Voos, L. Stagg Newman, and James Fox argue that non-traditional learners need to receive climate action and sustainability informa-tion when, where, and in a format that those learners can best access, leverage, and apply that information in their multiple roles throughout their lives. In Chapter 9, "You don't need a sign to protest: the rise of digital climate activism", Osiris Mancera advocates for digital climate activism as a means for personal engagement and connections between individuals (especially students) and sustainability movements. In Chapter 10, "Digital sustainability: tackling climate change with bits and bytes", Georg Reischauer and Lea Fuenfschilling explore the potential of digital technologies, such as big data analytics, online communities, and transaction platforms such as car sharing, to contribute to transformative climate actions. They paint an integrative picture that helps to advance our understanding of how organizations can leverage digital technologies to tackle climate change across multiple levels.

In Part III, Multi-level Climate Action Place and Pace, since obviously, on this planet, climate, whether benign, neutral, or threatening, is all around us on an ongoing basis, the authors in this part feature the tremendous diversity of climate scenarios our planet's species are experiencing or will soon experience, once again highlighting the critical and universal need for urgent and appropriate climate action everywhere, beginning yesterday. In Chapter 11, "Learning from city-level climate action planning," Bruce Paton draws upon his own city climate planning experience and climate action plans of other cities, in describing pathways to 2050 climate neutrality and making progress in those directions. He also highlights the roles of households, business, and state government in working with local governments on these plans and identifies entities that are either inhibitors or enablers of those approaches. In Chapter 12, "Multi-level sustainability from the perspectives of a developing economy: a case study on climate resilient communities of Bangladesh," Sakib Mahmud focuses on the climate action set of adaptation initiatives at different societal levels along the Bangladeshi southern coastal area and argues for coordination among those communities and their various stakeholders. In their very well-illustrated Chapter 13, "Multi-level climate action through circular supply chain management of ocean plastic," Andrea Neal, Michelaina Johnson, and Megan Havrda examine the global ocean plastic crisis, its relationship to climate-related emissions, and the several levels of stakeholders whose interaction could help solve both of these related issues. In Chapter 14, "The climate sprint: an agile process for catalytic collaboration towards a just transition," Dennis West and Jimmy Jia draw attention to the problem of *pace* in climate action that complements the more widely recognized challenges of the *scope* of change. They introduce the "Climate sprint model" to demonstrate the next decade as a ten-year program-ming phase of a 30- to 50-year roadmap to (carbon) net zero, thus allowing interim targets and phases to become aligned with long-term pathways.

In Part IV Multi-level Climate Action Economics and Finance, our authors focus on a key set of fields that are often associated with the realization of tangible human value – economics and finance. So it follows logically that, if multiple levels of human decision-makers in these fields are focusing on climate action, many of the rest of us may (and/or should) do likewise. In Chapter 15, entitled "An emerging multi-level approach to climate action in the US banking sector", Amy Townsend contends that the US banking sector is undergoing a significant change in its involvement in climate issues. She identifies numerous drivers of this change, including a wide range of actors at multiple levels in and around that sector. In Chapter 16,

"Harnessing the power of investors to drive climate innovation," Gabrielle Evans advances the idea of a Green Tax Incentive for developed economies to encourage individual and institutional sustainability investments, including those related to climate action. This incentive's possible impact on a multi-level set of economic, political, and social actors is also examined. In Chapter 17, "Culture, education, and sustainability: a systemic approach," Madhavi Venkatesan discusses each of those topics and their interactions, as well as the plastics–climate issue, connecting them to multiple levels of sustainability and climate stakeholders.

All told, we the co-editors think that this volume's contents exhibit a good balance between focusing on our central multi-level climate action theme and broadening that focus to include related social and environmental sustainability issues. We thank all of our authors and encourage all of our readers to contact them for further exploration and activation of their many crucial themes.

OTHER RELATED TOPICS IN OUR VOLUME (AND BEYOND) THAT COULD STILL BE ADDRESSED (BY YOU?)

While we are very pleased that our authors have highlighted a number of key multi-level climate action themes that we suggested in our initial Call for Proposal Submissions, readers and those researchers in their networks still have the opportunity to initially explore a number of other subjects to provide an even more complete picture of the multi-level climate challenges we face and possible solutions available to us. Here, we mention some of our primary recommended topics for further investigation and communication: climate impact scenarios, climate life cycle analyses, carbon tax/cap & dividend, the UN SDGs, the Paris climate agreement, enhanced climate collaboration/partnerships among networks of individuals, groups, and organizations, climate action and religion/spirituality, climate anxiety, climate lobbying/direct action, reducing overall consumption and/or population, climate and culture, climate and the arts, secondary benefits of climate action, climate justice, agroforestry climate solutions, drone usage, and the evolution of climate action over time. Of course, many other climate action topics could also be researched (and disseminated) including: climate justice, climate financial investments, carbon coins, various climate-related apps, such as personal energy efficiency calculators, registries of climate actions and tradeable (non-fossil fuel) credits, multi-level virtual tourism, potential vulnerabilities in renewable technology supply chains, and future uses of robotics and simulators (Girard, 2021). Perhaps one of the most significant multi-level topics that still needs to be addressed by climate action researchers and activists is whether the world's economic systems, especially those involved in its financial systems that helped create our climate crises, need to be questioned and reformed (Holmes et al., 2022; McKibbon, 2022), and, if so, how? Of course, the most challenging systems issue may be how we humans can best integrate our economic, social, and environmental sub-systems into one overarching sustainability system (Schnurr & Holtz, 1998; Santoyo-Castelazo & Azapagic, 2014; Folke et al., 2016). We encourage our readers to consider investigating these and related topics, to consider connecting them to the subjects explored in this volume, and to efficiently and effectively disseminate their findings and recommendations for maximum impact, as soon as appropriate.

Lastly, we would be remiss if we did not thank (profusely) our many reviewers, including each of our lead authors, and our outside reviewers, most of whom were selected from our personal/professional networks and all of whom have expertise in the general area of climate.

So, *thank you very much*, volume authors, and Eva Collins, Melissa Edwards, Ashish Gosain, Nardia Hague, Mark Heuer, Kate Kearins, William Knox, Ralph Meima, William Polley, Barb Ribbens, and Nicholas Hein.

A Final Thought (Cli-fi) and Three Requests: Your Letters to the Future, Ideas, and Continued Involvement

At the end of this introductory chapter, in addition to three requests, we would like to leave you with one last possibly provocative potential suggestion for motivating you the reader to consider beginning (or continuing) your journey in taking multiple climate actions, and that idea is for you to begin to explore a new genre in science-based fictional literature called "cli-fi" (pronounced kly'-fy). Increasingly over the past decade or so, numerous educational and entertaining-but-serious writers around the world have begun to produce novels, short stories, and screenplays focusing on climate change and how humans and others experience it, in our past and present, and how we/they may experience it in the future. Cli-fi characters and stories have ranged from climate migrations, through climate activism and preparations, to climate anxiety, geoengineering, and militarization. If readers are looking to explore climate action possibilities, this new genre is worth considering. You can find a full range of such recommendations by surveying the Cli Fi Global Report at cli-fi.net.

Finally, we have three multi-level climate action requests of you, the reader. The first is a "thought experiment" in which we ask you to consider writing "A letter to the future" perhaps to your descendants or students, about what you have done, are doing, or will do to address our climate crises while you still have the opportunity to take positive climate actions. Crafting such a letter may prompt you to upgrade your own climate efforts (as it did for one of our co-editors), perhaps along the lines of those actions suggested by our authors. Second, we invite all of our readers to communicate their intentions, their commitments, and their own actual solutions to addressing climate crises which they are implementing at one level or another. Please send your suggestions and your "Letters to the future" to the lead co-editor, Mark Starik, at mark.starik@gmail.com, who, with your permission, will collect and disseminate them in future publications, videos, and social media projects (with full credit to their respective authors, of course) and who will communicate individual responses of thanks to each reader who participates in either project. (He will also share his own "Letter to the future" and any collected multi-level climate actions with any reader who requests them). Third, we invite you to select from the list of excellent climate resources at the very end of this chapter to continue your climate action reading. In closing, we want to thank you for investing your time and attention on our volume, for promoting it throughout your networks, and also for indulging us in our final three requests. Let's hope our collective "Letters to the future", our respective initiating actions, and our further self-education and implementation efforts will be successful climate-action motivators for us all.

REFERENCES

Barnes, M. 2020. We must take climate change action now for future generations. *The Captimes.com*, December 16. p. 36.
B Corp Climate Collective. 2022. www.bcorpclimatecollective.org/about, accessed May 27.

B Lab. 2022. usca.bcorporation.net/benefit-corporation/?gclid=CjwKCAjw7cGUBhA9EiwArBAvolse ewNL8I3b5c-jdOajJncz1lg-4dt8d_P71pob_WnO98XFNJgmMhoCgcQQAvD_BwE, accessed May 27.

B Local Wisconsin. 2022. www.blocalwisconsin.org, accessed May 27.

Di Gregorio, M., Fatorelli, L., Paavola, J., Pramova, E., Nurrochmat, D.R., May, P.H., Brockhaus, M., Sari, I.M., & Kusumadewi, S.D. 2019. Multi-level governance and power in climate change policy networks. *Global Environmental Change*, 54, 64–77.

Earthwatch. 2022. *Earthwatch: Climate change at the Arctic's edge – EducationNC (ednc.org)*, accessed April 20.

Folke, C., Biggs, R., Norstrom, A.V., Reyers, B., & Rockstrom, J. 2016. Social-ecological resilience and biosphere-based sustainability science. *Ecology and Society*, 21(3), 41. http://dx.doi.org/10.5751/ES -08748-21034.

Girard, S. 2021. Madison West students tackle climate change with simulator activity. *The Cap Times*, September 1. p. 5.

Global Covenant of Mayors for Climate and Energy. 2022. *The Multilevel Climate Action Playbook for Local and Regional Governments*. www.globalcovenantofmayors.org/press/the-multilevel -climate-action-playbook-for-local-and-regional-governments/#:~:text=led%20by%20Parties .-,The%20Multilevel%20Climate%20Action%20Playbook%20for%20Local%20and%20Regional %20Governments,NDC%20implementation%20and%20investment%20plans, accessed May 22.

Green America. 2021. Climate victory gardens. www.greenamerica.org/climate-victory-gardens, accessed May 29 2021.

Holmes, R.M., Waldman, D.A., Siegel, D., & Pape, J. 2022. Declining trust in capitalism: Managerial, research, and public policy implications. *Academy of Management Perspectives*, May. https:doi.org/ 10.5465/amp2021.0011.

Intergovernmental Panel on Climate Change. 2022. IPCC report: 'Code red' for human driven global heating, warns UN chief. *UN News*, accessed January 24 2022.

Liss, S. M. 2013. CDC's anti-smoking ad campaign spurred over 100,000 smokers to quit: Media campaigns must be expanded nationally and in the states. https://www.tobaccofreekids.org/press-releases/ 2013_09_09_cdc, accessed May 22, 2019.

McKenzie-Mohr, D. 2011. *Fostering Sustainable Behavior: An Introduction to Community-based Social Marketing*. Gabriola Island, BC: New Society Publishers.

McKibbon, B. 2022. Could Google's carbon emissions have effectively doubled overnight? *The New Yorker*, May 20. www.newyorker.com/news/daily-comment/could-googles-carbon-emissions -have-effectively-doubled-overnight?utm_source=nl&utm_brand=tny&utm_mailing=TNY_Daily _052022&utm_campaign=auddev&utm_medium=email&utm_term=tny_daily_digest&bxid=6091 4454c3515c40dd02c443&cndid=64955964&hasha=f50abce4a8a82d218073f47bd32d59bd&hashb =b6d18ffb4284ef2dfa568158e19d96e044ce78c4&hashc=320a06089dc6a8b0867205ce1909318250 871522f3ca0a3d4a349d1f99119a11&esrc=register-page&mbid=CRMNYR012019&utm_content=A, accessed May 20.

MREA (Midwest Renewable Energy Association). 2020. *Rise up Midwest: Our Call to Action for a Midwest Clean Energy Transition*. RiseUpMidwest.org, accessed May 24, 2022.

Santoyo-Castelazo, E. & Azapagic, A. 2014. Sustainability assessment of energy systems: Integrating environmental, economic, and social aspects. *Journal of Cleaner Production*, 80, 119–138.

Schlossbergaug, T. 2016. English village becomes climate leader by quietly cleaning up its own patch. *New York Times* (on-line), August 21.

Schnurr, J. & Holtz, S. 1998. *The Cornerstone of Development: Integrating Environmental, Social, and Economic Policies*. Boca Raton, FL: Lewis Publishing.

Starik, M. & Kanashiro, P. 2020. Advancing a multi-level sustainability management theory. In D. Wasieleski & J. Weber (eds), *Business and Society 360: Part IV Sustainability*. Emerald Press, pp. 17–42. https://doi.org/10.1108/S2514-175920200000004003.

Starik, M., Kanashiro, P., Rands, G.P., & Deason, J. 2021. Call for proposal submissions: *Handbook of Multi-level Climate Action: Sparking and Sustaining Transformative Approaches*, June 19.

Starik, M. & Rands, G.P. 1995. Weaving an integrated web: Multilevel and multisystem perspectives of ecologically sustainable organizations. *Academy of Management Review*, 20(4), 908–935.

UNEP (United Nations Environment Program). 2022a. 10 ways you can help fight the climate crisis. www.unep.org/news-and-stories/story/10-ways-you-can-help-fight-climate-crisis, accessed May 24.

UNEP (United Nations Environment Program). 2022b. 16 ways to take action on climate. https://www.unep.org/news-and-stories/story/16-ways-take-action-climate, accessed April 19.

USEPA. 2022. *The Sources and Solutions: Fossil Fuels*. US EPA, accessed January 29.

World Meteorological Organization. 2022. *Climate Update 2022–2026*. UK Met Office/WMO. May 9, public.wmo.int/en/media/press-release/wmo-update-5050-chance-of-global-temperature-temporarily-reaching-15°c-threshold, accessed May 14.

Wynes, S. & Nicholas, K. 2017. The climate mitigation gap: Education and government recommendations vs. effective individual actions. *Environmental Research Letters*, 12 074024, iopscience.iop.org/article/10. … 088/1748-9326/aa7541.

Some Further Recommended Reading on Multi-level Climate Actions

Andre, R. 2020. *Lead for the Planet: Five Practices for Confronting Climate Change*. Toronto: University of Toronto Press.

Boswell, M.R., Greve, A.I., & Seale, T.L. 2019. *Climate Action Planning: A Guide to Creating Low-carbon, Resilient Communities*. Washington, DC: Island Press.

Commoner, B. 1976. *The Poverty of Power: Energy and the Economic Crisis*. New York: Alfred A. Knopf.

Dauncey, G. & Mazza, P. 2001. *Stormy Weather: 101 Solutions to Global Climate Change*. Gabriola Island, BC.

Funk, M. 2014. *Windfall: The Booming Business of Global Warming*. New York: Penguin Press.

Gates, B. 2021. *How to Avoid a Climate Disaster: The Solutions We Have and the Breakthroughs We Need*. New York: Alfred A. Knopf.

Goodall, C. 2010. *How to Live a Low-Carbon Life*, 2nd ed. London: Earthscan.

Gore, A. 2006. *An Inconvenient Truth: The Planetary Emergency of Global Warming and What We Can Do About It*. Emmaus, PA: Rodale.

Gore, A. 2017. *Truth to Power*. New York: Rodale.

Hawken, P. (ed.) 2017. *Drawdown: The Most Comprehensive Plan Ever Proposed to Reverse Global Warming*. New York: Penguin Random House, LLC.

Henson, R. 2019. *The Thinking Person's Guide to Climate Change*, 2nd ed. Boston: American Meteorological Society.

Jaccard, M. 2020. *The Citizen's Guide to Climate Success: Overcoming Myths that Hinder Progress*. New York: Cambridge University Press.

Kalmus, P. 2017. *Being the Change: Live Well and Spark a Climate Revolution*. Gabriola Island, BC: New Society Publishers.

Klein, N. 2014. *This Changes Everything: Capitalism vs. the Climate*. New York: Simon & Schuster.

Lappe, A. 2010. *Diet for a Hot Planet: The Climate Crisis at the End of Your Fork and What You Can Do About It*. New York: Bloomsbury USA.

Lovins, A. 2011. *Reinventing Fire: Bold Business Solutions for the New Energy Era*. White River Junction, VT: Chelsea Green Publishing.

Monbiot, G. 2006. *Heat: How to Stop the Planet from Burning*. Sudbury, ON: Doubleday Canada.

Nordhaus, W. 2013. *The Climate Casino: Risk, Uncertainty, and Economics for a Warming World*. New Haven, CT: Yale University Press.

Pittock, A.B. 2009. *Climate Change: The Science, Impacts and Solutions*, 2nd ed. Collingwood, Vic, Australia.

Robinson, K.S. 2017. *New York 2140*. New York: Orbit Hachette Book Group.

Robinson, K.S. 2020. *Ministry for the Future*. New York: Orbit Hachette Book Group.

Smith, M.E. 2021. *Inspiring Green Consumer Choices: Leveraging Neuroscience to Reshape Marketplace Behavior*. London: Kogan Page Limited.

Starik, M. & Kanashiro, P. 2021. *Personal Sustainability Practices: Faculty Approaches to Walking the Sustainability Talk and Living the SDGs*. Cheltenham, UK and Northampton, MA, USA: Edward Elgar.

Steele, P. 2019. *Analyzing Climate Change: Asking Questions, Evaluating Evidence, and Designing Solutions*. New York: Cavendish Square.

The Union of Concerned Scientists. 2012. *Cooler Smarter: Practical Steps for Low Carbon Living*. Washington, DC: Island Press.

PART I

THE MULTI-LEVEL CLIMATE ACTION MINDSET

2. Public–private climate actions for the built environment

Robert Sroufe and Emily Thiem

INTRODUCTION

This chapter aims to promote reflection, and challenge thinking. It is a collective call to action to secure a sustainable world for present and future generations. We purposefully look at a private–public partnership in the form of the 2030 Challenge as an example of climate actions with multiple benefits. Established in 2006, the 2030 Challenge set goals of reducing the usage of energy, water, and emissions from transportation attributed to the existing built environment by 50% in 2030. The districts emerging from this challenge now have over 520 million square feet of commercial building space. Over 1,200 member organizations are setting goals to reduce energy and water consumption and are rapidly emerging as a model for urban sustainability. This challenge and resulting districts have led to the zero-emissions movement in the global building sector and has since been adopted by architectural design firms, states, cities, counties. Within this chapter, we take a look at the 2030 Challenge, the impacts of this challenge to date, and the new arch of multi-level performance impacts for a rust-belt city in the Mid-Atlantic region. We hope to take measure of the current state of the built environment (i.e., buildings) and systems implications and provide a vision of a future where buildings and cities contribute to a resilient future. Buildings are an excellent place to start as we spend over 90% of our time inside of them.

Partnerships with defined goals can be the key to creating lasting climate action. The 2030 District Challenge is an example of this. These districts have found success across the country through clearly defined reporting measurements and goals and collaboration between stakeholders. The key to success here is the collaboration between many stakeholders that hold each other accountable to keep voluntary action impactful, despite government inaction. This drives action in a sector that contributes to 40% of global energy-related CO_2 and 77% of total US electricity consumption. Thus, the 2030 District Challenge can be a framework replicated in other industries to create effective and sweeping climate action as government policy continues to be inconsistent.

The built environment currently plays a significant role in global climate change, but the potential for decarbonizing this sector is within grasp. Current analysis has demonstrated that it is possible to eliminate emissions from buildings by 2050 with existing technology (United Nations Environment Programme, 2020). Doing so will require substantial effort and investments to improve building temperature regulation systems, building envelopes, and a focus on zero-carbon retrofits and new construction. In Paul Hawken's book *Regeneration: Ending the Climate Crisis in One Generation*, he writes that "global emissions goals cannot be attained unless more than one billion older buildings are upgraded to new energy standards" (Hawken, 2021). Thus, decarbonizing the building sector requires a system thinking focus and an evolution in the ways buildings have traditionally been constructed. Taking on a task such as this may seem daunting, but there is a value proposition to do so. For example, market analysis in the US demonstrated that if $279 billion were invested in retrofitting existing buildings, it would yield over $1 trillion in energy savings over ten years, create more than 3.3 million job-years of employment, and total US emissions would be cut by 10% (Hawken, 2017).

Government intervention has the potential to ignite efforts to decarbonize the building sector. Still, we posit that government intervention is too reactive and slow. Take, for example, expectations every November at the COP meeting, and for COP26 dubbed by Prince Charles as the "last chance saloon," yet the outcomes appear to be incremental and fall short of expectations. Private–public collaboration illustrates the ability to proceed on a local level even while national governments abdicate their responsibilities on climate change. On a local level, further consider how often the worst buildings are the ones that are built to code, as outdated legislation has perpetuated the creation and existence of inefficient and unhealthy buildings. While the COVID-19 pandemic could act as a turning point due to the attention of indoor air quality improvements and the creation of recovery packages, this chapter offers an alternative that does not set the government at the crux of climate action but as a player in a more extensive system.

Public and private partnerships with clear objectives, such as those illustrated by the 2030 District Challenge, offer opportunities for agile climate action solutions that simultaneously foster collaboration of local stakeholders across the value chain of the built environment and climate action. For example, the 2030 District Challenge requires that districts include at least 40% property owners, 20% professional stakeholders, and 20% community stakeholders (Nordman & Killeen, 2019). This creates opportunities for diverse stakeholder collaboration to meet goals, inspires innovation of best practices that keep the community in mind, and creates change at multiple systems levels. When we look for relationships spanning inputs, outputs, feedback loops, ecological, social, political, economic, organizations, and individuals (Starik & Rands, 1995), it provides the context for multi-level (global, regional, and local), multi-system (climate, cities, buildings, energy, water, air, and transportation) opportunities.

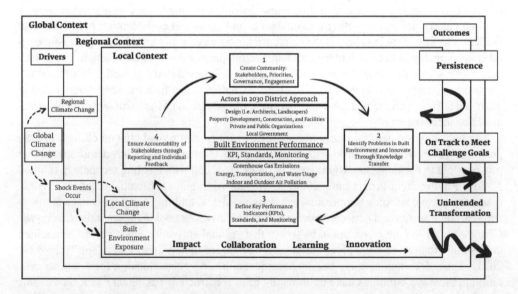

Figure 2.1   *Climate actions for the built environment*

As envisioned within Figure 2.1, the process of decarbonizing the building sector can yield positive outcomes when stakeholders respond to system changes and set action plans with measurable targets as metrics of success. The collaboration of these diverse perspectives and expertise can innovate higher standards and increase accountability for the group.

The successes of this methodology are evident from the 23 districts across the US and Canada participating in the 2030 District Challenge, which have already reduced energy consumption by 24% and water usage by 17% (Strength in Numbers, 2021). The Global Alliance for Buildings and Construction further supports multi-level actions such as this, saying, "To get the building sector on track to achieving net-zero carbon by 2050, all actors across the building's value chain need to contribute to this effort" (United Nations Environment Programme, 2020). The remaining sections of this chapter will focus on the impact and outcomes of this collaboration and its successes to illuminate the opportunity of other sectors to do the same to drive high-value, lasting climate action.

CURRENT "AS IS" STATE

When considering the current severity of the climate crisis, the impact of the built environment on both human and environmental health cannot be ignored. The International Energy Agency (IEA) reports that buildings account for nearly 40% of global energy-related CO_2 emissions, 55% of global electricity consumption, and 35% of global energy consumption (United Nations Environment Programme, 2020). In the United States, commercial buildings specifically consume almost 50% of the nation's total energy (Strength in Numbers, 2021). And why does the built environment have such a significant environmental footprint? There is no individual responsible, but instead a series of longstanding and outdated practices and embedded systems and value chains.

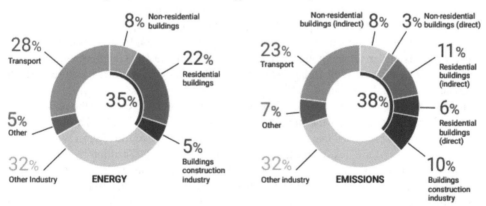

Global share of buildings and construction final energy and emissions, 2019

Notes: Buildings construction industry is the portion (estimated) of overall industry devoted to manufacturing building construction materials such as steel, cement and glass. Indirect emissions are emissions from power generation for electricity and commercial heat.

Sources: (IEA 2020d; IEA 2020b). All rights reserved. Adapted from "IEA World Energy Statistics and Balances" and "Energy Technology Perspectives".

Figure 2.2   Buildings and construction industry energy and emissions

At each stage of building development, design, construction, and use, there are opportunities to reduce the environmental impact from buildings (Figure 2.2). Take, for example, CO_2 emissions. Total CO_2 emissions are comprised of several sources, including construction (10%), indirect sources such as electricity consumption, heat by electrical devices, and the production and construction of buildings (19%), and direct emissions in buildings, such as fossil fuel combustion used for temperature regulation and water heating (9%) (United Nations Environment Programme, 2020). Further, consider the waste generated by the building sector. The building materials necessary to construct the built environment represent about half of the solid waste generated worldwide annually (*Annual Report 2021*, n.d.). By reconsidering the systems that create this impact, such as the carbon-intensive systems we currently rely on for heating and cooling, we can begin to unpack how to create a high-performing, healthy built environment.

These are critical systems to consider because of the projected growth of the population and built environment. It is estimated that by 2050, 6.7 billion people, about 68% of the population, will be living in cities, and an additional 2.5 trillion square feet of new and renovated building space will be required to accommodate the population (Hawken, 2021). If current practices do not evolve, this will likely worsen the climate crisis and many adverse effects on human health. Outdoor and indoor pollution is already a threat to human health, resulting in nearly 5 million premature deaths each year (International Energy Agency, 2021). Nine out of ten of us breathe polluted air every day. When we consider that many sources of indoor air pollution are from fossil fuel combustion necessary to power cooking and heating systems, it becomes clear that the built environment needs to transform (International Energy Agency, 2021). Only then can we begin to realize a world in which the buildings we interact with every day have a symbiotic relationship with our health and wellbeing.

Urgent action to decarbonize the built environment and invest in high-performance buildings is necessary. Cities are already experiencing some of the implications of climate change, such as rising temperatures, flooding, and increased intensity of storm systems. By 2050 it is expected that 1.6 billion urban citizens will be exposed to extremely high temperatures regularly, and over 800 million will be at greater risk from sea-level rise and coastal flooding (*Annual Report 2021*, n.d.). There is great hope in knowing that decarbonizing the built environment before 2050 is possible with existing technology. As the effects of climate change continue to test our current infrastructure, significant action by 2030 is crucial. Doing so can move us closer to achieving numerous UN Sustainable Development Goals (SDGs) such as Good Health and Well-Being (#3), Industry, Innovation, and Infrastructure (#9), and Sustainable Cities and Communities (#11).

The good news remains that stakeholders across the value chain recognize the opportunities and benefits of decarbonizing the building sector (Sroufe & Dole, 2021). The International Finance Corporation reported that "green buildings represent one of the biggest global investment opportunities of the next decade," estimated to be worth $24.7 trillion by 2030 (United Nations Environment Programme, 2020). In the US specifically, analysis by the Rockefeller Foundation and Deutsche Bank's climate change shop demonstrated that investments of about $280 billion now will yield more than $1 trillion of energy savings while creating jobs and reducing total US emissions (Hawken, 2017). While this may seem like a substantial investment, it is essential to understand that since 2015 the banking industry has already loaned and invested over $3.8 trillion dollars to the oil and gas industry, which is more than would be necessary to "retrofit every building in America to a zero-waste structure" (Hawken, 2021). Further, this industry gets $500 billion in subsidies globally every year. We know what global systems we have invested in over the last hundred years. The question is, what do we want to invest in for the next one hundred years? Identifying strategies and partnerships to help unlock these potential benefits will be vital to reaching carbon neutrality goals for the built environment and creating social and financial benefits for consumers.

While governments have a crucial role in decarbonizing this sector, we argue that reliance on their intervention alone is too optimistic as the creation of new legislation has historically been slow and unpredictable. Take, for example, the most recent rounds of Nationally Determined Contributions (NDCs) for the Paris Climate Accord. Of the submitted NDCs, 136 countries mentioned buildings, 53 said building efficiency, and 38 specifically called out building energy codes. Yet, only four countries mentioned putting plans in place to strengthen building codes after 2021 (United Nations Environment Programme, 2020). This indicates that while governments acknowledge the importance of building in their commitments to keep temperatures from rising above 1.5 degrees Celsius, very few have tangible or explicit action plans to realize the decarbonization of this sector. Further, in a recent World Green Building Council report, it was demonstrated that environmental regulations were the top motivating factor for encouraging green building. Still, simultaneously the lack of political support or incentives is the second-highest barrier to green building entry (Brady et al., 2021). While the government action has the power to spur change, relying on it as the sole change agent will lead to unmet expectations.

The COVID-19 pandemic may hasten government action due to the heightened public awareness surrounding the importance of indoor health and safety. Still, the exact implications of this are unclear. As we begin to exit the pandemic, the built environment can be an opportunity to improve health and stimulate the economy. From a health perspective, it is believed that about 1.6 million COVID-19 infections can be traced due to poorly ventilated environments (*Annual Report 2021*, n.d.). In combination with intense concern for workplace exposures leading to "work from home" scenarios, this fact has resulted in a hyperfocus on retrofitting outdated air quality systems and innovating ways to involve increased air circulation within buildings.

Economically, the pandemic slowed construction activity anywhere between 10 and 25% compared with 2019 (International Energy Agency, 2021). This resulted in about 2.5 million jobs being lost or at risk of loss in 2020, representing about 10% of the total construction workforce (United Nations Environment Programme, 2020). Retrofits, building renovations, and the new construction of high-performance buildings can provide economic stimulation by upskilling the construction industry and providing jobs. The International Energy Agency reports that, for every one million dollars invested in retrofits or efficiency measures, anywhere from 9 to 30 jobs would be created (United Nations Environment Programme, 2020). Therefore, government action such as recovery and stimulus packages provides an opportunity to increase the urgency for high-performance buildings, leading to health and economic improvements.

In the absence of consistent and robust legislation, there has been a response in increased action from the nonprofit and private sectors. These include the World Green Building Council, the World Business Council for Sustainable Development, The C40 Clean Construction Forum, the Green Building Alliance, the 2030 District Network, and more. Together, these organizations have created a lasting impact on the built environment and worked strategically with the public sector to create a healthier, more resilient, and high-performing built environment. Thus, this chapter will focus on the potential to drive rapid action in the built environment because of these partnerships enabled by the approach taken by the 2030 District Network.

THE PATH FORWARD – INTEGRATED SYSTEMS

From a systems thinking perspective, cities and buildings offer logical solutions to low energy and high performance. You need to look for and find the leverage points. Donella Meadows, author of *Thinking in Systems*, offers that

> a system is an interconnected set of elements that is coherently organized in a way that achieves something. Look at that definition closely for a minute. You can see that a system must consist of three kinds of things: elements, interconnections, and a function or purpose. (Meadows, 2008)

Buildings can be complex systems within larger city systems interconnected to produce a pattern of behavior over time. If you change the performance of the building envelope, the mechanical systems are impacted. For example, suppose you address lighting in the building. In that case, your final solution has a relationship between the windows and artificial lighting systems, which in turn impacts the heating and cooling systems. Simply addressing one element at a time can have significant unintended impacts to the building's function or purpose due to the complex interconnection of those elements. Buildings are also a pivotal opportunity to measure and manage ultra-low carbon intensity, movement away from carbon-intense energy sources, improvements in energy efficiency and climate action.

Meadows articulates in numerous examples that we cannot impose our will on a system. Yet, by understanding the systems relating to buildings and cities, we can monitor the system and discover how its properties and our goals can work together to bring forth something much better than could ever be produced by our will alone. When replacing a mechanical system or thoughts of considering a retrofit project arise, these leverage points or "triggers" can be used to enable changes and actions to move meaningfully toward whole-building performance. Because of the complexities of the systems relating to buildings and the difficulty of understanding such energy or mechanical systems without the benefit of technology connecting your equipment to dashboards, it is difficult if not impossible, to understand performance. Fortunately, the technology exists to model existing buildings to measure and connect those interrelationships. Using meters and sensors, and, more recently, artificial intelligence (AI) and the internet of things (IoT) to improve and calibrate building management has been underway for years (Sroufe et al., 2019).

Without the basic smart building infrastructure designed to provide feedback on the elements, interconnections, and a function or purpose, we find that building performance can be turbulent, chaotic, and full of surprises. This concept is not new to the built environment. Yet, most building owners and solution providers still attempt to improve the system by modifying the individual elements without respect to the system. More intelligent infrastructure provides an opportunity for building systems enabled by systems thinking. As Meadows established, the dynamic behavior of a system cannot be understood and controlled just by tweaking elements of the system.

Decision-makers facing the challenges of designing, building, improving existing, and managing buildings for a climate-resistant future must seek out more integrated solutions within the built environment. When owners, occupants, community, and decision-makers can see the whole-building solution and related performance, they have the confidence to address the planning challenges and implement solutions. This confidence means we can accomplish dynamic goals for the built environment and cities where most of the global population currently lives or will be living in the future.

Based on what we know about the built environment's footprint, energy consumption, air quality, system dynamics, and the science of climate change, the sooner we act, the more significant the impact and opportunity to diminish anthropogenic climate change. This is a challenge on a global scale and one that can be achieved with collaboration across socioeconomic sectors. Therefore, what happens by the year 2030 is essential. Fortunately, industry leaders, scholars, politicians, and activists already have a proven approach for changing cities and the built environment. This challenge is an intentional focus on buildings and what can be done by 2030 with existing technology. The "2030 challenge" has been around since 2006 when the members of the American Institute of Architects were early adopters and then worked with the US Conference of Mayors to approve a resolution adopting the challenge unanimously. This same decade was emphasized by the Intergovernmental Panel on Climate Change (IPCC, 2018) as some of the most critical years for reducing GHGs and limiting the detrimental impacts of climate change. Thus, COVID-19, the 2030 Challenge, and IPCC help to reinforce the fact that now is a good time to rethink the built environment.

BEST PRACTICES – THE 2030 CHALLENGE

The 2030 Districts Network represents a fraction of the potential successes possible in the built environment when local community stakeholders across a value chain commit to climate action. The 2030 District Network, currently comprising 23 "districts," is a voluntary community of property partners and sponsors who are dedicated to creating a "global network of thriving high-performance building districts and cities, uniting communities to catalyze a transformation of the built environment and the role it plays in mitigating and adapting climate change" (*About the Network | 2030 Districts Project Portal*, n.d.). To achieve this goal, each district has committed to meeting the 2030 Challenge for Planning goals of reducing the usage of energy, water, and emissions from transportation attributed to the existing built environment by 50% in 2030. For new construction, the goal is to be carbon-neutral by 2030. Through collaboration and accountability from the members of these districts, the 2030 District Network aims to make lasting climate action today.

To understand why the 2030 Districts Network has been successful, it is crucial to unpack what it is. The "network," which began in 2011, comprises a series of local "districts" that span North America. Each district is sponsored by a local organization and is made up of Property Partners and Sponsors within a specific geographical boundary, usually a downtown commercial area or city center. While each district develops its local standards for measurement and reporting, it is a ubiquitous requirement that all districts consist of at least 40% property owners, managers, and developers, 20% professional stakeholders, and 20% community stakeholders (Nordman & Killeen, 2019). As of 2021, the network encompasses 610 members, 340 professional partners, 252 community partners, 1,200 organizations, 2,400 buildings, and 520 million square feet of building space (Cieslak et al., 2020). Creating such a diverse network allows for insight into the complexities of the built environment. It provides excellent opportunities to utilize a system-thinking approach to solutions.

As was discussed previously, the built environment consists of a highly complex combination of systems that can make it challenging to innovate solutions without a systems approach. The 2030 Districts Network provides a solution to this. It brings together diverse stakeholders within a local area to collaborate and innovate solutions to meet the 2030 Challenge goals. Members of the district may include a range of members such as property developers, facilities managers, private businesses, nonprofit organizations, government officials, and more. By joining the district, each participant can access the wealth of knowledge, experience, and expertise that others have. In addition, the district can leverage its size to reduce costs for specific projects and tools and influence local civic leaders as a larger group. The result is a community of driven stakeholders who can view the built environment from a systems perspective because of community members' breadth and diversity of experience. Ultimately, by fostering collaboration and accountability from within the different stakeholder groups, we become less reliant on government intervention and view its role as an actor in a larger ecosystem.

Much of the success of the 2030 District Network has also been due to the collaborative nature of the nonprofit at the local and organizational levels. At a local level, districts are managed by local boards and wield influence over how they choose to interact, measure and report. This creates a sense of autonomy and flexibility as the district can decide how to govern themselves as they see fit. Further, the local nature of each district encourages knowledge transfer. It builds relationships as stakeholders are likely facing similar variables and experiencing the same obstacles that may impact their ability to execute change (*Knowledge Transfer Guide*, n.d.). For example, Architecture 2030 reported that several of the 2030 Districts are vulnerable to flooding. Therefore, they have also incorporated strategies focused on community and economic resilience into their operations (2030 Districts Take Next Step as Leaders on Local Climate Change Action, 2017). Thus, each district can use their knowledge and experience in the local area to support each other, innovate tailored solutions for their built environment, and provide each other with the measurement tools necessary to succeed.

To conceptualize this impact, let's evaluate two scenarios.

In *scenario one*, your employer has set mandatory objectives you must hit by a specific date, and returns to ensure you have met these in a year. Of course, meeting these objectives is up to you, but you know your performance will be measured in one year, and you will likely face repercussions if you fail.

In *scenario two*, your employer has set mandatory objectives you must hit by a specific date but offers support throughout this process to ensure these objectives are met. They provide you with baseline data, strategies that could be useful, introduce you to others who have gone through a similar task, and tools necessary to meet your goals. They will measure again in one year to see if you have met the objectives.

In which scenario are you more likely to meet the objectives? It is scenario two. Yet, when we rely solely on government intervention to address climate action, we end up with scenario one. Legislation is a powerful tool and enabler of change but often leaves actors responsible for change unsupported. The 2030 District drives change because it provides stakeholders with the community, information, and support to succeed. The objectives are not as daunting when approaching climate action in this way because we set ourselves up for success and have outlets we can turn to when we face challenges.

Two examples of this community approach were demonstrated by the Dallas 2030 District and the Seattle 2030 District. In Dallas, the district partnered with Dallas County to hold an educational session and tour of the Dallas County Record Building to educate the participants about the new building and how to include similar elements into their building portfolios. Doing so educated partners about best practices and the project's challenges and gave different perspectives on how to achieve the same objectives within a different setting. In Seattle, the 2030 district worked with policymakers to sign a new 2030 Challenge Pilot Program into legislation. The result of this legislation is a reward of up to two additional floors and a 25% floor area ratio bonus for developers if their project meets the performance goals of the 2030 Challenge for Planning (Strength in Numbers, 2021). These activities and successes can be found across the 2030 District Network and demonstrate the power of collaboration of stakeholders across the value chain. By sharing knowledge and access to resources, these districts have affected change across every level of the building process and considered the effects of different impacts on the entire system.

At the organizational scale, the 2030 District enables collaboration and knowledge transfer across all member districts. The network facilitates exchanges across the different districts, uses its size to influence national policies related to the built environment, creates national partnerships, secures reduced costs for members due to purchasing power, and acts as a central location to store and share data (2030 Districts Take Next Step as Leaders on Local Climate Change Action, 2017). Additionally, the centralized body provides toolkits to members that provide them with a host of discounts, measurement tools, project financing guides, and a wealth of resources to help them reach their goals.

Overall, the 2030 Districts Network has made substantial progress since creating the first district in 2011. The most recent reports revealed that there had been a 24% decrease in energy consumption and a 17% decrease in water consumption compared with the initial baseline for the entire 2030 Districts Network (Strength in Numbers, 2021). Although there still is a long way to go to 2030, as energy consumption is nearly halfway to its target of 50% reduction and water usage is about one-third of the way there, it is essential to acknowledge the network's successes. The data reported from the larger organization is an aggregate of all the district data. In 2017, there were only 16 districts, meaning that nearly one-third of the districts involved in the network have made substantial progress in the last four years.

When comparing organizational success to local success, an even more promising picture appears. For example, the Cincinnati 2030 District, which was established in 2018, has already reached a 30.4% reduction in energy compared with the baseline (Green Umbrella Regional Sustainability Alliance, 2020). Additionally, Pittsburgh, the largest 2030 District, has reached a 42.1% reduction in water compared with its initial baseline (Cieslak et al., 2020). Therefore, to understand how the 2030 Districts Network is transforming North America more specifically, we need to explore the impacts at the local level.

Case Study Example – Pittsburgh

An example of multi-level and multi-system collaborative success is the largest 2030 District in the US, in Pittsburgh, Pennsylvania. Once known for the steel industry that dominated the rust-belt city's economy, Pittsburgh is now transforming its industrial reputation into one of a healthy, resilient city. This is a unique challenge for the city as Pittsburgh experiences one of the highest energy burdens in the US. The built environment represents the vast majority of the city's greenhouse gas emissions at 81% (Pittsburgh's Climate Action Plan, Chapter 3; City of Pittsburgh, 2019. https://pittsburghpa.gov/dcp/climate-action-plan#). Pittsburgh is dedicated to addressing these issues with 550 buildings, representing 86 million square feet and 130 partners engaged in the 2030 district. The cumulative impact of this district thus far includes over 1,850,000 metric tons of carbon dioxide avoided, a reduction of total energy use by 28.9%, and a reduction of total water usage by 42.1%. In total, these reductions equate to a financial saving of $205.8 million. In 2020 alone, the district avoided 304,132 metric tons of carbon dioxide, equivalent to installing 84 wind turbines (Cieslak et al., 2020). While some of these reductions can be attributed to the impact of COVID-19, most are a result of its core tenet: community.

The Pittsburgh 2030 District attributes its success to the extensive community of property partners and sponsors involved in the 2030 District Challenge. To cultivate this environment, the district holds monthly meetings to invite policymakers, experts, service providers, and others to showcase technical expertise and success stories. They also encourage members to share the challenges they face in projects, best practices, and provide the community access to civic leaders and measurement tools. The District reports that this "forms a community of well-informed and purposeful leaders that have the knowledge to impact building development and operations throughout the region positively" (Cieslak et al., 2020). Creating an environment such as this provides the support and tools addressing particular issues to inspire change, enable impact, and create accountability amongst the district members.

At an individual member level, the district goes even further to support its members by providing confidential, individual performance feedback. This annual feedback allows them to see their current performance and strategize methodologies to stay on track to meet the 2030 Challenge goals. Within this meeting, members can see how their property compares to others in the district with the same "use-type." For example, a medical center could see on average how it compares to other medical centers in the area. Doing so gives the property owner a realistic understanding of how their performance compares with others and the possibilities for improvement. This type of support is integral to driving climate action because it helps members understand their current situation, demonstrates the growth opportunities, and then lays out a customized route to meet the objectives.

As part of fighting climate change in the city of Pittsburgh, the goal is to reduce energy and water consumption by 50% by 2030. This goal can be achieved through improving the quality of energy and water use data, ensuring all new buildings are carbon-neutral, mitigating high energy burdens in vulnerable communities, reducing sewer volume by 50% from 2013 levels, and improving the efficiency of public streetlights and traffic signals. (Pittsburgh's Climate Action Plan, Chapter 3; https://pittsburghpa.gov/dcp/climate-action-plan#). By combining these different methodologies, Pittsburgh can transform the built environment to improve the health of communities and the environment.

As the City's most significant contributor of greenhouse gas emissions, Pittsburgh's vertical built environment provides many opportunities for deep carbon reductions (Figure 2.3). Improving energy generation and distribution systems is one approach to reduce GHG emissions. However, improving end-user conservation and efficiency will also significantly reduce emissions. In 2020, the Community College of Allegheny County (CACC) realized these benefits when they altered the settings in their computer labs, forcing devices into sleep after a period of inactivity. As a result, the energy consumption from the computers dropped by 74%. It equated to financial savings of $60,000 to $75,000 in savings annually (Cieslak et al., 2020). For energy source and end-use demand, Pittsburgh's building stock offers many improvement opportunities in the commercial, residential, and industrial sectors; strategies specific to each end-use type abound and have much opportunity to be deployed at a grander scale.

In October 2016, the City of Pittsburgh adopted a new Building Benchmarking ordinance requiring all nonresidential buildings 50,000 square feet and larger to report annual water and energy consumption starting in June 2018. The first step to making any reductions in building energy and water use is to get a better understanding of how and where those resources are used. Benchmarking buildings allows owners, operators, and tenants to understand how each

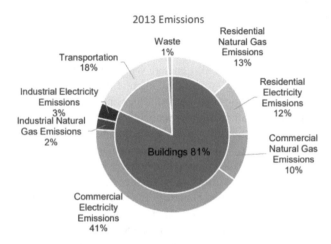

Figure 2.3   *Pittsburgh's GHG emissions inventory*

building is performing in relation to its local and national peers. This detailed benchmarking information can then help inform future decisions and investments, perpetuating cost and resource savings. In adopting building benchmarking legislation, Pittsburgh joined 16 cities across the US in requiring transparency toward measurable success. For example, in New York City, the first year of benchmarking legislation resulted in nearly 6% cumulative energy savings; San Francisco saw an 8% energy reduction with a similar policy. Since commercial buildings contribute 51% of the City's GHG emissions profile, Pittsburgh hopes to recognize the equivalent cost, resource, and emissions reductions (Pittsburgh's Climate Action Plan 3.0, p. 32).

It is the combination of Pittsburgh's public and public–private initiatives and commitment that help usher in a new era for the built environment in Pittsburgh. Together the resulting efforts present the opportunity to create a city of high-performing, healthy buildings that will only benefit the community and environment. As Pittsburgh looks to the future and its rapidly changing economy to a tech-focused city, it is imperative to transform the built environment to meet these needs. Ultimately, the 2030 Districts Network is just the beginning challenge for local stakeholders to imagine a new future for this industrial rust-belt city.

THE FUTURE "TO BE" STATE

Imagine a city where residents interact with and spend time inside and around healthy, high-performance buildings. With the right goals and planning in place now, not sometime in the future, we will realize a new value proposition from urban environments. There will be carbon neutral buildings, Passive House construction, WELL Buildings, and buildings that generate more energy than they consume, i.e., net positive buildings and Living Buildings. This built environment will be connected to smart infrastructure such as transportation systems, water, and energy systems in new ways enabled by artificial intelligence (AI) and the internet of things (IoT). Smart and sustainable buildings enable a future where environments do not just support our way of life with a focus on the lowest cost to construct but actually interact with and enhance our quality of life. Buildings have the potential to be connectors of social infrastructure interacting with occupants to improve air quality while bringing clean technology features, services, and information to a given location. In these environments, occupants not only occupy space but also engage with a place as architects help design the built environment as integral parts of systems and interactions (Carvalho & Macagnano, 2021).

This future can lead to interactions between buildings and occupants, creating opportunities to learn from and improve human health and productivity while simultaneously reducing the energy need of the systems that buildings and their occupants are connected to. Buildings are already moving toward this future "to be" state. They can be integrated like never before into the way we live, work, and play. A key element to help realize this future state is the setting of big goals. To this end, the Carbon Neutral Cities Alliance (CNCA) is a collaboration of leading global cities working to achieve carbon neutrality in the next 10–20 years – the most aggressive GHG reduction targets undertaken anywhere by any city. Examples of cities already working toward this bold GHG goal include Adelaide, Amsterdam, Boulder, Copenhagen, Glasgow, Hamburg, Helsinki, London, and others (CNCA, 2022). While it is possible for cities to achieve their interim carbon reduction targets through incremental improvements to existing systems, achieving carbon neutrality requires radical, transformative changes to core city systems. This is where CNCA is committed to a just carbon-neutral future that recognizes and redresses the disproportionate burdens and the disproportionate benefits of the fossil fuel economy. It does so by prioritizing climate action that advances the wellbeing of low-income people, Indigenous Peoples, communities of color, immigrants and refugees, and other historically marginalized communities and where cities of the future can make this possible.

Add to this list of carbon-neutral commitments those cities who have pledged to power their infrastructure with 100% clean energy commitments, and the future is already looking brighter. Over 180 cities, more than ten counties, and eight states across the US have goals to power their communities with 100% clean, renewable energy. These commitments – formalized in resolutions, climate action plans, renewable portfolio standards, and other policies – are the product of leadership from coalitions of civic champions, frontline activists, and Ready For 100 organizers nationwide. In total, over 100 million people now live in a community with an official 100% renewable electricity target (Sierra Club, 2022).

Over the past three decades, more than 600 local governments across the United States adopted their climate action plans setting GHG reduction targets. These pledges were in addition to America's commitment to the 2015 Paris Agreement, an international treaty signed by nearly 200 nations to limit the impact of climate change. But experts also say that many of those cities' plans were aspirational at best. Now they must work harder if they're going to curb the warming trend (Voyles Pulver, Bowman, Harvilla, & Wilson, 2021).

We also find hope and actions with a vision for a more sustainable future coming from the Resilient Cities Network. This network consists of 97 cities committed to building and investing in urban resilience, located in five geographical regions: Africa, Asia Pacific, Europe and Middle East, Latin America and the Caribbean, and North America. Urban resilience is "the capacity of a city's systems, businesses, institutions, communities, and individuals to survive, adapt, and grow no matter what kinds of acute shocks and chronic stresses they experience" (Resilient Cities Network, 2022). Shocks can be single-event disasters such as fires, earthquakes, and floods. Stresses are factors that pressure a city on a daily or reoccurring basis, such as chronic food or water shortage, an overtaxed transportation system, endemic violence, or high unemployment. Urban resilience is about making a city better, in both good times and bad, for the benefit of all its citizens, particularly the poor and vulnerable. The network's programs build capacity and scale resilience and investments in vulnerable communities and the critical systems that serve them. Programs are thematic action-oriented initiatives that are implemented to build capacity through peer-to-peer learning and the application of resilience tools and practices and to support the design and implementation of urban resilience projects. Pittsburgh was an early member of the Resilient Cities Network and hired a resiliency director position in the Mayor's office to support citywide actions.

The most robust commitments establish a vision for a more sustainable, clean energy future and do this alongside a plan to achieve it. Cities are forging their own paths to reach 100%, setting examples for others to follow, whether by pushing utilities to switch to more clean energy, powering city-owned buildings with renewables, or prioritizing energy efficiency to reduce energy waste with community workshops and weatherization for low-income homes. We can all do this in our homes by choosing an energy provider utilizing renewable sources. In addition, many cities are banding together to advocate for improved energy policies at the state level to meet their ambitious vision.

While some cities have made great strides, others have yet to get to begin the systems thinking approach necessary to uncover value that was once hidden but now more evident. Committing to 100% clean, renewable energy, green buildings, or the Paris Agreement are steps on a city's path to transition – each is a great place to start, but alone a tragic place to stop. To ensure that its benefits are felt community-wide, those most affected by environmental injustices must be at the center of planning a roadmap for reaching 100% renewables, carbon-neutrality, and ecological justice. The communities most impacted by fossil fuel pollution are critical to equitably achieving this vision. Decision-makers and diverse stakeholders need an action plan for how to create community, identify issues and opportunities, set performance targets, and have goals for accountability in the future. While it is inspiring to see all that is happening, these visions for smart, connected, clean energy, carbon-neutral and resilient built environments, increased powerful impacts, and increased progress will happen when these stakeholders can leverage a structured plan for action.

A MULTI-LEVEL ACTION PLAN FOR THE BUILT ENVIRONMENT

We have the capability, technology, and means to keep the global temperature rise under 1.5 degrees Celsius. Still, do we have the will, and a plan? Developing a vision and action plan for the future is an exercise the authors are familiar with. We do this within live, core required courses involving action-learning projects and with MBA Sustainability students at Duquesne University as part of the No. 1 ranked MBA Sustainability program in the US. It begins with understanding a "to be" vision of the future and then thinking about how to 'backcast' from that future and take action to change the current "as is" state of an organization, building, city, or system. We do this every semester in our live consulting project with corporate partners,

NGOs, and government entities, and this approach applies well to the built environment and cities.

It starts with asking three questions:

1. How do you think buildings, cities, and systems in the future will be more sustainable and how will they be different from today?
2. If the population levels off at ~12 billon people, what building systems and technologies will be necessary to provide for this population while not taking more from the earth than they give back?
3. What kinds of sustainable business practices will be part of this future?

The ability to envision a sustainable future supported by an evidence-based understanding of best practices for any system (in this case, buildings) sets the stage for people to realize multi-level (Starik & Kanashiro, 2020), multi-system goals. Recognizing opportunities for a more sustainable future allows designing, improving existing buildings, and constructing new buildings that align with global goals for more sustainable systems and infrastructure, i.e., the United Nation's Sustainable Development Goals (SDGs). The World Green Building Council sees buildings contributing to at least nine of the 17 SDGs (see Figure 2.4). These goals are guide rails for action plans and opportunities for a more sustainable future. These goals include but are not limited to No. 3 Good Health and Wellbeing; No. 7 Affordable and Clean Energy; No. 8 Decent Work and Economic Growth; No. 9 Industry Innovation and Infrastructure; No. 11 Sustainable Cities and Communities; No. 12 Responsible Consumption and Production; No. 13 Climate Action; No.15 Life on Land; and No. 17 Partnerships for the goals.

Efforts within cities align with other existing efforts to improve buildings. 2030 is a milestone date for carbon-neutrality set by Architecture 2030 and the 2030 Challenge for buildings to be part of a more sustainable society. The 2030 Challenge provides but one level of action focused on buildings, cities, and connected value chains that can propel the built environment toward meeting the UN SDGs.

As we pursue sustainability efforts and better building performance, we need a new way of thinking to evolve from the business-as-usual way of doing things in the past. By simply starting with three questions about the future, we can set the stage for discussions and planning for integrating systems. New strategies using a more dynamic return on investment, i.e., return on integration (ROInt) and performance measurements during operations, allow buildings connected to energy, water, and transportation systems to collaborate, learn, and innovate (Sroufe, 2018). In addition, buildings can connect with other buildings, communities, and other actors to enable city level, local, regional and global performance and operations that are on track to meet Challenges along with global goals.

With a focus on SDG Goal No. 11, Sustainable Cities and Communities, we see access to safe, affordable, and healthy housing and air quality is paramount to creating sustainable cities and communities. It is irrational to think that this goal will be accomplished through only new housing worldwide. With over 60% of the world's population living in urban areas in the near future, existing building owners and developers of multi-family buildings around the world must embrace the tools, techniques, and mindset so we can invest in making old buildings perform like new while setting high-performance climate action goals for any new buildings. Further advances of this goal will require city policies, homes, offices, schools, universities, and the built environment, in general, to support sustainable building practices across urban

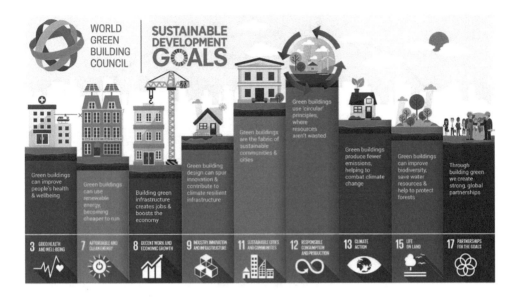

Figure 2.4   Action planning aligned with global goals

areas. Universities and their buildings can be living labs for best practices, carbon neutrality, and the integration of sustainability into curriculum and business schools (Sroufe, 2020; and see Sroufe, Hart, & Lovins, 2021). Existing actions contributing to this goal can be seen in the development of smart cities and registered living communities within the International Living Future Institute's living community challenge (ILFI, 2022) and all of the world's 2030 Challenge cities, Resilient Cities, and cities with goals of carbon neutrality. Tools already exist to ensure existing buildings are part of symbiotic relationships between people and all aspects of the built environment. Governments, campuses, planners, developers, and neighborhoods are coming together to create connected, symbiotic communities.

At a local level, understanding the current "as is" state, asking three questions, and capturing the outcomes from key actors will enable a vision of a more sustainable future. This sets up the beginning of an action plan, community engagement, opportunities prioritization, and thinking about governance. The key to success here is the collaboration and engagement of stakeholders that hold each other accountable to keep voluntary action impactful, enabled by government action. This local action and engagement drive actions in a sector that can impact 40% of global energy-related CO_2 and 77% of total US electricity consumption. If following the 2030 District Challenge guidelines, this engagement should include roughly 40% property owners, 20% professional stakeholders, and 20% community stakeholders (Nordman & Killeen, 2019).

The next step involves gap analysis between the vision of the future and any problems in the built environment or lack of innovation, the anticipation of climate change events, shocks to the system, and local impacts to systems related to the built environment. This builds knowledge of the current reality while recognizing that best practices and technology exist as part of a knowledge transfer opportunity.

Third, identifying key performance indicators, standards, and goals enables a plan-do-check-act approach to monitoring systems. The Global Alliance for Buildings and

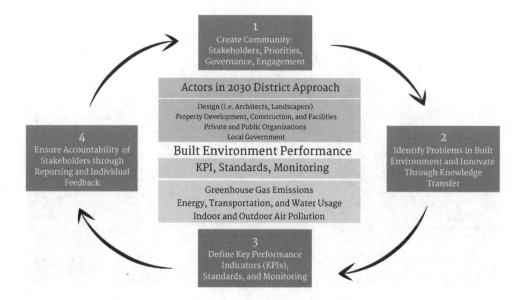

Figure 2.5   A multi-level action plan and value proposition

Construction support multi-level action knowing the building sector can achieve net-zero carbon by 2050, but all actors across the building's value chain need to contribute to the actions necessary to make this happen (United Nations Environment Programme, 2020).

A fourth action step looks at ensuring stakeholders are included in the measurement, management, and accountability processes and reporting outcomes with regular feedback loops. Performance metrics and progress towards goals are critical elements of any plan. The International Energy Agency (IEA) knows that buildings account for 40% of global energy-related CO_2 emissions, 55% of global electricity consumption, and 35% of global energy consumption (United Nations Environment Programme, 2020). These emissions and consumption levels set the bar for the "as is" state and opportunities to lessen impacts, show the ROInt, and provide the proving grounds for the value proposition necessary for changing business as usual. The value created forms a reinforcing loop of the action plan while revisiting each of the steps and outcomes regularly.

The World Green Building Council (Brady et al., 2021) proposes a multi-level value proposition as seven ways to identify value from a sustainable built environment. They find that seven themes consistently emerge in the financial business case and social value created. Together the themes outline the co-benefits that enhance the value proposition for a built environment. They are (1) the operating and lifecycle costs that include supply chains, construction, and the operation of buildings; (2) mitigation of environmental, financial, resilience, legislative changes, and reputational risks; (3) higher asset values linked to both performance and asset desirability; (4) return on investments, share prices, and increasing environmental, social and governance (ESG) requirements that we see as ROInt; (5) access to finance for green building funding and bonds; (6) the broader role of business in the development of environmental, social value beyond a traditional business case, to enable corporate social responsibility (CSR); (7) benefits to occupants in productivity and wellbeing. They go on to say, "you cannot afford not to be part of the sustainability movement – from an ethical, financial, risk mitigation or future-proofing perspective." The WGBC provides a nuanced way to look at the potential, and the value buildings and an action plan have to offer.

CONCLUSIONS

A multi-level perspective on ecological sustainability is necessary for many practical reasons (Starik & Rands, 1995). Support for the necessity of addressing climate-based sustainability at multiple levels is evident through both practitioner and scholarly literature on the topic of climate change and the negative impacts of human-made systems. In addition, there is a web of relationships highlighted by systems thinking, providing new opportunities for collaboration. These opportunities help us understand how and why high-performance buildings, entire cities, energy, water, and transportation systems, along with air quality, can be improved simultaneously through action. The phenomenon of city-level private–public climate action (both within and across cities) illustrates the power of actions on climate change. City-level actions help illustrate how much more powerful (and how much faster) progress will be when multi-level actions are included in policies delivered at a national level.

A number of well-intentioned global agreements and actions at multiple levels, including the United Nations Sustainable Development Goals (SDGs), the Paris Climate Agreement, regional compacts, national, state, and local government commitments, 2030 Challenges, Resilient Cities, business, nonprofit, community programs, carbon-neutral networks, and household level individual efforts have attempted to move civilization in the direction of climate stability. Paradoxically, as the co-editors indicated in their Call for Proposals,

> inaction to date across multiple systems, politics, and industries has fallen far short of achieving the short-term results necessary to prevent our persistent climate issues from worsening, let alone halting and/or moving us in a regenerative direction. What appears to be needed is a whole-species multi-level approach to this upheaval that requires the involvement of as many entities as possible to enlist all others at each level and to collaborate and connect with as many of those levels as possible. (Starik et al., 2021)

We think buildings, the places where we live, work and learn, provide an opportunity to engage and collaborate.

A purposeful part of this chapter is to push for more collaboration and advocate for connections through partnerships. Building solutions come from integrating and collaborating architects, engineers, construction professionals, community, and investments in smart building infrastructure. The UN SDGs provide actionable opportunities to strengthen global partnerships, to support and achieve the ambitious targets for all goals by 2030. This means bringing together national governments, the international community, civil society, the private sector, and other actors to show the business case for existing buildings. Despite advances in particular local, regional, and national areas of the built environment, more needs to be done to accelerate the progress of existing buildings. At a joint meeting of the UN Environment and Global Alliance for Building and Construction in Ottawa, a question was asked of Rob Bernhardt, CEO of Passive House Canada. The question: "What is the most significant development for building regulations and for enabling innovation?" His response, "The growing recognition that clearly defined building performance outcomes requiring the highest levels of efficiency, drive innovation and create economic opportunity. Such outcome-based codes combine efficiency and innovation to enable affordable, comfortable, healthy and resilient buildings" (Bernhardt, 2019).

Buildings and cities provide a platform and an action plan to solve wicked problems while exposing society to integrated management's dynamic new performance frontier (Sroufe, 2018). As Paul Hawken has said,

> We need to revise our economic thinking to give full value to our natural resources. This revised economics will stabilize both the theory and the practice of free-market capitalism. It will provide business and public policy with a powerful new tool for economic development, profitability, and the promotion of the public good.

With an integrated bottom line (IBL) approach to changing the built environment, environmental impacts, energy, water, and transportation systems, and air quality, the investments in infrastructure and what happens between now and 2030 have never been more critical.

When we reduce greenhouse gases (waste), conserve energy, and improve the overall health of buildings, we will have established one of the most impactful approaches to extending the life of our planet. Simultaneously, we will be providing an indoor environment for people, that irrespective of location, outdoor air quality, and socioeconomic position, should be healthy and high-performing. Making old and new buildings high-performance buildings is a matter of turning the traditional construction process on its head and using modern technology to shepherd investment such that every dollar has maximum impact on energy reduction and the improvement of indoor air quality. Actions taken on the built environment must be expected to improve the overall health and performance of that building, its occupants, and the systems to which it is connected.

Public–private partnerships can invest in high-performance buildings so that the places we spend over 90% of our time are healthier, ultra-low energy, and contribute to global sustainability goals. Climate action is an opportunity for performance improvement. Politicians, business leaders, and decisions makers can be enablers of innovative technology to apply to business processes, analyze data, solve complex problems, and lead change within any building or any city. Society will continue to demand more of its buildings, more sustainability across interconnected energy, water, and transportation systems, and more from the cities and places where people choose to live. Buildings can be partners in developing a more sustainable world, setting global goals while acting locally, and finding new environmental and social value in a more connected world. The information presented in this chapter is a call to action to further advance action planning, goal setting, collaboration, and multi-level climate action so that the goals of the 2030 Challenge and UN SDGs can become a reality.

REFERENCES

2030 Districts Take Next Step as Leaders on Local Climate Change Action. (2017, February). [Architecture 2030]. https://architecture2030.org/2030-districts-take-next-step-as-leaders-on-local-climate-change-action/.

About the Network | 2030 Districts Project Portal. (n.d.). Retrieved January 31, 2022, from https://www.2030districts.org/about-network.

Annual Report 2021. (n.d.). Retrieved January 30, 2022, from https://worldgbc.org/sites/default/files/WorldGBC%202021%20Annual%20Report.pdf.

Bernhardt, R. (2019). Personal communication between Craig Stevenson and Rob Bernhardt, United Nations Environment and Global Alliance for Building and Construction in Ottawa, February 21, 2019. Cited within R. Sroufe, B. Eckenrode, & C. E. Stevenson, (2019). *The power of existing buildings: Save money, improve health, and reduce environmental impacts.* Island Press.

Brady, C., Burrows, V., Al-Musa, A., Kawamura, S., Montano Owen, C., & Palmieri, A. (2021). *Beyond the business case: Why you can't afford not to invest in a sustainable built environment.* World Green Building Alliance. https://viewer.ipaper.io/worldgbc/beyond-the-business-case/?page=1.

Carbon Neutral Cities Alliance (CNCA). (2022). CNCA Alliance Members. https://carbonneutralcities .org/cities/.

Carvalho, S., & Macagnano, M. (2021). *Smart and sustainable buildings and infrastructure.* Deloitte. https://www2.deloitte.com/global/en/pages/public-sector/articles/urban-future-with-a-purpose/smart -and-sustainable-buildings-and-infrastructure.html.

Cieslak, C., Colao, P., Conrad, E., & Mendicino, A. (2020). Pittsburgh 2030 District 2020 Progress Report. Green Building Alliance. https://www.go-gba.org/wp-content/uploads/2021/05/GBA-2020 -2030-Report.pdf.

City of Pittsburgh. (2019). Pittsburgh Climate Action Plan Version 3.0. https://pittsburghpa.gov/dcp/ climate-action-plan.

Green Umbrella Regional Sustainability Alliance. (2020). Cincinnati 2030 District 2020 Progress Report. 2030 Districts Network. https://www.2030districts.org/sites/default/files/atoms/files/Cincinnati %202030%20District%202020%20Progress%20Report.pdf.

Hawken, P. (2017). *Drawdown: The most comprehensive plan ever proposed to reverse global warming* (First). Penguin Books.

Hawken, P. (2021). *Regeneration: Ending the climate crisis in one generation* (First). Penguin Books.

IEA (2020b), Energy Technology Perspectives 2020, IEA, Paris https://www.iea.org/reports/energy -technologyperspectives-2020.

IEA (2020d), World Energy Balances 2020, IEA, Paris https://www.iea.org/data-andstatistics?country= WORLD&fuel=Energy%20 supply&indicator=TPESbySource.

International Energy Agency. (2021). *Energy Technology Perspectives 2020.* IEA.

International Living Futures Institute (ILFI). (2022). See information on the living community challenge at https://living-future.org/lcc/.

IPCC. (2018). Summary for policymakers. In V. Masson-Delmotte, P. Zhai, H. O. Pörtner, D. Roberts, J. Skea, P. R. Shukla, A. Pirani, W. Moufouma-Okia, C. Péan, R. Pidcock, S. Connors, J. B. R. Matthews, Y. Chen, X. Zhou, M. I. Gomis, E. Lonnoy, T. Maycock, M. Tignor, & T. Waterfield (eds), *Global warming of 1.5°C. An IPCC Special Report on the impacts of global warming of 1.5°C above pre-industrial levels and related global greenhouse gas emission pathways, in the context of strengthening the global response to the threat of climate change, sustainable development, and efforts to eradicate poverty.* IPCC.

Knowledge Transfer Guide. (n.d.). BC Public Service Agency and Human Resources Community. Retrieved November 20, 2021, from https://www2.gov.bc.ca/assets/gov/careers/managers -supervisors/knowledge-transfer/knowledge_transfer_manager_guide.pdf.

Meadows, D. (2008). *Thinking in systems: A primer.* White River Junction, Vermont: Greenleaf Publishing, p. 327.

Nordman, E., & Killeen, R. (2019). Analyzing voluntary 2030 District energy programs using the Institutional Analysis and Development framework. Prepared for delivery at the Workshop on the Ostrom Workshop (WOW6) conference, Indiana University, Bloomington, June 19–21.

Resilient Cities Network. (2022). Connecting a city-led network. https://resilientcitiesnetwork.org/#.

Sierra Club. (2022). Committed. https://www.sierraclub.org/ready-for-100/commitments.

Sroufe, R. (2018). *Integrated management: How sustainability creates value for any business.* Emerald Group Publishing.

Sroufe, R. (2020). Business schools as living labs: Advancing sustainability in management education. *Journal of Management Education,* 44(6), 726–765.

Sroufe, R., & Dole, K. (2021). Operations management at the crossroads of innovation, sustainability, and the built environment. In T. Maak, N. Pless, M. Orlitzky and S. Sandhu (eds), *Routledge companion guide to corporate social responsibility,* Chapter 20. Routledge.

Sroufe, R., Hart, S. L., & Lovins, H. (2021). Transforming business education: 21st century sustainable MBA programs. *Journal of Management for Global Sustainability*, 9(1).

Sroufe, R., Stevenson, C.E., & Eckenrode, B. (2019). *The power of existing buildings: Save money, improve health, and reduce environmental impacts*. Island Press.

Starik, M., & Kanashiro, P. (2020). Advancing a multi-level sustainability management theory. In D. Wasieleski & J. Weber (eds), *Business and society 360 Part IV Sustainability*. Emerald Press. June 17–42. https://doi.org/10.1108/S2514-175920200000004003.

Starik, M., Kanashiro, P., Rands, G. P., and Deason, J. (2021). Call for proposal submissions – *Handbook of multi-level climate action: Sparking and sustaining transformative approaches*, pp. 1–2. June 19.

Starik, M., & Rands, G. P. (1995). Weaving an integrated web: Multilevel and multisystem perspectives of ecologically sustainable organizations. *Academy of Management Review*, 20(4), 908–935.

Strength in Numbers. (2021). *2030 Districts Network*.

United Nations Environment Programme. (2020). *2020 global status report for buildings and construction: Towards a zero-emission, efficient and resilient buildings and construction sector*. Nairobi with embedded sources for Figure 2.2 including; IEA (2019a), Energy Efficiency 2019, IEA, Paris https://www.iea.org/reports/energy-efficiency-2019 and IEA (2020b), World Energy Balances 2020, IEA, Paris https://www.iea.org/dataandstatistics?country=WORLD&fuel=Energy%20supply&indicator=TPESbySource.

Voyles Pulver, D., Bowman, S., Harvilla, B., & Wilson, J. (2021). Hundreds of U.S. cities adopted climate plans. Few have met them, but it's not too late. https://www.usatoday.com/story/news/investigations/2021/08/10/hundreds-u-s-cities-already-adopted-climate-plans-what-happened/5541049001/

3. Goal-based development: driving climate actions and sustainable development goals implementation within a holarchic model

John N. Telesford

LIST OF ABBREVIATIONS AND ACRONYMS

ACC	Anthropogenic Climate Change
AOSIS	Alliance of Small Island States
5Cs	Caribbean Community Climate Change Center
CARICOM	Caribbean Community
CCREEE	Caribbean Center for Renewable Energy and Energy Efficiency
COP	Conference of the Parties
GRENLEC	Grenada Electricity Company
IPCC	Inter-governmental Panel on Climate Change
LUCELEC	St. Lucia Electricity Company
NDC	Nationally Determined Contribution
OT	Overseas Territories
SDGs	Sustainable Development Goals
SIDS	Small Island Developing State
SIS	Small Island State
SNIJ	Sub-national Island Jurisdiction
UK	United Kingdom
UNFCCC	United Nations Framework Convention on Climate Change
VNR	Voluntary National Review

INTRODUCTION

Two hallmark events occurred in 2015 – the Paris Agreement, which called for all Nations to voluntarily commit to mitigate climate change by publicly declaring Nationally Determined Contributions (NDCs) (UN, 2015) and the United Nations Conference on Sustainable Development, where 193 Nations agreed to the global sustainable development agenda, 2030, driven by 17 sustainable development goals (SDGs). Among the SDGs is SDG-13 'take urgent action to combat climate change and its impacts' (climate action) and SDG 7 'ensure access to affordable, reliable, sustainable and modern energy for all'. Moreover, the intent of the NDCs is to demonstrate how the countries will mitigate climate change by systemically reducing greenhouse gases, from sectors such as energy. In this regard, Dzebo et al. (2018, p. 2) conducted an analysis of interactions between the SDGs and the NDCs, and found that:

"from the perspective of the NDCs, the SDG themes with the strongest synergistic connections included energy…". This proposed climate change mitigation/SDGs interface or "SDG-NDC connection", focuses this chapter on actions to mitigate climate change, while simultaneously meeting relevant SDGs (Dzebo et al., 2018, p. 2).

In this regard, a holarchic multilevel model is used to demonstrate an approach for identifying and analyzing interactions among actors and actions at this interface. The outcome is, to understand how these actions flow up and down the levels and integrate as a whole. Individuals, levels of government and organizations are recognized at multilevels where possible actions can occur (e.g. Starik and Rands, 1995). Chertow et al. (2020), proposed a holarchic system of the Hawaiian Islands in the context of physical flows of materials at holonic levels or holons (to be defined in subsequent sections). This holarchic system is re-conceptualized and adapted as five interacting holons: individuals; public and private organizations; island nation/territory government; inter-island organization, e.g. CARICOM; and global organization (United Nations organizations). It must be noted that the holarchic system can be re-defined for various contexts, but what is important are interactions within and more importantly between holons, thus offering a whole analytical frame. The holarchic multilevel model, referred to hereafter as the 'model', is applied in the case region of the Caribbean Community (CARICOM). The main goals of the analysis therefore, were to: (1) critically analyze actions within and between the holonic levels and (2) propose the idea of goal-based development as an innovative approach to engaging policymakers and stakeholders to implement these actions.

Goal-based development was introduced by Sachs (2015), and can be described as "a global thrust towards sustainable development, the pathway of which is clearly defined by the SDGs that are indivisible and were universally accepted by the majority of Nations on Earth". The overacting intent of this chapter, therefore, is to demonstrate how goal-based development can be applied as an innovative concept that can drive actions within the holarchic model to meet the dual outcomes at the SDGs–NDC interface.

To meet these aims and objectives, a case study was conducted in an island and archipelago context, as climate change impacts, described as a wicked problem, tend to be more severe and pose an existential threat to island peoples. Although islands' policymakers focus attention on climate change adaptation, it is also suggested that climate change mitigation should also be given consideration. As Cameron (2009) argued: adaptation to climate change on islands, and maybe globally, may only be a "temporary respite", if climate mitigation is not applied simultaneously. In this regard, a systematic review of key documents and websites that address climate change mitigation in chosen CARICOM island sates and at all the holonic levels was conducted. These documents include the NDCs submitted to the UNFCCC; the Voluntary National Reviews (VNRs), Nations' Sustainable Development Plans and other policy documents. The sustainable development plan for Grenada (this author was a part of the technical team that wrote the plan) was used to demonstrate how goal-based development can be integrated into the national plans. However, a simple alignment of goals must also be accompanied by integrated policy and stakeholder engagement, which is necessary to ensure that these actions are implemented, post plan.

This chapter consists of the following sections. A literature review is given in the next section. In the literature review a conceptual framework demonstrates how goal-based development is intended to be applied. In the third section materials and methods are presented. Results from the review are given in the fourth section. The fifth section discusses the results from two perspectives: (1) intra (top-down/bottom-up) and inter holonic interactions and (2) goal-based development as a driver of actions supported by integrated policy and stakeholder engagement. The final section summarizes the findings.

LITERATURE REVIEW

Climate Change Mitigation/SDGs Interface in the Holarchic Model

Two global events occurred in 2015. First, the Paris Agreement (UN, 2015), which was agreed to at the Conference of Parties (COP21), called for all Nations to voluntarily commit to mitigate climate change by publicly declaring Nationally Determined Contributions (NDCs). According to the Paris Agreement, article 2, a key goal is "Holding the increase in global average temperature to well below 2 deg C above pre-industrial levels and pursuing efforts to limit the temperature increase to 1.5 deg C above pre-industrial levels..." Article 4 further suggests how Parties are to meet these goals by developing and publicly displaying Nationally Determined Contributions (NDCs). Article 4 concludes: "Each Party shall prepare, communicate and sustain successive nationally determined contributions that it intends to achieve. Parties shall pursue domestic measures, with the aim of achieving the objectives of such contributions". Many countries have progressively developed NDCs that were submitted to the United Nations Framework Convention on Climate Change (UNFCCC), among them have been several island states.

The second event occurred at the United Nations General Assembly, where about 190 Nations agreed to the global sustainable development agenda, 2030, driven by 17 sustainable development goals (SDGs). According to the United Nations (UN, 2015, p. 3), "the 17 Sustainable Development Goals and 169 targets ... are integrated and indivisible and balance the three dimensions of sustainable development: the economic, social and environmental." Moreover, the SDGs "are intended to be universal, in the sense of embodying a universally shared common global vision of progress towards a safe, just and sustainable space for all human beings to thrive on the planet" (Osborn et al., 2015, p. 2). Two SDGs are at the locus of this chapter: SDG-13: climate action, and SDG-7: affordable and clean energy. Research has revealed the importance of understanding synergies between SDGs and their targets and the need to recognize and minimize trade-offs (Alcamo et al., 2020; Griggs et al., 2014; International Science Council, 2017; Nilsson et al., 2016; Prajal et al., 2017; Spangenberg, 2016; Weitz et al., 2018). In this regard, there is a synergistic relationship between SDG-7 and SDG-13, for as more sustainable energy is deployed, there is a strong likelihood that greenhouse gases such as carbon dioxide emissions will be reduced; which will assist with meeting the NDCs targets.

Therefore, there is also an important synergistic relationship between the SDGs and the NDCs, which has been explored in the context of climate action, SDG13, the NDCs and many of the other SDGs and the themes they support (e.g. Dzebo et al., 2017; Dzebo et al., 2018; Francesco et al., 2019; Northrop et al., 2016). In this regard, Dzebo et al. (2018, p. 2) concluded, "... that from the perspective of the NDCs, the SDG themes with the strongest synergistic connections, include, energy, ...", thus establishing an "SDG–NDC connection". But action at this nexus requires efforts at various levels within our world, including at the local, regional and global levels and more importantly understanding how these systems of actors and actions at various levels interact up and down the levels.

In this regard, Starik and Rands (1995) conceptualized multilevel/multi-system relationship webs, where system levels function as "… an environment for entities at other levels. Thus, the environments of individuals include relevant organizations, their political-economic environment, their social-cultural environment, and their ecological or natural environment" (p. 914). Similarly, Hitt et al. (2007, p. 1387), proposed "multilevel nesting arrangements" in which for example, "… individuals are nested in work groups, which in turn are nested in larger organizational units…, which are nested in a national organization. … organizations are nested in networks of interorganizational relationships … which in turn are nested in overall performance environments". These models provide excellent perspectives for understanding how multilevel systems work. However, they do not demonstrate how the multiple levels of the systems interact from the perspective of top-down environments to individuals and bottom-up, from individual to global environments. In this regard, Hitt et al. (2007), called for research and analysis that will address 'major real-world problems (such as climate change) and the bottom up approach'. From this perspective, this chapter will attempt to contribute to this nascent literature.

But climate change is a wicked-problem that exists at the social/human/nature interface (Incropera, 2016; Sun and Yang, 2016). Incropera (2016, p. 14) reiterated: "A wicked problem has many stakeholders, and any attempt at a solution will have multiple consequences as its implications ripple across parties." Such problems, therefore, may require a foundation that contextualizes the actions at global, regional, local and individual levels, in such a manner that global actions should be translated down to local/individual level, while actions at that level should lead and contribute to global solutions and actions, such as policymaking and implementation, for example, during conferences of the parties (COPs). The concept of panarchy provides such a foundation. In this regard, panarchy, suggests: "… a framework that characterizes complex systems of people and nature as dynamically organized and structured within and between scales of space and time" (Allen et al., 2014). Therefore, panarchy allows for appraising actions at multiple levels of complex systems. In other words, at the local level, how individuals are addressing the issue of energy use, can give an indication of how that individual is (not) contributing to climate change mitigation. Moreover, in the context of an ecosystem, "… panarchy is different from typically envisioned hierarchies in that control is not just exerted by larger-scale, top-down processes, but can also come from small scale or bottom-up processes" (Allen et al., 2014).

The Holarchic Multilevel Model or 'Model'

The holarchic model (Chertow et al., 2020) builds on the concept of panarchy. According to Chertow et al. (2020, p. 1: citing Koetler, 1976):

> "The holarchy framework" is an alternative to hierarchy in recognizing the semi-autonomous characteristic of components of biological and social systems, including organizations, organisms, and cells. Each of these entities is considered a holon since each is a complex system with operational and managerial independence wherein each system is seeking to optimize objectives at its respective holarchic level.

An important characteristic of holarchy therefore, is that social and ecological systems are interacting in complex systems in the holon and between the holons. The holarchic model has been variously applied in the manufacturing and computing sectors and recently to industrial ecology, where material flows were analyzed in the Hawaiian Islands (Chertow et al., 2020). In those applications, enterprises were the focus. However, the model works in a similar way in this application. First, five holons are relevant to the case, see Figure 3.1. Each holon forms a holonic level, within which key actors and actions are occurring. For example, at holonic level 2: organizations, private and public, are attempting to optimize their actions to mitigate climate change. A similar analysis can be envisioned at holonic level 4, in which regional actors are collaborating to ensure that climate actions are effective at that level. Therefore, each holon functions as a complex system of actors and actions. As Chertow et al. (2020) concluded: each holon is a nested system with relationships among actors (Chertow et al., 2020).

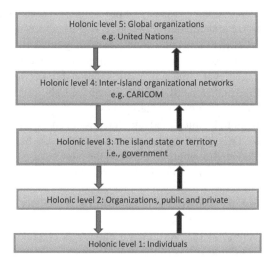

Figure 3.1   Holarchic multilevel model

However, and more importantly for this chapter, the holons are also interacting with each other. According to Chertow et al. (2020, p. 2): "… a holon is simultaneously a part and a whole in itself and arises from the collaboration of its complex sub-systems and super-systems". In this regard, the arrows in the model show flows of (policy, goals, targets) up and down the levels. It is assumed that higher level holonic level 5 is more influential with providing policy and goals to meet the key global challenges of climate change and suggesting actions for dealing with them. However, the actions and actors are also important at the lower levels, to ensure that the intent of the goals and polices handed down from above are achieved. Additionally, these lower level actors may influence policy change and direction. Thus, the holons interplay in a 'top-down'/'bottom-up' holarchy, with higher levels been perceived to be more influential; while bottom-up influence may be more difficult to achieve. For example, Chertow et al. (2020) concluded that material flows from enterprise/industry at the lowest holonic level were much less than that from the top levels, of global shipping. In this chapter, focus is on the bottom up approach or what Hitt et al. (2007) refer to as 'looking up'. The question drawn from this analysis is "What are the key (non-)actions occurring within and between these levels and how do they interact?"

Goal-based Development

Identifying and understanding (non-)actions and actors at the holonic levels are useful, but how these actions are stimulated to meet the intents of the SDGs/NDCs interface is of critical importance. Therefore, the idea of goal-based development, which was introduced by Sachs (2015), and can be described as "a global thrust towards sustainable development, the pathway of which is clearly defined by the SDGs which are indivisible and were universally accepted by the majority of Nations on Earth", is suggested to achieve this intent. According to Sachs (2015, pp. 490–491) there are compelling reasons to embark on goal-based development. Two of relevance to this chapter are that they: (1) "mobilize epistemic communities or knowledge communities [which] are networks of expertise, knowledge and practice around specific challenges…" and (2) "mobilize stakeholder networks". These reasons demonstrate that experts and networks should exist at each level of the model and they must be mobilized to participate in the design and implementation of policies that will drive the actions to meet the targets of the SDGs and NDCs. In this regard, the synergistic relationship between the goals, more specifically, SDG7 and SDG13 and at the SDGs/NDCs interface, should be driven by networks of stakeholders at all holonic levels and integrated policy.

As the SDGs are intended to be integrated and indivisible, and with the synergistic relationship between the SDGs/NDCs, their implementation should also be holistic. In this regard, Dzebo et al. (2018) concluded: the synergies between the NDCs and SDGs "underline the need for policymakers to consider the SDGs and climate action under the NDCs as linked and even integrated agendas; and to address them with coherent policy". This calls therefore for policy integration that will drive the synergistic relationship at the SDG7/SDG13 nexus. Policy integration design, challenges and ways to improve it, have been widely studied (e.g. Candel and Biesbroek, 2016; Peters, 2018). As climate change is considered a wicked problem, policy integration at the multiple levels of the holonic model may be even more challenging. According to Jensen, Nielsen and Russel (2020), climate policy is not only required at 'governance levels' (holonic level 3 in the model), but should also bring into play the various actors in the other holonic levels. Therefore, engaging stakeholders and attempting integrated policy are two features that are drawn out from and support goal-based development.

This leads to the second question: "how can goal-based (SDGs) development assist with driving these actions (identified within and between holons), in a holistic way?"

The Conceptual Framework

The overarching aim of the chapter is to demonstrate how goal-based development, can serve as an innovative approach to driving the actions and actors towards meeting the dual goals at the SDG–NDC connection. The conceptual model in Figure 3.2 demonstrates how this may occur. First, the holarchic model provides an understanding of actors and actions and establishes how they can interact in a holistic manner. But these actions may require a stimulus, and goal-based development, which is supported by integrated policy and stakeholder engagement, provides such an impetus. With this driver, meeting the SDGs, while mitigating climate change, may occur with minimized trade-offs between SDGs and the objectives of the NDCs.

It is envisioned that this framework can be applicable to any context, such as one relevant to the wider corporate world. For example, a global enterprise may wish to drive actions to mitigate its climate impact at the individual to inter-organizational networks at the global level. This framework could provide a visualization and practical map for effectively implementing a climate mitigation action plan that simultaneously focuses on meeting relevant SDGs. The remainder of the chapter demonstrates how this framework may be operationalized.

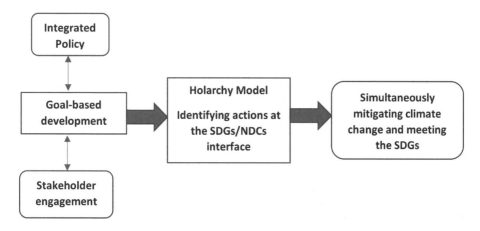

Figure 3.2   The conceptual framework

MATERIALS AND METHODS

The Case Region – CARICOM Small Island States and Territories

The Caribbean Community (CARICOM) was established on 4 July 1973, with the signing of the Treaty of Chaguaramas, which was revised to transition to a regional single market and economy. CARICOM consists of 20 members, with 15 Member States and five Associate Members. Many of the CARICOM member states form an archipelago, stretching from Trinidad and Tobago in the south to the Bahamas in the North. Three of the states – Belize, Suriname and Guyana – are located on the Americas continent. The five associate members and one full member (Montserrat) are non-sovereign jurisdictions or sub-national island jurisdictions (SNIJs). These islands are usually associated with a continental power such as the United Kingdom; for example, Bermuda, which is an overseas territory (OT) of the UK. SNIJs therefore, do not produce the requisite documents, such as NDCs and VNRs reviewed in the research, as they are included in such documents developed by the continental power. The full Member States or independent Small Island States (SIS) therefore, are the focus of this chapter. These are shown in Table 3.1.

Table 3.1   *Caribbean Community (CARICOM) member states*

CARICOM member states	NDC submission date	Acceptance speech delivered at UN General assembly endorsing the SDGs	VNR submission year
Antigua and Barbuda	2 September 2021	*	2021
The Bahamas	31 October 2016	No speech	2018
Barbados	30 July 2021	*	No submission
Belize	1 September 2021	*	2017
Dominica	21 September 2016	*	No submission
Grenada	1 December 2020	*	No submission
Guyana	20 May 2016	*	2019
Haiti	31 July 2017	*	No submission
Jamaica	1 July 2021	*	2018
St. Lucia	27 January 2021	*	2019
St. Kitts and Nevis	26 April 2016	*	No submission
St. Vincent and the Grenadines	29 June 2016	*	No submission
Suriname	9 December 2019	*	No submission
Trinidad and Tobago	22 February 2018	*	2020

Note: Information compiled by Author, showing CARICOM member states indicating recent NDC submission dates, source: https://www4.unfccc.int/sites/NDCStaging/Pages/All.aspx; * denotes acceptance speeches at the 2015 United Nations Sustainable Development Summit, source: https://sustainabledevelopment.un.org/post2015/summit and year of VNR submitted; source: https://sustainabledevelopment.un.org/vnrs/.

Actors and Data Sources

Table 3.2 summarizes the key actors and sources of information to inform actions at all the levels. At level 1, some key literature focused on island peoples and climate change was analyzed for climate mitigation actions. Moreover, secondary data from global islands future survey (Randall, 2021) were analyzed to glean an understanding of how individuals were (not) taking actions and their perceptions of how their islands' authority was dealing with climate change and the SDGs. Two of the CARICOM islands were a part of the research – Grenada and St. Lucia. The survey was conducted during the period 2019–2020. The results are summarized in Tables 3.3 and 3.4 at holonic level 1. At holonic level 2, key private actors are 'electricity service providers' and public organizations such as waste management authorities (as found in many states in the CARICOM region). Their importance in the 'whole' approach to climate mitigation is presented at holonic level 2. Two key documents reviewed at holonic level 3 were the countries' VNRs and NDCs. The countries that produced these reports are shown in Table 3.1. Seven states; Antigua and Barbuda, the Bahamas, Belize, Jamaica, Guyana, St. Lucia and Trinidad and Tobago, have both NDCs and VNRs. The key outputs from the review were the greenhouse gases emissions targets and the alignment of SDGs 7 and 13 to the NDCs. Additionally, the Grenada Sustainable Development Plan 2020–2035 was used to demonstrate how goal-based development is created within a national plan. The results of the review are shown in Table 3.5, at holonic level 3 in the results section.

Regional organizations and their roles in climate mitigation were identified at holonic level 4. As in the corporate world, which may have regional business units, in the public domain many regional organizations are established. In this regard, CARICOM as a political organization has created a number of institutions that focus on climate change. Two of these are the

Table 3.2   *Identification of actors and data sources at the holonic levels*

Holonic level	Key actors	Data sources
1	Individuals - population	Randall (2021)
2	Private organizations – electricity service providers; Renewable energy contractors; Public organizations – water companies; Waste management	GRENLEC (2020); LUCELEC (2020); Government of Grenada (2018)
3	Government of all CARICOM states	NDCs; VNRs; National Plans
4	Regional organizations – CARICOM and its sub-bodies	Websites and reports of: Caribbean Center for Renewable Energy and Energy Efficiency (CCREEE); Caribbean Community Climate Change Center (5Cs)
5	Global organizations – United Nations; AOSIS – Alliance of Small Island States	Websites of: UNFCC; IPCC; AOSIS

Caribbean Community Climate Change Center (5Cs) and the Caribbean Centre for Renewable Energy and Energy Efficiency (CCREEE), which, as the names imply, have a mandate to consider transitions in the energy sector to sustainable energy. Some grey literature and website reviews were conducted to present an understanding of the climate mitigation related work and actions of these organizations and key results are presented at holonic level 4. At the international level in holon 5, some United Nations organizations, such the Alliance for Small Island States (AOSIS), United Nations Framework Convention for Climate Change (UNFCCC) and the Inter-governmental Panel on Climate Change (IPCC) were identified. Key actions from these sources were summarized at holonic level 5.

Key Limitations and Cautions

Presenting the holarchic model in the context of islands and island political arrangements such as CARICOM may be useful to other regions. However, the lack of critical data to populate the results is a challenge faced by island researchers and researchers doing studies on islands. This would have limited the ability to provide more comprehensive results. Moreover, generalizing from this work and in the context of other settings outside of the regional island scope may be a challenge, and, if done, should be done with extreme caution. Specifically, the holonic levels suggested here may not be globally applicable, however, as was mentioned, it may be re-conceptualized based on the context in which other researchers may wish to apply it.

RESULTS AND ANALYSIS

Holonic Level 1: Individual

Individuals have a critical role to play in climate change mitigation actions and the simultaneous implementation of the SDGs, especially SDG-7 and SDG-13. These actions include using energy efficient products and services, installing renewable energy technologies, protecting carbon local syncs, such as trees and advocating for climate action. For example, in Grenada, the Grenada Electricity Services (GRENLEC, 2020) reported that 1.28% of electricity was generated by distributed renewable energy customers; while the St. Lucia Electricity Services Ltd reported 142 customers in St. Lucia had rooftop PV solar technology installed, (LUCELEC, 2020). These actions may be influenced by the upper levels, especially at level 3.

But there are key barriers to the uptake of these climate mitigation technologies. For example, in a study conducted in Grenada, barriers such as 'lack of access to affordable capital' and 'lack of appropriate tariffs to encourage renewable energy technologies' existed (Government of Grenada, 2018). Moreover, individuals can embark on actions, such as comfort and lighting control and behavior change in efforts to save energy and by extension mitigate the emissions of carbon dioxide. Behavior change, although complex, is identified as a necessary response to saving energy, which in turn serves as a climate mitigation action (Orland et al., 2014; Reveil, 2014; Staddon et al., 2016; Stephenson et al., 2010). Staddon et al. (2016) point out that behavior change in the household and workplace occur in differing contexts, which may require different approaches to invoking these changes.

Therefore, how individuals understand and perceive actions at level 3, may influence how they change behavior to reduce energy use and mitigate climate change. In this regard, Robinson (2018, p. 82) found in a literature review directed at climate change adaptation in the Caribbean that "... the governance of, as well as institutions and planning for, climate change and adaptation in Caribbean SIDS", was the most important issue researched. Another study investigated how individuals' "... perceptions influence actions to respond to climate change" (Thomas et al., 2020, p. 10), albeit relating mainly to adaptation action. Relating to energy, Stephenson et al. (2010) noted that external factors such as "legal, policy and market conditions" can affect how individuals behave in saving energy. From these perspectives, the perceptions of individuals on how governments are dealing with issues such as climate change, energy and the SDGs can hinder or support action at this level. In this regard, the author draws on the data captured in a global island survey, which included: Grenada and St. Lucia. Tables 3.3 and 3.4 summarize the responses to the questions related to this research.

Table 3.3   Perceptions of island people on SDGs in Grenada and St. Lucia

SDGs	How important are each of the following UN SDGs in relation to your island (1 = absolutely important and 7 = Not important)		How would you rate the success of your island government in striving to meet each of the SDGs by 2030 (1 = Extremely successful and 7 = Extremely unsuccessful)	
	Grenada ($n = 56$)	St. Lucia ($n = 54$)	Grenada ($n = 56$)	St. Lucia ($n = 54$)
7	1.98	2.38	4.61	4.76
13	2.06	2.42	3.81	4.50

Note: Table showing the perception of island peoples on the importance of the SDGs and success with their implementation by island authorities.
Source: Averages computed by the author, using data set taken from Island Sustainability Futures Project, 2019–2020.

Table 3.4 Perceptions of island people on climate actions in Grenada and St. Lucia

Statement of concern	To what degree do you agree with each of the following statements (Strongly agree = 1; Strongly disagree = 7)	
	Grenada ($n = 56$)	St. Lucia ($n = 54$)
Climate is addressed	4.68	5.10
Climate policy is in place	3.76	4.20

Source: Averages computed by the author, using data set taken from Island Sustainability Futures Project, 2019–2020.

Table 3.3 shows that although participants on both islands recognized the importance of the SDGs, especially SDGs 7 and 13 (average responses closer to '1'); their perception of the island governments' success with striving to meet them was less optimistic (average responses further from '1'). Additionally, in Table 3.4, respondents in both islands did not 'strongly agree' that issues of climate were being addressed or that there was effective climate policy in place, albeit from a tourism perspective.

Holonic Level 2: Organizations – Private and Public

In this holon, private actors, such as electric utilities and renewable energy providers are also important. It is not clear from the NDCs how these actors are intended to interact with the actions of government. However, a number of actions in the NDCs will require input and support from private entities, such as the privately-owned electric utility. In the NDCs, the governments outlined a number of targets that will require actions from the private utility. For example, to meet the target of "95% share of renewable energy in the electricity mix" (Government of Barbados, 2021), by 2030, actions on the part of the utility will be required. In this regard, the utility has begun to act. In a document titled: 'Our History, 1900–2019' the company revealed that it built "its first utility sizes photovoltaic solar plant," with "5 MW battery storage system" (Barbados Light and Power, n.d.). These complementary actions at the organizational level will enhance the move towards climate mitigation, especially in the energy and electricity sectors and assist with meeting the relevant SDGs. Similarly, the Grenada Electricity Services (GRENLEC) has made investments in solar PV plants for generating electricity.

Holonic Level 3: Island State and Territory Governments

The national governments of most island states drive and have the responsibility for climate mitigation and SDGs implementation policies and actions. In some islands there may be other levels of government. However, the majority of small islands have only one level, and as it is assumed that actions for NDCs/SDGs implementation lie only with the national government. In this regard, island governments have accepted the SDGs with speeches delivered at the UN Sustainable Development Summit in 2015; all states have created NDCs, signaling their intention to mitigate climate change, while some have prepared VNRs of how they intend to meet the SDGs and specifically SDG-13 and 7 (see Table 3.1).

The key results here are the targets established in the countries' NDCs to mitigate climate change and whether or not they are linked to the relevant SDGs. Table 3.5 shows that all countries have set targets, but six of 14 countries have explicitly linked their NDC actions to SDGs 13 and 7. For example, in Belize, an action to assess the need for fuel wood and its social impacts was clearly identified. Therefore, a country's VNR and in some cases their national plans that align to the SDGs, complements the NDCs. For example, in Antigua and Barbuda's VNR, a number of strategic actions for moving the country towards 100% renewable energy were identified (Government of Antigua and Barbuda (GoAB), 2021). Although Grenada did not do a formal VNR, the country adopted a National Sustainable Development Plan in 2020, which aligns its national goal of "energy security and efficiency" to SDG-13 and SDG-7 (Government of Grenada, 2019).

Table 3.5   CARICOM members, their GHG emission reduction targets and links to the SDGs

CARICOM member states	Greenhouse gas (GHG) emissions reduction targets	Connection to the SDGs?
Antigua and Barbuda	There was no overall emissions reduction target, but key and several sectoral targets were established.	Yes
The Bahamas	"an economy-wide reduction GHG emissions of 30% when compared to its Business as Usual scenario by 2030". (Government of the Bahamas, 2015)	No
Barbados	"an economy-wide reduction in GHG emissions of 44% compared to its business-as-usual (BAU) scenario by 2030". (Government of Barbados (GOB), 2021, p. 13)	Yes
Belize	"Targets included in this updated NDC are estimated to avoid cumulative emissions total across all sectors 5, 647 KtCO2e between 2021 and 2030…" (Belize Government, 2021, p. 2)	Yes
Dominica	"… total greenhouse gas (GHG) emissions [reduction] below 2014 levels", in a stepwise manner leading up to 2030 (Commonwealth of Dominica, 2016).	No
Grenada	"… reducing GHG emissions by 40% of the 2010 emission levels by 2030". (Government of Grenada, 2020, p. 4)	Yes
Guyana	Pledge to implement policies to reduce emissions from mining, logging and energy sectors (Republic of Guyana, n.d.)	No
Haiti	Not analyzed as document is in French	N/A
Jamaica	"25.4% reduction relative to business-as-usual emissions in 2030 (unconditional) • 28.5% reduction relative to business-as-usual emissions in 2030 (conditional)" (Government of Jamaica, 2020, p. 4)	Yes
St. Lucia	Commits to reducing GHG emissions by 37 GgCO2e by 2030 (Government of St. Lucia, 2021)	Yes
St. Kitts and Nevis	"… an emissions reduction target of 22% and 35% of … GHG emissions projected in the business as usual (BAU) scenario for 2025 and 2030 respectively. (Federation of St. Kitts and Nevis, 2021)	No
St. Vincent and the Grenadines	"… economy-wide reduction in greenhouse gas (GHG) emissions of 22% compared to its business as usual (BAU) scenario by 2025." (Government of St. Vincent and the Grenadines, 2015, p. 3)	No
Suriname	Commits to reducing emissions from the electricity, agriculture and transport and urban infrastructure sectors (Republic of Suriname, 2020).	Yes
Trinidad and Tobago	"… reduction objective in overall emissions from the three sectors by 15% by 2030 from BAU". (Republic of Trinidad and Tobago, n.d.)	No

Note: Information compiled from countries' NDCs taken from the UNFCCC repository.

Such actions may demonstrate a focus on goal-based development planning, and this is discussed using the Grenada National Plan. The plan is founded in the three pillars of sustainable development – economy, society and environment. These pillars support a number of national outcomes and goals and the 2035 vision. Three national goals were identified in the plan. The one of relevance to this chapter is "goal 3: environmental sustainability and security", which has "climate resilience…" and "energy security and efficiency" as national outcomes to be achieved. The plan goes on to further align these national goals and outcomes to the relevant SDGs, which are SDGs 7 and 13. This simple alignment provides a good foundation for goal-based development and planning. But there is a need to move beyond this simplistic alignment of goals and move towards continued stakeholder engagement and policy integration for plan implementation. However, there is need to deepen this approach and the importance of goal-based development from this perspective will be discussed in the subsequent section.

Holonic Level 4: Regional Organizations

One of the fundamental actions taken at the CARICOM level was the creation of a Regional Energy Policy in 2013, that focused on: "establishing regional and national targets for the reduction of greenhouse gas emissions in the energy sector and implementing appropriate mitigation actions relevant to the energy sector" (CARICOM, 2013, p. 56). First, this theme of CARICOM demonstrates the relationship between SDG-7 and SDG-13, although this was not relevant in 2013 as the SDGs and NDCs came into effect in 2015. Moreover, the evidence of such a target is not yet known by the author, but a comprehensive review of the NDCs of all CARICOM countries suggest that CARCIOM states have laid the foundation to create such a target. In this regard, it was suggested that: "Collaboration on the establishment of regional targets for emission reduction within the context…" of other regional projects, should be "… informed by international obligations and voluntary commitments under the UNFCCC (CARICOM, 2013, p. 56).

Stemming from this, the CCREEE was established to provide technical services to regional public and private sector organizations. One of the key interventions of the organization is on projects that have regional impacts or national ones that have the potential to be scaled-up regionally. From this perspective, CCREEE embarked on a number of strategic actions and projects to meet SDGs 7 and 13, with a regional focus. Two related projects include the 'climate resilience program' that considers building the resilience of regional electric utilities and 'sustainable transport programme', in which the organization has claimed to be instrumental in propelling strategies for the uptake of electric vehicles.

Holonic Level 5: Global Organizations

Globally, the efforts to combat climate change are driven by the United Nations Framework Convention for Climate Change (UNFCCC), and the many treaties and mechanism established since 1992. The Paris Agreement and Kyoto Protocol were born from the UNFCCC. Many arms of actions and actors have evolved within this framework including the science-based, Intergovernmental Panel on Climate Change (IPCC). The Panel has provided science-based evidence of anthropogenic climate change (ACC) and the need to limit global temperature rise below 1.5°C. Another key mechanism within the UNFCCC is the negotiation by the 197 Parties to the convention, convened annually as the Conference of the Parties (COP). At COP 21 in Paris, December 2015, 196 parties adopted the Paris Agreement, with the "… goal … to *limit global warming* to well below 2 deg. C, *preferably to 1.5 degrees Celsius*, compared to pre-industrial levels if ACC is to be halted" (UNFCCC, 2021; emphasis in original).

As it relates to islands globally, the Alliance of Small Island States (AOSIS) was established to provide island Parties with a united platform to champion the cause of islands. In 2018, the AOSIS recognized the link between climate action and the SDGs, noting that: "We recognize the critical linkage between climate change actions and achievement of the Sustainable Development Goals (SDGs)…" (AOSIS, 2018, p. 1). The island parties through AOSIS further "… welcomes with appreciation the ambitious NDCs submitted by SIDS and the recent announcements of SIDS to undertake and implement even more ambitious NDCs and reiterate our call for enhanced global cooperation for more urgent and more ambitious climate action" (AOSIS, 2018, p. 2). The AOSIS therefore mirrors and echoes the intentions and actions of the UNFCCC, the Paris Agreement and Kyoto Protocol and calls its members to action on a global scale.

Therefore, the development of NDCs and the pledges and actions to mitigate climate change, especially in the energy and electricity sector, is one championed by AOSIS. Moreover, the crucial need to integrate climate action with the SDGs is recognized and called for by AOSIS. This is important at this level, as it encourages islands to seek out synergies between the goals, especially SDGs-13 and 7.

DISCUSSION

The main aim of this chapter was to demonstrate how goal-based development can be conceptualized as a driver of actions in the model to meet the dual goals at the SDG-NDC nexus. There were two objectives, to: (1) critically analyze (non-)actions within and between the holonic levels, and (2) propose the idea of goal-based development as a key to engaging policymakers and stakeholders for implementing these actions to meet climate mitigation targets and the SDGs. These are now discussed.

Inter (Bottom-up/Top-down) Holonic Interactions – Completing the Whole

Inter (bottom-up/top-down) and intra holonic interactions are important to understanding how these multilevel actors function within holons, but more importantly between holons. In other words, understanding how these actions flow and influence actions from global, regional, local, individual levels and vice versa, to form a whole is the important outcome. Starting with holonic level 5, some key international organizations were identified, mainly within the United Nations set-up, that provide global guidance and platforms for climate action in general, and specifically for climate change mitigation. Foremost among these were the UNFCCC and the treaties and agreements that drive all UN Nations to act on climate issues. In this regard, the results show that the Paris Agreement, 2015, required that all Nations, including islands should publicly record in their NDCs how they would meet GHG reductions. Moreover, global islands saw the need to recognize and craft these actions in the context of the SDGs, which again was driven by the United Nations Conference on Sustainable Development held in the same year.

These actions appear to have filtered down to and influenced the next holonic level, in which a number of regional actors, enshrined within the Caribbean Community, provide guidance and practical suggestions for actors at the next level. It was noted in the results that: "Collaboration on the establishment of regional targets for emission reduction within the context…" of other regional projects, should be "… informed by international obligations and voluntary commitments under the UNFCCC (CARICOM, 2013, p. 56). Here the actors and actions at holonic level 5 are seen to be influencing the actions at the next holon. Moreover, closely coupled or embedded in the CARICOM, the regional actor CCREEE is focusing on actions on the regional level, but ensuring that these actions influence actions at holonic level 3 – government.

As shown in Table 3.2 and at holonic level 3, all the CARICOM states, represented by government actors, have already submitted at least a first NDC and are among the 194 states that have done so globally. Additionally, the majority of them have adopted the SDGs and have provided some analysis of how they are doing with their implementation, especially at the SDG-13/SDG-7 interface. Governments, seem to play a critical role in driving climate actions at a country level. But governments consisting of the various ministries and departments within the holon will have to forge key relationships with private and other public organizations at level 2. Moreover, how the actions/agreement of government influence actions at the holonic level 1 is also critical. In this regard, one of the key issues that arise, is how to turn the pledges for GHG reduction into actions at holonic level 1. This demonstrates the top-down interaction, moving from policies and pledges adopted by government from level 5 and moving it downwards to invoke individual action, which is much more difficult to accomplish.

There are 8 billion people inhabiting the World, with about 600 million living on islands. One can argue therefore, that holonic level 1 has the largest critical mass compared with the other levels. Therefore, their actions will be extremely important to meeting the SDGs and mitigating climate change. However, within the model, these actions can be influenced or hindered based on the perceptions of these individuals on actions at the upper levels, especially the 'government' actors at level 3. Although this cannot be generalized, the results show that the respondents in the case island perceive that governments are not doing well with achieving the SDGs, including SDGs 7 and 13 and are failing in climate action. Therefore, as individuals, they may not be motivated, at least by these perceptions to act on mitigating climate change. Moreover, barriers to the upscaling of renewable energy technologies and energy efficiency, already described in the results at holonic level l, may exacerbate the need to act. Stephenson et al. (2010), developed a useful framework which could be applied to understand individual energy behavior and culture, which may be applied to analyze and address this problem. Some issues previously identified by Stephenson et al. (2010), were policy, legal and market conditions which are mainly driven by governments.

However, actors at holonic levels 2 and 3, have recognized the need to act on involving individuals, especially in households and communities in the necessary actions on climate change and especially on mitigation. In this regard, in the United Nations synthesis report on NDCs, it was reported that (United Nations, 2021, pp. 6–7):

> Many Parties referred to formal arrangements in place for domestic stakeholder consultation. Most of them indicated that they conducted consultations and engagement in an inclusive and participatory manner, with some Parties specifically referencing gender sensitive consultations.
>
> Almost all Parties provided information on using one or more ACE [Action for climate empowerment] elements [education, training, public awareness, etc.] to promote implementation of mitigation and adaptation activities,...

This bottom-up approach is also important for making the model whole. The bottom-up approach was also recommended by Zang et al. (2020) as being important to China reaching its targets at the NDC-SDG connection. In this regard, Zang et al. (2020, p. 248) concluded that "Bottom up actions should emphasize on technology innovations, education by academia or non-governmental organization and public monitoring and participation". However, bottom up or looking up and integrating individuals' actions into the model, although challenging, will take the World closer to mitigating climate change and meeting relevant SDGs, country by country. This demonstrates how the bottom-up approach can be envisioned, moving from holon 1 up to holon 5. That is how Nations attempt to include and involve individuals in the actions that flow upstream to holonic levels 3, 4 and 5. It further shows how holonic level 3 serves as a pivot that can facilitate the actions at level 1, thus moving it up the levels. The 'looking-up' approach completes the holistic nature of the model.

However, the results did not reveal any explicit approach to including individuals' influence or interactions with policies and goals with the other levels of the model. For example, the interactions among levels 5, 4 and 3 appears to be much clearer, but a block appears when moving further down the model to levels 2 and 1. Furthermore, the interactions occurring from level 1 back up to level 5 or the looking-up interactions need further clarity. Moreover, both the bottom-up and top-down interactions, can be driven in a more systematic manner. Goal-based development may assist with driving these actions in a more systematic manner.

Goal-based Development – engaging Stakeholders, Integrating Policy for Climate Mitigation and SDGs

Stimulating actions at all the holonic levels and between levels requires a driver, which may be provided by goal-based development. Focused on integrated policy and stakeholder engagement, goal-based development can be applied to engaging stakeholders at all levels of the model, and can also demonstrate to governments how policies may be integrated and developed with wider stakeholder involvement. Sachs and colleagues (2019) suggest that: "The implementation of the [SDGs] requires close coordination among several government ministries, …". Goal-based development therefore sets the stage to involve stakeholders within a holonic level, such as ministries in the government at level 3 and between other levels of the holarchic model, such as individuals (holon 1) and organizations in holon 2; albeit driven by government.

First, the model should be relevant to policymakers at holonic level 3, who have the ability to leverage actions at the upper and lower holonic levels. The results at holonic level 3, show that some governments have embedded the SDGs into their national plans, by aligning local objectives and outcomes with the SDGs. In this regard, it was shown how Grenada attempted to align its national goals and outcomes, with relevant SDGs. But governments must move beyond this simplistic alignment, towards full engagement of actors at the other holonic levels, especially levels 2 and 1. In this regard, the model can be used to uncover a number of actors and actions and more importantly describes how these actions flow and influence each other up and down the model. These stakeholders therefore, must be mobilized to participate in the design and implementation of policies that will move all stakeholders towards meeting the dual outcomes of the SDGs and mitigating climate change. In this regard, the synergistic relationship between the goals and the SDG/NDCs interface, comes into play. Francesco et al. (2019, p. 678), noted that the vast majority of countries globally have mentioned the SDGs in their NDCs, but "none discuss in detail the impact of climate policy on the achievement of the SDGs." Goal-based development can assist with detailing these discussions by providing a foundation for integrated policy planning and implementation.

More specifically, this 'leveraging by governments' relates to policies that will drive climate mitigation action (SDG-13) and energy transition to affordable and clean energy (SDG-7). But involving the massive population at holonic level 1 in policymaking to meet the dual outcomes is no easy feat. NDCs and the SDGs are driven globally, but must be implemented locally and country-by-country if they are to be achieved. Here, bottom up planning and policymaking is crucial. Goal-based development and the model can contribute to this effort in that they will provide governments with an approach to identify and involve actors and actions within the holons and offers a holistic understanding of the interactions that are occurring up and down the model. With this approach, engaging individuals may become less cumbersome. For example, at holonic level 2, all key private and public actors will be identified and engaged with an integrated policy implementation plan that includes relevant actions to meet the dual goals at the NDC/SDS interface.

Finally, the polices for driving the dual goals of climate mitigation and meeting the relevant SDGs and NDCs targets, may have different policy developers and owners within government, as is the case in states such as the islands focused upon in this research. Using Grenada as an example, the country has an energy policy and a climate change policy that were developed and owned by separate ministries within government. What goal based development will do is use the SDGs as a common platform from which all ministries can integrate policies towards the dual goals. Goal-based development therefore suggests that countries should move beyond "ticking off SDGs; as met or not met", towards grasping a more comprehensive understanding of how the SDGs interact among themselves and with other key directives, such as the NDCs. This allows for the SDGs to drive an integrated policy direction that builds synergies and minimizes trade-offs with other relevant SDGs. According to Sachs et al. (2019: p. 805) "many policy interventions … are needed to achieve each SDG, and each intervention generally contributes to several goals". Integrated policy and stakeholder engagement are critical issues that support goal-based development, which will drive actions towards meeting the dual goals of climate change mitigation and relevant SDGs.

CONCLUSION

If the wicked problem of climate change is to be addressed then understanding what actors are (not) doing at multiple levels will be important. Using the case region of CARICOM, key holons of actors and actions were framed within a holarchic multilevel model. The conceptual framework developed for this chapter suggests that actions within the model required to mitigate climate change and meet the SDGs, can be stimulated by goal-based development. The first section of the chapter identified a number of actions at the five holonic levels of the model, from global organizations at level 5 to individuals at level 1. The actions were crafted within the dual context of the SDG–NDCs connections established in the literature. It was found that global agreements generally flowed down the model, thus influencing actions at regional and government levels 4 and 3, respectively. However, governments as a pivot in the model may struggle with getting the actors at the lower levels 1 – individual and 2 – public and private organizations to act. At these levels, actions were minimal and the perceptions of individuals on how their governments were doing with climate change and the SDGs may be stymying actions at levels 1 and 2. But the importance of actions at the lower levels were necessary, as this is where the masses are and their action will play a vital role in meeting the dual goals. The model therefore provided a 'whole picture' of (non-)actions, actors and how they interface with each other, up and down the model.

Goal-based development supported by stakeholder engagement and integrated policy was then discussed as a means to drive collective actions that will mitigate climate change and meet the SDGs. As a key owner of the NDCs and SDGs, governments' role in galvanizing other stakeholders cannot be underscored. Governments therefore must involve stakeholders at all levels in policy planning and in getting buy-in on the targets and goals they have agreed to. Additionally, within government itself, different ministries are developing policies and plans that will lead towards the dual goals and targets. Not seeing the SDGs in particular as individual goals, but rather as integrated among themselves and the NDC targets, is a foundational approach to integrated policy. In conclusion therefore, goal-based development can stimulate government to act and engage all stakeholders at all holonic levels, in order to develop policies that integrate SDGs and NDCs, in an effort to meet the required outcomes at the NDCs–SDGs interface.

REFERENCES

Alcamo, J., Thompson, J., Alexander, A., Antonialadies, A., Delabre, I., Dolley, J., Marshall, F., Manton, M., Middleton, J. and Scharlemann, J. P. W. (2020). Special issue editorial: Analyzing interactions among the sustainable development goals: Findings and emerging issues from local and global studies. *Sustainability Science*, 15, 1561–1582. https://doi.org/10.1007/s11625-020-00875-x.

Allen, G., Angeler, G. D., Garmestani, A. S., Gunderson, L. H. and Holling, C. S. (2014). Panarchy: Theory and application. *Ecosystems*, 17, 578–589. https://doi.org/10.1007/s10021-013-9744-2.

AOSIS (2018, November, 1). Samoa declaration on climate change in the context of sustainable development for SIDS. https://sdgs.un.org/sites/default/files/documents/21091CC_Declaration.pdf.

Barbados Light and Power (n.d.). Our history 1900–2019. https://www.blpc.com.bb/images/pdfs/OUR _HISTORY_1900_2019.pdf?type=file.

Belize Government (2021). Updated nationally determined contribution. https://www4.unfccc.int/sites/ ndcstaging/PublishedDocuments/Belize%20First/Belize%20Updated%20NDC.pdf5.

Cameron, E. (2009). Small island developing states at the forefront of global climate change. In R. Engelman et al. (eds), *State of the World: Into a Warming World*. New York and London: W.W. Norton and Company.

Candel, J. J. L. and Biesbroek, R. (2016). Toward a processual understanding of policy integration. *Policy Science*, 49, 211–231. https://doi.org/10.1007/s11077-016-9248-y.

CARICOM (2013). CARICOM energy policy. https://www.ccreee.org/wp-content/uploads/2020/06/ 10862-caricom_energy_policy.pdf

Chertow, M. R, Graedel, T. E., Kanaoka, K. S. and Park, J. (2020). The Hawaiian islands: Conceptualizing industrial ecology holarchic system. *Sustainability*, 12, 3105. https://doi.org/10.3390/su12083104

Commonwealth of Dominica (2016). Intended nationally determined contribution. https://www4.unfccc .int/sites/ndcstaging/PublishedDocuments/Dominica%20First/Commonwealth%20of%20Dominica- %20Intended%20Nationally%20Determined%20Contributions%20(INDC).pdf

Dzebo, A., Brandi, C., Janetschek, H., Savvidou, G., Adams, K., Chan, S. and Lambert, C. (2017). Exploring connections between the Paris Agreement and the 2030 Agenda for Sustainable Development. https:// transparency-partnership.net/system/files/document/SEI_2017_Exploring%20Paris%20Agreement %20and%20SDG%20connections.pdf.

Dzebo, A., Janetchek, H., Brandi, C. and Iacobuta, G. (2018). The sustainable development goals viewed through a climate lens. https://www.sei.org/publications/the-sustainable-development-goals-viewed -through-a-climate-lens/.

Federation of St. Kitts and Nevis (2021). Updated nationally determined contribution. https://www4 .unfccc.int/sites/ndcstaging/PublishedDocuments/Saint%20Kitts%20and%20Nevis%20First/St. %20Kitts%20and%20Nevis%20Revised%20NDC_Updated.pdf.

Francesco, F. N., Sovacool, B., Hughes, N., Cozzi, L., Cosgrave, E., Howells, M., Tavoni, M., Tomei, J., Zerriffi, H. and Milligan, B. (2019). Connecting climate action with other sustainable development goals. *Nature Sustainability*, 2, 674–680. https://doi.org/10.1038/s41893-019-0334-y

Government of Antigua and Barbuda (2021). Voluntary national review. https://sustainabledevelopment .un.org/content/documents/279502021_VNR_Report_Antigua_and_Barbuda.pdf.

Government of the Bahamas (2015). Intended nationally determined contribution (INDC) under the United Nations Framework Convention for Climate Change (UNFCCC). https://www4.unfccc.int/ sites/ndcstaging/PublishedDocuments/Bahamas%20First/Bahamas_COP-22%20UNFCCC.pdf.

Government of Barbados (GOB) (2021, June). Barbados 2021 update of the first nationally determined contribution. https://www4.unfccc.int/sites/ndcstaging/PublishedDocuments/Barbados%20First/2021%20Barbados%20NDC%20update%20-%2021%20July%202021.pdf.

Government of Grenada (2018). TNA mitigation: Barrier analysis and enabling framework report. https://unfccc.int/ttclear/misc_/StaticFiles/gnwoerk_static/TNA_key_doc/47552afa0ce140e09e43f0a205f7a227/2179026821574311f8e82a6b4c5d1bcd9.pdf.

Government of Grenada (2019). National sustainable development plan. https://gov.gd/sites/default/files/docs/Documents/others/nsdp-2020-2035.pdf.

Government of Grenada (2020). Second nationally determined contribution. https://www4.unfccc.int/sites/ndcstaging/PublishedDocuments/Grenada%20Second/GrenadaSecondNDC2020%20-%2001-12-20.pdf.

Government of Jamaica (2020). Update of the nationally determined contribution (NDC) of Jamaica to the United Nations Framework Convention on Climate Change (UNFCCC). https://www4.unfccc.int/sites/ndcstaging/PublishedDocuments/Jamaica%20First/Updated%20NDC%20Jamaica%20-%20ICTU%20Guidance.pdf.

Government of St. Lucia (2021). St. Lucia's nationally determined contribution. https://www4.unfccc.int/sites/ndcstaging/PublishedDocuments/Saint%20Lucia%20First/Saint%20Lucia%20First%20NDC%20(Updated%20submission).pdf.

Government of St. Vincent and the Grenadines (2015). Intended nationally determined contribution. https://www4.unfccc.int/sites/ndcstaging/PublishedDocuments/Saint%20Vincent%20and%20the%20Grenadines%20First/Saint%20Vincent%20and%20the%20Grenadines_NDC.pdf..

GRENLEC (2020). Grenada Electricity Services Ltd. Annual Report 2020. https://grenlec.com/wp-content/uploads/2021/10/GRENLEC-2020_AR-web.pdf.

Griggs, D., Stafford-Smith, M., Rockström, J., Öhman, M. C., Gaffney, O., Glasser, G., Kanie, N., Noble, I., Steffan, W. and Shyamsundar, P. (2014). An integrated framework for sustainable development goals. *Ecology and Society*, 19(4), 49. http://dx.doi.org/10.5751/ES-07082-190449.

Hitt, M. A., Beamish, P. W., Jackson, S. E. and Mathieu, J. E. (2007). Building theoretical and empirical bridges across levels: Multilevel research in management. *Academy of Management Journal*, 50(6), 1385–1399.

Incropera, F. P. (2016). *Climate change: A Wicked Problem: Complexity and Uncertainty at the Intersection of Science, Economics, Politics and Human Behavior.* 1st ed. Kindle. Cambridge University Press.

International Science Council (2017). *A guide to SDG interactions: From science to implementation.* International Science Council. https://council.science/publications/a-guide-to-sdg-interactions-from-science-to-implementation/.

Jensen, A., Nielsen, H. Ø. and Russel, D. (2020). Editorial: Climate policy in a fragmented World-Transformative governance interactions at multiple levels. *Sustainability*, 12(23), 10017. https://doi.org/10.3390/su122310017.

LUCELEC (2020). 2020 Annual Report. https://www.lucelec.com/sites/default/files/annual-reports/LUCELEC_2020_Annual_Report.pdf.

Nilsson, M., Griggs, D. and Visbeck, M. (2016). Map the interactions between Sustainable Development Goals. *Nature*, 534, 320–322. https://www.nature.com/news/polopoly_fs/1.20075!/menu/main/topColumns/topLeftColumn/pdf/534320a.pdf.

Northrop, E., Biru, H., Lima, S., Bouye, M. and Song, R. (2016, September). Working Paper: Examining the alignment between intended nationally determined contributions and sustainable development goals. https://www.wri.org/research/examining-alignment-between-intended-nationally-determined-contributions-and-sustainable.

Orland, B., Ram, N., Lang, D., Houser, K., Kling, N. and Coccia, M. (2014). Saving energy in an office environment a serious game intervention. *Energy and Buildings*, 74, 43–52. http://dx.doi.org/10.1016/j.enbuild.2014.01.036.

Osborn, D., Cutter, A. and Ullah, F. (2015). *Universal Sustainable Development Goals: Understanding the Transformational Challenge for Developed Countries.* Stakeholder Forum. https://sustainabledevelopment.un.org/content/documents/1684SF_-_SDG_Universality_Report_-_May_2015.pdf

Peters, G. B. (2018). The challenge of policy coordination. *Policy Design and Practice*, 1(1), 1–11. https://doi.org/10.1080/25741292.2018.1437946l.

Prajal, P., Costa, L., Rybski, D., Lucht, W. and Kropp, J. P. (2017). A systematic study of Sustainable Development Goal (SDG) interactions. *Earth's Future*, 5, 1169–1179. https://doi.org/10.1002/2017EF000632.

Randall, J. E. (2021). *An Introduction to Island Studies*. Island Studies Press/Rowan and Littlefield.

Republic of Guyana (n.d.). Guyana's revised intended nationally determined contribution. https://www4.unfccc.int/sites/ndcstaging/PublishedDocuments/Guyana%20First/Guyana%27s%20revised%20NDC%20-%20Final.pdf.

Republic of Suriname (2020). Nationally determined contribution 2020. https://www4.unfccc.int/sites/ndcstaging/PublishedDocuments/Suriname%20Second/Suriname%20Second%20NDC.pdf.

Republic of Trinidad and Tobago (n.d.). Intended nationally determined contribution under the United Nations Framework Convention on Climate Change. https://www4.unfccc.int/sites/ndcstaging/PublishedDocuments/Trinidad%20and%20Tobago%20First/Trinidad%20and%20Tobago%20Final%20INDC.pdf.

Reveil, K. (2014). Estimating the environmental impact of home energy visits and extent of behavior change. *Energy Policy*, 73, 461–470. http://dx.doi.org/10.1016/j.enpol.2014.05.049.

Robinson, S. (2018). Adapting to climate change at the national level in Caribbean small island developing states. *Island Studies Journal*, 13(1), 79–100. https://islandstudies.ca/sites/default/files/ISJRobinsonNationalClimateChangeAdaptationCaribbean.pdf.

Sachs, J. (2015). *The Age of Sustainable Development*. Columbia University Press.

Sachs, J., Schmidt-Traub, G., Mazzucato, M., Messner, D., Nakicenovic, N. and Rockström, J. (2019). Six Transformations to achieve the Sustainable Development Goals. *Nature Sustainability*, 5, 804–814. https://doi.org/10.1038/s41893-019-0352-9.

Spangenberg, J. H. (2016). Hot air or comprehensive progress? A critical assessment of the SDGs. *Sustainable Development*, 25(4), 311–321. https://doi.org/10.1002/sd.1657.

Staddon, S. C., Cycil, C., Goulden, M., Leygue, C. and Spence, A. (2016). Intervening to change behavior and save energy in the workplace: A systematic review of available evidence. *Energy Research and Social Sciences*, 17, 30–51. http://dx.doi.org/10.1016/j.erss.2016.03.027.

Starik, M. and Rands, G. (1995). Weaving and integrated web: Multilevel and multi system perspectives of ecologically sustainable organizations. *Academy of Management Review*, 20(4), 908–935.

Stephenson, J., Barton, B., Carrington, G., Gnoth, D., Lawson, R. and Thornes, P. (2010). Energy cultures: A framework for understanding energy behaviors. *Energy Policy*, 38, 6120–6129. https://doi.org/10.1016/j.enpol.2010.05.069.

Sun, J. and Yang, K. (2016). The wicked problem of climate change: A new approach based on social mess and fragmentation. *Sustainability*, 8, 1312. https://doi.org/10.3390/su8121312.

Thomas, A., Baptiste, A., Martyr-Koller, R., Pringle, P. and Rhiney, K. (2020). Climate change and small island developing states. *Annual Review of Environment and Resources*, 45, 1–27. https://doi.org/10.1146/annurev-environ-012320-083355.

UNFCCC (United Nations Framework Convention on Climate Change) (2021, November 22). The Paris Agreement. https://unfccc.int/process-and-meetings/the-paris-agreement/the-paris-agreement

United Nations (2015). *Transforming our World: The 2030 Agenda for Sustainable Development* [A/RES/70/1]. https://sustainabledevelopment.un.org/content/documents/21252030%20Agenda%20for%20Sustainable%20Development%20web.pdf.

United Nations (2021, November, 17). Nationally determined contributions under the Paris Agreement: Synthesis report. FCCC/PA/CMA/2021/8. https://unfccc.int/sites/default/files/resource/cma2021_08E.pdf.

Weitz, N., Carlsen, H., Nilsson, M. and Skånberg, K. (2018). Towards systemic and contextual priority setting for implementing the 2030 Agenda. *Sustainability Science*, 13, 531–548. http://dx.doi.org/10.1007/s11625-017-0470-0.

Zang, C., Cai, W., Liu, Z., Wei, Y.-M., Guan, D., Li, Z., Yan, J. and Gong, P. (2020). Five tips for China to realize its co-targets of climate mitigation and sustainable development goals (SDGS). *Geography and Sustainability*, 1, 245–249. https://doi.org/10.1016/j.geosus.2020.09.001.

4. Motivations toward sustainability in manufacturing at multiple levels

Markéta Svobodová

INTRODUCTION

The qualitative research summarized in this chapter concerns the motivations of private sector employees towards sustainability and their perceptions of their company's motivations toward sustainability. It involved more than 60 in-depth, semi-structured interviews with 60 individuals from the Czech operations of an international large-scale manufacturing company.

The focus of the research summarized was on determining differences among employees in various hierarchical layers of organization: manual workers, administrative workers, managers and/or coordinators without subordinates, lower management, and middle and top management. The objective was to better understand the context and perceptions of motivations toward sustainability for the individual as well as the organization. In both areas, gaps were found in the literature (see the following section of this chapter for details). A better understanding of such motivations within organizations could help various actors (government, media, etc.) to motivate companies more effectively.

It was found that interviewees' childhood experiences, and the opinions of those who raised and influenced them, were crucial in building their internal motivations toward sustainability. Thus, the importance of family, relatives, school, and the surrounding community is critical for building sustainability motivation in an individual. Additionally, the interviewees' children often were mentioned as the primary motivating factor towards sustainability, especially in the case of manual workers.

This research also suggests that, when motivated individuals start working for a company, they may develop ideas for sustainability improvements. However, if such efforts are not welcomed positively by the company, especially management, individuals typically stop coming up with new ideas and focus only on their required work. Thus, the research suggests that organizations should try to motivate their employees to develop ideas for improvements in the company's sustainability. Otherwise, workers often will not voice their views without being asked, will not feel empowered, and will lose their enthusiasm.

In the end, the most sustainability motivated employees are the most demotivated by the lack of sustainable activity in the company for which they work. To get their support and willingness to help with their ideas, the company must convince them that it wants to make fundamental changes in its core business. Otherwise, the organization could lose potential ideas that could help the company be more sustainable and, in the longer term, also more competitive.

Notably, business cases supporting sustainability could help motivate the companies to make sustainability improvements at multiple levels of their core businesses when intrinsic motivation in the company (represented by the relevant management) is lacking. One such business case could be a situation involving recruitment of new employees (as sustainability helps attract them, and at the same time also helps prevent current employees from leaving).

Another useful business case could include the public relations impact of positive media messages and word-of-mouth that could take place as soon as the company starts to improve sustainability truly.

Companies, however, need to be careful not to employ greenwashing, which is a short-sighted activity of some companies defined in literature as being purposefully untrue. (A lack of knowledge of what is and what is not sustainable could also lead to greenwashing in some cases.) Greenwashing is short-sighted in the sense that when people become knowledgeable they will see that it was not genuinely sustainable behavior. They will lose trust in that company, harming the company brand, a parameter that is widely considered valuable property of any well-known company.

Organizations also can be motivated toward sustainable behavior of the company via the key performance indicators (KPIs) of the employees, or a similar system—motivating people toward sustainable functioning of the company financially. (This insight was one of the sustainability improvement ideas from several interviews, although that aspect of the interviews is not the focus of this handbook chapter.) This is crucial, especially for employees who are motivated toward sustainability mainly externally, thus requiring external incentives.

Based on the interview results, the government plays a vital role in motivating organizations toward sustainability. Some managers and other employees think it is the responsibility of the public sphere to protect the environment. In their opinion, businesses exist to make a profit and employ people. Through taxes, penalties, subsidies, and other incentives, the government pushes companies to behave responsibly toward the environment. Legislation, related restrictions, and the risk of penalties were, according to the findings of this research, the most powerful tools for making companies more sustainable in the short term than would be the case without any external influence.

Let us examine an example of negative externalities to illustrate the need for the public sphere to motivate organizations to behave more sustainably. If a company decides to internalize its negative externalities (or even better, to understand them as part of the whole system from the beginning) and include them in their business plans, resulting increased prices of their products could make the company less competitive in the market. Thus, such a company sooner or later may cease to exist, as its efforts to become more environmentally sustainable did not correspond with the sustainability for that company in the sense of surviving in the long term. Consequently, we currently cannot expect companies to commit to such policies if not supported by the public sector.

There are various definitions of sustainability. In this chapter, we will be viewing sustainability as a concept comprising all three pillars: environmental, social, and economic. What needs to be ensured is the sustainable development, that "meets the needs of the present without compromising the ability of future generations to meet their own needs," as described by the report called *Our Common Future* (UN Secretary-General & World Commission on Environment and Development, 1987).

Note: some parts of the research described in this chapter on the motivations of organizations toward sustainability were also covered in its author's conference proceedings from the 15th International Days of Statistics and Economics Conference (Svobodová, 2021).

The following sections include:

- a literature review on organizational motivations toward sustainability,
- methodology covering details and the context of the research,

- detailed findings with specifics on motivations of companies as well as the individuals themselves for sustainability actions at different hierarchical layers, and
- a deductive coding example in the appendix.

LITERATURE REVIEW

A substantial amount of literature on sustainability and topics relevant to this umbrella term has been written in the last few years. That includes organizational or corporate sustainability, also known as corporate social responsibility (CSR).[1] This phenomenon has recently gained significant attention from the public, governments, and other stakeholders.

Nevertheless, literature on the motivations of organizations toward sustainability is far less available. However, it has been continuously emergent and evolving in recent years, so a continuous literature review in this area is necessary. The literature review was conducted for motivations toward sustainability, focusing on organizations and differences among stakeholders (particularly management and other employees).

The sustainable behavior of individuals depends on various factors, and the most effective way to influence employee behavior depends on the individual and their organizational context. Interventions in the context are usually functioning more than verbal appeals "because a variety of factors influence behavior, creative approaches involving multiple influences on behavior offer the greatest potential for change" (Stern, 2005).

Some academic papers, for example, one by Windolph et al. (2014), attempt to summarize the literature concerning motivations toward sustainability strategies of companies. The literature by Babiak and Trendafilova (2011), Bansal (2005), Delmas and Toffel (2008), Ditlev-Simonsen and Midttun (2011), Frondel et al. (2008) and Moon (2007), was also found to be particularly relevant.

The above-mentioned paper by Windolph et al. (2014) primarily discusses three motivational drivers for the management of environmental as well as social issues by companies found in selected literature (Bansal & Roth, 2000; Darnall, 2003; Epstein, 2008) regarding the area of corporate sustainability management: corporate legitimacy seeking, market success, and internal improvement.

The paper does not consider the ethical or moral attitudes of individuals in focusing on motivations relevant to businesses and organizations. The authors examined differences among departments, finding low engagement in sustainability in the finance and accounting department. On the other hand, public relations showed greater levels of attention. This pointed out that legitimacy is an important motivator toward sustainability when compared with some prior research findings.

A paper by Khan et al. (2018) classified motivational drivers into five dimensions and ranked them based on their impact on sustainability. However, this research was conducted only on social sustainability in the healthcare supply chain. The five dimensions mentioned are organizational practices, media and reputation, excellence and awards, technology and innovation, and attitudes.

Paulraj et al. (2017) suggested that *relational and moral motivators* are the essential drivers for sustainability. According to this study, morally motivated companies perform better than those which are not.

Other authors, Shum and Yam (2011), came up with a structural equation model that tries to identify essential factors, including their interactions that can influence managers who are profit-motivated toward corporate responsibility voluntarily. This study attempts to validate Carroll's four-dimensional (economic, legal, ethical, and discretionary) CSR framework that is intended to explain why and how such managers do voluntary CSR.

In some papers, organizational readiness also is considered in addition to motivations. In another selected article, written by Law and Gunasekaran (2012), "the relationships between motivating factors (management, internal and external) and company's willingness and readiness (supportive measures) to adopt sustainable development strategies" is studied.

One of the papers mentioned above (Ditlev-Simonsen & Midttun, 2011) compares what three panels think motivates managers for Corporate Responsibility from a positivist and normative perspective. The motivation of managers is also discussed in other papers (e.g., Kitsis & Chen, 2020), in some with a focus only on sustainability managers (Schaltegger & Burritt, 2018; Visser & Crane, 2010). Another paper (Williams & Schaefer, 2013), focused on the context of SMEs, and highlighted the importance of "personal values and beliefs" for environmental sustainability motivations.

The motivation of workers is studied in other papers. For example, Felo indicated: "Companies that talk about the importance of sustainability and back up that talk with their performance management systems motivate their employees to accept sustainability projects..." (Felo et al., 2015). The role of incentives was scrutinized in another study (Merriman et al., 2016). Another paper discusses how culture de-/motivates employees for sustainability (Galpin et al., 2015). Nevertheless, the role of line managers is also important, "an engaged line manager was essential for promoting employee motivation and involvement in the longer term" (Saksvik et al., 2020).

There are relevant gaps and ideas for future research identified in the literature. The following names a few examples in the areas of motivations of companies and employees.

Regarding perceptions of motivations of organizations: "… Triangulation strategies could be employed to tap the perceptions of various corporate stakeholders regarding corporate motives for adopting a social agenda. These might reveal very different outcomes than research reporting only the perceptions of top management" (Brønn & Vidaver-Cohen, 2009).

Nevertheless, findings from different papers on how motivations for corporate sustainability are relevant differ. Windolph stated that

> these challenges call for further profound analyses of … the reasons why companies care about sustainable development – or why they do not. Particularly in the realm of a normative topic like sustainable development, it is of vital importance that researchers keep in touch with practice... (Windolph et al., 2014)

This research was locally and role-wise focused: it looked at German companies and gained responses only from those responsible in the sustainability area: CSR, Sustainability, or EHS (Environment-Health-Safety).

It is essential to know the motives for organizational sustainability for various reasons, such as public policy effectiveness, developing relevant and practical tools for management, and consulting (Bansal & Roth, 2000).

Concerning *motivations of employees for sustainability*, another paper shows how little can be found in the literature regarding sustainability motivations at *individual workers' level*: "How to integrate sustainability efforts throughout the organization, however, remains a challenge… understanding of organizational sustainability efforts at the individual employee level of analysis, a conspicuously small part of the organizational research surrounding this topic" (Merriman et al., 2016).

According to a recent paper (Lee & Chen, 2018), "little attention has been devoted to employees' behavior toward CSR" so far. Their article showed that "an organization's efforts on CSR could enhance the fulfillment of employees' ERG needs."[2] This interconnection of workers' needs with the sustainability of the company they work for links back to the motivations toward sustainability of employees as well as the company.

A literature focusing in detail on differences in motivations toward sustainability at a large industrial organization concerned various stakeholder groups and internal divisions, as well as various managerial layers and employees, is notably absent, except for the previously mentioned papers (Svobodová, 2021).

METHODOLOGY

Qualitative research is used as it enables researchers to go into more detail regarding the explanation of the motivations, including *Why* questions. In-depth, semi-structured interviews were used. Refer to the relevant part of the interview guide for the in-depth semi-structured interview questions below in Table 4.1. The presented guide represents a framework to explore the motivations of interviewees for sustainability as well as their opinions about the motivations for sustainability of their company. The interview guide is a list of high-level topics and high-level questions that are planned to be covered during the interviews. During the interviews, relevant other additional questions were asked to understand the details. In addition, the wording of the questions stated below was adjusted after a few pilot interviews.

One of the pieces of literature mentioned in a paper by Longhurst (2009) states,

> In-depth, semi-structured interviews are useful for investigating complex behaviors, opinions, and emotions and for collecting information on a diverse range of experiences. They do not offer researchers a route to 'the truth,' but they do offer a route to partial insights into what people do and think.

Thus, the data collected from the interviews are opinions of the participating interviewees, helping us to understand some complex topics more thoroughly.

As stated earlier, this chapter is based on qualitative research—62 in-depth semi-structured interviews (with 30–60 minutes per interview, most of them taking 60 minutes) with 60 employees from the Czech operations of an international large-scale manufacturing company. Interviewees represented various layers of the organizational hierarchy (different management levels, administrative workers, and manual workers; see the details about the sample in Table 4.2). The reason for selecting a large manufacturing company was to be able to include as many relevant hierarchical layers as possible (to have manual workers and to be a large company with various hierarchical layers).

The aim was to have a proper number of interviewees from all hierarchical layers while also including both females and males represented as evenly as possible. However, as manual workers in the selected company were predominantly male, males also were predominantly represented among the interviewees from this hierarchical layer. Similarly, middle and top managers in the selected organization also were mainly men, even though a bit less as a rule than in the manual workers' group. On the other hand, in the group of administrative/office

Table 4.1   *In-depth semi-structured interviews—interview guide (the part concerning motivations toward sustainability)*

	SECTION 0 – Introduction
	The researcher introduction
	Thank you for your participation
Introduction by the Researcher	"Data will be used in anonymized form. Do you agree with recording and personal data processing?"
	Interview duration
Introductory/'same ground' questions	What is sustainability in your view?
	Do you deal with sustainability somehow at your company? If so, how?
	SECTION 1 – Motivations
General motivations toward sustainability	What motivates you for sustainability?
	Does your employer want to be sustainable? If so, why?
Internal stakeholders' influence	Which departments motivate/inspire you for sustainability?
	Which internal stakeholder/s motivate/s you for sustainability? Any role models?
External stakeholders' influence	Which external stakeholders motivate you/your company for sustainability?
Sustainability pillar preference	In which aspect of sustainability (economic, environmental, or social) is your company motivated the most? Why?
	In which aspect of sustainability (economic, environmental, or social) are you motivated the most? Why?
Motivations differences among hierarchical layers	Are there in your opinion differences in motivations toward sustainability among manual workers, administrative workers, and different levels of management? If so, which ones?
	DEMOGRAPHICS

Position	What is your position in the company?
	 ● Manager – if so, please specify:
	   ● Junior management
	   ● Middle management
	   ● Top management
	
	 ● Employee / specialist – if so, please specify:
	   ● Manual work
	   ● Office work

Number of years in the company	How many years have you worked in this company? ● ≤1 ● >1–3 ● >3–5 ● >5–10 ● >10
Age	Please share your age range? ● ≤25 ● 26–35 ● 36–50 ● 51–65 ● >65
Gender (not asked)	● Female ● Male

	Which department do you work in?
	● Public relations
	● Communications
	● Marketing
	● Sales
Department	● Research and development (R&D)
	● Purchasing
	● Logistics
	● Production
	● Finance/Accounting
	● Human resources (HR)
Nationality (if relevant to ask)	Where do you come from?

workers, female employees were represented by more than half of the participants in the interviews. Of the total number of interviewees, female employees were represented by 35%.

The number of interviews conducted was the result of data saturation. It means that with new interviews, no more relevant useful data was gained. Therefore, for the topic of this handbook chapter, further follow-up interviews were not deemed useful.

Table 4.2   Sample description table—interviewees according to their hierarchical position in the organization and gender

Workers according to	Number of Interviewees		
hierarchical layers	Female (%)	Male (%)	Total
Manual workers	0 (0)	8 (100)	8
Administrative/office workers	11 (57,9)	8 (42,1)	19
Managers/coordinators without subordinates	5 (35,7)	9 (64,3)	14
Lower management	4 (40)	6 (60)	10
Middle and top managers	1 (11,1)	8 (88,9)	9
Total	21 (35)	39 (65)	60

Interviewees were chosen in the following manner: the researcher contacted an employee from the Sustainability division and this person helped to disseminate the call to find interviewees throughout the company, especially regarding all hierarchical layers.

The non-probability (typical for qualitative research—with non-representativity of the sample) sampling was done in several ways: mainly, purposive/judgment (concretely expert) sampling guided by criteria of saturation (i.e., adding more interviewees in needed hierarchical categories to reach data saturation) was undertaken. It was done in two ways: first, via the researcher's main contact in the Sustainability department—to select whom to directly contact from middle and top managers as well as some of the representatives of lower management and managers/coordinators without subordinates and some office workers. Candidates for interviews were contacted by the Sustainability representative directly, by email. Second, coordinators from all various divisions transferred the message in their respective areas/divisions to people who they thought would be amenable for such an interview with a researcher. In addition, since the coordinator in the Production Division did not know all relevant employees, some manual workers were selected to participate via manual workers supervisors/foremen who suggested workers to contact.

From those people who were contacted by the coordinators as described above, a portion signed up to participate via an Excel spreadsheet with possible intervals for the interviews;

so in this expert sampling, self-selection played a role as well, as not all people who were contacted, accepted the invitation to take part in the interview.

It is worthwhile to mention that, before using mainly expert sampling, purely convenience sampling (concretely self-selection) was discussed with the Sustainability Division employees to send a general request to all employees to appoint themselves to an interview. However, because of strict rules regarding emailing workers, this idea was rejected at the beginning of the sampling process.

In addition to the previously mentioned sampling techniques used, a Snowball (chain) technique was used to obtain additional relevant contacts for interviews. Some interviewees recommended contacting one or several colleagues directly, without action by the researcher.

Data were gathered in the Czech Republic by recording the interviews conducted via MS Teams, Zoom and mobile phone when previously mentioned tools were technically impossible for an interviewee. Interviews for the most part were conducted individually.

Thematic analysis was used to analyze the data from the interviews, structuring codes sequentially, funneling them down to get themes and categories with common patterns. Codes were created particularly inductively from the data gained. As the researcher expected from the previous literature, few codes were created deductively (more general or common codes)—see an example in Appendix 1. The codebook was developed to help with the analysis of the collected data.

The researcher looked at the data inductively. However, some theoretical background to build on is needed to have a basis for what is already out there in the literature. For interpreting data, different *theoretical lenses* can be put on.

The most relevant theories for the subject matter of Motivations of Organizations for Sustainability are connected to needs and motivations: particularly McClelland's Three Needs Theory—*Achievement, Power*, and *Affiliation* (McClelland, 1988), Alderfer's Theory of Motivational Needs—ERG, standing for *Existence, Relatedness*, and *Growth* (Alderfer, 1969), and Vroom's Expectancy Theory (1964, as cited in Van Eerde & Thierry, 1996)—where *Expectancy, Instrumentality*, and *Valence* are essential, and behavior is according to the outcome's desirability (Hinze Courses, 2010). As a note, the Theory of Motivational Needs is very close to Maslow's Theory of Human Motivation—Hierarchy of Needs with levels representing physiological, social, and self-actualization needs (Maslow, 1943). Those theories help to explain the motivations of people to do something in this research concerning sustainability.

Concerning the reliability of this qualitative research from a data collection view, triangulation was used. Most importantly, checking selected archival data such as previous email communications on sustainability topics allowed the researcher to observe some motivations and connected limitations. In addition, the researcher was invited to participate in several meetings of the sustainability strategy team, being able to observe "live" their motivations and obstacles they expect about sustainability improvements in the future. Those meetings were connected in follow-up after most in-depth interviews had been conducted.

FINDINGS

The interviews examined the individuals' motivations and their perceptions why and how their employer was motivated to behave sustainably. As described in the previous section, different levels of employees were interviewed. This section examines the findings to determine similarities and, most importantly, differences.

As a general finding, sustainability is often viewed as primarily connected to nature and environmental topics. Overall, there was a strong pattern in the employees' views from different levels. Some employees offered the opinion that their company tries to behave sustainably because of external forces such as laws and the risk of penalties and that the organization counts the economic pillar as the most critical pillar of sustainability. Others mentioned that all three pillars (economic, environmental, and social) are of the same importance to the company.

Interestingly and maybe for some also surprisingly, employees as motivational drivers for the sustainability of the organization was hardly mentioned—either by management or by other employees. That is connected to the further findings of employees not feeling engaged and thus not motivated about the company's view of sustainability.

Relation to the Selected Motivation and Needs Connected Theories

Regarding the theories mentioned in the methodology section above, *Achievement* from McClelland's Three Needs Theory can be seen at the administrative and manual workers' levels. *Affiliation* and sometimes also *Power* needs can be encountered especially at the top and middle management level. *Affiliation* particularly because sustainability behavior is expected from the middle and especially top management by the mother company.

When looking at Alderfer's Theory of Motivational Needs, the *Existence* need was seen primarily in some manual workers' answers as they demonstrated interest/fear of (not) keeping pure nature for the future, and not being sure about securing a healthy environment for their children and future generations. *Relatedness* needs were (like *Affiliation* described above) more evident at the top and middle managers' levels. At that level, sustainability matters were viewed as more important for interpersonal relationships in management positions. *Growth* need was seen among management representatives and a bit at other levels, usually mentioned by a few individuals. In this need, not only personal development but also, for example, morality is included.

Regarding Vroom's Expectancy Theory in coming up with sustainability improvement ideas, interviewees articulated attempts to suggest sustainability improvements even though they were not welcomed, or have not seen any follow-up actions from suggestions. Thus, even though sustainability behavior was in some cases viewed as something rather unexpected, they tried anyway to influence corporate behavior.

Based on the results of this research, Vroom's Expectancy Theory can be enriched by adding the parameter of time connected to the persistence of the individual, who does not expect a positive outcome anymore but is trying to influence it anyway. Some people continue striving even when experiencing a lot of pain—demotivation—by trying to change something even when hearing "No" again. And even though after years of trying and getting apathetic and "ground" by the company (this term was mentioned during interviews: to keep the original linguistic meaning in the Czech language: "semletý firmou"), they still wanted to participate in a sustainability interview, which shows that they did not stop caring about this topic. However, it appeared to the researcher that they expected some pain to be alleviated by discussing it anonymously with somebody external to the company. Valence as an anticipated reward value of the outcome could be viewed as driving those employees in the sense that, even though they no longer expect any positive outcome, they still try to make positive changes, since the potential result is so important for them.

Motivations of Individuals Toward Sustainability

The individuals interviewed who were the most motivated toward sustainability also viewed the company as not doing enough in this area, which discouraged them from trying again or even more. Those most motivated for environmental sustainability stated that the company was doing too little in this area. Those focusing more on the social aspect of sustainability thought that the company was not doing enough, particularly in the social area.

Interviewees often mentioned misinformation about sustainability solutions, especially from manual and office workers who have learned about sustainability but often not from trusted sources.

In the following sections, we take a closer look at some specifics and similarities concerning the motivations of individuals for sustainability, divided according to the different stakeholder groups that took part in the interviews.

Middle and top management
Several patterns for internal motivations toward sustainability were seen. Children, for example, were also mentioned as a main driver. Trends and obligations were stated as motivating factors more than in other interviewees' groups. Some managers exhibited little motivation for sustainability as it does not always pay off and could limit them.

A pragmatic view was also expressed: "I am not naive. It must pay off—it must have an added value for the organization (e.g., in PR—it must be seen that the company has done something in sustainability)." This interviewee also stated that they were a realist who always looked at what they could get out of it. Another interviewee stated that their motivation is to create new economic values while caring about the surroundings.

Most of the people in this group mentioned internal motivators for sustainability, as represented by the following selected quotations:

- "To keep humankind and the state of the planet at least as it is currently."
- Not doing bad things—"to be able to look myself in my eyes in the mirror."

Some mentioned children as the primary motivation for sustainability, or that it is something we "must" do:

- "We need to try to keep a beautiful world for our children and grandchildren."
- "The health of my children is my motivation (breathing clean air, etc.)."
- "It is a must—to save this planet."
- It is a trend in the EU.

Lower management
Lower management interviewees were more critical about the company's endeavor to behave more sustainably. The pattern in this group of stakeholders indicated a view that management

seems not to care much about sustainability. Few of them do anything in the sustainability area and only do because it is included in their job-related tasks. Thus, it is clear that for those who are not motivated toward sustainability by other means, having it as a task, an obligation, is a source of motivation. Therefore, it is crucial to set the rules from the top of the company to show the desirable direction toward sustainability.

A hedonist approach also was seen in trying to live life without any limits, which could be potentially limited by taking sustainability into account (like driving a car at high speed and thus with high consumption). On the other hand, motivation for sustainability because of children or having clean nature came during a few interviews with lower management representatives.

Managers and coordinators without subordinates
Proportionally more interviewees in this group were motivated to behave sustainably compared with the previously described group of lower management. The motivations for the people motivated toward sustainability in this group were mainly related to nature, children, and being raised in such a way or influenced by family and friends.

Office workers
Office workers were the most represented group in the sample (19 employees). Out of these, only one worker did not have much personal motivation for sustainability owing to their financial insecurity and not being satisfied with their free time (not having enough). This confirms that people first need to have secured the basic physiological needs before focusing on higher needs in the hierarchy.

For office workers, internal motivation and interest were the most significant drivers for sustainability. Surroundings and media were encountered as motivational sources mainly by this group of interviewees.

Selected quotations to show the representation of positive motivation, are as follows:

- "Something must be done—we have only one planet." They also like that sustainability comes up with something new, like bringing new products.
- "I think we need to stop and think about what we need—just quality things, not to act according to trends."
- Nevertheless, original motivation can be positive but already turning into a demotivation state: "At work, I retreated from some of my principles, as it is easier."

Manual workers
Children were stated to be the primary motivation toward sustainability for manual workers. To go with them for a walk and show them examples of how to behave. The second most significant motivational driver for sustainability in this group had to do with their upbringing by their parents. Saving costs was also among the motivators for this employee group interviewed.

Manual workers felt that not being heard in their attempts for sustainability improvements was an important demotivator. As bringing the products to life is the task they are paid for and evaluated by, they cannot do anything else if there is no spare time. Thus, sustainability rules need to come from top management and be included in the tasks or job descriptions. In addition, sustainability needs to be made easy and logical to do. For example, waste disposal containers should be accessible for all workers, instead of them having to go a long way to throw something away. Otherwise, they cannot behave sustainably even though they want to, as they must manage their tasks on time.

Motivation Toward Sustainability of the Organization

Middle and top management

Legislation (mainly Czech and from the EU, including Green Deal) and regulations were the number one reason for taking responsibility for the company's wanting to behave sustainably and doing it faster than the company would otherwise, according to the interviewees from the top and middle management. The Paris Agreement was also said to have some impact.

Public Relations or the brand and image of the company was mentioned as the second most important reason for the organization's activity in the sustainability area. Additionally, some interviewees connected it with a positive impact on sales as well.

Some quotations are included to clarify the interviewees' opinions:

- "Legislation was needed to kick the ass of the industry. Now market demand is rapid—it is different in regions, however."
- "Externally, it seems like the company is trying to be more sustainable. Then people buy our products more. It is a trend."
- "The primary aim is to comply with legislation and sell more products. Maybe it is correct like that."
- "Set conditions from the external world are needed to push the company to go beyond its comfort zone."
- "Now it is also starting to make financial sense to be sustainable, as technologies are getting cheaper."
- "Sustainably managed companies are the same as or outperform the rest in terms of profitability and business success."
- "Anything bad can harm the brand."

Additionally, it is helpful to add quotations that state the reasons why the company is not intrinsically acting sustainably, without external "pushes":

- "Transformation is costly—to do old and new things at the same time. Innovations cost money."
- "How to bring the workforce with us is an issue, since fewer people will be needed for the innovations (easier production, new technologies used). It is difficult to motivate them to support such a change."
- "You don't make money on ecology—otherwise, it would return hard cash."

Lower management

Existential motivation, meaning being essential for the company to survive in the long term, was stated mostly by lower management representatives. Legislation, both national and EU-related, was labeled as the most crucial reason for sustainable behavior very often by this group, although comparably less so than by the higher-level managers described above.

Nevertheless, profit as a driver was seen by this group to be relatively more significant when compared with other respondents' groups.

Selected quotations follow, to give a few examples:

- "The claims of customers who look at responsible businesses are better than those who are not interested in the planet and pretend to be a separate island which has nothing to offer back to society."
- "To survive in the long run, the company has to behave sustainably and adapt to new, sustainable ways of doing business."

Managers and coordinators without subordinates

Some representatives of this group mentioned optimization as the most important motivator toward sustainability—to lower company costs. This was in contrast to the group of lower management, which looked at the financial aspects from the profit-selling point of view rather than internal costs.

Otherwise, similar motivators were highlighted as in the previous group: (1) the EU and Czech legislation, (2) keeping the continuity of the business, (3) being a trend, and (4) customers' perception.

Several respondents were critical of how the company does things in sustainability versus what is presented externally. Some citations:

- "The organization is only doing what needs to be met, not looking at the whole ecosystem—not looking long term in 10 years."
- "The company is more and more aware of the influence and responsibility for products; it has become a political topic and is being discussed on top levels."
- "Not to get fined."
- "It is often greenwashing. The company is only taking care of topics seen externally (PR), not the little things inside the company, to be seen in a good light. With all activities, image is important. Priority is put where the company can show off."
- "It's taken as an on-the-top topic, not a priority one. Only what we are pushed into by the outside is done."

Office workers

Office workers who took part in the interviews viewed both legislation and PR as the critical drivers for the sustainability of the selected organization. In general, office workers are essential in the company's attempts connected to sustainability and view it all as to be done just because of external pressure.

Some office workers showed positive views of the company because it employs many people, which they view as a major responsibility towards society. However, most interviewees from this group of employees would prefer that the organization be more motivated toward sustainability.

A couple of quotations can be mentioned here for this group too, for example:

- "Unequivocally, the company has to be sustainable, since that is the trend—legislation, customers."
- "Competitive pressure from those who are further than the company."

Manual workers

Manual worker interviewees mentioned continuing the company's existence as the main reason for the company to act sustainably. Moreover, complying with all legislation was often seen as an important motivator as well. This group mentioned responsibility for its workers as well, in contrast to other groups participating in the interviews. Selected quotations follow:

- "If you don't do business environmentally, socially, you won't succeed."
- "To be talked about positively."
- "The motivators are that it is a trend and customers and the EU want it. If you want to go with the trends, you must go in that direction. Also, for example, water recycling leads to the fact that it is worth it—in a while, it will start to earn money."
- "Existence—to do business in the future too."

Perceived Differences in Motivations Toward Sustainability among Different Hierarchical Levels

Middle and top management

This group indicated that the top and middle management (themselves) have the highest motivation toward sustainability. They also see ensuring sustainability as one of the managers' roles. Selected quotations follow:

- "The higher in the organization, the higher the motivation for sustainability since they must act as a role model for others—i.e., they must behave according to rules. For manual workers, the main motivator is salary. In practice, however, I had the experience that people like the sustainability topic, and so they start to come up with ideas whenever they get some space for it."
- "However, people are shy here, and so management needs to initiate that sustainability ideas are welcomed to make them come up with such ideas which they have."

Lower management

Differences were seen mainly in the possibilities to influence things as the lower managers have good access to the lower and higher positions. They also think top management has sustainability in KPIs, so they are motivated by them too, whereas specialists and manual workers cannot influence things much. Some quotations as examples:

- "It is important to motivate the bosses to make their subordinates in the team feel they can influence something."
- "If it is not really uncomfortable, people try to behave sustainably no matter the position—but it depends on each person's opportunities."
- "Communication is on the top management. How employees see that management is behaving, they behave similarly as they think that is expected from them too. So it always depends on which character the manager is."
- "Better sympathy for sustainability is by top management rather than middle management."
- "Each person is motivated by something different—e.g., people in top positions do not look at money, unlike manual workers."

Managers and coordinators without subordinates

Views from this group were found to be similar to those of the previous group. Some quotations:

- "Some higher management now view the topic as important because of their children who view it more sharply."
- "A manual worker is motivated differently than an administrative worker, rather by money. Some people grew up with sustainability values, and then the position is not important."
- "The lower in structure, the less they care. Nobody cares for sustainability at the company if it is not their task"—based on tasks and targets.

Office workers

It was often mentioned that office workers could not influence much. They do not have the power or time for such things, even though they would like to do so. Personal motivation is often significant, but their role is limiting them. KPIs are not sustainability-related, so thus trying to improve sustainability at the organization is just "a nice thing to do", something extra beyond employees' regular work duties. The prevalent view is that it should be in the KPIs so that all hierarchy levels would be motivated in that way. Selected quotations are as follows:

- "If one manager says something, the rest of the people 'shut up.' Voicing ideas is seen as a risk of getting bad feedback. Micromanaging is also a big issue for the potential of sustainability ideas."
- "Sustainability has to come from top management, but it is not coming now."
- "There is excellent personnel in the company, but there is also a hierarchy, so people at lower positions are not trusted. I see this as the biggest problem for the company. Over two to three years, they all 'model' themselves in the same opinion."
- "People are in management sometimes 20 years—sustainability is something new and sometimes a 'foul word.' I think managers do not have internal motivation for it."
- "The opinion of an expert is often overshadowed by the opinion of the manager's ego."
- "Position is only one factor in the motivation of a person. Also, character, values… are playing an important role."
- "There is a different focus on specific sustainability areas according to the position."
- "Middle managers see it sometimes as current tasks."

Manual workers

Manual workers mainly stated that it is not about position but the person. And if the company wants all layers to do it, it needs to be mentioned in internal regulations, which need to be followed. Selected quotations follow here as well:

- "People who have it in them will do it. Not the rest." Control is needed according to them.
- "A worker goes home at the end of the working hours. Employees in higher positions are afraid of inheriting problems."
- "It depends on how people were raised and their consciences."

The Sustainability Pillar's Preferences by Individuals Versus the Selected Organization (as Perceived by Individuals)

The generally recognized pillars of sustainability—economic, environmental, and social—were considered. Most interviewees mentioned that the environmental pillar is the most important. However, there were preferential views according to division/team: economic for sales-oriented people, and social for people connected with Human Resources and Integrity.

Middle and top management
This group almost always perceived the organization's motivation to be economic and connected to legal regulations. Still, to the direct question about pillars, nearly half of them replied that all three pillars are equally important. So the theory they have in mind is that all three pillars matter equally, but when discussing how it works in practice in the organization, the economic pillar prevailed when decisions were rendered. As an example from the quotations: "They all [pillars] go together. Environment and society create consumer demand. The economic pillar [money] goes with it."

In comparison, when talking about the preference of the pillar regarding the importance for them personally, the majority stated that all three pillars were essential for them. Several preferred the environmental pillar, and one mentioned the economic one to be the preferred one.

Lower management and managers/coordinators without subordinates
Most of this group's representatives stated the economic pillar to be the crucial one for the company and the environmental one or all three to be the most important for them.

Office workers
The environmental pillar was the most important for most office workers interviewed. For several, it was the social pillar or all three. It was also stated that the economic pillar is not important as "society has enough money." The economic pillar as the primary motivation for the company was mentioned as a strong pattern in this group.

A few quotations follow:

- "Economic pillar is motivation number one, especially now with the COVID-19 virus."
- The economic pillar is the most important for the organization—and "sustainability is increasing prices." It is a capitalist company—the focus is on the financial part only. The organization, "does not care about social and environmental pillars—it is just forced to do it. Just some individuals who want to change something are trying."

Manual workers
The economic pillar was mentioned as the most important for the company's motivation, whereas for the individual's motivation, mainly the social or the economic pillar was mentioned, connected also to the other one or two pillars. The economic pillar was stated to be the most important for the company as, if there will be no profit, the company will not survive. Most of manual workers also saw the connection with environmental and social areas.

The hierarchy of needs was clear: first, workers need to have enough money to care about society and the environment.

Compared with other layers, manual workers think more often that it is not right to focus primarily on the economic pillar. On the other hand, they view current changes in sustainability at the company positively. The environmental pillar was mentioned the least by manual workers. They view primarily the economic and then the social pillars as the most important.

Some economic pillar related examples:

- "Social and economic are the most important for me. But the social pillar is connected to environmental aspects—the system has to work as a complex."
- "We are humans, and we all need money. It is not correct that all is connected to money, however. When there is money, we can also care about the environment—it should be set by the state as rules."
- "When there will be money but no community and environment, money will be of no use. We will not have air to breathe. Money will exist, but we will not."
- "The environment is the most important because when I'm old, I'll still want to be able to go to a clean forest for a walk."
- "Economic for me because when I have enough money, I can also be active in other areas."

Findings Regarding Data from Selected Organization's Divisions

One finding of this research was that people working in areas mainly responsible for sustainability matters of the company were highly motivated toward sustainability but few turned out to be interested in getting such a position/opportunity at the company. Only divisions from which a significant percentage of respondents came are discussed in this paper to ensure anonymity. Interviewees from the Sales and External Relations-related departments were more optimistic about the organization's sustainability efforts and behavior than interviewees from other divisions.

Production

Interviewees in this category viewed sustainability very narrowly, related to production, mainly sorting waste. Furthermore, most of them stated they could not influence the sustainability of the company. One citation: "When there is a container for plastics, I am sorting plastics there. But I cannot influence having, e.g., more containers there to avoid mixing plastics with other waste."

External stakeholders influencing the organization's motivation toward sustainability mentioned were NGOs, close-by communities and mayors. Workers from production perceived the company as going in the right direction with the sustainability of the production site compared with the past.

Not having time for sustainability was mentioned significantly more often by people working in production than by other workers interviewed. "We do not have time to care about sustainability. We have to produce pieces and pieces."

Misinformation about some sustainability topics occurs in this stakeholder group more often than in others. Furthermore, workers from production mentioned more that they are working at this company because of a good salary and stability.

Limitations

Concerning demographic aspects, the data were analyzed focusing on similarities and differences by position, respectively its hierarchy in general, and not other factors such as age, gender, or the number of years the interviewees worked at the company.

Interviewees took part in the discussions with the researcher voluntarily. However, this does not have to be seen as a limitation since, for discussing motivations, it was beneficial that people with some opinions about their and company's motivation take part in the research. Besides interviewees' nominations by the coordinators from various divisions, some interviewees from the production division were nominated by their managers. Additionally, some interview participants were recommended by their colleagues during interviews (the "snowball" technique) as those interviewees thought that they would have something interesting to share regarding the motivations and limitations of the company for sustainability.

As the research was conducted qualitatively, the data gathered serves to represent opinions of the interviewees, not as generalizable findings that could be applied to the general population. However, we could expect similar results at companies in similar contexts and conditions (manufacturing, large international companies, etc.). On the other hand, compared with quantitative research, the data from interviews offer strong internal validity (details helping to explore and understand the subject matter thoroughly).

IMPLICATIONS AND RECOMMENDATIONS FOR RELEVANT STAKEHOLDERS

The following implications and recommendations for the selected relevant stakeholders are based on the conducted qualitative research in the selected company, going in-depth regarding the sustainability motivations with the interviewees. Connecting the dots was done using the author's long-term experience in sustainability (working, volunteering, as well as continuously studying corporate sustainability in detail).

Policymakers

This qualitative research showed the social contract concept in the data from the participants. The social contract signifies that some of the personal freedoms are taken by a state to protect or gain some civil rights, as viewed in the past by Locke as well as Rousseau. Among such private or civil rights, we can also count protecting the environment. As stated by some interviewees, the government (meaning not the business) is responsible for taking good care of the environment.

Furthermore, even those employees who were motivated toward sustainability view the role of the government as more crucial in protecting the environment than the role of the company for which they work. Some interviewees highlighted that it is the state's role to make sure that the environment is protected. Thus, it was generally felt by the interviewees that the public sphere motivates companies to behave more sustainably and faster, through legislation and enforcement.

Organizational Leaders

The research results indicate that organizational leaders should try to keep employees of their companies motivated and wanting to speak up with their ideas for improvements, try to implement them, and not penalize employees for being brave and honest with their thoughts and opinions.

Sustainability should be incorporated in all resources in the company: not only people in all divisions but also in all assets from the tangible area, and in the accumulated experience, culture, and knowledge of the employees.

Media Influencers

The media should try to communicate various motivations of organizations regarding sustainability to make this information available to the public. It is also helpful if the public knows of different possible motivations and can thus challenge the company they work for in this area. Discussing this topic in the media might help motivate organizations for sustainability as well.

Teachers and Students

It is recommended to include sustainability in curricula to make current and future students aware of organizational motivations toward sustainability. This also could help them see the broader view of possible motivations toward sustainability when looking for a job or cooperating with companies.

CONCLUSION

In conclusion, the motivation of employees toward sustainability in organizations does not depend on the position in the company or department but on the individual's conviction. Whether the motivation materializes in their actions depends mainly on whether a person has the time and capacity to do so, and whether demotivators, which arose gradually due to negative experiences, exist. However, how much impact they have depends on the position—how much power a person has to enforce something within the organization.

Most employees interviewed perceived the company to focus mainly on the economic pillar (less on the environmental and social ones). The interviewees also viewed the company as needing external motivation (especially EU and Czech legislation) to focus on sustainability and move faster with sustainability efforts.

Usually, those most passionate about sustainability were primarily demotivated by what the company was doing in this area (by its insufficient activity in sustainability). Moreover, this research suggests that employees who are more interested in environmental aspects usually view the company as doing too little in the ecological area (similar to the case of social aspects). In addition, employees are often motivated toward sustainability in a hidden and passive form. Also, employees are happy to work more on sustainability if they have time and approval to do so.

Let us summarize the key points from the selected levels of interviewee groups. Lower management did not show much motivation for sustainability compared with other groups—

they seemed to not care so much about it (the second least "caring about sustainability" group consisted of managers and coordinators without subordinates). From the most represented group of administrative workers, only one person showed little personal motivation for sustainability, which signifies that this interviewee's group showed relatively the highest push for sustainability. It is also noteworthy that this group had the largest representation, proportionally, of female interviewees. For manual workers, children were most named the primary motivator to behave sustainably. Manual workers interviewed are typically motivated toward sustainability, but they feel that they are not able to influence things at work.

From the findings, we can also conclude that the *achievement* motivation is prevalent regarding McClelland's Three Needs Theory. According to Alderfer's Motivational Needs Theory, the need for *growth* is the primary motivation. From Vroom's Expectancy Theory, *instrumentality* and *expectancy* are very low, and in terms of *valence*, the outcome is sometimes not expected by the interviewees anymore.

NOTES

1.   Currently the term CSR is not used much as it is seen as a concept which does not cover all three pillars of Sustainability (refer to the name "Social")
2.   Alderfer's ERG theory suggests that there are three groups of core needs: existence (E), relatedness (R), and growth (G)—you can find more on this theory in the Methodology section of this chapter.

REFERENCES

Alderfer, C. P. (1969). An empirical test of a new theory of human needs. *Organizational Behavior and Human Performance*, *4*(2), 142–175. https://doi.org/10.1016/0030-5073(69)90004-X

Babiak, K., & Trendafilova, S. (2011). CSR and environmental responsibility: Motives and pressures to adopt green management practices. *Corporate Social Responsibility and Environmental Management*, *18*(1), 11–24. https://doi.org/10.1002/csr.229

Bansal, P. (2005). Evolving sustainably: A longitudinal study of corporate sustainable development. *Strategic Management Journal*, *26*(3), 197–218. https://doi.org/10.1002/smj.441

Bansal, P., & Roth, K. (2000). Why companies go green: A model of ecological responsiveness. *Academy of Management Journal*, *43*(4), 717–736. https://doi.org/10.5465/1556363

Brønn, P. S., & Vidaver-Cohen, D. (2009). Corporate motives for social initiative: Legitimacy, sustainability, or the bottom line? *Journal of Business Ethics*, *87*(1), 91–109. https://doi.org/10.1007/s10551-008-9795-z

Darnall, N. (2003). Motivations for participating in a voluntary environmental initiative. The multi-state working group and EPA's EMS pilot program. In S. Sharma & M. Starik (eds), *Research in Corporate Sustainability*. Cheltenham, UK and Northampton, MA, USA: Edward Elgar Publishing, 123–154.

Delmas, M. A., & Toffel, M. W. (2008). Organizational responses to environmental demands: Opening the black box. *Strategic Management Journal*, *29*(10), 1027–1055. https://doi.org/10.1002/smj.701

Ditlev-Simonsen, C. D., & Midttun, A. (2011). What motivates managers to pursue corporate responsibility? A survey among key stakeholders. *Corporate Social Responsibility and Environmental Management*, *18*(1), 25–38. https://doi.org/10.1002/csr.237

Epstein, M. J. (2008). *Making Sustainability Work. Best Practices in Managing and Measuring Corporate Social, Environmental, and Economic Impacts*. Sheffield, UK: Greenleaf.

Felo, A. J., Merriman, K. K., Sen, S., & Litzky, B. E. (2015). Encouraging employees to support corporate sustainability efforts. *Management Accounting Quarterly*, *16*(4), 25–31.

Frondel, M., Horbach, J., & Rennings, K. (2008). What triggers environmental management and inno-vation? Empirical evidence for Germany. *Ecological Economics*, *66*(1), 153–160. https://doi.org/10.1016/j.ecolecon.2007.08.016

Galpin, T., Whitttington, J. L., & Bell, G. (2015). Is your sustainability strategy sustainable? Creating a culture of sustainability. *Corporate Governance*, *15*(1), 1–17. http://dx.doi.org/10.1108/CG-01-2013-0004

Hinze Courses. (2010, October 27). *Expectancy* [Educational. Archived copy]. https://web.archive.org/web/20101027133712/http:/web.dcp.ufl.edu/hinze/Expectancy.htm

Khan, M., Hussain, M., Gunasekaran, A., Ajmal, M. M., & Helo, P. T. (2018). Motivators of social sus-tainability in healthcare supply chains in the UAE—Stakeholder perspective. *Sustainable Production and Consumption*, *14*, 95–104. https://doi.org/10.1016/j.spc.2018.01.006

Kitsis, A. M., & Chen, I. J. (2020). Do motives matter? Examining the relationships between motives, SSCM practices and TBL performance. *Supply Chain Management*, *25*(3), 325–341. http://dx.doi.org/10.1108/SCM-05-2019-0218

Law, K. M. Y., & Gunasekaran, A. (2012). Sustainability development in high-tech manufacturing firms in Hong Kong: Motivators and readiness. *International Journal of Production Economics*, *137*(1), 116–125. https://doi.org/10.1016/j.ijpe.2012.01.022

Lee, L., & Chen, L.-F. (2018). Boosting employee retention through CSR: A configurational analysis. *Corporate Social Responsibility and Environmental Management*, *25*(5), 948–960. https://doi.org/10.1002/csr.1511

Longhurst, R. (2009). Interviews: In-depth, semi-structured. In *International Encyclopedia of Human Geography*. Elsevier, 580–584. https://doi.org/10.1016/B978-008044910-4.00458-2

Maslow, A. H. (1943). A theory of human motivation. *Psychological Review*, *50*(4), 370–396. https://web.archive.org/web/20170914183817/http:/psychclassics.yorku.ca/Maslow/motivation.htm. https://doi.org/10.1037/h0054346

McClelland, D. (1988). *Human Motivation*. Cambridge University Press.

Merriman, K. K., Sen, S., Felo, A. J., & Litzky, B. E. (2016). Employees and sustainability: The role of incentives. *Journal of Managerial Psychology*, *31*(4), 820–836. http://dx.doi.org/10.1108/JMP-09-2014-0285

Moon, J. (2007). The contribution of corporate social responsibility to sustainable development. *Sustainable Development*, *15*(5), 296–306. https://doi.org/10.1002/sd.346

Paulraj, A., Chen, I. J., & Blome, C. (2017). Motives and performance outcomes of sustainable supply chain management practices: A multi-theoretical perspective. *Journal of Business Ethics*, *145*(2), 239–258. https://doi.org/10.1007/s10551-015-2857-0

Saksvik, P. Ø., Christensen, M., Fossum, S., Lysklett, K., & Karanika-Murray, M. (2020). Investigating managerial qualities to support sustainable intervention effects in the long term 1. *Nordic Journal of Working Life Studies*, *10*(2), 81–99.

Schaltegger, S., & Burritt, R. (2018). Business cases and corporate engagement with sustainability: Differentiating ethical motivations. *Journal of Business Ethics*, *147*(2), 241–259. https://doi.org/10.1007/s10551-015-2938-0

Shum, P. K., & Yam, S. L. (2011). Ethics and law: Guiding the invisible hand to correct corporate social responsibility externalities. *Journal of Business Ethics: JBE*, *98*(4), 549–571. http://dx.doi.org/10.1007/s10551-010-0608-9

Stern, P. C. (2005). Understanding individuals' environmentally significant behavior. *Environmental Law Reporter News & Analysis*, *35*, 10785.

Svobodová, M. (2021). Motivation of organizations for sustainability – the case of a large industrial company in the Czech Republic. *The 15th International Days of Statistics and Economics*, 1008–1018.

UN Secretary-General & World Commission on Environment and Development. (1987). *Report of the World Commission on Environment and Development*. United Nations. https://digitallibrary.un.org/record/139811

Van Eerde, W., & Thierry, H. (1996). Vroom's expectancy models and work-related criteria: A meta-analysis. *Journal of Applied Psychology*, *81*(5), 575–586. https://doi.org/10.1037/0021-9010.81.5.575

Visser, W., & Crane, A. (2010). *Corporate Sustainability and the Individual: Understanding What Drives Sustainability Professionals as Change Agents* (SSRN Scholarly Paper ID 1559087; Issue ID 1559087). Social Science Research Network. https://doi.org/10.2139/ssrn.1559087

Williams, S., & Schaefer, A. (2013). Small and medium-sized enterprises and sustainability: Managers' values and engagement with environmental and climate change issues: SMEs and sustainability - managers' values and engagement. *Business Strategy and the Environment, 22*(3), 173–186. https://doi.org/10.1002/bse.1740

Windolph, S. E., Harms, D., & Schaltegger, S. (2014). Motivations for corporate sustainability management: Contrasting survey results and implementation. *Corporate Social Responsibility and Environmental Management, 21*(5), 272–285. https://doi.org/10.1002/csr.1337

APPENDIX

Deductive Coding – Example

1. In which aspect/pillar of sustainability is your company motivated the most?
    1.1. Economic
    1.2. Environmental
    1.3. Social
    1.4. All three
    1.5. Economic and environmental
    1.6. Economic and social
    1.7. Environmental and social
    1.8. None (it is not motivated toward sustainability)
2. In which aspect/pillar of sustainability are you motivated the most?
    1.1. Economic
    1.2. Environmental
    1.3. Social
    1.4. All three
    1.5. Economic and environmental
    1.6. Economic and social
    1.7. Environmental and social
    1.8. None (I am not motivated toward sustainability)

5. Content analysis of nationally determined contributions: multi-level climate action to achieve the goals of the Paris Agreement

Erin Rae Hoffer

INTRODUCTION

As public organizations around the world struggle to meet the challenge of global warming, increasing reports of environmental disaster and instability drive concerns for stronger action. Research on multi-level climate action (MLCA), the application of multi-level governance (MLG) theory to environmental issues and climate change, is needed to shed light on the actions of international groups, governments, and non-governmental organizations in addressing the crisis of climate change.

Multi-level Governance Theory and Climate Action

In the past decades, MLG research has explored the impact of globalization and the influence of non-governmental stakeholders (Hooghe & Marks, 2003). MLG theories explain the way policy instruments, strategies, and plans interconnect global institutions, nations, regional governments, and local authorities to achieve shared goals (Adriázola et al., 2018). Much the way that horizontal and vertical elements underpin the theory of multi-level governance (Hooghe & Marks, 2003), MLCA theory provides insight into complex structures with conflicting perspectives about solutions to the problems of global warming, illuminate the way public and private stakeholders negotiate and share power, make decisions, and implement policies with long-term social and economic impacts (Potluka & Liddell, 2014).

Betsill and Bulkeley (2006) remind us that urban climate action was called out as fundamental to environmental sustainability in the Brundtland Report (World Commission on Environment and Development, 1987). In an earlier publication, these authors (Bulkeley & Betsill, 2005) determined that "a perspective informed by multilevel governance can examine the ways in which urban sustainability is being constructed and contested at a variety of scales of governance and through multiple political spaces" (p. 59). The contributions of subnational actors at city, regional, or provincial level do not weaken national power, but rather, call for new definitions, scope, and scale of national policymaking, and for refocusing responsibility through environmental discourse, as advocated by Hajer and ProQuest (1995).

Global Policy Context for Multi-level Climate Action

An important context for MLCA theory is the work of the United Nations. In 1988, the United Nations Environment Programme and the World Meteorological Organization gathered a worldwide group of scientists, the Intergovernmental Panel on Climate Change (IPCC), to formulate reports on climate change, including the scientific knowledge, the social and economic impacts, responses, and solutions (IPCC, n.d.b). The IPCC's First Assessment Report (FAR) was presented at the first international convention, the Conference of the Parties, in Berlin in 1995 (IPCC, n.d.a). After that first conference, the United Nations Framework Convention on Climate Change (UNFCCC) gathered international policymakers and scientific experts annually for Conferences of the Parties (COPs) to negotiate agreements to address climate change.

As Pahl-Wostl (2009) observes, multi-level structures with many decision-making centers and alternative modes of coordination can address the policy issues associated with the governance of natural resources. Zürn (2020) extends the MLG typology by enumerating four different types defined by strong versus weak centralized authority and dominant identity versus multiple identities. Decentralized federalism (dominant identity, weak center), centralized federalism (dominant identity, strong center), and strong supranational integration (multiple identities, strong center) are three of the four types. The fourth, global governance (multiple identities, weak center) reflects the structure of the UNFCCC, the international organization formed to address the climate crisis (DeLeo, 2017).

Climate Policy Action of the Paris Agreement

The UNFCCC's Paris Agreement on Climate Change was adopted by the representatives of 196 nations at COP 21 in Paris in 2015 (Rogelj et al., 2016). The Paris Agreement became legally binding in 2016. The agreement's aim was to commit nations to actions that would limit climate change, described in 15 Articles.

Article 1 explains the definitions applied throughout the treaty. Article 2 reaffirms the goal of limiting global temperature increase to ensure a sustainable future. Article 4 asks Parties to restrict emissions and mitigate greenhouse gases (GHG) through domestic measures. Article 5 focuses on the ability of Parties to conserve sinks, forests, and reservoirs. Article 6 calls for transfer of mitigation outcomes through cooperation, environmental integrity, and transparent accounting. Article 7 sets out a goal for adaptation, the development of infrastructure and social systems to withstand global warming. Article 8 describes the need for Parties to counteract current economic and environmental destruction resulting from climate change. Articles 9, 10, and 11 articulate the obligations of developed countries to contribute resources so that developing countries would be capable of supporting the agreement. Articles 12, 13, and 15 focus on education, awareness, and transparency. Article 14, the "global stocktake" requires all Parties to contribute data towards a collective progress assessment every 5 years, starting in 2023 (United Nations Framework Convention on Climate Change, n.d.a, n.d.c, n.d.d).

Nationally Determined Contributions

Article 4 also requires Parties to report national plans to reduce emissions through formal statements of intention every 5 years, known as Nationally Determined Contributions (NDCs). NDCs enable each country to meet emissions reductions targets in ways suited to national circumstances. Pauw and Klein (2020) point out that the NDC model overcame the difficulties of previous UN climate negotiations by enabling countries to address climate change in different ways. This was a breakthrough that enabled agreement, a significant departure from previous UNFCCC policies, a device that enabled countries to drive their own action plans, recognizing the unique circumstance of each nation, emphasizing 'contributions' as opposed to 'commitments' (Rajamani, 2016).

The NDCs describe national strategy, envision a positive future, and assess the social, economic, and environmental context for policy change. These documents commit nations to common goals, reiterate the ambition to continued emissions reductions over time, and disclose vulnerabilities and risks. Detailing action plans, mitigation strategies, policy implementation intentions, the NDCs describe intentions to transform industry sectors, and explain the means to adapt as the climate shifts the environment. Each nation determines the degree to which programs and investments are disclosed, the need for financial support from other parties is articulated and plans for innovation and technology transfer are explained. Transparency of progress is established through the global stocktake.

Prior to the twenty-first Conference of the Parties (COP21) in 2015, countries drafted Intended Nationally Determined Contributions (INDCs), preliminary documents that described the climate actions the countries intended to take following 2020. By August 2017, 165 INDCs were published by the UNFCCC (Stephenson et al., 2019).

The IPCC's 2018 Special Report warned that limiting global warming to the Paris Agreement goal of 1.5°C above pre-industrial levels would require the transformation of economic and social systems to drive change across business sectors and governmental boundaries, to ensure sustainable development for the future (IPCC, 2018).

The 2021 Conference of the Parties (COP26)

In November 2021, the twenty-sixth Conference of the Parties (COP26) convened in Glasgow to make progress toward the overarching goals of the Paris Agreement, to limit global emissions and adapt to climate change. The UK Presidency of the Conference negotiated deals aimed at addressing deforestation and land degradation, coal phase-outs, methane emissions reductions, vehicle electrification, gas and oil reductions. Criticism that these deals were lacking in policy detail diminished the sense of progress. Finalizing the Paris rulebook to support future carbon trading, along with a joint declaration by China and the US on increased ambition, yielded a positive perception of conference outcomes (Davy, 2021).

In the run-up to the 2021 conference, 143 of the 192 signatories to the Paris Agreement had submitted new or updated NDCs, reflecting increased ambition and new action plans (COP26, 2021). The text of this updated set of NDCs provides an opportunity to gain knowledge about the multi-level climate action that Parties to the Paris Agreement will pursue to achieve their commitments and prevent global climate disaster (United Nations Framework Convention on Climate Change, n.d.b).

LITERATURE REVIEW

Theories of Multi-level Governance

The study of multi-level climate action builds upon literature on governance structures incorporating divided jurisdiction, power-sharing across tiers, and influence of non-state actors. A seminal paper by Marks (1993) incorporated the term 'Multi-Level Governance' (MLG) to explain the structural policy of the European Commission, emphasizing the importance of systemic negotiation between different tiers of government. Bache and Flinders (2004) described the shift in decision-making from authoritative to dispersive in the application of MLG to the restructuring of the British State from a state-centric model to one based on the tenets of decision-making shared across governmental levels, loss of control as states share decision-making with sub-national entities such as states, and interconnected arenas for policy and public administration.

Piattoni (2009) presents the history and concepts of multi-level governance, describing the theoretical, empirical, and normative challenges of MLG as these governance models span processes, situations, strategies, and structures. Empirically, Piattoni finds that MLG describes phenomena explained by traditional governance, leading to ambiguity. Normatively, the author questions whether MLG leads to decisions with greater legitimacy than those achieved through traditional governance structures. A reliance on ad hoc networks, haphazardly constituted, incorporating non-government actors, drives MLG outside the bounds of representative democracy, equivalent to special purpose jurisdictions with non-governmental organizations, requiring new criteria for judgement.

Type 1 and Type 2 Categories

By exploring a body of articles on MLG, Hooghe and Marks (2003) found two distinct categories of multi-level governance. Type 1 describes a federal governance system, such as that found in the United States or Canada, in which national, provincial, regional, and local jurisdictions exercise clearly demarcated authority. The second category, Type 2, describes a fluid intersection of groups across jurisdictions aimed at accomplishing specific tasks. The tension between community and scale is fundamental to the differences between Type 1 and Type 2 multi-level governance. The understanding of responsibility and authority within the elements of a Type 1 governance structure revolves around the shared communications and identity. In contrast, the Type 2 governance structure operates at potentially overlapping scales. This categorization sheds light on approaches to multi-level climate action, in particular the Type 2 approaches pursued by global organizations such as the UNFCCC. Analogous activity occurs at national, cross-national, subnational, and non-state levels as nations drive sustainable development to reach the goals of the Paris Agreement.

Multi-level Climate Policy Factors and Actions

Wamsler et al. (2020) conducted a qualitative study of mindset as a factor in climate policy change among participants at the twenty-fifth UNFCCC Conference of the Parties (COP25) in 2019. The researchers found significant agreement among subjects that a mindset shift can foster communication and collaboration. The results emphasized the need for transformative skills and safe spaces to foster change. The transformative skills framework incorporates openness, self-awareness, and reflection, compassion and empathy, perspective-seeking and rationality, agency, empowerment, and sense-making, and values-based courage and engagement.

The literature on mindset and competencies led to research on the actions taken to formulate climate policies. Related to the foundational concepts of policy design, Linder and Peters (1989) explored the cognitive factors that influence the perception of performance information and technical data and shape the choice of policy instruments. Brown (2012) commented on the common condition of overlap and division in domestic governance on greenhouse gas emissions and climate change. Reviewing scholarly papers describing MLG Type 1, or federal-type, approaches to climate change policy, the author noted the common feature of competition among and between subnational governments and national or federal governments. After the creation of the Kyoto Protocol in the UN Convention on Climate Change in 1997, Rabe (2007) noted the limitations of institutional capacity of national or subnational governments to respond to GHG emissions with effective policies in Canada and America.

Daniell and Kay (2017) stated that this perspective on government is applied in the literature of environmental policy and resource management "along with the terms 'adaptive governance', 'polycentric governance' and 'collaborative governance', to emphasize the transfers of power and responsibility to a variety of stakeholders and scales of governance" (p. 4). The authors observe the pattern of authority dispersion across levels and boundaries of government, negotiations across tiers of government, and the influence of non-state actors, such as market actors and civil society. Moser and Boykoff (2013) described multi-level climate action to enable jurisdictions to adapt to the changing climate through the interactions of actors, policies, and institutions, working collectively, independently, and at times at cross-purposes.

Knill et al.'s (2007) textbook on environmental policy in the EU highlighted the challenges of multi-level climate action. The authors observed that the outcomes of EU policymaking on the environment are influenced by interests and capacities at national and supranational levels, frustrating the aspiration for a uniform approach, shifting by issue, economic interests of member states, and national priorities for action. The large number of varied actors, from administrators to decision-makers, interest groups, and stakeholders along the implementation chain, exert influence and prevent effective policy outcomes. Rather than the result of a coherent set of principles and paradigms, the environmental policy at the time was a collection of individual measures resulting from the influence of many disparate actors, the consequence of member state competition rather than strategic vision.

Research shed light on the interaction of non-state actors (NSA) in multi-level government. Piattoni (2009) explained the involvement of civil society, trade unions and industry groups as an element of MLG. However, the presence of non-governmental stakeholders is not a consistent element in the theoretical construct of MLG among other scholars, including Hooghe and Marks (2003). Tortola (2017) suggested that the importance of non-state actors as an axis of ambiguity remains to be clarified.

Climate Policy Research and NDCs

Researchers have employed the text of the NDCs to support a range of studies on issues of international policy and politics, including this question of non-state actors. Hsu et al. (2020) studied the text of the Nationally Determined Contributions to assess the prominence of non-state actors and found that most developed countries made little mention of non-state actors, instead finding the data biased toward NSA in the NDCs of developing countries. The researchers observed that NDCs often put commitments in conditional terms, making actions dependent on the financial support, technology transfer, or assistance to build capacity and expertise provided by other Parties. The study found multi-level elements in several NDCs. Canada proposed to leverage provincial initiatives as the basis of carbon pricing policies, and South Africa incorporated content provided by civil society and business associations.

Collado et al. (2019) gained an understanding of the role of urban slums in the climate action of developing countries through content analysis of 28 of the NDCs that were publicly available prior to the COP21 conference in 2015. The researchers found that developing countries with a significant presence of urban slums did not have mitigation or adaptation policies for informal settlements. Tobin et al. (2018) employed Discourse Network Analysis to identify concepts in the language of the 162 documents submitted to the UNFCCC by 16 May 2016. Manual coding revealed the map of common climate mitigation targets. The researchers noted the prevalence of business as usual (BAU) targets, and the prominence of adaptation elements, suggesting an awareness of the challenge in reaching collective emission goals.

The NDCs provided data for studies of agriculture. Hönle et al. (2019) applied a mixed methods approach to a study of the 46 countries representing 90% of global agricultural emissions to determine how these nations would prioritize adaptation and mitigation in agriculture. Qualitative coding of the text of these 46 NDCs focused on shedding light on each country's perceptions of the role the nation would play in climate mitigation in agricultural sectors. Coding of supporting documents, such as Biennial Update Reports (BURs), was added to the analysis. The researchers found that commitment to climate policy to mitigate emissions in agriculture appears to be dependent on technology solutions, efficiency gains, and modernization.

Taking another approach to NDC-based research into agriculture, Paim et al. (2020) conducted a document analysis of the NDCs for China, India, the EU, and Mexico, focusing on the potential for water–energy–food synergies. Keyword searches and content analysis of selected passages were combined with analysis of related documents. The researchers concluded that the capacity to mainstream the Water–Energy–Food Nexus approach varied within the four countries, with India and China classified as minimally capable, Mexico classified as hybrid, and the EU determined to be sufficient.

Research on the Sustainable Development Goals (SDGs), 17 articulated ambitions developed by the United Nations in 2015 to drive public and private sectors toward a shared vision of a sustainable world has also benefitted from studies of the NDCs (United Nations, n.d.). Antwi-Agyei et al. (2018) explored the alignment of SDGs among 11 West African states through iterative content analysis, identifying sectoral keywords that aligned with specific SDGs. The researchers determined that the energy sector was the top priority for mitigation among the West African states whereas agriculture was the focus of adaptation efforts.

Along similar lines, Janetschek et al. (2020) conducted detailed content analysis of the NDCs by breaking all 164 documents into 7,000 activities representing actions. These activities were mapped to the 17 SDGs, manually analyzed, and coded based on an assessment of whether the activity was or wasn't applicable to SDG content categories. The study determined that five of the SDGs were mentioned more prominently than the others, namely the goals for Zero Hunger (SDG2), Clean Water and Sanitation (SDG6), Affordable and Clean Energy (SDG7), Sustainable Cities and Communities (SDG11), and Life on Land (SDG15).

Researchers have found the NDCs useful for studies of governance priorities and mechanisms. Stephenson et al. (2019) noted that the NDCs reveal the climate commitments and political positions of nations post-Paris, asserting that these documents are the key to understanding international climate policy dynamics. The team applied a quantitative content analysis to the text of 165 NDCs submitted prior to 1 August 2017 to reveal areas of convergence and divergence. The researchers concluded that the Parties to the Paris Agreement had not achieved the bottom-up mobilization needed for effective climate action, but rather the top-down institutional affiliations, patterns, and isolation persisted, limiting success.

Jernnäs et al. (2019) commented that the "pledge and review model" of the NDC process enabled the research team to gain information on the mechanisms that governments would employ to support their commitments (p. 1240). The researchers studied all 145 NDCs that had been submitted to the UNFCCC by 30 July 2018. First identifying governance mechanisms with qualitative content analysis, then coding based on mechanism, such as legislation or behavior influence of citizens. The governance mechanisms were clustered and examined with descriptive statistics. The study revealed the significant number of mechanisms that nations intended to use to make their contributions. The role of the state in climate action is highly variable, dependent on a range of public resources. Contradictory mechanisms such as market programs and legislative actions were proposed. The NDC approach to gaining global commitments appeared to retain the top-down divisions that existed in the UNFCCC prior to the Paris Agreement. The authors observed that the concept of contribution, while sufficiently open to enable compromise, resulted in a global agreement too ambiguous to prevent economic concerns from overshadowing urgent climate actions.

METHODS

This chapter describes an empirical study of the elements of global climate action, multi-level governance, and management theory. The purpose of the study was to conduct a content analysis of the NDCs and develop a theory about the way multi-level climate actions reflect institutional theory, resource-based theory, agency theory, and stakeholder theory. The content analysis focused on the updated NDCs submitted to the UNFCCC in 2020 and 2021 prior to COP26.

Theory

To provide insight on multi-level climate action, Starik and Kanashiro (2013) identified the sustainability connections and omissions of prominent management theories, four of which will inform this study – agency theory, stakeholder theory, institutional theory, the resource-based view (RBV) of organizations.

First, agency theory illuminates the relationships between parties engaged in organizational transactions by explaining the interactions between principals who benefit and the agents who represent them. Agency theory was fundamental to the study of the impact of climate change mitigation policies on financial performance conducted by Secinaro et al. (2020). The researchers assessed the relationship between corporate environmental performance and financial performance among publicly traded European firms. Secinaro et al. concluded that firms that engaged in company-wide sustainable practices realized financial benefits of lower production costs and profit increases. Starik and Kanashiro (2013) point out that misaligned interests in environmental action between principals and agents might lead decision-makers to emphasize risk without sufficient awareness of the opportunity afforded by climate action.

Second, Parviainen et al. (2017) applied stakeholder theory in an extensive review of the scholarly literature of corporate social responsibility in the shipping industry. The researchers explored power and interdependence of stakeholders, including customers, employees, partners, suppliers, academics, and NGOs to gain insight into the role that a group of interested parties can play in driving environmental practice change. Starik and Kanashiro (2013) connect stakeholder theory to larger obligations to groups and individuals, noting that organizations struggle to address quality of life over the longer term.

Third, institutional theory suggests that an organization results from social interactions, external pressures, and occurrences. The theory has been applied in environmental studies; Jo et al. (2020) studied factors affecting payment in a voluntary forest carbon market in South Korea. Institutional theory revealed a sequential relationship from initial perception to the intention to pursue forest carbon offsets by environmental stakeholders, such as forest owners and government employees. The study concluded that market or regulatory factors drove the steps from intention to action and explained intensity variations.

Fourth, Yurdakul and Kazan (2020) utilized the resource-based view (RBV) of organizations to shape a study of the impact of eco-innovation on the environmental and financial performance. The researchers selected the natural-resource-based view (NRBV) theory articulated by Hart (1995) to structure interviews with manufacturing sector representatives. Surveys gathered data on resource savings and utilization, and considered energy use, carbon dioxide emissions, total greenhouse gas emissions, waste, pollution, recycling, among others. Eco-innovation was found to have direct and indirect impacts on financial performance, cost performance, and environmental performance, suggesting the value of environmentally focused investments for competitive advantage in organizations. This study underscores Starik and Kanashiro's (2013) observation that sustainability improves competitiveness through effective resource utilization.

These theories describe the influence of agents, stakeholders, institutional constraints, and resources to achieve objectives. Multi-level climate commitments described in the NDCs of Parties to the Paris Agreement provide data to explore the interactions, influence, and dynamics of these interrelated factors.

Sample

Prior to the COP26 event in Glasgow in 2021, 165 NDCs had been registered to meet the requirements of the Paris Agreement, representing all Parties (United Nations Framework Convention on Climate Change, 2021b). Each document reflects unique decision-making processes for the nation or, in the case of the European Union, a multi-national group, reflecting the urgency and commitment to climate action.

The UNFCCC reported that 90% or more of the NDCs provided information in accordance with COP guidance for clarity, transparency, and understanding. All NDCs discussed mitigation targets or co-benefits. Over 71% of the documents expressed strengthened GHG emissions reduction commitments, included numeric mitigation targets, and economy-wide targets across sectors. Qualitative strategies, plans, and actions were included in fewer than 40% of the NDCs (United Nations Framework Convention on Climate Change, 2021c).

This study was conducted on a sample of 30 NDCs. The 30 were selected by ranking the documents by the emissions percentage each represented (Worldometers.info, n.d.). The complete list appears in the Appendix. Reflecting the unified approach to multi-level climate action and the commitment to achieving the goals of the Paris Agreement, 27 of the Parties registered the same European Union NDC. Since these 27 nations are represented by one of the NDCs in the sample, the inclusion brings the sample to 56 Parties, representing a combined population of 5,788,492,036, and, based on 2020 measurements, responsible for 94.8% of global carbon emissions (World Population Review, n.d.).

Analysis

The documents registered by the Parties in the selected sample were downloaded from the UNFCCC interim NDC registry from October 1 through October 31, 2021. The files were loaded into NVivo 12 in PDF format.

Content analysis enables the discovery of intentions through the observation of patterns and relationships (Krippendorff, 2019). This research methodology has been successfully applied to the study of climate actions through analysis of INDCs and NDCs (Ekholm & Lindroos, 2015; Collado et al., 2019; Stephenson et al., 2019). This study applied inductive coding to analyze the NDCs with a focus on governance actions that shed light on multi-level climate mechanisms. The binding nature of the NDCs reflects the commitment and intentions of Parties that have joined the Paris Agreement. The emphasis on public policy analysis builds on the cycle of relationships between corporations, and public interest groups (DiMento, 1986).

Thirty NDCs were analyzed during the initial open coding phase, with words and passages highlighted and labeled according to topic. Codes were manually applied in NVivo to flag observations about the impact of climate change, country vulnerabilities, needs, and aspirations. In addition, codes were created and attached to text expressing the strategies, action plans, commitments, and policies of each Party. The research questions of multi-level climate action drove coding on governance action, stakeholder engagement, sub-national and international mechanisms. In addition, the passages included in each NDC to meet the Paris Agreement's requirements that each Party provide Information for Clarity, Transparency, and Understanding were flagged to enable cross-comparison.

The coding scheme emerged inductively using a grounded approach until all 30 NDCs had been reviewed and an initial set of over 1000 codes and sub-codes had been identified and further grouped into clusters. Salient terms with significance in the context of the Paris Agreement, such as adaptation ambition, capacity-building, leakage, loss and damage, mitigation, resilience, were noted in the coding process (United Nations Framework Convention on Climate Change, n.d.d).

A significant code cluster was identified with the overarching theme of Government Action (Tables 5.1a and 5.1b). These included descriptions of action plans, commitment, education, access to finance including investment and funding, industry transformation programs across a range of industries, policies to regulate and enforce standards, and protections for vulnerable populations, endangered resources, and precious assets. Multi-level mechanisms were discerned among governance action codes such as cross-sectoral implementation, cross-province collaboration, outreach to the private sector, fostering of market mechanisms, and the development of ministries or agencies to foster and control emissions reductions within national economies.

Table 5.1a *Government Action Codes, instances, sub-codes, part 1, action-improve*

Code	Instances	Sub-codes
Government Action		
action plan	48	adaptation, agriculture, capacity-building, carbon control, climate plan, cooling, economic recovery, energy, gender action, green economy, heat wave, implementation tools, integrated resources, just transition, landscape restoration, management plan, methane, national adaptation, national advancement, development, regional adaptation, short-lived climate pollutants, strategic framework, sustainable consumption, sustainable development and sustainable production
adaptation	7	agriculture, air quality, forest, health, land, strategy, waste, water
carbon trading	3	statistics, verification
collaboration	2	cross-province, indigenous
commitment	11	actions, coal, NDC, flood risk reduction, increase protected areas, land-use changes, renewable energy, stretch goals, transportation
conserve	2	biodiversity, ecosystems
control	2	coastal zone development, methane
economic development	8	equitable access, industry diversification, job creation, skills training, worker transition
education	11	blue carbon, build capacity, education impacts, indigenous knowledge, international learning, low carbon consumption, professional training
efficiency initiatives	2	energy trading, zero defect
emissions control	5	tracking, accounting, reporting
engage stakeholders	8	Engagement
access to finance	41	bonds, Climate Investment Funds, disaster risk management, domestic investment, Global Environment Fund (GEF), green accessible retrofit funding, Green Climate Fund (GCF), green credit, green finance instruments, households, IDB loan, limitations, low-cost financial resources, low-income retrofits, grant investment, rapid access to finance, results-based financing (RBF), risk guarantee fund, support to developing countries, transportation fund, attract foreign investment
access to finance-funding	9	bond, domestic, international, needs, sector-based
access to finance-investment	28	afforestation, buildings, carbon capture, clean agriculture technology, clean fuels, community energy efficiency, homeowner assistance, indigenous communities, indigenous areas, industry decarbonization, land rehabilitation, low emission vehicles, low emissions tech, methane reduction, nature, transportation, vehicles, wetlands
financing and funding	19	budgeting and estimating, capital markets, climate finance accelerator (CFA), debt forgiveness, expenditures, financial strategy, government investment, green alignment, ineffectiveness of loans, mechanisms, public–private partnerships, rebates, energy efficiency support, research support
market mechanisms	4	allocation, emissions trading, international markets
global contribution	3	capacity-building, disaster mitigation, alternative fuels in developing countries
governance structure	2	
improve resilience	33	agriculture, biodiversity, cities, coastal resources, energy, fisheries, food production, forests, infrastructure, marine disasters, public health, health systems, transport, wastewater, water

Table 5.1b   *Government Action Codes, instances, sub-codes, part 2, incentives-tax*

Code	Instances	Sub-codes
Government Action		
incentives	11	challenge large emitters, subsidy reform, tariff, tax incentives
industry transformation	30	additional sectors, agriculture, building design, coal, coastal shipping, consumer vehicles, environmental dispatch, finance, food, forestry, freight, hard to mitigate sectors, heating and cooling, industrial processes, infrastructure planning/engineering, land management and forestry LULUCF, lighting, manufacturing, marine, natural resource, practice adoption, public transportation, service, 30 tourism, urban planning, waste management, wastewater, water system
industry transformation – energy	46	bagasse, clean energy, coal, decarbonize electricity, demand–supply cap, diesel, domestic oil to electric, efficiency struggles, electricity, emissions reduction, enterprise development, green refineries, Erid, hydro, measures, needs, net-metering, net-zero, nuclear, off-grid electrification, oil efficiency, oil reduction, performance standards, power generation, renewable, solar, transmission, wind, zero carbon
industry transformation – transportation	10	air, compressed natural gas, fuel policy, government vehicles, rail system
industry transformation – vehicles	9	electric, highway charging
legislation	11	CSR, emissions accountability, enforcement degree, environmental protection, establish goals, framework act, GHG management, hazard protection, motion, water resources
limiting factors	4	
ministries	13	
monitoring and warning	5	
national policy	7	adaptation, biofuels, climate change, forests
operations improvement	4	
partnership	3	electricity transformation, indigenous peoples, NDC
policy	5	climate change, evaluation, renewable energy, transit, electric vehicles
policy implementation	13	climate resilience, cross-agency policymaking, enable green ecosystem, geothermal, NDC, quantitative assessment, reduce emissions, training
policy instrument	14	climate change, climate risk, decarbonization, environmental, methane reduction
policy or regulation	22	adaptation strategy, anti-pollution, circular economy, climate change law, emissions management framework, energy supply mix, fly ash, fuels, MRV, net-zero carbon emissions, planning, REDD+ (forest), regulatory harmonization, solid waste
programs	8	bioshield, coastal management, desalination, energy efficiency, forced displacement, health, rural employment
promote	40	adaptation mitigation awareness, biodiversity, circular economy, climate change awareness, emissions reduction, energy efficiency, energy transformation, sustainable lifestyle, urban development, voluntarism, voluntary reductions
protect	40	blue carbon, ecosystem, flora/fauna areas, food security, forests, grassland, habitat, health, historic/cultural sites, land, marine areas, river, soil quality, vulnerable social groups, vulnerable cities, indigenous, water resources, wetlands, workers
research and innovation	25	hydrogen, low-carbon, public–private, transfer, water
restore	17	afforestation, degraded areas, economic opportunity, ecosystem, grassland, groundwater, watershed
standards	36	adaptation, building code, carbon pricing, clean fuel, effluent discharge, energy efficient ratings, fuel efficiency, GHG, large emitter performance, product standards and labeling, renewable energy, vehicle

Code	Instances	Sub-codes
strategy	37	adaptation in infrastructure, adaptation in spatial planning, adaptive capacity building, agriculture, clean air, climate adaptation, climate preparedness and resilience, coastal zone management, community capacity building, community engagement, degraded land, disaster preparedness and recovery, ecosystem improvement, emissions reduction, energy efficiency, forestry, hydrogen, IT systems for risks and impacts, land conservation, low emissions, mitigation, policy coordination and communication, risk management, transportation, watershed management
tax	3	avoidance, carbon

FINDINGS

Analysis of the most recent NDCs reveals multi-level governance at work in multiple directions, through vertical coherence and horizontal cooperation. The complexity and depth of the policy descriptions show the ambitious range of strategies that Parties have devised to achieve commitments. This agrees with the findings of previous NDC research (Eberl et al., 2021). In an earlier study of multi-level climate policy integration, Mickwitz et al. (2009) stated the need for alignment of signals and incentives across levels of government so that policies are coherent. The researchers found that strategies and decisions enacted at different levels of government must demonstrate consistency to achieve change in a particular sector, such as transportation or energy.

As illustrated in Table 5.2, NDC passages reflect the intention to foster vertical policy coherence through sub-national policy alignment, commitment to capacity-building across boundaries, ministries with climate-action-relevant oversight, stakeholder engagement, public–private partnerships, and whole of government programs. Horizontal cooperation with the international community was expressed in terms of trust, awareness of vulnerability to the effects of climate change, expectations for support, and openness to transparency.

The analysis suggests that the pattern of multi-level climate action that Parties pursue is designed to create a social context and drive change by leveraging the insights of frameworks discussed earlier. Agency theory, stakeholder theory, institutional theory, and resource-based view of organizations explain the mechanisms that further behavior change and resource development across the public sphere, private industry, and civil society.

Agency Theory was studied by Martinez and Bowen (2013) in the context of the United Nations' Clean Development Mechanism, a climate action encouraging greenhouse gas reduction projects in developing countries that predated the Paris Agreement. The authors applied the framework to assess the risk, uncertainty, and incentives, and found ethical issues in the failure of agents to act in the interests of principals. The most recent set of NDCs demonstrates that Parties structure formal incentives to motivate agents, from national to sub-national actors, to act in the interests of society.

Government action codes that appear in the NDCs were mapped to one or more categories based on whether that action reflects a principal/agent relationship, a stakeholder involvement, an institutional constraint, or a tactic to provide access to resources.

Table 5.2   *Multi-level action codes reflecting vertical policy coherence and horizontal cooperation. Table courtesy of the author*

Code	Instances	Code	Instances
Multi-level		Multi-level	
Vertical policy coherence		Vertical policy coherence	
accounting	2	collective action	1
agreement	1	Conference of the Parties authority	1
apex policymaking integration	1	continent	1
barrier removal	1	country vulnerability	10
budget mechanism	1	cross-cutting elements	2
capacity framework	1	cross-referencing	1
capacity-building	1	CROSS-UN-org synergy	1
climate justice architecture	1	developed countries support for mitigation	9
communities	1	devolution of funds	1
constituted bodies	1	differentiated responsibility	1
cooperation	1	European Union organizations	5
coordination	1	global convention	1
cross-sectoral implementation	3	global cooperation	18
federal	4	historic responsibility	5
focal agency	1	intergovernmental collaboration and support	2
funding	2	International conflict	2
implementation success factors	3	international conventions and frameworks	1
inclusiveness	1	international funding, Just Transition	2
indigenous framework	1	international investment in adaptation and mitigation	4
mandate	1	International Transferred Mitigation Outcomes (ITMOS)	1
mechanism	1	member states	1
ministries	3	monitoring report evaluation (M&E)	2
partnership	1	multilateral cooperation	2
policy integration	1	multi-level climate action	4
private sector, public–private partnership	14	multi-national leadership and support for economic advising	2
provincial	2	multisectoral	1
ratification	1	NDC accountability	2
reporting	1	negotiation	1
shared jurisdiction	1	support for collective effort	1
shared responsibility	3	synergy	1
stakeholder engagement and validation	5	trust in international cooperation	9
sub-national	9	UN program support	4
whole of government	4	UNFCCC accountability	1
whole of society, social resilience	2		

Implications

The implications of the study are that multi-level climate actions undertaken by governments prioritize two overarching aspirations – to transform behavior and to provide resources. Government actors will invest time and resources to manage principal/agent relationships, engage stakeholders, institutionalize sustainable development practices, and motivate the development of economic, environmental, and technological resources to make good on commitments, such as those articulated in the Paris Agreement.

Parties will pursue myriad strategies and actions to change the way individuals and companies live and work. Achieving deep reductions in global emissions will require industry transformation. The sample named over 20 sectors ranging from agriculture to water systems. Regulations and standards will place constraints and provide opportunities in the private sector, shift the expectations of the public, and engage civil society in societal change. Government-initiated programs articulate a vision for a sustainable future and build capacity to influence behavior change across the public sphere, private industry, and civil society.

In addition, Parties intend to employ financing for ambitious undertakings by establishing economic incentives and providing access to funding sources. Expressions of commitment to protect vulnerable populations and environments, to overcome the tragedy of the commons by increasing the perceived value of shared environmental assets, are prominent as well. NDCs tout the potential of social and technological innovation to provide intellectual property for sustainable development. Each proposed climate policy action influences behavioral and resource change through a complex set of relationships spanning the public sphere, private industry, and civil society (Figure 5.1).

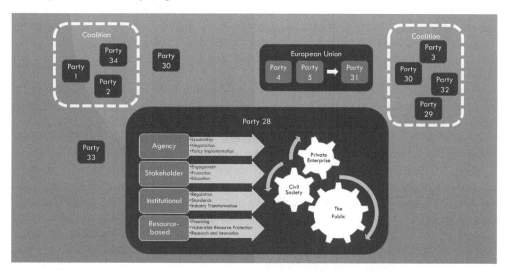

Figure 5.1   *NDCs articulate multi-level climate action that reflects agency, stakeholder, institutional, and resource-based theories of change propagating through the public sphere, private industry, and civil society. Figure courtesy of the author*

CONCLUSIONS

The study explored the language of multi-level climate action as expressed in NDCs, the formal documents by which Parties to the Paris Agreement articulate commitments to reduce emissions and meet goals. Content analysis of these texts revealed that agency theory, stakeholder theory, institutional theory, and resource-based views of organizations provided insight to inform the way a global community of nations with differing political structures, economic positions, demographics, and cultures intends to transform society.

Parties expressed concern about the impacts of climate change, and the vulnerabilities to which their people are exposed. Strategy descriptions and explanations revealed intentions to implement policy, provide incentives, educate, promote positive behavior, and constrain the decisions of public and private industry to meet the challenges of systemic risk and outcome uncertainty. The large number of plans included in each NDC suggests that climate action in the future will require experimentation and innovation, expertise-building, and resource-sharing across international boundaries.

For each Party, actions of leadership, such as programs and promotion to influence behavior, interact with stakeholder engagement that brings private actors and civil society into policy discussions. Institutional actions such as regulation and standardization that enforce behavior change depend on resource-building to ensure that financing, innovation, and natural resources are in place.

The data collection was limited to the registered NDCs provided online by the UNFCCC in the timeframe prior to October 1, 2021. Thirty NDCs representing the highest emitting Parties formed the sample for content analysis. New NDCs are registered with the UNFCCC on an ongoing basis. Each document provides a rich source of data for the study of multi-level climate action. In addition to national aspirations of 192 Parties to achieve the goals of the Paris Agreement, these documents provide insight about national ambition and limits, social and governance structures, and the opportunities and obstacles for social, economic, and cultural change.

Since the data collection was completed, over 60 parties have registered new or updated documents, including Parties that represent significant percentages of the global emissions total. So, the analysis does not include these more recent updates. In addition, the study was limited by the time and resources of a single researcher. Additional time, collaborators, and resources could expand the analysis to cover the NDCs of all Parties.

There is a need for further research to better understand the dynamics of these interactions as Parties move forward. Practices of measurement and transparency will be key as Parties work to implement strategies and determine whether the breadth and scope of this first set of contributions and commitments will achieve the collective goals of the Paris Agreement. The completion of the global stocktake, the process that assesses progress toward emissions reduction goals, will take place in November 2023. The results of this assessment will drive the timeframe for increased ambition and updated strategies in the next round of NDCs (United Nations Framework Convention on Climate Change, n.d.d).

A follow-up study might enlist a team of researchers to expand the scope of the research by reviewing a complete, current set of NDCs, assessing the validity of the findings of this subset. Related work could apply a quantitative method, to apply the quantitative methodology of Stephenson et al. (2019) on the updated set of NDCs, to apply multi-level governance theories and determine whether progress has been made in addressing the obstacles identified by that research team. Alternatively, adding theories or multi-level climate action to an exploration of Party characteristics and governance mechanisms could expand the study of Jernnäs et al. (2019) based on the newest NDCs from all 192 Parties.

System dynamic modeling and causal mapping, methods that illuminate qualitative and quantitative interactions between factors, could explore or measure the impact of agency actions, stakeholder engagement, institutional constraints, and resource-building. Grounded theory derived from a content analysis of the full set of current NDCs could support the development of a complex multi-level climate action theory. As recommended by Starik and Kanashiro (2013), such a theory should incorporate five features, a focus on natural and socio-economic environments, consideration of policy approaches at multiple levels from individual to organization to society, an analysis of the underlying systems as reflected by systems analysis, perspectives on expectations for the quality and timeframes of human life, and awareness of the impacts of environmental transformations and disasters.

Just prior to COP26 in Glasgow, the UNFCCC confirmed that the 2021 aggregation of NDCs suggests a concerning 16% increase in global emissions by 2030 (UN Climate Press Release, 2021). This is an important moment to apply research to illuminate the outcomes of the negotiations at the conference, employ multi-level climate action research to make recommendations and inform policymakers, national leaders, and negotiators. Non-governmental stakeholders, industry leaders, and civil society advocates can benefit from a deeper understanding of the implications of the NDCs to align organizational practices. By reflecting on the theoretical insights of agency theory, stakeholder theory, institutional theory, and the resource-based view of the firm, corporate leaders can better prepare strategies and plans to secure their companies, the economic health of their own stakeholders, and contribute to climate action.

REFERENCES

Adriázola, P., Dellas, E., & Tänzler, D. (2018). Multi-level climate governance supporting local action. Retrieved December 5, 2021, from http://star-www.giz.de/cgi-bin/getfile/53616c7465645f5f8c1 4142fe94f844319ab2ab675c1eccb18a06dcb7b07a9f5c11efca781e793e04c0df6e4acbc8fc6b6b 21ee75b463d47a0143beb46e62a3f/giz2018-0318en-cpmud-multi-level-climate-governance.pdf.

Antwi-Agyei, P., Dougill, A. J., Agyekum, T. P., & Stringer, L. C. (2018). Alignment between nationally determined contributions and the sustainable development goals for West Africa. *Climate Policy*, 18(10), 1296–1312. https://doi.org/10.1080/14693062.2018.1431199

Bache, I., & Flinders, M. V. (2004). *Multi-level Governance* [electronic resource]. Oxford University Press.

Betsill, M. M., & Bulkeley, H. (2006). Cities and the multilevel governance of global climate change. *Global Governance*, 12(2), 141–160. https://doi.org/10.1163/19426720-01202004

Brown, D. M. (2012). Comparative climate change policy and federalism: An overview. *The Review of Policy Research*, 29(3), 322–333. https://doi.org/10.1111/j.1541-1338.2012.00562.x

Bulkeley, H., & Betsill, M. (2005). Rethinking sustainable cities: Multilevel governance and the 'urban' politics of climate change. *Environmental Politics*, 14(1), 42–63. https://doi.org/10.1080/09644010042000310178

Collado, J. R. N., Wang, H.-H., & Tsai, T.-Y. (2019). Urban informality in the Paris Climate Agreement: Content analysis of the nationally determined contributions of highly urbanized developing countries. *Sustainability (Basel, Switzerland)*, 11(19), 5228. https://doi.org/10.3390/su11195228

COP26: Updated NDC Synthesis Report: Worrying Trends Confirmed (2021). Greentech Lead.

Daniell, K. A., & Kay, A. (2017). Multi-level Governance: An Introduction. In K. A. Daniell and A. Kay (Eds), *Multi-level Governance Conceptual Challenges and Case Studies from Australia*, (pp. 3–32). ANU Press. http://doi.org/10.22459/MG.11.2017

Davy, C. (2021). COP26: What was agreed at the Glasgow climate talks? In *China Dialogue [BLOG]*. Newstex.

DeLeo, R. A. (2017). Anticipatory policymaking in global venues: Policy change, adaptation, and the UNFCCC Futures. *Journal of Policy, Planning and Futures Studies*, 92, 39–47. https://doi.org/10.1016/j.futures.2016.09.001

Di Gregorio, M., Fatorelli, L., Paavola, J., Locatelli, B., Pramova, E., Nurrochmat, D. R., May, P. H., Brockhaus, M., Sari, I. M., & Kusumadewi, S. D. (2019). Multi-level governance and power in climate change policy networks. *Global Environmental Change*, 54, 64–77. https://doi.org/10.1016/j.gloenvcha.2018.10.003

DiMento, J. F. (1986). *Environmental Law and American Business: Dilemmas of Compliance.* New York: Plenum Press.

Eberl, J., Gordeeva, E., & Weber, N., (2021). The policy coherence framework approach in a multi-level analysis of European, German and Thuringian climate policy with a special focus on land use, land-use change and forestry (LULUCF). *World*, 2(26), 415–424. https://doi.org/10.3390/world2030026

Ekholm, T., & Lindroos, T.J. (2015). An analysis of countries' climate change mitigation contributions towards the Paris Agreement. White Paper. Available online: https://www.vtt.fi/inf/pdf/technology/2015/T239.pdf (retrieved January 15, 2021).

Hajer, M. A., & ProQuest. (1995). *The Politics of Environmental Discourse Ecological Modernization and the Policy Process.* Clarendon Press; Oxford University Press.

Hart, S. L. (1995). A natural-resource-based view of the firm. *Academy of Management Review*, 20, 986.

Hönle, S. E., Heidecke, C., & Osterburg, B. (2019). Climate change mitigation strategies for agriculture: An analysis of nationally determined contributions, biennial reports and biennial update reports. *Climate Policy*, 19(6), 688–702. https://doi.org/10.1080/14693062.2018.1559793

Hooghe, L., & Marks, G. (2003). Unraveling the central state, but how? Types of multi-level governance. *The American Political Science Review*, 97(2), 233–243. https://doi.org/10.1017/S0003055403000649

Hsu, A., Brandt, J., Widerberg, O., Chan, S., & Weinfurter, A. (2020). Exploring links between national climate strategies and non-state and subnational climate action in nationally determined contributions (NDCs). *Climate Policy*, 20(4), 443–457. https://doi.org/10.1080/14693062.2019.1624252

IPCC (n.d.a). *Climate Change: The IPCC 1990 and 1992 Assessments.* Retrieved January 8, 2022, from https://www.ipcc.ch/report/climate-change-the-ipcc-1990-and-1992-assessments/

IPCC (n.d.b). *History of the IPCC.* Retrieved January 8, 2022, from https://www.ipcc.ch/about/history/

IPCC (2018). Summary for Policymakers of IPCC Special Report on Global Warming of 1.5°C approved by governments. Retrieved December 12, 2022 from https://www.ipcc.ch/2018/10/08/summary-for-policymakers-of-ipcc-special-report-on-global-warming-of-1-5c-approved-by-governments/

IPCC Special Report on Climate Change and Land (n.d.). Global warming of 1.5°C. Institute for Global Environmental Strategies. Retrieved December 5, 2021, from https://www.ipcc.ch/sr15/.

Janetschek, H., Brandi, C., Dzebo, A., & Hackmann, B. (2020). The 2030 Agenda and the Paris Agreement: Voluntary contributions towards thematic policy coherence. *Climate Policy*, 20(4), 430–442. https://doi.org/10.1080/14693062.2019.1677549

Jernnäs, M., Nilsson, J., Linnér, B.-O., & Duit, A. (2019). Cross-national patterns of governance mechanisms in nationally determined contributions (NDCs) under the Paris Agreement. *Climate Policy*, 19(10), 1239–1249. https://doi.org/10.1080/14693062.2019.1662760

Jo, J.-H., Roh, T., Hwang, J., Lee, K., & Lee, C. (2020). Factors and paths affecting payment for forest ecosystem service: Evidence from voluntary forest carbon market in South Korea. *Sustainability (Basel, Switzerland)*, 12(17), 7009. https://doi.org/10.3390/su12177009

Knill, C., Liefferink, D., & ProQuest. (2007). *Environmental Politics in the European Union: Policy-making, Implementation and Patterns of Multi-level Governance.* Manchester University Press.

Krippendorff, K. (2019). *Content Analysis: An Introduction to its Methodology* (4th ed.). SAGE.

Linder, S. H., & Peters, B. G. (1989). Instruments of government: Perceptions and contexts. *Journal of Public Policy*, 9(1), 35–58.

Marks, G. (1993). Structural policy and multi-level governance in the EC. In A. Cafruny & G. Rosenthal (Eds), *The State of the European Community. Vol. 2, The Maastricht Debates and Beyond,* (pp. 391–410). Boulder, CO: Lynne Rienner.

Martinez, C. A., & Bowen, J. D. (2013). The ethical challenges of the UN's clean development mechanism. *Journal of Business Ethics*, 117(4), 807–821. https://doi.org/10.1007/s10551-013-1720-4

Mickwitz, P., Aix, F., Beck, S., Carss, D., Ferrand, N., Görg, C., Jensen, A., Kivimaa, P., Kuhlicke, C., Kuindersma, W., et al. (2009) *Climate Policy Integration, Coherence and Governance; PEER Report No 2.* Partnership for European Environmental Research: Helsinki, Finland.

Moser, S. C., & Boykoff, M. T. (2013). *Successful Adaptation in Climate Change Linking Science and Policy in a Rapidly Changing World.* Routledge.

Pahl-Wostl, C. (2009). A conceptual framework for analysing adaptive capacity and multi-level learning processes in resource governance regimes. *Global Environmental Change*, 19(3), 354–365. https://doi.org/10.1016/j.gloenvcha.2009.06.001

Paim, M.-A., Salas, P., Lindner, S., Pollitt, H., Mercure, J.-F., Edwards, N. R., & Viñuales, J. E. (2020). Mainstreaming the water-energy-food nexus through nationally determined contributions (NDCs): The case of Brazil. *Climate Policy*, 20(2), 163–178, https://doi.org/10.1080/14693062.2019.1696736

Parviainen, T., Lehikoinen, A., Kuikka, S., & Haapasaari, P. (2017). How can stakeholders promote environmental and social responsibility in the shipping industry? *WMU Journal of Maritime Affairs*, 17(1), 49–70. https://doi.org/10.1007/s13437-017-0134-z

Pauw, W. P., & Klein, R. J. (2020). Beyond ambition: Increasing the transparency, coherence and implementability of Nationally Determined Contributions. *Climate Policy*, 20(4), 405–414. https://doi.org/10.1080/14693062.2020.1722607

Piattoni, S. (2009). Multi-level governance: A historical and conceptual analysis. *Journal of European Integration*, 31(2), 163–180. https://doi.org/10.1080/07036330802642755

Potluka, O., & Liddle, J. (2014). Managing European Union structural funds: Using a multilevel governance framework to examine the application of the partnership principle at the project level. *Regional Studies*, 48(8), 1434–1447. https://doi.org/10.1080/00343404.2014.898837

Rabe, B. G. (2007). Beyond Kyoto: Climate change policy in multilevel governance systems. *Governance (Oxford)*, 20(3), 423–444. https://doi.org/10.1111/j.1468-0491.2007.00365.x

Rajamani, L. (2016). Ambition and differentiation in the 2015 Paris Agreement: Interpretative possibilities and underlying politics. *The International and Comparative Law Quarterly*, 65(2), 493–514. https://doi.org/10.1017/S0020589316000130

Rogelj, J., den Elzen, M., Höhne, N., Fransen, T., Fekete, H., Winkler, H., Schaeffer, R., Sha, F., Riahi, K., & Meinshausen, M. (2016). Paris Agreement climate proposals need a boost to keep warming well below 2°C. *Nature (London)*, 534(7609), 631–639. https://doi.org/10.1038/nature18307

Secinaro, S., Brescia, V., Calandra, D., & Saiti, B. (2020). Impact of climate change mitigation policies on corporate financial performance: Evidence-based on European publicly listed firms. *Corporate Social-Responsibility and Environmental Management*, 27(6), 2491–2501. https://doi.org/10.1002/csr.1971

Starik, M., & Kanashiro, P. (2013). Toward a theory of sustainability management. *Organization & Environment*, 26(1), 7–30. https://doi.org/10.1177/1086026612474958

Stephenson, S. R., Oculi, N., Bauer, A., & Carhuayano, S. (2019). Convergence and divergence of UNFCCC nationally determined contributions. *Annals of the American Association of Geographers*, 109(4), 1240–1261. https://doi.org/10.1080/24694452.2018.1536533

Tobin, P., Schmidt, N. M., Tosun, J., & Burns, C. (2018). Mapping states' Paris climate pledges: Analysing targets and groups at COP 21. *Global Environmental Change*, 48, 11–21. https://doi.org/10.1016/j.gloenvcha.2017.11.002

Tortola, P. D. (2017). Clarifying multilevel governance. *European Journal of Political Research*, 56(2), 234–250. https://doi.org/10.1111/1475-6765.12180

UN Climate Press Release (2021, October 25). Updated NDC Synthesis Report: Worrying Trends Confirmed. Unfccc.int. (n.d.). Retrieved January 16, 2022, from https://unfccc.int/news/updated-ndc-synthesis-report-worrying-trends-confirmed

United Nations (n.d.). Transforming our world: the 2030 Agenda for Sustainable Development. Retrieved December 7, 2021, from https://sdgs.un.org/2030agenda.

United Nations Framework Convention on Climate Change (2021a, September 17). *Nationally: Determined Contributions under the Paris Agreement: Synthesis Report by the Secretariat*. Retrieved January 2, 2022, from https://unfccc.int/sites/default/files/resource/cma2021_08E.pdf

United Nations Framework Convention on Climate Change (2021b). *NDC Synthesis Report*. Unfccc. int. Retrieved January 12, 2022, from https://unfccc.int/process-and-meetings/the-paris-agreement/nationally-determined-contributions-ndcs/nationally-determined-contributions-ndcs/ndc-synthesis-report

United Nations Framework Convention on Climate Change (2021c). *Nationally Determined Contributions under the Paris Agreement: Revised Synthesis report by the Secretariat*. Retrieved January 15, 2022, from https://unfccc.int/sites/default/files/resource/cma2021_08r01_E.pdf

United Nations Framework Convention on Climate Change (n.d.a). Key aspects of the Paris Agreement. Unfccc.int. Retrieved December 5, 2021, from https://unfccc.int/process-and-meetings/the-paris-agreement/the-paris-agreement/key-aspects-of-the-paris-agreement

United Nations Framework Convention on Climate Change (n.d.b). Nationally determined contributions (NDCs). Retrieved December 5, 2021, from https://unfccc.int/process-and-meetings/the-paris-agreement/nationally-determined-contributions-ndcs/nationally-determined-contributions-ndcs

United Nations Framework Convention on Climate Change. (n.d.c). Glossary of climate change acronyms and terms. Unfccc.int. Retrieved January 15, 2022, from https://unfccc.int/process-and-meetings/the-convention/glossary-of-climate-change-acronyms-and-terms

United Nations Framework Convention on Climate Change. (n.d.d). Global stocktake. Unfccc.int. Retrieved January 16, 2022, from https://unfccc.int/topics/global-stocktake

Wamsler, C., Schäpke, N., Fraude, C., Stasiak, D., Bruhn, T., Lawrence, M., Schroeder, H., & Mundaca, L. (2020). Enabling new mindsets and transformative skills for negotiating and activating climate action: Lessons from UNFCCC conferences of the parties. *Environmental Science & Policy*, 112, 227–235. https://doi.org/10.1016/j.envsci.2020.06.005

World Commission on Environment and Development (1987). *Our Common Future*. Oxford University Press.

World Population Review (n.d.). *2021 world population by country*. Retrieved January 12, 2022, from https://worldpopulationreview.com/

Worldometers.info. (n.d.). *CO_2 emissions by country*. Worldometer. Retrieved January 15, 2022, from https://www.worldometers.info/co2-emissions/co2-emissions-by-country/

Yurdakul, M., & Kazan, H. (2020). Effects of eco-innovation on economic and environmental performance: Evidence from Turkey's manufacturing companies. *Sustainability (Basel, Switzerland)*, 12(8), 3167. https://doi.org/10.3390/su12083167

Zürn, M. (2020). Unravelling multi-level governance systems. *British Journal of Politics & International Relations*, 22(4), 784–791. https://doi.org/10.1177/1369148120937449. Data sources: https://www.globalcarbonproject.org/carbonbudget/20/data.htmhttps://www.icos-cp.eu/science-and-impact/global-carbon-budget/2020

APPENDIX

Table 5A.1 *UNFCCC Party Names for 31 of the NDCs selected for analysis, with UNFCCC registration dates, 2019 emissions percentage, and 2021 population. European Union is listed for reference, since the 27 member states registered the EU NDC on behalf of the country. Table courtesy of the author*

	2019 emissions %*	12 December 2015 emissions %*	Party	Submission date	2021 Population**
1	1.14	1.46	Australia	Thu Oct 28 2021	25,788,215
2	0.19	0.21	Austria***	Fri Dec 18 2020	9,043,070
3	0.29	0.27	Bangladesh	Thu Aug 26 2021	166,303,498
4	0.17	0.24	Belarus	Mon Oct 11 2021	9,442,862
5	0.27	0.32	Belgium***	Fri Dec 18 2020	11,632,326
6	1.26	2.48	Brazil	Wed Dec 09 2020	213,993,437
7	0.11	0.15	Bulgaria***	Fri Dec 18 2020	6,896,663
8	1.54	1.95	Canada	Mon Jul 12 2021	38,067,903
9	0.24	0.25	Chile	Thu Apr 09 2020	19,212,361
10	30.34	20.09	China	Thu Oct 28 2021	1,444,216,107
11	0.05	0.07	Croatia***	Fri Dec 18 2020	4,081,651
12	0.02	0.02	Republic of Cyprus***	Fri Dec 18 2020	1,215,584
13	0.28	0.34	Czechia***	Fri Dec 18 2020	10,724,555
14	0.08	0.15	Denmark***	Fri Dec 18 2020	5,813,298
15	0.05	0.06	Estonia ***	Fri Dec 18 2020	1,325,185
	35.45		***European Union (comprised of 27 countries)		
16	0.11	0.17	Finland**	Fri Dec 18 2020	5,548,360
17	0.83	1.34	France***	Fri Dec 18 2020	65,426,179
18	1.85	2.56	Germany***	Fri Dec 18 2020	83,900,473
19	0.17	0.28	Greece***	Fri Dec 18 2020	10,370,744
20	0.14	0.15	Hungary***	Fri Dec 18 2020	9,634,164
21	6.83	4.1	India	Sun Oct 2 2016	1,393,409,038
22	1.65	1.49	Indonesia	Thu Jul 22 2021	276,361,783
23	0.10	0.16	Ireland***	Fri Dec 18 2020	4,982,907
24	0.18	0.2	Israel	Thu Jul 29 2021	8,789,774
25	0.87	1.18	Italy***	Fri Dec 18 2020	60,367,477
26	3.03	3.79	Japan	Fri Oct 22 2021	126,050,804
27	0.26	0.09	Kuwait	Tue Oct 12 2021	4,328,550
28	0.02	0.03	Latvia***	Fri Dec 18 2020	1,866,942
29	0.04	0.05	Lithuania***	Fri Dec 18 2020	2,689,862
30	0.03	0.03	Luxembourg**	Fri Dec 18 2020	634,814
31	0.65	0.52	Malaysia	Fri Jul 30 2021	32,776,194

* Report of the conference of the Parties on its twenty-first session, held in Paris from 30 November to 13 December 2015 https://unfccc.int/resource/docs/2015/cop21/eng/10.pdf#page=30.
** World Population in Review. Retrieved 12 January 2022 https://worldpopulationreview.com/.
*** European Union Member State.

Table 5A.2   UNFCCC Party Names for 25 of the NDCs selected for analysis, with UNFCCC registration dates, 2019 emissions percentage, and 2021 population

	2019 emissions %*	12 Dec 2015 emissions %*	Party	Submission date	2021 Population**
32	0.00	0.01	Malta***	Fri Dec 18 2020	442,884
33	1.26	1.7	Mexico	Wed Dec 3 2020	130,262,216
34	0.09	0.05	Mongolia	Tue Oct 13 2020	3,329,289
35	0.41	0.53	Netherlands***	Fri Dec 18 2020	17,173,099
36	0.26	0.575	Nigeria	Fri Jul 30 2021	211,400,708
37	0.24	0.06	Oman	Thu Jul 29 2021	5,223,375
38	0.59	0.43	Pakistan	Thu Oct 21 2021	225,199,937
39	0.40	0.34	Philippines	Thu Apr 15 2021	111,046,913
40	0.84	1.06	Poland***	Fri Dec 18 2020	37,797,005
41	0.13	0.18	Portugal***	Fri Dec 18 2020	10,167,925
42	0.28	0.17	Qatar	Tue Aug 24 2021	2,930,528
43	1.71	1.85	Republic of Korea	Thu Dec 23 2021	51,305,186
44	0.21	0.3	Romania***	Fri Dec 18 2020	19,127,774
45	4.71	7.53	Russian Federation	Wed Nov 25 2020	145,912,025
46	0.09	0.12	Slovakia***	Fri Dec 18 2020	5,460,721
47	0.04	0.05	Slovenia***	Fri Dec 18 2020	2,078,724
48	1.30	1.46	South Africa	Mon Sep 27 2021	60,041,994
49	0.68	0.87	Spain***	Fri Dec 18 2020	46,745,216
50	0.12	0.15	Sweden***	Fri Dec 18 2020	10,160,169
51	1.09	1.24	Turkey	Mon Oct 11 2021	85,042,738
52	0.52	1.04	Ukraine	Sat Jul 31 2021	43,466,819
53	0.59	0.59	United Arab Emirates	Tue Dec 29 2020	9,991,089
54	0.96	1.55	United Kingdom of Great Britain and Northern Ireland	Sat Dec 12 2020	68,207,116
55	13.43	17.89	United States of America	Thu Apr 22 2021	332,915,073
56	0.80	0.72	Viet Nam	Fri Sep 11 2020	98,168,833
	94.8		Total population		5,788,492,036
			World population		7,577,130,400
			Sample percentage of world population		76.39%

* Report of the Conference of the Parties on its twenty-first session, held in Paris from 30 November to 13 December 2015 https://unfccc.int/resource/docs/2015/cop21/eng/10.pdf#page=30.
** World Population in Review. Retrieved 12 January 2022 https://worldpopulationreview.com/.
*** European Union Member State.

6. Climate action: from multilateral negotiations to implementation

Mukes Kapilashrami

INTRODUCTION – AN 'EXECUTIVE SUMMARY' TO LEVEL THE PLAYING FIELD

Recognized as one of the most pressing challenges in the history of modern civilization, *global warming* and *climate change* is a subject matter most individuals, irrespective of their socioeconomic and cultural background, have come across in one way or the other. What once was "exclusively" discussed among scientists and environmentalists has, today, entered every household, national debate stage, and executive boardrooms across the globe.

While there are several well-crafted definitions describing climate change in depth, in simple words climate change can be summarized as "a change in the weather pattern impacting the environment and the natural habitat". "A change in the weather pattern" sounds innocent and harmless. However, concerns arise when such "manufactured" change in the environment becomes incorrigible.

The early notation of global warming was made by a Swedish physicist and Nobel Laureate Professor Svante A. Arrhenius back in the late 19th century (at a time when fossil fuel was becoming mainstream, and an integral part of a new and modern society) (Afework et al., 2019). In an article ('On the influence of carbonic acid in the air upon the temperature of the ground') published in the journal *The London, Edinburgh and Dublin Philosophical Magazine and Journal of Science* in April 1896; Professor Arrhenius presented his research on the correlation between the greenhouse effect and combustion of fossil fuels, and concluded that global temperatures could increase by as much as 5°C (or 9°F) as atmospheric concentrations of carbon dioxide increased two-fold (Arrhenius, 1896). While the initial studies were driven by scientific curiosity, the severe impact of combustion of fossil fuels on the environment was not really foreseen, and the study remained conceptual. Today, nearly 130 years later, climate change is considered one of the biggest crises in the history of human civilization.

Climate Change in a Nutshell

Given the attention climate change has drawn in recent times, some may believe that climate change is a new phenomenon. However, the "foundation" for its origin can be traced back to the time humankind first explored natural resources for self-serving purposes, such as deforestation for human settlement and timber trade, mining and extraction of metals and minerals, extraction of fossil fuels etc. However, such exploitation of natural resources initially occurred very locally, and at significantly smaller scale. Following the mid-19th century industrial revolution, the widespread use of fossil fuels to produce energy contributed to advances in manufacturing processes, and exponentially increased production throughput. The impact of the human society on the environment scaled accordingly.

As our environmental footprint reaches the point that it impacts nature's natural ability to recover from any intrusion on the environment, slowly our footprint starts becoming irreversible. This results in an imbalance in the eco-system where abnormal weather patterns and extreme off-seasonal weather conditions start occurring. At this point, climate change is neither a concept nor a prediction; it becomes a stark reality.

Contributing Factors to Global Warming and Climate Change

Among the many contributing factors to climate change e.g. increasing atmospheric concentrations of greenhouse gases, deforestation, utilization of toxic fertilizers in agriculture, increasing livestock farming, and so on, increasing atmospheric concentrations of greenhouse gases (or, GHGs) has been recognized as the pre-eminent cause for climate change as ensuing from increasing (average) temperature of the earth's surface (Pachauri & Meyer, 2014), or *global warming*.

So, what? ... does a one or two degree rise in the average atmospheric temperature really matter?

With over 70% of the earth's surface covered by water (serving as the planet's 'air conditioner', together with the Arctic and Antarctic), it would clearly require a significantly large amount of energy to heat the earth's average surface temperature even by half a degree. Yet, an increase of nearly 2°C (or 3.6°F) has occurred since late 19th century (Lindsey & Dahlman, 2021). The reported change in the earth's average surface temperature represents just what it sounds like, an average change, while actual regional temperature fluctuations may tell an entirely different story.

Connecting the Dots – Ozone Layer, Greenhouse Effect and Rising Temperature

The ozone layer in the stratosphere (at approximately 20–30 km, or 12–20 miles above the earth's surface) is a "reciprocal" filter composed of ozone gas (i.e., trioxygen, or O_3) that plays a critical role in maintaining a natural balance in our planet's temperature. While it (i) absorbs the harmful ultraviolet (UV) rays from the sun (preventing them from entering the earth's atmosphere), it (ii) also contributes to the *greenhouse effect*. The greenhouse effect refers to a process in which greenhouse gas molecules trapped in the ozone layer absorb certain concentrations of the radiation (thermal and solar) reflected from the earth's surface, preventing them from exiting the earth's atmosphere (NASA, Science Mission Directorate, 2010). The greenhouse effect itself is the underlying process that makes our planet habitable by allowing it to maintain an average surface temperature of around 15°C (or 59°F), whilst protecting it from the sun's harmful UV radiation.

The naturally occurring greenhouse effect is imperative for our planet's survival, but as result of the world's increasing emission of greenhouse gases the ozone layer is continuously accumulating more and more heat. This human-induced intensification of the greenhouse effect contributes to anomalous heat absorption, and thus excess heating of our planet (i.e., global warming).

Among the recognized greenhouse gases (e.g., carbon dioxide, water vapor, carbonhydride, nitrous oxide, and chlorofluorocarbons), water vapor is the most abundant greenhouse gas, but carbon dioxide (or CO_2) has been recognized as the most prevalent and harmful greenhouse gas fueling global warming. According to the US National Oceanic and Atmospheric

Administration (NOAA), the average atmospheric concentrations of CO_2 reached nearly 413 ppm in 2021 (with recorded CO_2 emissions exceeding 35 Gton) which is nearly 130% higher than that in 1960 (with recorded CO_2 emissions below 10 Gton). Concurrently, the average surface temperature has increased by over 0.8°C (or 1.4°F) during the same time period (Lindsey, 2021).

The impact of climate change extends far beyond the environment and affects all facets of our society; human health, agriculture and cultivation, economic growth, gender inclusion, political stability etc. While the debate continues over the root-cause of climate change, its existence as well as the severity of its impact, one thing is however clear – climate change does not discriminate, it affects us all! But with more severe impact on the most vulnerable states, island nations, and coastal communities. The latter can be best described by reflecting on the melting of the Arctic and its impact down in the mid-latitudes.

Arctic Warming and Climate Change

'Surface Albedo' (SA) refers to the Earth's surface reflection of solar radiation and is described by a fraction between 0 (for zero reflection) and 1 (for 100% reflection). While the Earth's average surface albedo has been estimated to be ~0.30 (NASA Earth Observatory, 2021), actual absorption varies greatly by geographical region (Table 6.1).

Table 6.1   Regional surface albedo across the Earth's surface

Geographical region	Surface albedo	Reference
Open sea	~0.06	NSIDC (2020)
Desert sand	<0.4	Tezlaff (1983)
Green grass	0.15–0.26	Tezlaff (1983)
Ice, and ice covered with snow	~0.5–0.9	NSIDC (2020)

With higher reflectivity, the Arctic region is reportedly heating up at a higher rate (up to three times) than anywhere else across the Earth's surface (Beer, Eisenman, & Wagner, 2020), contributing 30–50% of the warming of our planet (Turton, 2021). According to the 2020 Arctic Report Card by NOAA, the highest temperature over Arctic land in the past century was recorded between October 2019 and September 2020, with Arctic annual mean temperature 1.9°C (or 3.4°F) above the average temperature between 1981 and 2010 (Figure 6.1) (Ballinger, 2020).

In addition to rising sea levels and the impact on the aquatic eco-system, rising temperatures in the Arctic region have been correlated with disruption to the polar vortex and an imbalance in weather patterns down in the mid-latitudes (NOAA, 2021). Increasing concentrations of atmospheric water vapor and moist air often manifests in irregular regional weather patterns, where some regions experience heat waves and severe drought, whilst for others temperature fall (as the polar jet stream is destabilized, polar winds propagate toward the southern hemisphere), intensified rainfall and flooding, hurricane and storm winds (European Environment Agency, 2018; Means, 2021). Figure 6.2 highlights selected climate anomalies worldwide as reported in the October 2021 Global Climate Report (NOAA National Centers for Environmental Information, 2021).

To further emphasize on the impact of climate change in a much broader context, one needs to look at the impact on the most vulnerable communities; communities and individuals already suffering from inadequate infrastructure, economic development and political governance.

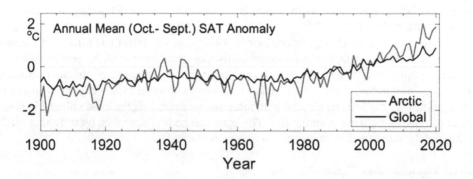

Figure 6.1   Recorded mean surface air temperatures (SAT) over Arctic land between 1900 and 2020 relative to 1981 to 2010 mean temperatures, as indicated by horizontal line at 0°C (Ballinger, 2020)

A good example is the regional areas in Sub-Saharan Arica where extreme and irregular weather patterns have not only resulted in intensified conflicts among (already conflict ridden) communities over access to (already) limited resources, but also resulted in forced displacements and migration of individuals impacting their safety and security (in particular women and children, making them subject to violence, and forced recruitment by armed groups and militias) (de Coning, Krampe, & Grand, 2021; Krampe, 2019). Similarly, extreme weather conditions in South and East Asia have often forced individuals (and at times entire communities) to migrate and travel long distances on foot in search of basic livelihoods while posing severe health risks over extended time periods; from inadequate access to clean water and basic sanitation, and food insecurity, to elevated exposure to air- and water-borne diseases, and other vector-borne diseases (Majra & Gur, 2009).

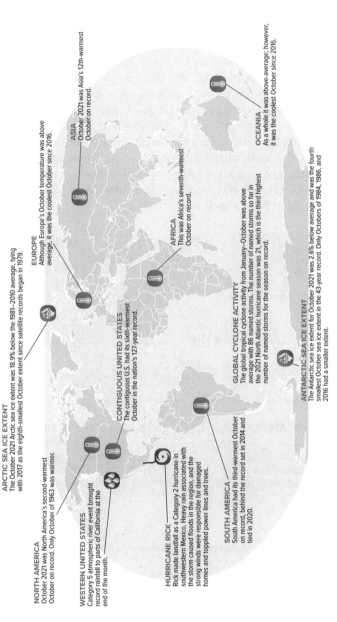

Figure 6.2   Selected climate anomalies and related events reported in Global Climate Report October 2021 (NOAA National Centers for Environmental Information, 2021)

Future Projection of Climate Change

Future projection on the impact of human and societal activity on climate change is an important measure to understand how to best formulate most relevant, and effective policies and mitigation strategies. Socioeconomic driving forces considered in such analyses often include economic growth, technological advances, political stability, and population growth. Different scenarios and pathways have been applied in the past to understand the future state of climate change, including the *Special Report on Emission Scenario* (or, SRES), and *Representative Concentration Pathway* (or, RCP). While the SRES projects future emission scenarios based on socioeconomic driving forces, the RCP does not include any specific socioeconomic contributing/driving factors, and instead focuses on quantitative analyses of atmospheric concentrations of GHGs over time. The RCP can be described as a 'reverse engineering' approach in which specific emission rates and concentrations (at certain times in the future) are assumed, and research is directed to understand the various societal changes and directions to reach such emission rates. In striking contrast, the SRES approach projects future emissions around four key scenarios (A1, A2, B1, and B2) based on the socioeconomic driving forces (Figure 6.3) (Hanania & Donev, 2022; Nakicenovic et al., 2000).

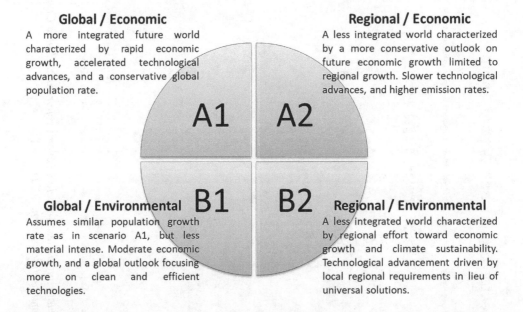

Global / Economic

A more integrated future world characterized by rapid economic growth, accelerated technological advances, and a conservative global population rate.

Regional / Economic

A less integrated world characterized by a more conservative outlook on future economic growth limited to regional growth. Slower technological advances, and higher emission rates.

Global / Environmental

Assumes similar population growth rate as in scenario A1, but less material intense. Moderate economic growth, and a global outlook focusing more on clean and efficient technologies.

Regional / Environmental

A less integrated world characterized by regional effort toward economic growth and climate sustainability. Technological advancement driven by local regional requirements in lieu of universal solutions.

Figure 6.3   *Key scenarios for projection of future GHG emissions following the SRES approach*

An important difference between SRES and RCP is that RCP takes into consideration the possible existence of climate policies and mitigation strategies to achieve net negative emission, which often results in lower emission scenarios.

To complete the RCP, a shared socioeconomic pathway (or, SSP) was introduced in 2016. The SSP models how socioeconomic factors, e.g., population, economic growth and technological advancement, may evolve over time, and impact future efforts toward climate change mitigation and adaptation. Specifically, five narratives are summarized within the SSP (Table 6.2), each narrative defining a unique baseline in the absence of climate mitigation strategies. The SSP projects pathways (based on each unique socioeconomic scenario) that may either facilitate or impede future climate change mitigation and adaptation strategies, depending along which socioeconomic trajectory the world evolves in the future.

Table 6.2   *Summary of the SSP narrative, as presented by Riahi et al. (2017)*

Narrative	Summary
SSP1	Sustainability – Taking the Green Road (Low challenges to mitigation and adaptation) wherein the world shifts gradually, but pervasively, toward a more sustainable path, emphasizing more inclusive development that respects perceived environmental boundaries. Management of the global commons slowly improves, educational and health investments accelerate the demographic transition, and the emphasis on economic growth shifts toward a broader emphasis on human well-being. Driven by an increasing commitment to achieving development goals, inequality is reduced both across and within countries. Consumption is oriented toward low material growth and lower resource and energy intensity
SSP2	Middle of the Road – The world follows a path in which social, economic, and technological trends do not shift markedly from historical patterns (Medium challenges to mitigation and adaptation). Development and income growth proceeds unevenly, with some countries making relatively good progress while others fall short of expectations. Global and national institutions work toward but make slow progress in achieving sustainable development goals. Environmental systems experience degradation, although there are some improvements and overall the intensity of resource and energy use declines. Global population growth is moderate and levels off in the second half of the century. Income inequality persists or improves only slowly and challenges to reducing vulnerability to societal and environmental changes remain.
SSP3	Regional Rivalry – A Rocky Road (High challenges to mitigation and adaptation). A resurgent nationalism, concerns about competitiveness and security, and regional conflicts push countries to increasingly focus on domestic or, at most, regional issues. Policies shift over time to become increasingly oriented toward national and regional security issues. Countries focus on achieving energy and food security goals within their own regions at the expense of broader-based development. Investments in education and technological development decline. Economic development is slow, consumption is material-intensive, and inequalities persist or worsen over time. Population growth is low in industrialized and high in developing countries. A low international priority for addressing environmental concerns leads to strong environmental degradation in some regions.
SSP4	Inequality – A Road Divided (Low challenges to mitigation, high challenges to adaptation). Highly unequal investments in human capital, combined with increasing disparities in economic opportunity and political power, lead to increasing inequalities and stratification both across and within countries. Over time, a gap widens between an internationally-connected society that contributes to knowledge- and capital-intensive sectors of the global economy, and a fragmented collection of lower-income, poorly educated societies that work in a labor intensive, low-tech economy. Social cohesion degrades and conflict and unrest become increasingly common. Technology development is high in the high-tech economy and sectors. The globally connected energy sector diversifies, with investments in both carbon-intensive fuels such as coal and unconventional oil, but also low-carbon energy sources. Environmental policies focus on local issues around middle and high income areas.
SSP5	Fossil-fueled Development – Taking the Highway (High challenges to mitigation, low challenges to adaptation). This world places increasing faith in competitive markets, innovation and participatory societies to produce rapid technological progress and development of human capital as the path to sustainable development. Global markets are increasingly integrated. There are also strong investments in health, education, and institutions to enhance human and social capital. At the same time, the push for economic and social development is coupled with the exploitation of abundant fossil fuel resources and the adoption of resource and energy intensive lifestyles around the world. All these factors lead to rapid growth of the global economy, while the global population peaks and declines in the 21st century. Local environmental problems such as air pollution are successfully managed. There is faith in the ability to effectively manage social and ecological systems, including by geo-engineering if necessary.

Road to Climate and Carbon Neutrality

As we reflect on key fundamentals of climate change and global warming, one might conclude that a solution may be as simple as to end the world's use of fossil fuels and thereby end the world's emission of GHGs. Although the elephant in the room has been identified; the road ahead toward carbon neutrality is unfortunately not as straightforward.

Due to the world's continuously increasing energy demands and consumption, climate change (and related global warming) is a very complex challenge. There are currently no viable solutions that allow a complete transition from fossil fuels to zero carbon energy alternatives. Nor can one ignore the fact that many of the world's economies have been built (and still rely) on fossil fuels. Having said that, a future clean energy infrastructure cannot solely rely on transitioning to low and zero-carbon energy technologies, or instituting policies applying a price on carbon. An entire sustainable clean energy economy needs to be designed that will reduce our dependence on fossil fuels. This would mean enabling integration of renewable energy sources into existing energy grids, facilitating offshore production of clean fuel, advancing technologies for storage and transportation of clean fuel, as well as improving efficiencies of current infrastructure and grid, whilst concurrently enabling a fossil-fuel free workforce. Such ambitious goals require that all stakeholders come together on a common platform and work in concert to devise inclusive and sustainable solutions readily adaptable by all economies and communities.

A multilateral approach can be summarized as a vehicle for communication between stakeholders, enabling them to join forces (cross borders and economic systems) to further lay out strategies and targets toward achieving common climate goals that align with national interest and objectives.

While one needs to appreciate the diversity and unique requirements of each individual nation and economy, it often comes with the challenge of convening the world's leaders to objectively work toward common goals, since many such leaders are often driven by an agenda supporting national interests. Given the complexity of a multilateral approach, a comprehensive "near future solution" is a difficult proposition. Instead, multilateral negotiations focus on bringing parties a compromised solution while leaving room to negotiate the pathway and short-term solutions toward common goals.

Although globalization has, to a considerable extent, brought the world together, socioeconomic dynamics do yet play an important role and pose many challenges in the final roll-out and implementation of climate policies formulated through multilateral agreements.

MULTILATERAL NEGOTIATIONS AND GLOBAL AGREEMENTS

Hosted in Stockholm Sweden in 1972, the United Nations Conference on the Human Environment (a.k.a. the Stockholm Conference) was the first major United Nations driven meeting focusing on the impact of human society on the environment, and with that it became the first steppingstone towards a multilateral approach in international environmental affairs.

The Stockholm Conference focused on 26 key principles within the broader context of the Global Environmental Assessment Programme; Environmental Management Activities; and International Measures to Support Assessment and Management Activities Carried out at the National and International Levels, emphasizing the rights and responsibilities of the individual as well as the state (United Nations Conference on the Human Environment, 2021). Based on these key principles, 109 recommendations and action points were outlined within the framework of:

- Planning and Management of Human Settlements for Environmental Quality
- Environmental Aspects of Natural Resources Management
- Identification and Control of Pollutants of Broad International Significance
- Educational, Informational, Social and Cultural Aspects of Environmental Issues
- Development and Environment

The conference also laid the foundation for a dialogue between industrialized and developing countries on the correlation between economic growth, environmental impact, and the well-being of human society (United Nations Conference on the Human Environment, 2021).

Another milestone of the Stockholm Conference was the formation of United Nations Environment Programme (or, UNEP) with the mandate to "provide leadership and encourage partnership in caring for the environment by inspiring, informing, and enabling nations and peoples to improve their quality of life without compromising that of future generations" (UNEP, 2021a). With UNEP, there was now a direct link between environmental affairs at grass-roots and policy level.

A lot has happened since the Stockholm Conference and the formation of UNEP in 1972. With the growing awareness on the environmental impact of the further development of human society and associated economic growth, a number of international organizations and panels have been formed over the years to further strengthen the engagement of the world's leaders and other stakeholders. This includes the formation of the Intergovernmental Panel on Climate Change (or, IPCC) in 1988 and the United Nations Framework Convention on Climate Change (or, UNFCCC) in 1994.

Since its inception in 1988, the IPCC has played an important role in educating governments, private sector and civil society on the "current state" of our planet by tracking human-induced changes and irregularities across the environmental landscape (air, land and sea). Composed of working groups focusing on (i) the scientific basis of climate change; (ii) impact of climate change and adaptation; and (iii) climate change mitigation, the IPCC has provided the world with assessments on future risks and the implications of climate change on the natural habitat and human society, as well as identified targets for mitigation of environmental risks based on scientific merit.

The IPCC is only one example; several other non-government organizations and academic institutions have, over the years, brought the world data and assessments on the condition of our planet, as well as long-term projections with actionable recommendations to further mitigate any related environmental risk. These data lay the foundation for the dialogue as leaders come together under the pretext of a multilateral approach.

In its sixth and most recent assessment report (published in August 2021) the IPCC sent the world an alarming message on the rates at which human society has warmed our planet in the past centuries (Masson-Delmotte et al., 2021). The findings reflect very well how the modern human civilization and economy has evolved over the years, since the industrial revolution in the mid-19th century (Figure 6.4).

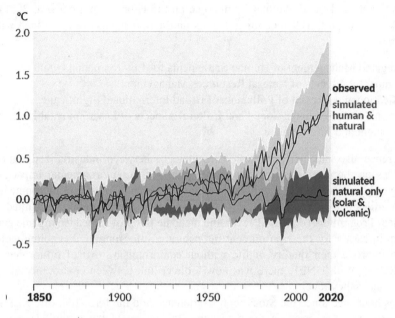

Source: Masson-Delmotte et al. (2021).

Figure 6.4   *Change in global surface temperature (annual average) as observed and simulated using human and natural, and only natural, factors (both 1850–2020)*

Table 6.3   *Projected long-term (2080–2100) temperature rise relative to 1850–1900 (Masson-Delmotte et al., 2021)*

Pathway	Socioeconomic scenario	Projected temperature rise
SSP5–8.5	Very high range of GHG emissions	4.4°C (or 7.9°F)
SSP3–7.0	High range of GHG emissions	3.6°C (or 6.5°F)
SSP2–4.5	Intermediate range of GHG emissions	2.7°C (or 4.9°F)
SSP1–2.6	Low range of GHG emissions	1.8°C (or 3.2°F)
SSP1–1.9	Incredibly low range of GHG emissions	1.4°C (or 2.5°F)

Looking forward, global temperatures are expected to rise (relative to the average temperatures between 1850 and 1900) at least until the mid-21st century irrespective of what socioeconomic pathways (Table 6.3) the world evolves along (Figure 6.5) (Masson-Delmotte et al., 2021). An important message here is that even under a scenario of intermediate future GHG emission rates, average global temperatures are yet projected to rise far beyond 2°C (or 3.6°F). A question one may (rightfully) ask, seeing the predictions for future GHG emissions (Figure 6.5) is that "even if the world was to assume significant measure today to reduce global GHG emission from current rates, would it really suffice"?

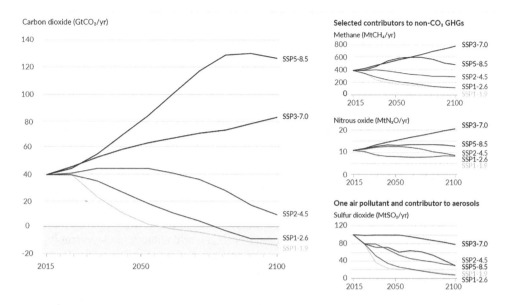

Figure 6.5   *Future annual emissions of CO_2 (left) and of a subset of key non-CO_2 drivers (right), across five illustrative scenarios*

Tasked to support the global response to the threat posed by climate change – UNFCCC has been the driving force behind convening nations and stakeholders on the key challenges, and intergovernmental climate meetings through annual negotiations, a.k.a. Conference of the Parties (or, COP).

Bringing the parties to the negotiation table is one thing, but reaching an agreement on goals, targets, and related policies for reduction of global GHG emissions is more complex (given that the parties often try to protect and maintain their respective national interests during the negotiations).

The COP is an annual assembly that convenes heads of state, private sector, and civil society leadership from across the globe under one roof with one ultimate goal; to agree on a universal solution to end global warming and related climate change. With the last COP in 2022, there have been 27 meetings in total. While each meeting has been a step in the right direction, none has resulted in an immediate solution that would prevent continued warming of our planet.

Bringing all signatory stakeholders to an agreement and 100% ratification has thus far proven incredibly challenging. In fact, to date, only one agreement (or protocol) has achieved 100% ratification.

The Effectiveness of a Multilateral Approach

In the early 1980s, the world was alarmed by the discovery of a large hole – over 9.5 million square miles in size! – in the ozone layer over the Antarctic. With growing evidence for the correlation between the use of ozone depleting substances (ODSs) e.g., chlorofluorocarbons and hydrochlorofluorocarbons, and the deterioration of the ozone layer, the world had to come together to address the threat.

Adopted in 1987, the Montreal Protocol on Substances that Deplete the Ozone Layer (or, Montreal Protocol) mandated regulation on the production and use of ODSs. Specifically, it set targets phasing-out ODSs that are typically found in cooling applications, fire extinguishers, building insulations etc. This was the first treaty that achieved ratification of all countries in the world, following the final ratification of South Sudan in 2012.

Among other things, what made this Protocol successful was that it included provisions for trade and agreements for countries that ratified the treaty, offered industries sufficient leverage to plan for long-term ODS-free solutions, and allowed developing economies extended time to phase out ODSs. In addition, through the "Multilateral Fund for the Implementation of the Montreal Protocol" that was established in 1991, developing economies were offered financial and technical assistance to meet the targets to phase out ODSs (UNEP, 2021b).

Today, our planet is on a recovery path, and is expected to revert to levels where it was in the 1970s by 2070 (Figure 6.6). As reported by UNEP, a world without the Montreal Protocol would have had catastrophic consequences on human health, food security, life on land and in water, and the eco-system in its entirety (UNEP Ozone Secretariat, 2021).

The Montreal Protocol can be described as a "textbook case" that exemplifies how effective a multilateral approach can be if the need and capacity of each individual stakeholder is acknowledged and targets are set accordingly (although it eventually took nearly 15 years, since inception, for it to get fully ratified).

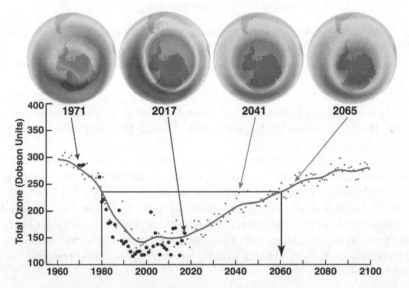

Figure 6.6   *Simulated data of the ozone hole above the Antarctic suggesting that the ozone hole is on a recovery path as result of the Montreal Protocol, and expected to regress back to its levels recorded in 1970 by 2070 (Morgan et al., 2015)*

Reduction of Ozone Depleting Substances versus Reduction of Greenhouse Gases

One may ask, if the Montreal Protocol worked out so well and our planet is now on a recovery path, then why hasn't the same strategy been applied to reducing global GHGs emissions?

Well, there is a difference.

While both a depleting ozone layer and global warming are very alarming concerns, there is a significant difference in the root cause behind these environmental threats, and the extent to which the world's economies are willing to go in effort to phase out substances causing such threats.

Let us look at the ODSs. These are manufactured chemical substances used in niche applications and sectors. Although they can be found in our day-to-day applications (cooling and refrigeration, medical and safety applications), they are *not* an integrated part of our economy nor have any of the world's economies been built on these. Thus, weighing the short-term threat these substances pose to human health and society against the economic impact of banning the same, clearly a decision to phase out ODSs is indisputable.

If we, on the other hand, consider GHG emissions (which arise from combustion of fossil fuels), one cannot ignore the fact that most of the world's developed economies have been built on fossil fuels, and many still depend on fossil fuels to support domestic energy infrastructure, workforce, manufacturing, and export of the same for economic gains. Fossil fuels have been and are an integral part of our modern society and civilization, and an important commodity in the global economy. A unanimous agreement on a path toward climate neutrality is, unfortunately for some parties, in direct conflict to concurrently safeguarding national interests and requirements. To best exemplify this further, let us review the Kyoto Protocol.

Adopted in 1997, the Kyoto Protocol (often referred to as the first international treaty for reduction of global GHG emissions) mandated reduction of human-activity-increased concentrations of atmospheric carbon dioxide. Emphasizing the responsibility of the industrialized economies (recognized as the predominant contributors to global GHG emissions) to reduce their GHG emissions, the Kyoto Protocol suggested applying a cap regulating the annual carbon dioxide emissions of the industrialized economies, while only requiring developing economies to participate on voluntary basis (UNFCCC, 2021a).

To further persuade industrialized countries to commit to the Kyoto Protocol, the protocol outlined three pathways (or Kyoto Mechanisms) (UNFCCC, 2021a) through which such countries could earn additional emission reduction credits.

- *International emissions trading*
  An industrialized country that has already met its annual GHG emission cap may buy additional emission credits from a developing economy if it exceeds its annual emission target.
- *Clean development mechanism*
  An industrialized country may earn additional emission reduction credits toward meeting its annual emission target by working with developing economies on emission reducing projects (e.g., installing solar or wind power, or supporting rural development).
- *Joint implementation*
  An industrialized country may earn additional emission reduction credit toward meeting its annual emission target upon contributing toward GHG emission reduction offshore (i.e., reducing another industrialized economy's GHG emission).

The concept of emission trading (or carbon trading) changed the playing field as entities now looked at carbon as a commodity (UNFCCC, 2021b). In addition to emission trading, putting a price on carbon (or applying a carbon tax) has been another way to regulate carbon emissions.

The core difference between the two paths is that the latter defines a price on carbon and allows the market to regulate the emission quota, whereas carbon trading directly regulates concentrations of allowed carbon emissions and instead allows the market to regulate the price (Frank, 2014).

Notwithstanding the many strategies that were rolled out to support industrialized economies to reduce their annual GHG emissions, the Kyoto Protocol did not unfold as expected and several parties that initially ratified the *protocol* later withdrew from the same.

Among the various arguments for why the Kyoto Protocol was not successful, one of the primary concerns with the Kyoto Protocol was the fact that only industrialized economies were being held accountable and subject to the binding targets, while developing economies were exempt. Criticism was directed at exempting India and China (as two of the world's largest contributors to global GHG emissions) from regulating their GHG emissions. Another issue was the fact the economies that could afford it would buy their way out through the emission trading system, and continue emitting GHGs at levels beyond their annual emission cap. Given the many challenges with the Kyoto Protocol, the parties could not even come to an agreement on the implementation of the protocol, even the following year at COP4 in Buenos Aires.

As of 2020, the average surface temperature of our planet had increased by an additional ~0.55°C (or 1°F) since the inception of the Kyoto Protocol in 1997 (NASA Goddard Institute for Space Studies, 2021).

The Copenhagen Climate Conference in 2009 brought together nearly 115 of the world's leaders (and set a landmark as one of the largest international political meetings) in an effort to streamline the Kyoto Protocol. While there was further progress in that the developed economies committed to fund projects and strategies reducing global GHG emissions, there was still resistance among the parties in terms of who should be subject to the annual emission cap and who not. While the parties representing the industrialized economies maintained their stand and criticized the agreement for not holding developing economies accountable, the counter argument emphasized the developing economies' right to develop their economies utilizing fossil fuels the same way the developed economies had been doing in the last century.

Another important aspect contributing to the challenge is an economy's direct and indirect carbon footprint. With 98% of its domestic energy produced from renewable sources (Norwegian Ministry of Petroleum and Energy, 2016), Norway is (amongst the developed economies) one of the least GHG emitting economies and in many ways considered a "poster child" for climate sustainability. However, Norway's export of natural gas accounts for nearly 20–25% of the EU's gas demand (Norwegian Petroleum Directorate, 2021), and 7% of the EU's import of crude oil (Eurostat, 2021). Similarly, Saudi Arabia accounts for nearly 20% of the world's crude oil export but the country on its own only accounts for less than 1.5% of the world GHG emissions.

Norway and Saudi Arabia are only two examples among many. With Asia becoming the manufacturing hub of the world in the last two decades, not only has the service and production sector been outsourced there but a large fraction of the environmental footprint of the western economies can today be found in Asia, and in other developing economies. This raises questions on the accountability for domestic GHG emissions versus GHG emissions offshore.

Paris Agreement – A New Hope

With the Paris Agreement (or COP21) in 2015 came a new hope for containing global warming within 2°C (or ideally within 1.5°C) from pre-industrial time as it rolled out a binding climate treaty that was adopted by 196 parties, with the ambitious goal to achieve carbon neutrality by 2050.

Different from the Kyoto Protocol, the Paris Agreement held all parties (developed and developing economies) accountable for reducing global GHG emissions. Under the Paris Agreement, parties are to set their individuals targets (a.k.a. nationally determined contributions, or NDC), both short-term (2030) and long-term (2050) goals (goals that are to be reviewed every five years). In layperson language, one can summarize the Paris Agreement as "you know what needs to be achieved and by when, you have to find your own path forward, and we'll review your progress every five years".

Following this new approach, some parties have formulated NDCs focusing on regulating GHG emissions through taxes and investments in GHG emission reducing projects offshore, while others have focused on investing in green infrastructure and transportation, integrating renewable energy alternatives into the national energy grid, as well as on national capacity building (UNFCCC, 2021c).

An important milestone of the Paris Agreement was the fact that the parties were now not only discussing strategies to reduce global GHG emissions, but also rolling out strategies on how to achieve net zero carbon emissions within a foreseen future (something previously unheard of!).

An important lesson learnt from past COPs has been the fact that there is no "one size fits all" solution to global warming and climate change. Nor do the parties have the ability to undertake the same path toward reducing their own net annual GHG emissions.

Phase Out or Phase Down

Different from the Paris Climate Meeting in 2015, the tone at COP26 in Glasgow (2021) had changed as world's leaders now firmly emphasized the severity of global warming and the urgent call for global action in an effort to maintain the 1.5°C target from the previous COP meeting. In addition, there was a call to gravitate away from carbon trading and establish an integrated mechanism for (i) *climate adaptation* to protect natural habitat and communities, (ii) *climate finance* to mobilize economic support mitigating climate change, and (iii) funding for *loss and damage* to aid developing economies recover damage from climate change (UN Climate Change Conference (COP26), 2021).

What made the headlines was that COP26 explicitly called to end deforestation by 2030 and phase out coal and fossil fuels by 2050. Momentarily, the world seemed to be on a track to a historic climate agreement, but things took a dramatic turn at the end as a final draft of the Glasgow Agreement was being finalized by all the parties. India (later support by China) intervened at the last minute with an appeal to change the language in the agreement from *phase out* to *phase down* the use of coal and fossil fuels in order for them to move forward and sign the agreement, arguing that they are not at the point to completely phase out coal by 2050 given its dominance in their economy and their status as a developing nation. This is a notable example of how national interests at times overcome global objectives.

Under current circumstances, where island nations and coastal communities are already experiencing early climate change warning signals and seeing what a future with increased average global temperatures exceeding 2°C (or 3.6°F) holds, just the notation that some of the world's largest GHG emitting economies seek to revise the wording in the agreement to phase out fossil fuels is very daunting. To the great disappointed of the global community, the parties eventually had to adhere to India's request in order for India and China to sign the agreement and commit to the remaining targets.

Why was it so important to consider India's motion to change the wording from *phase out* to *phase down* coal? Together with China and the United States, India represents one of the world's largest GHG emitting economies. So how effective would an agreement (and the strategies therein) to reduce global GHG emissions really be if two of the largest sources of the global GHG emissions would not be part of the solution?

In addition to reaffirm their commitment to limit global temperature rise to 1.5 degrees Celsius above pre-industrial levels, at COP27 (in Sharm El-Sheikh, Egypt) the parties agreed to establish a loss and damage fund that would support most vulnerable countries recover from damage caused by climate change. In addition, it was also decided that a special fund should be established to assist developing nations respond to *loss and damage*.

Currently, the world is already on the verge of exceeding temperatures beyond 2°C (or 3.6°F) by 2030 even if all the parties were to meet their individual NDCs. In fact, in order to meet the 1.5°C (or 2.7°F) goal of the Paris Agreement coal would have to be completely phased out by the OECD by 2030, and globally by 2040 (Climate Action Tracker, 2021). But this is the name of the game. A multilateral agreement often means finding the most integrated solution. It may not be the ideal solution for the short-term, but it is sufficient to create momentum in the right direction toward climate change mitigation and adaptation. Such an agreement is typically an open-ended solution that requires parties to regularly revisit the agreement and revise the terms of reference (or NDCs) based on progress and limitations. Figure 6.7 presents a broad overview of selected climate meetings, and outcome since the Stockholm Conference in 1972.

Moving forward, policies and climate pledges alone will not solve the climate crisis. Equally important is the contribution of the private sector and scientific community that together will translate policies and guidelines to actionable items. With private sector engagement an entire climate economy can be mobilized, including leveraging technological advances in line with government policies and climate pledges, mobilizing a workforce that was previously working in sectors heavily dependent on fossil fuels, improving infrastructure and efficiencies reducing energy waste, supporting national capacity building, as well as mobilizing investments supporting education and technology research.

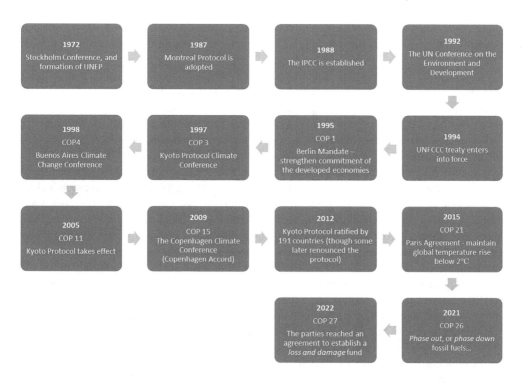

Figure 6.7   *Overview of selected of climate meetings since the Stockholm Conference in 1972*

MULTILATERAL APPROACH BEYOND POLICY

Over the past centuries, the world has witnessed many important technological advances that have laid the foundation for our modern civilization. One such key innovation is the ability to transform and contain energy in a controlled way to further enable processes and pursuits impacting all facets of human life and society.

The use of fossil fuels to produce electrical energy gained ground in the middle of the 19th century and revolutionized all aspects of modern life, establishing an entire new global economy. Today, fossil fuels have become an indispensable commodity, and their widespread use has exceeded far beyond nature's ability to recover from the elevated atmospheric concentration of carbon dioxide.

From Fossil Fuels to Zero Carbon Energy Alternatives

Some may argue that multilateral negotiations don't have a track record of being effective, in light of the many challenges associated with bringing leaders from various socioeconomic demographics to consensus on climate targets and goals. In all fairness, it is important to acknowledge the fact that the meetings have impacted society in raising awareness of the severity of climate change, and on the impact of each individual's action on the same. A good example of this is the continuously increasing global capacity of installed renewable energy alternatives driven by joint public–private sector partnerships, and continuously increasing private sector engagement through climate sustainable business models and corporate climate pledges.

In the last decade alone, the global capacity of installed renewable energy sources have more than doubled, from approximately 1.3 TW in 2010 to over 3.0 TW in 2020 (Figure 6.8) (The International Renewable Energy Agency, Abu Dhabi, 2021). While green alternative energy sources offer many important environmental benefits, there are also issues impeding their implementation, e.g., initial cost, impact on the surrounding environment and civil society, as well as performance (i.e., efficiency) against requirements. For instance, while hydropower offers one of the cheapest and most efficient pathways to produce clean energy, with energy conversion rates up to 90%, limitations associated with its implementation include large principal investments, location restrictions (need for access to a water reservoir), and consequences on aquatic life. Such limitations often become a topic of debate when negotiating new installations with investors and municipal leaders, and often also meet resistance from environmental groups due to concerns for the surrounding natural habitat.

On the technical side, two key factors that impede large-scale deployment of many of today's green energy alternatives is the ability to store and transport clean energy produced off-grid and offshore and off-grid. Mobile large-scale energy storage capacity holds the future for clean energy sustainability as it would open new avenues for utilization of, for example, solar and wind power, and with that an entire new clean energy economy.

Policy plays an important role in pushing green technological advances through the 'economic pipeline' by directing investments in technology research and infrastructure, formulating tax breaks and economic benefits contingent on investments in clean energy technology, as well as regulating GHG emissions. However, policies alone will not translate climate goals and strategies to action, 'solution architects' need to be brought to the table and be made an active part of climate negotiations.

Scientists need to be Part of Multilateral Meetings and Negotiations

The basis for multilateral meetings and negotiations relies on the findings presented by the scientific community, whether that be through organizations such as the IPCC, academic institutions or related international organizations. But the participation of the scientific and research community at the negotiation table has, however, been very modest. Scientists are the solution architects that need to be made an active negotiating partner around the negotiation table to deliver the most realistic and actionable climate change mitigation and adaptation strategies, and goals. Such an approach would allow technology design and deployment to be customized based on the actual requirements of the individual party. Specifically, to review available technologies and advise on how to redesign them to best "fit" individual end user's requirements in terms of relevance, functionality and cost, as well as quantity investments against wider impact. With that ensure delivery of climate targets that carry more merit and would bring more parties to an agreement. Specifically, to review available technologies and advise on how to redesign them to best "fit" specific 'market requirements' in terms of relevance, functionality and cost, but also investment against wider impact. This is crucial since there is a significant discrepancy in the economic and infrastructural background between the parties (industrialized economies versus developing economies), and how each party is impacted by climate change (mainland territories versus island nations). Doing so would

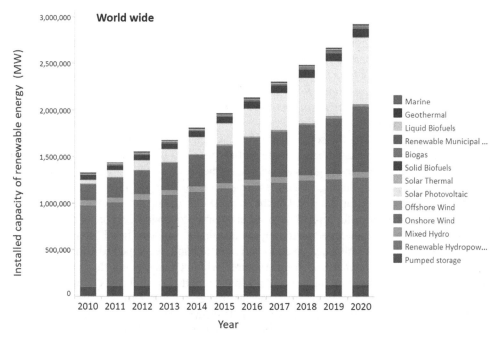

Source:　The International Renewable Energy Agency, Abu Dhabi (2021).

Figure 6.8　*Global capacity of installed renewable energy between 2010 and 2020*

incentivize and accelerate investments (both national and offshore) in green innovations and related technologies, as well private sector engagement.

To best exemplify the importance and impact of "tailored technology implementation" is by reviewing how the telecom industry has evolved over the years. The invention of the telephone revolutionized the prospects of human interaction and communication. In the years following the late 19th century, hard-wired phone lines were drawn across cities and borders, connecting individuals, communities and nations. As technology matured telephone lines were improved and updated, communication networks expanded and, in more recent years, also replaced by base-stations (or, cellphone towers) as we entered the era of wireless communication technology.

While western and developed economies have been part of this renaissance in telecommunication, many developing economies bypassed this entire path, and instead directly rolled-out mobile and wireless communication networks custom-tailored to meet the end-users' unique prerequisites and needs. Today, while many in the developing parts of the world may lack access to water, sanitation, and adequate infrastructure, they are yet connected to a global community and market through 2G and 4G mobile networks (some regions even gravitating toward 4G and 5G) (Wyrzykowski, 2020). Developing economies and island nations are important stakeholders at the climate negotiation table as they are more severely impacted by climate change, and the first to record early warning signals for what climate change brings along. With energy demand on the continuous rise in these economies (as a result of economic development and growth), so are their GHG emissions. While they recognize the environmental impact of their use of fossil fuels, many are still building their infrastructure with the same, given their availability and economic viability.

As world leaders negotiate strategies and investments in clean energy technologies to phase out fossil fuels, parties representing developing economies often make the argument: *the developed economies have fully utilized and benefited from fossil fuels for over 150 years to build their economy and modern infrastructure, why are the developing economies being deprived the same opportunity (in particular) when their environmental footprint is nowhere near that of the developed economies.*

While no one is arguing the severity of climate change and use of fossil fuels, but given the socioeconomic discrepancy between the parties there is a fundamental difference in their ability to meet *universal* climate goals and targets as these may necessarily do not consider the many challenges that developing economies are already suffering. This emphasizes the need to tailor climate goals and targets based on the *weakest link* around the negotiation table, while leaving opportunities open for more developed economies to tap in with greater contributions. This is an important argument, emphasizing the fact that a "one size fit all" solution does not exist, nor would it work. Pathways need to be identified and developed to allow developing nations build their economies and infrastructures without undertaking the same route the developing economies have in the past century (but yet both time and cost effective).

Many of today's fastest growing economies are represented by African nations. In a study by World Finance in 2019, Ethiopia (8.5% GDP growth rate), Côte d'Ivoire (7.4% GDP growth rate), Senegal (7% GDP growth rate), Tanzania (6.4% GDP growth rate) and Ghana (6.3% GDP growth rate) represent five of the fastest growing economies in Africa (Newell, 2019). With a population of over 115 million, Ethiopia has been ranked as the fastest growing economy in Africa by the World Economic Forum in 2019 (Gray, 2018). Ethiopia's annual domestic energy consumption has increased from approximately 1 TW in 1990 to over 10 TW in 2019 (IEA, 2019a), while access to electricity has increased from 5% to over 45% (IEA, 2019b). The country's annual CO_2 emissions have scaled concurrently with its economic growth, and increased nearly 600% since 1990 (IEA, 2019a).

On a positive note, the installed capacity of solar technology, in particular, in Ethiopia has increased from nearly 2 GW in 2010 to over 4.5 GW in 2020 (Figure 6.9). Installed capacity of solar technology in Ethiopia has increased from 0.03 MW in 2010 to over 20 MW in 2020 (The International Renewable Energy Agency, Abu Dhabi, 2021). Although these numbers indicate that we are on right track, we are still far from the goal.

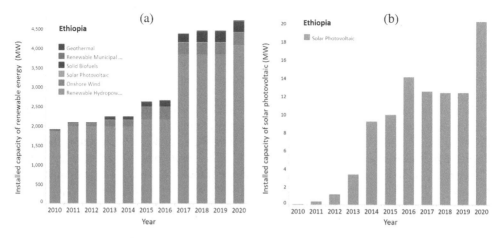

Source: The International Renewable Energy Agency, Abu Dhabi (2021).

Figure 6.9   *(a) installed capacity of renewable energy in Ethiopia between 2010 and 2020; and (b) installed capacity of solar photovoltaic in Ethiopia between 2010 and 2020*

Understanding Wider Impact of Climate Neutral Technologies

Another argument for the need to include scientists and related subject matter experts around the negotiation table is the importance to understand the wider impact of often suggested climate change mitigation and adaptation strategies.

For instance, in an effort to reduce global carbon emissions from the transportation sector (contributing to nearly one third of global GHG emissions), transitioning to electric vehicles (or, EVs) is a strategy that has widely been discussed. While EVs would, from the end-user side, cut down GHG emissions to nearly zero, there are other serious consequences regarding the environment and society that need to be understood and acknowledged.

Although still in its infancy, EV technology has revolutionized the transportation industry, and demonstrated how a future clean energy transportation sector can transform the role of fossil fuels in our society and economy. As auto manufacturers are today directing their man-ufacturing toward EVs, some even pledging transitioning to 100% EV in the next few decades (Motawalli, 2021), there are still a number of concerns that need to be addressed before EV technology can truly go mainstream.

Mining of raw materials and minerals (e.g., lithium and cobalt) for batteries needs to be made more ethical and environmentally sustainable. With over half of the world's lithium resources found beneath salt flats in the Andean regions, local and indigenous communities have to compete for access to ground water (in an otherwise already dry region) with the larger mining corporations that require a large volume of ground water to extract lithium (*Nature* (Editorial), 2021; UNCTAD, 2020). Similarly, a vast amount of the world's cobalt reserves can be found in Central Africa, where the mining often involves young children working under very dangerous and unhealthy conditions (Searcey & Lipton, 2021; UNCTAD, 2020).

Challenges on the application side with EVs include; (i) the limited energy storage capacity of current battery technology; (ii) EV charging stations are still (predominantly) relying on power from national energy grids; (iii) infrastructure needs to be developed at the pace at which EV technology is advancing to allow for more charging stations with clean energy sources; and (iv) the technology is still far too expensive to be adapted by a larger audience (Stringer & Park, 2021).

The application of energy storage technology reaches far beyond the transportation sector, and is an integral part of a future zero carbon energy infrastructure where energy produced off-grid/offshore through green energy sources (wind, water, and solar) can readily be stored off-grid at high capacity, and transported with minimum energy loss. With the growing call for high-capacity batteries at larger volumes, extraction of the core minerals is being intensified by the day. While this very promising technology will play an important role in supporting the quest to phase out carbon, policies and regulations safeguarding human lives and the surrounding environment at extraction sites need to be in place. Beyond any doubt, this emphasizes the important interplay between science and policy to devise climate change mitigation and adaptation strategies that are sensitive to their wider impact and consequences on the environment, human health, peace and security, political stability, and local economies.

CONCLUDING REMARKS

Considering the continuous globalization of the world's economies, the growing cross-border inter-dependency between individuals and communities, and outsourcing of production of goods and services offshore, global warming and climate change have become more complex than ever before. It is thereby imperative that a solution to these challenges includes the representation of all economies, and socioeconomic stakeholders (in particular those most vulnerable), in order to deliver more comprehensive and relevant climate agreements and solutions.

As discussed, no single party or entity alone can be held accountable for global warming and climate change. While some parties may have a larger environmental footprint, and others have less, climate change impacts everyone irrespective of their own contribution.

Given the discrepancy in the economic and infrastructural background between the parties, and how each party is impacted by climate change, there is no universal solution to the challenge. Climate targets and goals need to be devised based on individual party's own capacity and socioeconomic infrastructure, with a focus on those parties with most limitations.

While policy may be the force behind driving societal change, policy alone will not resolve the current climate crisis. Solution architects, representing and carrying the voice of the scientific community, need to be part of the climate negotiations, to advise on the impact and consequences of climate strategies and targets, and, moreover, to advise on targets and goals tailored to the individual capacity of each party based on scientific merit. Such an approach would bring more stakeholders to a consensus, while incentivizing and accelerating both private and public sector investment.

Finally, one needs to be reminded that a multilateral approach often means finding the lowest common denominator that all parties can agree on as starting point; it may not be an ideal solution for the short-term, but it needs to be a solution that allows all stakeholders to work in concert and in the same direction (one step at a time), toward a common long-term goal.

REFERENCES

Afework, B., Campbell, A., Hanania, J., Sheardown, A., Stenhouse, K., & Donev, J. (2019, January 4). *Discovery of the greenhouse effect – Energy education*. Retrieved from https://energyeducation.ca/encyclopedia/Discovery_of_the_greenhouse_effect

Arrhenius, S. (1896). On the influence of carbonic acid in the air upon the temperature of the ground. *Philosophical Magazine and Journal of Science*, 237–276.

Ballinger, T. J.-B.-J. (2020). *NOAA Arctic Report Card 2020: Surface air temperature*. The National Oceanic and Atmospheric Administration. doi:10.25923/gcw8-2z06

Beer, E., Eisenman, I., & Wagner, T. (2020). Polar amplification due to enhanced heat flux across the halocline. *Geophysical Research Letters*, *47*(4), 1–10.

Climate Action Tracker. (2021, November 9). *Glasgow's 2030 credibility gap: Net zero's lip service to climate action | Climate Action Tracker*. Retrieved from Glasgow's 2030 credibility gap: net zero's lip service to climate action: https://climateactiontracker.org/publications/glasgows-2030-credibility-gap-net-zeros-lip-service-to-climate-action

de Coning, C., Krampe, F., & Grand, A. O. (2021, April 29). *The impact of climate change on Africa's peace and security – training for peace*. Retrieved from https://trainingforpeace.org/analysis/the-impact-of-climate-change-on-africas-peace-and-security/

European Environment Agency. (2018, August 30). *Climate change and water — Warmer oceans, flooding and droughts*. Retrieved from https://www.eea.europa.eu/signals/signals-2018-content-list/articles/climate-change-and-water-2014

Eurostat. (2021, November 25). *Shedding light on energy in the EU – A guided tour of energy statistics | 2021 edition*. Retrieved from https://ec.europa.eu/eurostat/cache/infographs/energy/bloc-2c.html#carouselControls?lang=en

Frank, C. (2014, August 12). *Pricing carbon: A carbon tax or cap-and-trade?* Retrieved from https://www.brookings.edu/blog/planetpolicy/2014/08/12/pricing-carbon-a-carbon-tax-or-cap-and-trade

Gray, A. (2018, May 4). *Ethiopia is Africa's fastest-growing economy | World Economic Forum*. Retrieved from https://www.weforum.org/agenda/2018/05/ethiopia-africa-fastest-growing-economy/

Hanania, J., & Donev, J. (2022, April 3). *Energy Education – Emission scenario*. Retrieved from https://energyeducation.ca/encyclopedia/Emission_scenario

IEA. (2019a). *Ethiopia – countries & regions – IEA*. Retrieved from Key Statistics: https://www.iea.org/countries/ethiopia

IEA. (2019b, November 8). *Ethiopia energy outlook, Analysis IEA*. Retrieved from Ethiopia Energy Outlook, Analysis from Africa Energy Outlook 2019: https://www.iea.org/articles/ethiopia-energy-outlook

Krampe, F. (2019, September 13). *Climate change, peacebuilding, and sustaining peace | IPI global observatory*. Retrieved from https://theglobalobservatory.org/2019/09/climate-change-peacebuilding-and-sustaining-peace/

Lindsey, R. (2021, October 7). *Climate change: Atmospheric carbon dioxide*. Retrieved from https://www.climate.gov/news-features/understanding-climate/climate-change-atmospheric-carbon-dioxide

Lindsey, R., & Dahlman, L. (2021, August 12). *Climate change: Global temperature*. Retrieved from https://www.climate.gov/news-features/understanding-climate/climate-change-global-temperature

Majra, J. P., & Gur, A. (2009). Climate change and health: Why should India be concerned? *Indian Journal of Occupational and Environmental Medicine*, 11–16.

Masson-Delmotte, V., Zhai, P., Pirani, A., Connors, S. L., Péan, C., Berger, S., Caud, N., Chen, Y., Goldfarb, L., Gomis, M. I., Huang, M., Leitzell, K., Lonnoy, E., Matthews, J. B. R., Maycock, T. K., Waterfield, T., Yelekçi, O., Yu, R., and Zhou, B. (Eds.). (2021). IPCC 2021: Summary for policymakers. In: *Climate change 2021: The physical science basis. Contribution of Working Group I to the Sixth Assessment Report of the Intergovernmental Panel on Climate Change*. Cambridge University Press.

Means, T. (2021, August 18). *Climate change and droughts: What's the connection? Yale Climate Connections*. Retrieved from https://yaleclimateconnections.org/2021/08/climate-change-and-droughts-whats-the-connection/

Morgan, A., Newman, P., Nash, E., Stranhan, S., Oman, L., & Hanson, H. (2015, June 4). *Hyperwall: The Antarctic ozone hole will recover*. Retrieved from https://svs.gsfc.nasa.gov/30602

Motawalli, J. (2021, October 4). *Every automaker's EV plans through 2035 and beyond - Forbes Wheels.* Retrieved from https://www.forbes.com/wheels/news/automaker-ev-plans/

Nakicenovic, N., Alcamo, J., Davis, G., de Vries, B., Fenhann, J., Gaffin, S., ... Dadi, Z. (2000). In *Special report on emissions scenarios: A special report of Working Group III of the Intergovernmental Panel on Climate Change* (p. 599). Cambridge, UK: Cambridge University Press. Retrieved from http://www.grida.no/climate/ipcc/emission/index.htm

NASA Earth Observatory. (2021, November 25). *Measuring Earth's albedo.* Retrieved from https://earthobservatory.nasa.gov/images/84499/measuring-earths-albedo

NASA Goddard Institute for Space Studies. (2021, November 18). *Global climate change, vital signs of the planet.* Retrieved from https://climate.nasa.gov/vital-signs/global-temperature/

NASA, Science Mission Directorate (2010). (2021, November 26). *The Earth's radiation budget | Science Mission Directorate.* Retrieved from https://science.nasa.gov/ems/13_radiationbudget

Nature (Editorial). (2021, June 29). *Lithium-ion batteries need to be greener and more ethical | Nature.* Retrieved from https://www.nature.com/articles/d41586-021-01735-z

Newell, M. (2019, March 21). *Top 5 fastest-growing economies in Africa | World Finance.* Retrieved from https://www.worldfinance.com/markets/top-5-fastest-growing-economies-in-africa

NOAA. (2021). *What is the polar vortex | NOAA.* Retrieved from https://scijinks.gov/polar-vortex/

NOAA National Centers for Environmental Information. (2021, November). *Global climate report – October 2021.* Retrieved from https://www.ncdc.noaa.gov/sotc/global/202110

Norwegian Ministry of Petroleum and Energy. (2016, November 5). *Renewable energy production in Norway – regjeringen.no.* Retrieved from https://www.regjeringen.no/en/topics/energy/renewable -energy/renewable-energy-production-in-norway/id2343462/

Norwegian Petroleum Directorate. (2021, March 24). *Exports of oil and gas – Norwegianpetroleum.no.* Retrieved from https://www.norskpetroleum.no/en/production-and-exports/exports-of-oil-and-gas/

NSIDC. (2020, April 3). *Thermodynamics: albedo | National Snow and Ice Data Center.* Retrieved from https://nsidc.org/cryosphere/seaice/processes/albedo.html

Pachauri, R. K., & Meyer, L. A. (2014). *IPCC, 2014: Climate change 2014: Synthesis Report. Contribution of Working Groups I, II and III to the Fifth Assessment Report of the Intergovernmental Panel on Climate Change.* Geneva: Intergovernmental Panel on Climate Change.

Riahi, K., van Vuuren, D. P., Kriegler, E., Edmonds, J., O'Neill, B. C., Fujimori, S., ... Tavoni, M. (2017). The Shared Socioeconomic Pathways and their energy, land use, and greenhouse gas emissions implications: An overview. *Global Environmental Change, 42,* 153–168.

Searcey, D., & Lipton, E. (2021, November 29). Hunt for the 'blood diamond of batteries' impedes green energy push. *The New York Times.* Retrieved from https://www.nytimes.com/2021/11/29/world/congo-cobalt-albert-yuma-mulimbi.html

Stringer, D., & Park, K. (2021, November 2). Why an electric car battery is so expensive, for now. *Bloomberg.* Retrieved from https://www.bloomberg.com/news/articles/2021-09-16/why-an-electric -car-battery-is-so-expensive-for-now-quicktake

Tezlaff, G. (1983). Albedo of the Sahara. In *Satellite measurements of radiation budget parameters* (pp. 60–63). Bonn.

The International Renewable Energy Agency, Abu Dhabi. (2021). *IRENA (2021), Renewable energy statistics 2021.* Retrieved from https://www.irena.org/solar

Turton, S. (2021, June 1). *Climate explained: Why is the Arctic warming faster than other parts of the world?* Retrieved from https://theconversation.com/climate-explained-why-is-the-arctic-warming -faster-than-other-parts-of-the-world-160614

UN Climate Change Conference (COP26). (2021, November 25). Retrieved from https://ukcop26.org

UNCTAD. (2020, July 22). *Developing countries pay environmental cost of electric car batteries | UNCTAD.* Retrieved from https://unctad.org/news/developing-countries-pay-environmental-cost -electric-car-batteries

UNEP. (2021a). Retrieved from https://www.unep.org/

UNEP. (2021b, November 25). *About Montreal Protocol.* Retrieved from https://www.unep.org/ozonaction/who-we-are/about-montreal-protocol

UNEP Ozone Secretariat. (2021, November 25). *Ozone and you | Ozone Secretariat.* Retrieved from https://ozone.unep.org/ozone-and-you

UNFCCC. (2021a, November 25). *What is the Kyoto Protocol? | UNFCCC*. Retrieved from https://unfccc.int/kyoto_protocol

UNFCCC. (2021b, November 25). *Emissions trading | UNFCCC*. Retrieved from https://unfccc.int/process/the-kyoto-protocol/mechanisms/emissions-trading

UNFCCC. (2021c). Retrieved from NDC Registry: https://www4.unfccc.int/sites/NDCStaging/Pages/Home.aspx

United Nations Conference on the Human Environment. (2021, November 25). Retrieved from United Nations Conference on the Human Environment, 5–16 June 1972, Stockholm: https://www.un.org/en/conferences/environment/stockholm1972

Wyrzykowski, R. (2020, November 16). *GSMA | Mobile connectivity in Sub-Saharan Africa: 4G and 3G connections overtake 2G for the first time*. Retrieved from https://www.gsma.com/mobilefordevelopment/blog/mobile-connectivity-in-sub-saharan-africa-4g-and-3g-connections-overtake-2g-for-the-first-time/

PART II

MULTI-LEVEL CLIMATE ACTION EDUCATION AND INFORMATION SYSTEMS

7. Multi-level carbon literacy in management education: an approach to address climate change in the classroom

Cathy A. Rusinko

INTRODUCTION

Research across disciplines strongly suggests the appropriateness of multi-level models for education in general, and for education for sustainability, in particular. According to You and Sharkey (2009), multi-level models facilitate student engagement. Starik and Kanashiro (2020) propose that multi-level approaches—in both management education and practice—can provide a more realistic and holistic approach to crises, such as climate change, that occur on multiple levels. They further propose that multi-level models can facilitate simultaneous learning at multiple levels, and can reinforce that individual well-being is connected to well-being at other levels. Likewise, they argue for a multi-level approach to sustainability solutions for policymakers, educators, researchers, and practitioners.

A multi-level approach to carbon literacy in the classroom can facilitate continuous commitment to sustainable practices beyond the classroom, especially if individual-level sustainable practices and impacts are used as a bridge to practices and impacts at other levels (e.g., organizational, societal). Correspondingly, multi-level approaches to carbon literacy can facilitate lifelong learning and practices to address climate change. One of the most crucial but challenging goals of education for sustainability is continuity of sustainable practices beyond the classroom and beyond university life (e.g., Rands, 2009). Recent work (e.g., Cordero et al., 2020; Molthan-Hill et al., 2019) suggests that higher education may play an important role in laying the groundwork for lifelong sustainable practices.

This chapter presents an explanatory multi-level approach, including an assignment and resources and tools to teach multi-level carbon literacy in management classes at the undergraduate and graduate levels. The chapter is useful and accessible to educators with varying levels of resources and opportunities for teaching carbon literacy in their classes, and is compatible with different delivery formats (e.g., on-ground, hybrid, virtual, online). Readers of this chapter will gain resource materials for integrating carbon literacy into their undergraduate and graduate classes, as well as ideas for developing new assignments or adapting existing assignments to address a multi-level approach to carbon literacy. This multi-level approach to carbon literacy can facilitate transfer of sustainable practices beyond the classroom and throughout work, life, and social systems.

In the literature that addresses climate change and the temperature of the Earth, various verbs are used, including *decrease* and similar verbs that indicate reversing the Earth's temperature, as well as *mitigate* and similar verbs that indicate stopping or slowing the increase of the Earth's temperature. Since the complex and scientific issues that underpin the options for impacting the Earth's temperature are beyond the scope of this chapter, the more neutral term of *address* will be used with respect to climate change, with the exception of citations from other sources.

The chapter begins with a brief justification and literature review, and then presents a generic multi-level approach (Figure 7.1) to illustrate a multi-level approach to carbon literacy and climate change. A sample assignment (Figure 7.2) is provided that applies Figure 7.1, and more specifically illustrates how to use a multi-level approach to carbon literacy as education for sustainability in the management classroom. Additional resources for teaching and learning carbon literacy are also provided (Box 7.1).

The purpose of this chapter is to provide one multi-level approach to teaching and learning carbon literacy, as one means to address climate change and sustainability in the classroom. A full-blown curriculum and assessment plan for teaching carbon literacy is beyond the scope of this chapter, but may be included in future and more expansive work.

JUSTIFICATION AND LITERATURE REVIEW

Carbon literacy can be defined as:

> An awareness of the carbon dioxide costs and impacts of everyday activities, and the ability and motivation to reduce the emissions, on an individual, community and organisational basis. Carbon literacy is a term used to describe an awareness of climate change, and the climate impacts of mankind's everyday actions. (Carbon Literacy Project)

Hence, carbon literacy is defined as a multi-level phenomenon, so it is appropriate to address it with a multi-level approach.

As researchers and non-researchers continue to observe, results of the ongoing increase in the Earth's temperature include rising sea levels and greater frequency of extreme weather, such as heat waves, droughts, and floods. These events will continue to affect local, national, and global economies, as well as human and environmental health, and national and global security (e.g., Fernando et al., 2012). Some researchers cite climate change as a contributing factor to the severity of the Covid-19 Pandemic and its effects on human and economic systems (e.g., Barouki et al., 2021). Therefore, it is crucial for all members of society to understand the relationship between carbon and climate change so that they can take multi-level actions to reduce carbon emissions and address climate change. This chapter represents one contribution, within the context of education for sustainability, to help undergraduate and graduate students to understand and address—at multiple levels—the crisis of carbon emission and climate change through an assignment on carbon literacy.

Sustainability has been defined in many different ways, and one of the oldest and most cited definitions can be paraphrased as satisfying current needs while still preserving resources to satisfy the needs of future generations (Brundtland, 1987). This generic definition can be applied to education for sustainability, and particularly with respect to carbon literacy, since future generations depend upon today's members of society to decrease carbon emissions in order to address climate change in the future. Mitigation of climate change is included in the United Nations Sustainable Development Goals (UN SDGs), as well as in the UN Principles for Responsible Management Education (PRME).

The importance of education for sustainability as a means to inform and empower today's students, so that they can preserve the planet for themselves and future generations, has been a prominent topic in management and business education, as reflected by several edited volumes (e.g., Arevalo and Mitchell, 2017; Starik and Kanashiro, 2021; Wankel and Stoner, 2009) and journal special issues (e.g., Areavalo et al., 2020; Rusinko and Sama, 2009; Starik et al., 2010), and scores of articles and chapters in volumes not specifically dedicated to education for sustainability.

This chapter presents a multi-level approach to carbon literacy as a way of educating for sustainability, so that management students can address climate change on individual, organizational, and societal levels.

AN APPROACH FOR ADDRESSING CARBON LITERACY AT MULTIPLE LEVELS

Figure 7.1 illustrates a multi-level approach to carbon literacy and climate change, including practices at three different levels: individual, organizational, and societal. As indicated by the arrows in Figure 7.1, practices at each of the three levels can facilitate and/or engender practices at each of the other two levels; this is explained further below.

Figure 7.1   *A multi-level approach to carbon literacy and climate change*

At the individual level, practices to address climate change by reducing carbon emissions can include a wide array of personal choices connected to resource usage, including cooking and eating (choose mostly foods that are local, in-season, and have a low carbon footprint; minimize food waste; compost); transportation (walk/bike/public transport); housing (efficiently sized space with access to public transportation; resource efficient heating, cooling, water heating, etc.); waste conservation and disposal (reduce/reuse/recycle), and all other aspects of personal life. See the Resources section (Box 7.1) at the end of this chapter for more information on individual practices to decrease carbon emissions and address climate change.

Since individuals are also members of organizations, they can transfer—and/or advocate to transfer—their individual practices, such as those listed above, to their organizations, as indicated by the arrows in Figure 7.1. Additionally, as more individuals participate in carbon saving practices, these practices will become more accepted by society overall, and hence, will facilitate societal practices, as also indicated by the arrows in Figure 7.1. Societal practices are discussed below.

At the organizational level, employees can advocate for practices at their workplaces to reduce carbon emissions and address climate change; this can also include advocating for their organizational unit or department to participate in practices that are already being undertaken in other organizational units within the organization, or in other organizations. Organizational practices to reduce carbon emissions can include a wide range of actions, such as choices about waste conservation and disposal (reduce/reuse/recycle); eliminating purchase of disposable water bottles in favor of a water dispenser to fill reusable water bottles; and using post-consumer office supplies. When it is within their span of control, employees and managers can expand the practices listed above to larger organizational segments or to the whole organization. Given a wide span of control, upper-level managers can adopt farther-reaching practices that focus on resource efficiency and reduction of carbon emissions across the organization, e.g., strategies for structures and employee work spaces, heating and cooling, computing, lighting, dining, product production/service delivery, etc. Organizations can also leverage work-from-home strategies as a means to conserve resources and decrease carbon emissions, especially since Covid-19 forced many organizations to learn how to operate efficiently with most or all employees working from home. See the Resources section at the end of this chapter (Box 7.1) for more information on organizational practices to decrease carbon emissions and address climate change.

Organizations can also request or require practices to reduce carbon emissions by suppliers, customers, and other stakeholders, which can help to further spread carbon-saving practices to other individuals, organizations, and society, as indicated by the arrows in Figure 7.1. For example, some organizations require that suppliers meet specific resource and carbon savings practices, which causes those supplier organizations to embrace these practices. Some manufacturers provide low carbon refills for detergents and other household products, while other manufacturers of food and cosmetics use re-fillable containers; these organization-level practices also engage individual users in practices to reduce carbon emissions, as indicated by the arrows in Figure 7.1. As more and more individuals and organizations participate in low carbon practices, these practices become more established and accepted as societal practices or norms, as also indicated by the arrows in Figure 7.1.

At the societal level, groups of citizens can lobby for low carbon emissions practices to replace high carbon emissions practices. For example, in some communities, citizens have successfully lobbied to ban the use of plastic bags in retail stores. Citizens' groups have also lobbied for purchase of alternative energy by their governments, as well as for other government purchasing policies and practices that reduce carbon emissions. As more societal practices to reduce carbon emissions are adopted, the concept of reducing carbon emissions can become more institutionalized, and hence more accepted by organizations and individuals who will further embrace practices to reduce carbon emissions at their levels, as indicated by the arrows in Figure 7.1. See the Resources section (Box 7.1) at the end of this chapter for more information on societal practices to decrease carbon emissions and address climate change.

The next section presents an assignment, based on Figure 7.1, and designed to address climate change by teaching carbon literacy at multiple levels.

A MULTI-LEVEL ASSIGNMENT TO ADDRESS CLIMATE CHANGE BY TEACHING CLIMATE LITERACY IN THE MANAGEMENT CLASSROOM

Today's students are the future members, decision-makers, and managers in organizations, and future policymakers and leaders of society. A multi-level approach to carbon literacy in management education—starting with individual practices, but including organizational and societal practices—will increase the probability that students embrace sustainability as a lifelong practice by transferring these practices to their organizational lives, and helping to establish them as societal practices. Correspondingly, a multi-level approach can increase the probability that students will continue to practice and advocate for pro-climate actions long after they have graduated from their management and business programs. Such continuity is encouraged as a major goal of education for sustainability (e.g., Cordero et al., 2020; Molthan-Hill et al., 2019; Rands, 2009) and is crucial in order to address climate change for current and future generations (Starik and Kanashiro, 2020).

Students work on the assignment in two stages, as illustrated in Figure 7.2. To successfully complete the assignment and address climate change, students are required to use materials provided by the Carbon Literacy Project and other sources; sample materials are listed in the Resources section of this chapter (Box 7.1). Some of these materials help students to assess their carbon footprint, and learn how to reduce it in order to engage in individual practices to decrease carbon emissions and address climate change. Other materials help students to translate their individual practices into organization and societal practices. Some materials provide background information on carbon literacy, carbon emissions, and climate change. Additionally, the Carbon Literacy Project provides training and certification in carbon literacy to instructors and other interested professionals for a very nominal fee.

Figure 7.2 summarizes the assignment, and provides a few sample outcomes and additional instructors' comments about the assignment. The sample outcomes represent some of the students' ideas for reducing carbon emissions and addressing climate change with respect to individual and organizational practices in Stages I and II. These ideas illustrate how students were able to transfer and adapt individual practices in Stage I of the assignment to organizational practices in Stage II of the assignment, as indicated by the framework in Figure 7.1. The student outcomes also reinforce perspectives by earlier researchers who propose that multi-level models can facilitate simultaneous learning at multiple levels in management education (e.g., Starik and Kanashiro, 2020).

In Spring 2021, the assignment was launched in an undergraduate management elective on current management topics. However, the assignment could be integrated into a wide variety of management courses, including core courses such as management principles and capstone. The assignment can be adapted for diverse teaching formats, levels, and class sizes. It would work equally well in on-ground, hybrid, or virtual class environments, although different accommodations would be needed for different formats. Likewise, higher expectations would be set at the graduate level, relative to the undergraduate level.

	Instructions	Sample Outcomes	Comments
Stage I: Individual-Level Plan	Students create an individual lifestyle plan to address climate change in their own lives. 1. Answer: What can I do in my own life to address climate change? 2. Do research to inform and justify your plan. 3. Present your plan as a PowerPoint presentation.	Install timers on home/apartment thermostats to conserve energy. Create weekly shopping and menu plans to reduce food waste in home/apartment. Take shorter showers to save water in home/apartment.	Use materials in Resources section to teach/learn about carbon literacy & climate change.
Stage II: Organization-Level Plan	Student teams create an organization-level plan to address climate change. 1. Teams choose an organization/part of an organization as a consulting site. 2. Teams use and extend Stage I individual-level plans to craft and present (as a PowerPoint presentation) a plan to address climate change for the site. Additional site/industry-specific research is required. 3. Can/how can your plans in Stages I & II impact society?	Increase temperature for AC & decrease temperature for heat in public areas and offices to conserve energy. Eliminate trays in dormitory dining halls to reduce food waste. Install low-flow shower heads and water-conserving washing machines on campus.	Use materials in Resources section to teach/learn about carbon literacy & climate change. Can be assigned to individuals. Can use library research on existing organizations if real-world sites are not available. See text for responses/outcomes to question #3.

Figure 7.2   Multi-level assignment: carbon literacy and climate change

If teams are not practical, both Stages I and II could be assigned to individuals. In working through Stages I and II, an inverted classroom pedagogy—in which students or student teams read materials and use tools such as the carbon footprint calculators independently and before class, and class time is used for discussions, applications, extensions, and questions—works effectively. However, the assignment can be adapted for diverse pedagogies.

Since many researchers have argued that sustainability is a "wicked" topic which is multi-disciplinary by nature (e.g., Rusinko, 2010; Waddock, 2013), this assignment would be even more impactful if undertaken by a multi-disciplinary team of students, including management students and students from other disciplines within and/or outside of business. However, this type of approach would require a special topics course, short course, or alternative structure.

Figure 7.2 does not include student responses to question 3 in Stage II, "Can/how can your plans in Stages I and II impact society?" Since obtaining sites for societal-level projects is more challenging than obtaining sites for organization-level projects for a variety of reasons, students were instructed to hypothesize with respect to societal practices that could follow from their individual and organizational practices in Stages I and II. When hypothesizing about how their individual practices to reduce carbon emissions could facilitate societal practices to do the same, students offered that practices to reduce carbon emissions by a growing number of individuals—such as installing timers on home thermostats—could result in these practices being accepted as the norm by a significant portion of society at large; after all, society is a collection of individuals. When hypothesizing about how their recommended organizational practices to reduce carbon emissions could facilitate societal practices to do the same, student teams pointed-out that organizational practices—and especially those that impacted consumers and other stakeholders along the value chain—would simultaneously be impacting carbon reduction practices of society at large, since society is also a collection of organizations. Correspondingly, when hypothesizing about how societal practices to reduce carbon emissions could facilitate individual and organizational practices to do the same, students responded that society represented the sum of individuals and organizations. In addition, societal practices can become more widespread norms, which are then more readily accepted by increasing numbers of organizations. All of these student responses reinforce past research which posits that multi-level models can illustrate how individual well-being is connected to well-being at other levels and vice versa (e.g., Starik and Kanashiro, 2020).

The next section provides some resources for teaching and learning carbon literacy.

RESOURCES

Box 7.1 lists some resources that are helpful for teaching and learning about carbon literacy. Resources are listed according to the level (individual, organizational, societal) to which they are most directly related. However, the carbon footprint calculators can be useful at all levels. Instructors and interested others are encouraged to explore these resources and choose those that best meet their needs. Box 7.1 also provides some background resources and more general reading (articles and chapters) on education for sustainability, climate change, climate literacy and related topics; the references in these readings can be leveraged to expand and build a library and resources for teaching and learning about carbon literacy, climate change, and related topics.

CONCLUDING COMMENTS AND LIMITATIONS

This assignment, which is informed by the framework in Figure 7.1, allows students to gain an understanding—at multiple levels—of climate literacy and the relationship between carbon emissions and climate change. The multi-level approach allows a more holistic and realistic approach to climate change, which occurs on multiple levels. The assignment can facilitate simultaneous learning at multiple levels, and can reinforce that individual well-being is connected to well-being at other levels and vice versa (e.g., Starik and Kanashiro, 2020).

This chapter and assignment can be helpful to college-level educators and undergraduate and graduate students; the former are training the future decision makers and leaders, and the latter will be the future decision makers and leaders. In teaching about addressing climate change, it is crucial to help students to carry out and apply lessons learned far beyond the classroom and long after graduation (e.g., Rands, 2009). This assignment can facilitate this end by engaging students to think beyond their current practices to organizational and societal practices, and by helping students to understand the relationships and interdependence between and among individuals, organizations, and society. In addition, this chapter and assignment may also provide a framework and exercise for current organizational decision makers and policymakers who are seeking a starting place for addressing carbon emissions and climate change in their department or organization.

A possible limitation to the assignment is the time required for the multi-stage process which, as specified in Figure 7.2, is designed to yield one individual assignment and one team assignment, with time for reflection between the two assignments. A quicker, alternative approach when time is constrained could present the assignment as a sprint or brainstorming exercise in one or two classes, depending upon length of the class. In addition, the assignment is most engaging when students have access to real-world sites and organization members for Stage II. Since this type of access is not always available, students can do library research to fulfill the requirements for Stage II. Of course, this chapter and assignment can also be used to inform and adapt existing class discussions and assignments on climate literacy and climate change.

Additionally, it is important to acknowledge that this assignment, as developed for a management class in a business school, is oriented toward individuals and organizations in more industrially developed environments. It is equally important to acknowledge other types of environments in other parts of any given country and in other parts of the world. While adaptation of this assignment to these other environments is beyond the scope of this chapter, future work should focus here.

BOX 7.1   SOME RESOURCES FOR TEACHING & LEARNING CARBON LITERACY

For Multi-level Practice

Climate   Generation,   https://www.climategen.org/take-action/act-climate-change/take-action/

For Individual Practices

WWF Carbon Footprint Calculator (Individual: UK and select countries), https://footprint.wwf.org.uk/#/

Carbon Footprint Calculator (US zip code: Individual, Household, Event, Trip), https://www.conservation.org/carbon-footprint-calculator#/

For Organizational Practices

What Offices Can Do to Address Climate Change (US EPA), https://19january2017snapshot.epa.gov/climatechange/what-you-can-do-office_.html

What Organizations Can Do to Address Climate Change (Center for Climate & Energy Solutions), https://www.c2es.org/content/business-strategies-to-address-climate-change/

For Societal Practices

One Way to Reduce Community-Level Carbon Footprint, https://pcc.uw.edu/blog/2020/05/05/how-can-communities-reduce-their-carbon-footprint-an-introduction-to-community-choice-aggregation-and-community-science/

For Resources from the Carbon Literacy Project

https://carbonliteracy.com/trainer-consultant/the-carbon-literacy-resources-library/

For Certification in Carbon Literacy by The Carbon Literacy Project

https://carbonliteracy.com/individual/

(Box 7.1 continued)

For General/Background Reading—Education for Sustainability and Climate Change

Journal Special Issues

Rusinko, C.A. and Sama, L.M. (2009) 'Greening and sustainability across the management curriculum', *Journal of Management Education*, 33(3).

Starik, M., Rands, G., Marcus, A.A., Clark, T.S. (2010) 'Sustainability in management education', *Academy of Management, Learning & Education*, 9(3).

Arevalo, J.A., Mitchell, S.F., Rands, G., Starik, M. (2020) 'Sustainability in management education', *Journal of Management Education*, 44(6).

Edited Volumes

Arevalo, J.A. and Mitchell, S.F. (eds) (2017). *Handbook of Sustainability in Management Education*. Edward Elgar Publishing.

Wasieleski, D.M. and Weber, J. (eds) (2020). *Sustainability (Business and Society 360, Vol. 4)*. Emerald Publishing Limited.

REFERENCES

Arevalo, J.A. & Mitchell, S.F. (eds) (2017). *Handbook of Sustainability in Management Education*. Edward Elgar Publishing.

Arevalo, J.A., Mitchell, S.F., Rands, G. & Starik, M. (eds) (2020). Special issue: Sustainability in management education. *Journal of Management Education*, 44(6).

Barouki, R., Kogevinas, M., Audouze, K. et al. (2021). The COVID-19 pandemic and global environmental change: Emerging research needs. *Environment International*, 146, 106272, ISSN 0160-4120, https://doi.org/10.1016/j.envint.2020.106272.

Brundtland, G.H. (1987). What is sustainable development? *Our Common Future*, 8(9). World Commission on Environment and Development.

Carbon Literacy Project. https://carbonliteracy.com/what-on-earth-is-carbon-literacy/.

Cordero, E.C., Centeno, D. & Todd, A.M. (2020). The role of climate change education on individual lifetime carbon emissions. *Plos One*, 15(2), e0206266. https://doi.org/10.1371/journal.pone.0206266.

Fernando, H.J., Klaic, Z.B. & McCulley, J.L. (2012). National security and human health implications of climate change. *Proceedings of the NATO Advanced Research Workshop on Climate Change, Human Health and National Security*. Dubrovnic, Croatia, April 2011.

Molthan-Hill, P., Worsfold, N., Nagy, G.J., Leal Filho, W. & Mifsud, M. (2019). Climate change education for universities: A conceptual framework from an international study. *Journal of Cleaner Production*, 226, 1092–1101, https://doi.org/10.1016/j.jclepro.2019.04.053.

Rands, G.P. (2009). A principle-attribute matrix for environmentally sustainable management education and its application: The case for change-oriented service-learning projects. *Journal of Management Education*, 33(3), 296–322.

Rusinko, C.A. (2010). Integrating sustainability in management and business education: A matrix approach. *Academy of Management Learning & Education*, 9(3), 507–519.

Rusinko, C.A. & Sama, L.M. (eds) (2009). Special issue: Greening and sustainability across the management curriculum. *Journal of Management Education*, 33(3).

Starik, M. & Kanashiro, P. (2021). Introduction to personal sustainability practices. In *Personal Sustainability Practices*. Edward Elgar Publishing.

Starik, M. & Kanashiro, P. (2020). Advancing a multi-level sustainability management theory. In D.M. Wasieleski & J. Weber (eds), *Sustainability (Business and Society 360, Volume 4)* pp. 17–42. Emerald Publishing Ltd., https://doi.org/10.108/bas.

Starik, M., Rands, G., Marcus, A.A., Clark, T.S. (eds) (2010). Special issue: Sustainability in management education. *Academy of Management Learning & Education*, 9(3).

Waddock, S. (2013). The wicked problems of global sustainability need wicked (good) leaders and wicked (good) collaborative solutions. *Journal of Management for Global Sustainability*, 1(1), 91–111.

Wankel, C. & Stoner, J. A. (eds). (2009). *Management Education for Global Sustainability*. IAP.

You, S. & Sharkey, J. (2009). Testing a developmental–ecological model of student engagement: A multilevel latent growth curve analysis. *Educational Psychology*, 29(6), 659–684. https://doi.org/10.1080/01443410903206815

8. Non-formal sustainability, resilience, and climate-change education for professionals and life-long learners

Gerard Voos, L. Stagg Newman, and James Fox

INTRODUCTION

A movement is happening. It is one without placards and smart sayings. Rather, it is a campaign that expands non-formal learning opportunities across the country. Pulitzer Prize winning journalist, Farah Stockman (2021), expects that in our fast-changing technical world employees will constantly have to learn new skills to remain competitive in their workplaces and that those proficiencies will be acquired more from short technical certification classes than from formal college degrees. In other words, the future workforce—and communities in general—will need continuous educational opportunities and will look for more affordable and schedule-friendly alternatives to traditional college to obtain them. Our emphasis here is on a subset of these alternatives—the expansion of educational endeavors focused on sustainability, resilience, and climate change (SRC) issues in communities throughout the United States.

As a nation, we cannot come to a consensus on SRC solutions without mutual recognition of our environmental challenges. Where can individuals and groups go to receive the instruction and mentorship to help them reach that understanding? The answer to that provides the basis for this chapter.

The goal of any SRC education program should be to increase positive SRC actions. Developing an erosion control plan, designing an electrified mass-transit system in a densely populated urban zone, or publishing a municipal climate change adaptation and resilience plan qualify as positive SRC actions. These have long-term constructive outcomes for current and future generations of humans, and—just as importantly—other species and their habitats. We recognize that the capacity to dwell on SRC issues and enroll in courses about them is a privilege. It is a privilege of wealth, a privilege of time, and a privilege of culture.

We present these programs as in-person proceedings, as a profusion of online SRC educational opportunities is available, at low to no cost, to prospective students around the world. These online offerings are not included here but are described by Voos et al. (2021). That account—the premise upon which this chapter originated—was a business plan developed for specific types of businesses in a distinct geographic and demographic setting. Here we include similar participant groups, but expand that inclusion across the United States.

What is Non-formal Education?

Non-formal learning is an educational experience that occurs outside mainstream academic settings. Falk and Dierking (2010) estimate that the average American spends less than five percent of their lifetime in a classroom environment. This leaves the majority of people's lives devoid of formal learning experiences. That does not mean they stop learning. While formal academic training (from kindergarten through graduate school) and degrees are important and convey to society meaningful accomplishment, they do not represent how most middle-age and older adults learn. Where then, should people turn who don't need a degree, but do need information to advance in their workplace, acclimate to new geographic settings (e.g., immigrants), make a positive difference in their communities, or simply wish to continue learning about their world? Non-formal education can fill that void. Definitions for different types of education can be vague and nuanced, so we use those put forward by the Organisation for Economic Co-operation and Development (OECD):

- Formal learning is always organized and structured, and has learning objectives. From the learner's standpoint, it is always intentional: i.e., the learner's explicit objective is to gain knowledge, skills and/or competences.
- Informal learning is never organized, has no set objective in terms of learning outcomes and is never intentional from the learner's standpoint. Often it is referred to as learning by experience or just as experience.
- Mid-way between the first two, non-formal learning... is rather organized and can have learning objectives. The advantage of the intermediate concept lies in the fact that such learning may occur at the initiative of the individual but also happens as a by-product of more organized activities (OECD, 2021).

The International Commission on Education for the Twenty-first Century (1996) developed a set of ideas put forth to address what the Commission determined was the discounting of lifelong educational opportunities for young people and those generations yet born. They wrote that education was,

> ... at the heart of both personal and community development; its mission ... to enable each of us, without exception, to develop all our talents to the full and to realize our creative potential, including responsibility for our own lives and achievement of our personal aims. (p. 17)

The principles embodied by the Commission very much reflect the values and goals of the SRC non-formal education program we describe here; by which learning must be prepared for, never ceases, and is often more effective when done communally.

Why SRC Education Instead of Simply Climate Change Education?

Americans must grasp and appreciate the limits of our planet—for taking resources from, and disposing wastes to—and how to live with the consequences. To date, we have been the world's "bad actors." We created a lifestyle (e.g., our food, transportation, housing, clothing) more comfortable and convenient than any other, and have not paid the true cost for it. We shifted environmental and financial damages to the far reaches of the globe, meanwhile enjoying our largesse and repeating the mantra "out of sight, out of mind." Today, that unpaid bill is coming due, sooner than we had hoped, and with a ferocity that we didn't know enough to fear. Its name is climate change.

The Doughnut graphic (see Figure 8.1) depicts major parts of the biosphere's highly complex system—a visual summation that leads us to infer that "economies, societies, and the rest of the living world, are complex, interdependent systems that are best understood through the lens of systems thinking" (Doughnut Economics Action Lab, 2020). It is through that systems' lens that we must view and understand climate change. It cannot be singled out as a standalone problem; it is an aggregation of actions, reactions, and impacts from decades of human activity. Any SRC educational effort must cover those topics that help explain the current condition of the biosphere—where we are and how we got to this point—so we don't repeat our mistakes, and also where, and with what velocity, we are going—i.e., how do we fix this and how long do we have to do that?

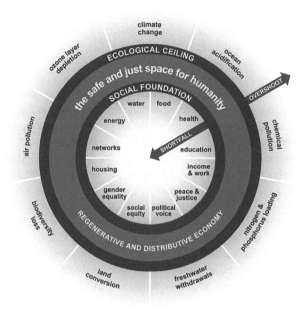

Source: Doughnut Economics Action Lab, 2020.

Figure 8.1   *The doughnut*

We cannot successfully address climate change without addressing the long-term sustainability of any proposed solution. Since 1987, sustainability—in its most simplistic terms—has been defined by the United Nations as "meeting the needs of the present without compromising the ability of future generations to meet their own needs" (United Nations, 2021). During the ensuing 34 years, the term has been used to describe the supply of resources used by man, including land, food, water and air, as well as the built environment, and those resources used (and created) by organisms other than man.

Related to sustainability, resilience is the ability of a system to withstand and adapt to short-term and long-term disruptions while still maintaining that system's uniqueness (Post Carbon Institute, 2018). Resilience thinking, meanwhile, takes the topic of resilience to a more complex level. It reflects the ability of humans to "adapt or even transform" their behavior during incremental and/or abrupt changes in their daily environment (Folke, 2016).

Who Benefits from Non-formal SRC Education?

Learning about SRC issues can lead to innovative behavior and a higher level of environmental consciousness and action. This requires education at all ages and stages of life. Our aim, then, is to educate a broad swath of the adult populace on SRC topics and involve for-profit businesses, non-profit organizations, and community groups in the process.

Almost anyone with a thirst for learning can benefit from a non-formal SRC education program. These programs will require a broad expertise to develop and deliver, based on regional variation of natural resources, population distribution, and impacts from climate change. There are significant differences across the country in adaptation and transformation needs, and as Moss et al. (2019), conclude, one size does not fit all.

For our purposes we have narrowed the number of categories of target student populations to five, but that could easily be parsed into many more separate groups should one choose. Our emphasis in the ensuing sections is on adult learners in the following categories: life-long learners; tourists; business, industry, and their employees; members of professional societies; and community leaders, decision makers, and local governments.

We assume that members of each of these groups are self-motivated to learn about SRC issues and solutions. This may be a result of personal interest, a need for additional knowledge to advance professionally, and/or a requirement for continued employment. In most cases, the participating individuals and organizations will provide payment for these educational programs. At times, grants and donations may be secured to fund a program (for an individual or group), but most likely that will be the exception rather than the rule.

In addition to how non-formal SRC education should be delivered to these groups, we'll discuss two subgroups that can be included within each: train-the-trainer and trusted sources. Trainers, teachers, trusted sources and practitioners all require education regarding their local and regional assets, threats to those assets, and potential solutions. The trainer is a professional educator with expertise not only in various fields, but in how to deliver the right amount of material at the appropriate level of depth. As we will see, the five groups of learners require vastly different levels of SRC information delivered in an assortment of ways.

Creating trusted sources of accurate SRC information may be the most difficult task of a non-formal SRC education program, because many people today depend on personal feelings rather than scientific evidence and objective facts when reviewing a situation and making decisions (Cormick, 2020). A recent Pew Research Center study (2019) found that Americans trust those individuals and organizations who display competence, honesty, and benevolence. The researchers found Americans also value empathy, openness, integrity, and accountability in those from whom they seek guidance. Public school principals, police officers, military leaders, and religious leaders topped their list of people who care about others. Developing an ever-growing pool of these information providers would benefit public policy on SRC issues in every geographic area of the country. Trusted sources of information on SRC issues will vary per individual, and by family, region of the country, and religious (or non-) affiliation.

A glance at Figure 8.1 shows how many disciplines and subdisciplines are involved. Cultivating and identifying talented teachers who already know—or are willing to learn—SRC issues will take a conscious effort by organizers. Educators must be familiar with the SRC topic and the group they are teaching. Topics will range from a general understanding of SRC issues and the impacts society faces (for life-long learners and tourists) to specific issues that will impact a particular industry or professional group. In the middle are community leaders, decision makers, and activists from across the country—each with local and/or regional needs and abilities to respond.

SRC education can change the way people see the world and how they fit into it—as a system. As Donella Meadows (1999, p. 13) points out, "delivering information to a place where it wasn't going before and therefore causing people to behave differently," is a very strong leverage point. You can't ask people to support new policies, pay new or greater taxes, or change their lifestyles if they don't understand why they are being asked to do so.

What Skills Should be Taught?

The concepts and skills that educators can teach through a non-formal SRC education program are many. They include the obvious: sustainability, resilience, and climate change. We would also include subsets and nuanced aspects of those subjects: adaptability, transformability, and dealing with uncertainty. Kwauk and Casey (2021) listed skills they believe will be needed to participate and succeed in a world of fluctuating climate and ecological shifts. In Table 8.1, we included their suggestions and added several of our own.

Why is a Multi-level Response to SRC Challenges Important?

Climate change did not arrive—as we now recognize it—on the world's doorstep one dark stormy morning. It began as a series of solutions; a solution to growing crops faster and more reliably; a solution to moving people and products faster across land, sea, and sky; a solution to making our buildings more comfortable and to lighting them without open flames; and so on. Those "solutions" have now turned into problems vastly more complex than anything mankind has experienced.

As it arrived at multiple times and on multiple scales, so must we address it. As Starik and Kanashiro (2020) note, no one person, one government, or one organization can solve such a multifaceted, byzantine problem. Creative solutions will be developed and acted upon by a panoply of individuals, organizations, and government groups during the next century.

That variety begins with this chapter's authors. We include a theoretical mathematician, an energy geologist, and an environmental soil scientist. Our interdisciplinarity represents the connection between disciplinary silos that will be required to solve current and future SRC issues.

Table 8.1   Skills and concepts that can be addressed in a non-formal SRC education program (modified from Kwauk and Casey, 2021)

	Environmental & ecosystem management
SRC skills that will be helpful for green jobs	Environmental knowledge & awareness
	Science skills
	Adaptability
	Collaborative thinking
	Communication
	Coping with uncertainty
SRC and green life skills	Critical thinking & reasoning
	Decision-making
	Effective stewardship (meaningful vs feel good)

	Problem solving
	Resilience
	Strategic thinking
	Disruptive vs normative thinking
	Effective philanthropy
	Environmental stewardship
	Future and anticipatory thinking
Knowledge skills helpful for a green transformation	Integrative thinking
	Inter- & multi-disciplinary thinking
	Respecting diverse viewpoints
	System thinking
	Valuing traditional & indigenous knowledge
	Working within complexity

Our goal here is to outline SRC education programs that will inform multiple adult student populations, create overlap in those groups, and to ensure that the SRC message is not only getting to, but absorbed by, as many people and organizations as possible.

NON-FORMAL SRC EDUCATION PROGRAMS

Below, we describe five non-formal education programs aimed at different target audiences. We begin with life-long learners, a group that may be the most zealous students. We then move on to tourists who can partake of SRC information through *edutainment* programs. In these programs, educators use the entertainment value of a setting (e.g., a beautiful vista, a working farm, a turbulent river) as a draw for visitors, then deliver educational information as the participants interact with their surroundings. Following that, we address the growing demand for in-depth information on SRC issues by delving into programs for specific commercial and government services groups. Participants of these programs will be motivated to learn, either from personal interest or as a requirement set by their employer for continued employment.

The primary assumptions we make are that non-formal instruction is mainly performed in-person, the students are accompanied by people they know, and the class is supported by online resources.[1] Because the SRC field has become very deep and broad, a student who begins the process as self-motivated and self-taught may find that a non-formal educator is required to provide structure and focus to the learning experience.

The non-formal educator must translate standard content into a format and vocabulary students will relate to. The American Society of Adaptation Professionals published its *Living Guide* in 2021. They recommend educators use language and concepts that are familiar to the intended audience. In particular, they suggest considering the cultural and political implications of using the phrase *climate change*. For this reason, a growing base of literature is calling these educators *science translators*, people who can take the complexity of a scientific topic and relate it to groups of learners. As they teach cohorts of learners, these science translators must be transparent and iterative, and all facts they present should be clearly cited so participants can later access the information. From an implementation reality then, there might be two areas of non-formal education specialty—one group that creates robust content, and another group that delivers that content to the learners.

To be successful, SRC education programs must work for the participants, work for the environment, and work financially.

Working for participants entails providing the knowledge students want and require. A talented educator who becomes a trusted source can fill that role and help students develop critical thinking skills, which will provide benefits far beyond the classroom.

Working for the environment is what SRC education is all about, bringing the principles of the Doughnut (see Figure 8.1) to as many people as possible. Whenever feasible, educators should develop course topics that use local and regional examples of SRC issues. This has the dual effect of providing the students with easily referenceable subjects (e.g., solid waste disposal, storm water runoff, erosion control) that are part of their daily lives, and offers them opportunities to participate in problem resolution activities. These programs should also incorporate storytelling whenever possible. Stories use the intuition one has gained in life to understand complex topics. Moreover, stories enable students to take the messages to others.

Storytelling consists of written and verbal accounts of lives and cultures past, and legends of civilizations—some real, some fictional—long gone. It can also include fictional narratives of future societies and the challenges they face. This is especially true of science fiction. Kim Stanley Robinson, in a recent article in *Bloomberg Green Daily* (2021, p. 4), discussed the basic premise of science fiction and its ability to bring the future to the present:

> Imagine that you're in the future. You look around at a changed world. Very interesting. Then you look back at your own time, seeing it as if it were already history. *Those people, back in 2021—what were they thinking?! How did they do what they did, and why?* You begin to judge those people of the past, a judgment we are always too quick to make. *Oh, they were so ignorant and stupid! Why didn't they see the danger? Why didn't they act? How could they have been so foolish, so selfish*—But wait. That's actually us! This is science fiction's great temporal reorientation.

We should not underestimate the value of a story to deliver a serious and vital message.

Finally, non-formal SRC education programs must be financially viable, either through tuition, donations, and/or grants. Voos et al. (2021) provide a detailed financial analysis of similar programs. They analyzed start-up costs, revenue generating opportunities, operating expenses, and offer multiple financing scenarios for each target sector.

Life-long Learners

Life-long learning is a broad term that encompasses both goal-oriented learning experiences (i.e., employment optimization, certification, permitting, etc.) and learning for personal fulfillment. Those seeking personal fulfillment may be motived by the sheer joy of discovering new topics. As they learn about SRC issues and solutions, this group addresses both intellectual and emotional needs.

Life-long learners may also be trying to *do the right thing*; that is living their personal life to help, albeit in a small way, in the quest to solve our shared SRC challenges. Jared Diamond in his book *Collapse* (2011, pp. 579–584) spoke to specific actions that individuals can take in their day-to-day life to make a difference in their communities and become trusted sources of SRC information to friends and relatives. Among the actions he suggested, the first and most important was educate yourself.

Life-long learners also include people who are finding a new focus in life, what David Brooks calls the "second mountain" (Brooks, 2020). These students include retirees and empty nesters—those who have recently found time along with the energy to pursue new causes to give added meaning to their lives. They have the time and life experience to understand the safe space as depicted in the Doughnut (see Figure 8.1), and what they need to do to live within that place and mitigate environmental risks.

Non-formal education is well suited to meet the needs of life-long learners, who, in general, will not partake of formal academic programs to satisfy their educational objectives. As we discussed above, these programs range widely in structure, fulfilling the desires of a broad spectrum of the population. Non-formal education programs are also extremely flexible, and can quickly install almost any subject into their SRC curriculum. One item to note is that most programs offered to a set audience will saturate the market (i.e., demand will project upwards at first, then decline to a lower level over time). Program administrators can interchange topics, introduce new subjects, and continuously stay current with cultural, political, and economic viewpoints and scientific improvements to avoid or delay such a decrease (Voos et al., 2021).

Tourists and Edutainment

This target sector has the greatest financial and creative potential of all the programs we describe. It is limited only by the geographic and cultural allure of the host region—those intangible assets that draw tourists in the first place. Tourism serves as the backbone of many local economies and can provide a constant supply of potential participants during portions of the year or in some locales, year-round. There is a wide variety of programming that could be offered including environmentally-themed meals, day-long seminars and short courses, and multi-day interactive events led by local experts (Voos et al., 2021).

Tourists are a specific subset of learners and many seek educational programs to enhance their traveling experience. SRC edutainment programs are designed to entertain, educate, and motivate. Most include a resident expert; one who knows the local geography, history, and demographics, and can extend that knowledge to incorporate regional SRC issues.

Tourists in search of an edutainment program typically have both the time and financial resources to embrace these experiences. They also have an expectation for high quality. Thus, for an SRC education program to succeed, it must provide an appropriate level of food, lodging, transport and other amenities. Typically, participants in such programs are not likely to be price sensitive and are willing to support productions that spark their curiosity and stimulate their intellects. This affords project administrators the opportunity to build into the overall fee structure support for additional organizational activities or provide financial assistance in the form of scholarships.

Business, Industry and their Employees

The goal for this audience is to develop and deliver courses that focus on a specific business or industry, and to provide their employees what they need to know about SRC topics and issues. This is an important distinction compared with the community groups discussed later, where we want learners to move beyond knowing to doing (i.e., moving from non-formal education to training).

This group is interested in acquiring knowledge to support their businesses as they adapt to a changing climate and move toward more sustainable and resilient practices. These learners will pursue courses in clusters and build their knowledge from a shared understanding of issues and resources. For some, SRC will become part of their job, and they will need to rapidly increase their skill sets, and promptly apply their new knowledge to work-related applications.

A course under this heading would be populated by a specific company, a group of similar companies, or very closely related groups (which becomes an industry). Depending upon the size of the company, it is possible that the business will hire a consultant to create tailored content to focus on larger SRC issues that address key pain points. For instance, an individual business or company has its own issues of location, supply chains, etc. A group of companies might share some general issues (e.g., supply chains), but with varied locations it would be harder to describe particular hazards and impacts.

This relationship between content creators and educators quickly becomes complex and multi-level. Content creation and teaching require different skill sets—people who know the topic deeply and people who know how to teach. They are not mutually exclusive, but having one skill does not automatically beget the other. To implement effective programs, it may be that we need to *train the trainer*. In other words, a content creator, knowledgeable of SRC topics, would work with professionals who are familiar with the business or industry sector (e.g., energy) in question. The content creator would provide SRC-related content to educators who would tailor that curriculum to specific businesses and deliver the instruction.

Some trade associations, such as those that represent automobile manufacturing, might hire consultants to create content applicable to the entire industry and then provide that content to individual companies with their own educators. This bundling of services could create some efficiencies in non-formal programs as they scale up to meet the demands of society.

Members of Professional Societies

This scenario is like the previous one, except that the educational product is provided to members of professional societies. A professional society exists to develop or further the work in a particular profession. Its members are both individuals and organizations who are interested in setting standards for their professional work, networking with fellow professionals, and developing best practices to further their careers or business interests.

Non-formal education courses would provide professional certification and/or continuing education units to specific groups within a professional society, such as the American Society of Adaptation Professionals, the American Planning Association, or the American Institute of Architects. Many businesses rely on their related professional societies to provide guidance and best practice on SRC topics. Some industries are new to SRC issues, and do not have an established *preferred methods* to integrate fundamentals into industry protocols. For this reason, the professional society would play a large role in vetting of instructors, approval of curricula, and coordination of course schedules.

The result of society members attending SRC courses would be professional certification and/or professionally recognized continuing education units. However, the instruction might be segmented or tiered. Leaders of an organization would need to set industry standards if practices have not been formally defined for such a member education program. Then a curriculum could be offered in a second tier to interested members. These courses would evolve over time based on audience feedback regarding the usefulness and applicability of the knowledge gained.

One strategy for professionals interested in providing SRC-related education to professional societies would be to pursue this scenario in parallel with another educational effort. This is not an enterprise for which the provider simply publicizes a course and participants enroll. This setting requires an in-depth knowledge of the professional organization and its goals.

In principle, each endeavor should be treated like a service, rather than a good promoted to a mass market (Voos et al., 2021). For example, the educator could create content and offer an educational program to a business in the sector that the professional society represents, and then market or sell this content to the professional society.

Community Leaders, Decision Makers, and Local Governments

This is the most complex of the five target populations. Both the diverse set of actors and the interrelated system of elements that must be considered when addressing community resilience create this complexity.

We define a community as any municipal, county, tribal, regional, or state government entity; or any group that is working with one of these entities (e.g., non-profits or activists). Within a community, educators may need to treat differently several types of participants in regard to non-formal education. We grouped these into three categories, but realize that in certain communities some people have multiple responsibilities.

- Decision-makers are people who are willing to accept responsibility and assign resources. In local government, this group can include county managers and staff, city managers and staff, elected officials, planning boards, emergency responders, etc. These individuals are the main consumers of non-formal education.
- Community champions are people the community views as *trusted messengers* to communicate SRC issues and engage the appropriate groups. They are often the *point* people who work with practitioners and decision makers. The champions are willing to be conversant in the concepts of community resilience, and they are often the first people who pursue opportunities for SRC education. Although they are usually passionate learners, the champions don't often become non-formal educators.
- Science translators are individuals in state, local, and tribal governments, non-profit organizations, and private sector companies who evaluate climate risks, develop resilience strategies, and access federal funding. They are experts who convey to municipal governments actionable climate-change data and information. They can take climate, vulnerability, and risk assessment data and apply the results locally. The translators are the ones who provide most of the non-formal education for this sector (Moss et al., 2019).

Funding educational programs for this group is often included in a larger project to build a risk and resilience plan for the community. Local governments usually provide this funding, but it can be supplemented from a unit of state or federal government. The community will often release a request for proposals for the resilience plan and incorporate items such as workshops and community outreach. A contractor who submits a proposal will often bring together a group of professionals to create the resilience plan, and also include in it educators and communicators to deliver the non-formal education program.

Finally, there is a big difference for this target audience in non-formal education and training. Non-formal educators provide information on *what to do*. Training provides information on *how to do it*. There are many opportunities for more in-depth training on all the topics we discussed. It can be delivered at a variety of scales and by a collection of institutions including community colleges, non-profit organizations and for-profit businesses.

SUMMARY

We've discussed in this chapter non-formal SRC education and how it can help address our environmental challenges. Hopefully, we've demonstrated the nimbleness of non-formal education, its ability to be regionally specific, and its accessibility and applicability to a fairly broad range of the population. Individuals and groups can access SRC-related courses and workshops at any point in their lives, although our emphasis here is on adults of post-college age. Our work is limited to five target populations, but this is merely a small subset of potential student groups.

We wanted to list model SRC programs for each of our target populations but, at this time, they don't exist or are not known to us. The potential programs, as described, are meant to be provided in-person, and serve populations of students who live within a geographic region, or visit that region (as with edutainment offerings) for several days or more. Our original effort was meant to offer ideas to entrepreneurial enterprises, both non-profit and for-profit, in one geographic region. That is how we wish you the reader would interpret these pages—through your imaginations while considering your home cities, states, and regions. Potential audiences for educational offerings may not be present exactly as described here, and may exist in your area as conglomerations of the groups mentioned above or as totally different arrangements of ages, professions, incomes, etc. Not getting bogged down trying to fit your population(s) into one of our definitions is important. Flexibility of thinking is key.

We did not include here a discussion on SRC education for underrepresented groups in this country. These groups include the economically disadvantaged, many people of color, those who are physically and mentally challenged, and non-English speakers. Members of these groups did not create climate change, but it will affect them to an equal or greater extent than the target populations we discussed above. Their ability to adapt to worsening conditions will no doubt be restricted in comparison. We appreciate the importance for all people to understand the intricacies of a warming planet, and be empowered to act accordingly. We do not have—and therefore did not propose here—solutions for creating financially sustainable non-formal education programs and recruitment of participants for those programs. This is an area of non-formal SRC education that requires much additional research and extensive outreach. Our concerns regarding future inclusion of this population include, how to get information about local SRC issues to them? How to sustainably pay for the programs? And, what information do these individuals and groups need (and want) to enhance their and their families' lives?

We mentioned storytelling and its value in a non-formal educational setting. Storytelling can also help educators address a condition known as Shifting Baseline Syndrome. It is a situation in which each generation bases their view of the biosphere and its current vigor on comparisons with how it existed when they were born—i.e., their personal eco-baseline (Pauly, 1995). For most, history plays no part in that judgement. Shifting baseline syndrome, also known as generational amnesia, can lead to concessions made, generation after generation, that result in ecological devastation. For example, a concession to a developer to drain 50 acres of a 1000-acre wetland may seem reasonable at the present time. If that reasonable concession is made every 20 years (or once per generation), it won't take many generations before those wetlands are irreversibly damaged. Society has long titled this fate: *death by a thousand cuts*. When we hand down stories that relay how the earth was generations, even centuries, ago, that personal eco-baseline can be shifted and caution on environmental matters encouraged.

A closing word on program evaluation. Each program offered in every town, city, and region should be evaluated per its success in delivering SRC information. Was it financially feasible? Was the level of information appropriate for that audience? Were the instructor(s) informed and did they present the information in an understandable manner? Did the course motivate the individual, the group? Quality is key; time is of the essence and waste is the enemy.

NOTE

1.   The online resources as described by Voos et al. (2021) are numerous and of such variability in subject, depth, and cost, that individuals may require a wayfinder or guide to choose the program right for them.

REFERENCES

American Society of Adaptation Professionals (2019). *ASAP living guide to the principles of climate change adaptation*. Retrieved from https://adaptationprofessionals.org/wp-content/uploads/2019/12/ASAP-Living-Guide-2.pdf

Brooks, D. (2020). *The second mountain: The quest for a moral life*. New York, NY: Random House.

Cormick, C. (2020). Top tips for getting your science out there. *Career column: Nature*. https://doi.org/10.1038/d41586-020-00239-6

Diamond, J.M. (2011). *Collapse: How societies choose to fail or succeed*. New York, NY: Penguin.

Doughnut Economics Action Lab (2020). About Doughnut Economics: Meet the Doughnut and the concepts at the heart of Doughnut Economics. Retrieved from https://doughnuteconomics.org/about-doughnut-economics

Falk, J.H. and Dierking, L.D. (2010). The 95 percent solution: School is not where most Americans learn most of their science. *American Scientist*, 98(6). Retrieved from https://www.americanscientist.org/article/the-95-percent-solution

Folke, C. (2016). Resilience (Republished). *Ecology & Society*, 21(4), 44. https://doi.org/10.5751/ES-09088-210444

International Commission on Education for the Twenty-first Century (1996). *Learning the treasure within: Report to UNESCO of the International Commission on Education of the Twenty-first Century*. Retrieved from https://www.gcedclearinghouse.org/sites/default/files/resources/%5BENG%5D%20Learning_0.pdf

Kwauk, C. and Casey, O. (2021). *A new green learning agenda*. The Brookings Institution. https://www.brookings.edu/wp-content/uploads/2021/01/Brookings-Green-Learning-FINAL.pdf

Meadows, D. (1999). *Leverage points: Places to intervene in a system*. The Sustainability Institute. https://www.donellameadows.org/wp-content/userfiles/Leverage_Points.pdf

Moss, R.H., Avery, S., Baja, K., Burkett, M., William, S., Chischilly, A.M., Dell, J., ..., Zimmerman, R. (2019). Evaluating knowledge to support climate action: A framework for sustained assessment. *Weather, Climate, and Society*, 11(3), 465–487. https://doi.org/10.1175/WCAS-D-18-0134.1

Pauly, D. (1995). Anecdotes and the shifting baseline syndrome of fisheries. *Trends in Ecology & Evolution*, 10(10), 430.

Pew Research Center (2019). *Why Americans don't fully trust many who hold positions of power and responsibility*. https://www.pewresearch.org/politics/2019/09/19/why-americans-dont-fully-trust-many-who-hold-positions-of-power-and-responsibility/

Post Carbon Institute (2018). Think resilience online course overview. Retrieved from https://education.resilience.org/wp-content/uploads/2018/08/TR-course-overview.pdf

Robinson, K.S. (2021). Guest column. *Bloomberg Green Daily Newsletter*, October 23. New York, NY: Bloomberg.

Starik, M. and Kanashiro, P. (2020). Advancing a multi-level sustainability management theory. In D.M. Wasieleski and J. Weber (Eds), *Sustainability (Business and Society 360, Vol. 4)*. Bingley: Emerald Publishing Limited, pp. 17–42. https://doi.org/10.1108/S2514-175920200000004003

Stockman, F. (2021, November 11). You know the saying: You are the product/Interviewer: K. Swisher. *New York Times*. New York, NY.

United Nations (2021). *Sustainability*. Retrieved from https://www.un.org/en/academic-impact/ sustainability

Voos, G., Rogers, K., Fox, J. and Newman, L.S. (2021) *The non-formal education project: Final report*. Retrieved from https://drive.google.com/file/d/1brcNwaafYVt7_FH-lY08v_nKgVn2vkbu/view?usp =sharing

9. You don't need a sign to protest: the rise of digital climate activism

Osiris Mancera

INTRODUCTION

It is the mid-1960s and you are carrying a picket sign in a crowd of hundreds (maybe thousands), stifled by the summer heat, and marching proud and lively. This sense of unity is remarkable, unforgettable. Gratitude washes over you and the pride is evident in each "Hoorah" and slogan your voice echoes. Flash forward a half-century and it is 2020. You stare at your screen as the votes come in, post a story on Instagram about the hard work you and your friends have done sharing online petitions and retweeting speeches, and relish in your ability to gain hundreds of views in minutes.

The realm and reality of what protesting and being an activist means have changed over the years, transformed into something unique, and increased inclusion in terms of what "counts". And while additions to the activism sphere have been made, this by no means discounts the effectiveness and modernity of in-person protesting, as shown in the Flint Water Crisis protests of 2017 and, most recently, in the Black Lives Matter marches whose peak re-emerged and became "news fire" during the summer of 2020. However, the digitization of the 21st century has percolated into areas beyond personal quotidian use and into the ways we learn, the ways we connect with one another, and the ways we campaign for what we believe in.

Thus, this chapter focuses on the digitization of climate change activism and the youth-led changes seen within sustainability over the past decade, from 2010 to today. As can be seen in the 'Defined Terms', the focus will be on students and youth within Generations Y and Z not only in the United States but around the world. Not meant to alienate or exclude, this narrowing of scope allows for a deeper look at a particular form of activism, one led by individuals whose lives have, for the most part, been digital and engulfed in eco-anxiety.

For many, reading a chapter about student activism might seem confusing. Many of us live under the assumption that the "big changes" are made by large corporations with billion dollar wallets or, at least, by professionals who are, incidentally, older and with more experience. This belief might come from years of conditioning in our own lives, or it may come from our own experience, seeing occurrences such as The Bill and Melinda Gates Foundation[1] donating millions (over $310 million, to be more or less exact) to fight climate change (Candid, 2019). On the other hand, we are doing a beach cleanup and are left believing our actions are but a speck in the grand scheme of things. However, that is not the case. Young people and students all over the world have proved that they are tremendous, brave, and incredibly resourceful in the impact that they can make in the climate activist realm. The purpose of a chapter focused on and prioritizing student activism stems from the power that comes from and the immense change that has been enacted by young people all over the world, especially over the past decade. At the same time, there is continuing rhetoric surrounding stereotypes and misconceptions of young people that paint us as entitled, unmotivated, and lazy, which is simply untrue.

In this chapter, the efforts of students and young people will be elevated in importance and impact. As the planet transforms every day and as more and more unexpected and harrowing environmental crises spring up across the globe, it becomes even more imperative that positive change be encouraged. This change comes from and will continue to be grounded in the movement and passion of young people, both students and otherwise. Moreover, another reason for a chapter on youth activism is there is so much material published through blogs, social media, and news outlets on standalone stories on youth-led activism, but not much consolidated work focused on promoting and celebrating the real and positive impact that student-led climate action has had.

CLIMATE CHANGE: A 20TH AND 21ST CENTURY BRIEF (RE) VIEW

For many of us, especially those that are a part of Generations Y and Z, the term 'climate change' is nothing new. We may have learned about it in AP Environmental Science, been a part of the Climate March in Washington DC, or have recycled at home since we could walk. But do we really know the story? At least, the story beyond what we see in the news, the microaggressions directed towards the planet, and singular events that serve to collectively harm the planet?

To begin, climate change refers to the shifting of weather patterns over time. While the changes were generally mild in the early 19th and 20th centuries, the past few decades have seen rapid increases in global temperatures beyond what cannot be attributed to naturally occurring warming. The anthropogenic warming of the planet is a result of the greenhouse effect, whereby an increase in CO_2 (and other greenhouse gasses[2]) trapped in our atmosphere leads to heat retention from the sun's rays (as opposed to its reflection) (BBC News, 2021). While a 1°C increase[3] might not seem like much, it has had a tremendous impact on our natural environment. In the past decade, it has been suggested that sensitive fish with Temperature-Dependent Sex (TDS) determination such as Argentinian silverside have been affected by increasing ocean temperatures[4] (Ospina-Álvarez and Piferrer, 2008). Not only does the climate crisis threaten their reproductive viability, but it also threatens to permanently alter the sex ratio of the young, which can lead to overall species decline and marine community destruction (Hardt, 2016). Similarly, unsustainable fishing practices have led vulnerable species to adjust evolutionarily, becoming smaller and smaller in response to overfishing[5] (Conover et al., 2009). From food scarcity to natural disasters and animal species declines, there is scarcely an entity that goes unaffected by the climate crisis. Luckily, over the past couple of years, our climate crisis has entered public knowledge so much so that a majority of Americans view climate change as a major threat[6] (Fagan and Poushter, 2020). In fact, it would prove difficult to find someone who could not list at least some key drivers of climate change, including the burning of coal and fossil fuels, overpopulation, and laggard legal protections.

Throughout this time, it is undeniable that humans have had a tremendous impact on the warming of the planet and its accompanying disasters, from erratic weather to changing wildlife populations and reduced agricultural production[7] (Environmental Protection Agency, 2017). It is entirely likely that poorer and developing countries will suffer the most, an unfortunate by-product of the hyperconsumption of the Global North already satiated and comfortable in their industrial history. In addition, fast-growing regions, low-lying nations and islands, and urban areas will be (and are currently being) most affected[8] (BBC News, 2020). And while plenty of people have yet to embrace and acknowledge the reality of the climate crisis, there is an increasing amount of undeniable evidence at our disposal. For instance, the 2021 United Nations Climate Change Report is most notable in its detailed science-based explanation (IPCC, 2021). According to the report, reducing the negative impact of climate change is physically possible with intentional change.[9] Of course, this is nothing new, but has been at the forefront of many young people and students' activism for years.

CHANGE THAT STEMS FROM CAMPUS PASSION

A beacon of social activism, college campuses have led the way to environmental stewardship for decades. Of course, the biggest leaders have nearly always been the students fueled by a need for action, educated about global injustices, and pumped with empowerment. Whether arriving on campus with knowledge of the climate crisis, having faced certain consequences themselves, or being surrounded by college courses on environmental sociology and economics, college students are ready to take action[10] (Kovacs, 2020). Of course, it helps that, generally, college campuses represent safe spaces for practicing activism with a reasonable belief of protection and non-harm before, during, or after engaging, a by-product of Social Safety Theory. With the incredible and unceasing efforts of college students, colleges and universities have been able to make great strides. For example, Georgetown University was able to cut its carbon emissions by 70% from 2006 to 2013[11] (Miller, 2015). The university's student-led initiative "Solar Street" supported this effort and involved the installation of rooftop solar panels on select student townhouses around campus[12] (Georgetown University, 2013). With projects focused on carbon emissions reduction and solar energy implementation, schools such as Georgetown University have led the way in college and university environmental activism and stewardship.

Moreover, from the very first Earth Day celebrated in 1970[13] to the 2006 Carnival of Climate Chaos in London,[14], students have led the way to enacting positive eco-friendly change. This momentum does not look like it is going anywhere (Lane, 2020). From the very beginning of climate activism, students have led the charge because they are among the most negatively affected by the climate crisis. This insatiable desire to enact positive change can only increase and the impact become even greater as the digital age develops and unfolds, eventually encouraging corporations and larger-scale businesses to adopt similar practices for a multi-level approach to solving climate change, similar to CSR movements within business (Georgallis, 2017). In fact, this greater access to online platforms not only enhances the influence and reach of calls to action but also unites international and intersectional youth-led movements. According to the United Nations, over 1.8 billion people worldwide are between the ages of 10 and 24 (UNFPA, n.d.). On a planet with roughly 7.8 billion individuals, a 23% chunk is not half bad. In the United States, 92% of all college and university students are under the age of 24, comprising about 12.8 million individuals (Education Data, 2021). It is no wonder that a big force in climate activism over the years has always been youth, working on movements from fossil fuel divestment to food security.

Fossil Fuel Divestment

In December of 2019, students at the University of Pennsylvania, wearing beanies and warm winter jackets, stormed a Board of Trustees meeting demanding change, fueled by prior demands for town hall meetings, intentional university planning, and overall greater transparency (Snyder and Orso, 2019). Their focus was fossil fuel divestment, and it was not their first time demanding alternative energy. Back in 2016, the Board of Trustees was asked to reconsider their stance on fossil fuel investments, which then amounted to $10.7 billion, a jump from its $1.9 billion the year prior (Snyder, 2016). After a month-long sit-in, the Board unanimously decided against divestment on morality grounds, and highlighted its alternative plans for environmental change on campus. Turning back to this chapter's introduction, protests and demonstrations have been led by students for many, many years in the form of chants, marches, sit-ins, and petitions. As a prime educator of critical thought and self-awareness, colleges and universities are excellent battlegrounds for student-led positive change. For climate activists, it often means being surrounded by thousands or hundreds of thousands of like-minded change-makers wanting to leave their mark and taking responsibility for making this planet habitable and enjoyable to live on. Of course, that does not come without great pushback and harrowing drive, as we have seen in the activist history at the University of Pennsylvania.

At Duke University, a similar issue on fossil fuel divestment reigns true. While the school's Advisory Committee on Investment Responsibility (ACIR) created the Board of Trustees Strategic Task Force on Climate Change to promote climate-friendly decision-making, the university has continued to refuse full fossil fuel divestment (Golchin, 2021). Instead, the ACIR's climate-focused initiatives have centered on curated fossil fuel investment, where the selected companies from the Carbon Underground 200 are limited and thus the university's portfolio has potentially lower carbon emissions (Fossil Free Funds, n.d.). Alternative climate-positive initiatives, such as the university's alternative energy policies, were believed to fulfill the institution's eco-responsibility given the higher perceived risk and high initial cost of full fossil fuel divestment. Students, however, perceive the university's stance to be irresponsible and to fall short of the university's scope of responsibility, given the negative accumulated impact since the university's inception in 1838. Given the scale and community (and sometimes global) effect of colleges and universities, however, it would be unfair to deem their efforts miniscule or futile.

While many education institutions are currently fighting to create equitable and climate-friendly solutions to years of planet harming, others are paving the way and leading by example. Across the Atlantic, the University of Edinburgh pledged to reach carbon neutrality by 2040. A prominent first step for them was divesting wholly from fossil fuels (The University of Edinburgh, 2021). A notable leader in the university-led climate activism movement, The University of Edinburgh has actively campaigned for and supported climate change policies and initiatives for years. For them, the only way to be value-based was to not only support others' efforts to low-impact operations, but to reflect those values themselves. These momentous actions were, without a doubt, a result of the tremendous and years-long effort by students, including the school's Students' Association. Beyond divesting from fossil fuels, the university founded a Responsible Investment Network in 2020 to empower higher-education bodies to invest sustainably and ethically. Additionally, since 2010, they have invested over £170 million (or over US$235 million) into low carbon technology, climate research, and

forward-thinking businesses, exemplifying that responsible investments are the most beneficial both in the short and long term (The University of Edinburgh, 2020).

Food Access and Security

In addition to fossil fuel divestment, food access and security has proved a momentous cause
on college campuses. In recent years, colleges across the United States have turned their attention to food waste culture on campus as well as food insecurity in surrounding communities.
While I was an undergraduate student at Johns Hopkins University, student organizations
such as Real Food Hopkins and the school's Office of Sustainability would regularly host
food waste audits in the campus' cafeteria, have a table on student quads to educate on proper
recycling, and welcome students to the university's community garden, Blue Jay's Perch,
to garden and enjoy an assortment of fresh vegetables. Nestled in Baltimore City, where
one in four individuals experience food insecurity, Johns Hopkins University has plenty of
real-world examples of what food insecurity and wealth inequities look like in communities,
especially college-town communities (Saint Vincent de Paul Baltimore, n.d.). It is no wonder
that Johns Hopkins University is one of the leaders in the food security movement in colleges
and universities.

One monumental player in the university-based food waste movement is the Bon Appétit
Management Company. While the company offers its services to corporations and museums,
many college and university students will tell you their awareness of Bon Appétit is their role
in universities (the University of Pennsylvania and Johns Hopkins University are just two of
them). In 2019, the company's partnership with the non-profit Natural Resources Defense
Council (NRDC) led to a fruitful and in-depth research study on university food waste, the
first of its kind. In the study, called *Towards Cleaner Plates: A Study of Plate Waste in
Food Service*, they found that each student wasted 112 pounds of edible food waste per year
(Cardwell et al., 2019). The study also provided implementable recommendations for food
service providers, including proper portion size training for staff *and* offering tasting spoons at
food stations. While a sizable difference requires systemic change in how society approaches
food access and food waste, this research study supported the empowerment of the users or
students themselves in making a difference one meal at a time.

Students at the University of Delaware are using their voices to start conversations on food
waste and food security on campus and in their neighboring community. One student-led
group, a chapter of the Food Recovery Network (FRN), actively works to salvage edible food
waste from its on-campus dining halls to the Newark Empowerment Center, which aims to
tackle issues around food insecurity in Delaware (Wagner and Kang, 2019). In 2019, the group
collected over 1,000 pounds of edible food waste. However, this result as well as the overall
food waste impact of the university is largely suppressed by university-wide policies and the
protocols of the university's food service provider, Aramark. This does not mean the university denies responsibility to promote campus-wide environmental stewardship. For instance,
one university tactic to mitigate food waste was the implementation of BioHiTech food waste
digesters in the main student dining hall. A way to reduce improper food disposal, these
immense food digesters make the waste easier to dispose of and use as fertilizers for the university's South Campus for instance. However, while this gargantuan apparatus has digested
and repurposed over 9,500 pounds of food waste, it is not enough.[15] Additional contributing
variables to the food waste problem include overproduction stemming from poor inventory

and production management, as well as lack of proper training and access to composting services. To combat food waste innovatively, students, such as doctoral student Elvis O. Ebikade, are following the academic path to problem-solving our climate epidemic. Ebikade's work focuses on using potato peel waste (and potentially, other food waste) as energy alternatives to fossil fuels (Roberts, 2021). With over 1.3 billion tons, or over 30%, of edible food being wasted annually worldwide, solutions that help tackle both food waste and fossil fuel divestment are more than welcomed (UN Environmental Program, n.d.).

As we have seen, climate activism is hardly ever solely about protecting the planet, at least not in the superficial sense. Climate activism deals with issues beyond itself, and instead is interwoven with issues of racial justice, ability access, gender equity and more. We next turn to the movement towards intersectional climate activism and the ways this new focus in climate spaces is influencing and guiding current and future endeavors towards environmental stewardship both within and outside of college and university campuses.

INTERSECTIONALITY FUELS MEANINGFUL CHANGE

Throughout virtually all social movements and groups, especially in the past few years, intersectionality has become a big focus. In the past decade, conversations around the future and evolution of activism have revolved around collaboration and layered activist practices. Causes such as Black Lives Matter are the epitome of such an approach, as the group showcased that black lives include black trans lives, black Muslim lives, and black Cuban lives[16] (Felipe-Gonzales, 2021). Not only are there a multitude of layers within "black lives", but there is a reality that true black liberation involves liberation for all.[17] As we will show in the following sections, environmental justice goes beyond minimizing one's use of single-use straws and taking shorter showers. While these efforts are incredibly important for prolonging the integrity of our planet, they are not the only aspects that merit climate crisis advocacy. Additional layers within environmental justice include racial equity in education and ableism within climate movements to name a few.

During the 2020 US presidential election, school kids across the country joined hands through the Teens Take Charge[18] initiative in support of integration in New York City Schools as well as to unveil inequitable conditions across public schools in the city (Richards, 2020). A tradition of sectioning students based on race and class has left New York City schools with student populations wholly unreflective of the city itself, hailed as one of the most culturally diverse and racially mixed in the country. Beyond being an issue on segregation, race-based discrimination in school systems highlight environmental concerns as well. Public schools, which have disproportionately more black students, are also more likely to have older buildings with unrenovated piping and lead-tainted water[19] (Nuñez and Molloy, 2017). While stakeholders have refused to remain silent, treatment of the issue varies across lines of identity difference. When the parents of an affluent Montessori school in Washington DC discovered the school had lead in their water, there was an uproar. Within weeks, the school adopted a filtration system. Of course, they were not the first parents to demand justice, they were just the whitest and the wealthiest. This example reminds us that taking a racial (or other identity-based) lens when discussing environmental crises is essential, lest we forget key aspects within this movement that play a pivotal role in how environmental destruction manifests itself. Or course, race is not the only identifier we must consider when approaching matters from an intersectional lens, but it is one easier to approach and from which to comprehend issues in the United States (Atewologun, 2018).

Various environmental groups and movements have been criticized for taking a binary or single lens approach to the climate crisis. This begs the need for involving diverse perspectives and experiences in any and every activist space, not only because this leads to additional insights into the struggles different groups face in various situations, but it also ensures that the "savior complex"[20] that plagues activism spaces is eradicated. An excellent example is the "ban plastic straws" movement, which will be mentioned briefly in the coming sections. While a fantastic movement in theory, its execution has been rife with socioeconomic status (SES)-based and ableism discrimination. While plastic single-use straws are a challenge within the climate crisis, and especially in its harrowing effect on marine life when improperly disposed of, the plastic straw has become an icon for the movement. However, the issues that arise with this particular movement are its exclusion and neglect of differently-abled individuals, some who physically cannot drink a soda without using additional tools such as straws[21] (Danovich and Godoy, 2018). Some alternative approaches to the plastic straw movement could have included bringing in voices from disability spaces to the conversation, supporting legislation around increased access to the various forms of sustainable straws (such as silicone, compostable corn-based straws, and single-use recycled plastic straws), and educating consumers around a customized low-impact approach to climate activism. As the climate activist space continues to be white and middle-class,[22] the solution is diversity as a first step. Several youth movements around the world are working on making that happen. These young activists teach us that enacting meaningful change in one's community and in the world does not require one to be a student, but does require heart and dedication to the movement.

ACTIVISM NEED NOT ARISE FROM BRICK AND MARBLE

In the sphere of activism, whether working to combat workplace inequity, the building of a landfill near a daycare, or otherwise (although all issues are interconnected in some way or another, as we learned in the previous section), it can be easy to silo ourselves into "doing" activism in one way. In response to the term "activism", it can also be easy to picture college students engaging in a sit-in on campus or marching with picket signs painted in red with "Stop Nukes" in bold lettering. However, that is not the only way to enact change and express disapproval of the status quo. Countless others have found creative and innovative ways of calling attention to injustices everywhere. Some include bold teenagers addressing world leaders at the UN for their inaction, while some protest mightily and steadily, and still, others involve full-fledged lawsuits.

Many of us can recall the countless articles populating our newsfeed and displayed on cable TV of the young Swedish girl striking at school in August 2018. She could be seen holding up a sign that read "Skolstriejk För Klimatet", which translates to "School Strike for Climate" in English, just a month before the Swedish general election. For Greta Thunberg, this was only the beginning. It grew to weekly protests outside of the Swedish parliament, known as "Fridays for Future" and skyrocketed in 2019 when she stood before millions (including in-person and virtual supporters), daring world leaders to enact change during our climate crisis. After writing a number of books about her experiences and climate change activism, including *Our House is on Fire: Scenes of a Family and a Planet in Crisis* and *No One is Too*

Small to Make a Difference, Greta continues to inspire young people to stand for what they believe in, as she continues doing so herself. Amidst the heatwave that plagued countless countries in the summer of 2021, Greta called out the climate hypocrisy of world leaders during the 2021 G7 Leaders' Summit via Twitter (Hanson, 2021). Using this quick and effective method has served Thunberg and other activists and influencers to both connect with their supporters and communicate with those who were previously untouchable before the boom of the Social Media Age.

When viral media attention (either through traditional outlets such as TV news or modern platforms such as Facebook) cannot be garnered, brave activists have worked tirelessly to organically gain attention to their causes. Activist and Japanese native Mayumi Sato is just one example. After receiving the Princeton in Asia fellowship, she spent over two years in Thailand learning about gender and social inclusion in Bangkok and in indigenous tribes (Shalom, 2021). Like a true trailblazer, Mayumi champions climate conservation practices to protect the most vulnerable populations, those who suffer when their forests are burned and homes desecrated to connect intersectional social injustices such as climate change and gender equity. Others, such as Toronto-based Kehkashan Basu, create foundations from which youth can learn and practice their climate activism to have a more meaningful and lasting impact. In founding the Green Hope Foundation, Kehkashan has supported numerous reforestation projects, such as mangrove replanting in the Bay of Bengal (Klimaatadaptatie Groningen, n.d.). In a similar way, Indigenous Mexican artist Xiuhtezcatl Martinez (known as X) has been fighting climate change since he was six (Xiuhtezcatl, n.d.). Through fashion design and musical rebellion,[23] X has brought light to climate issues surrounding identity clashes and minority treatment (McPherson, 2017). And while he has worked with renowned artists such as Willow Smith and Bassnectar, his calls to action have found niche support. As the youth director of Earth Guardians (originally founded by X's mother in 1992), he heralds the next generation of climate liberators through artistic expression and civic engagement. This does not mean his incredible climate activism has been for naught, given X's grand support network and reach; he is now going so far as to combat in the court system, to which we turn to next.

Engaging the legal system through formal pathways is a tiring, long-winded, and expensive process. As an institution built on precedence, the US legal system is often a follower and not a leader when it comes to ethics and social justice, a shepherd that corrals by waiting for its sheep to whine for fencing and their own food. To file a lawsuit, especially for a much-debated cause as climate change, can be a harrowing ordeal and is tremendously laudable when led by youth. Known as the "Inconvenient Lawsuit", *Alec L. et al. v. Lisa P. Jackson et al.* was filed in May 2011 by then 17-year-old Alec Loorz (Ellison, 2012). Alec, a climate activist since the age of 12, demanded greater carbon dioxide regulation and went after those directly in charge of it, including Environmental Protection Agency Administrator Lisa Jackson. Refusing to see themselves as powerless, the plaintiffs and their non-profit partners Kids vs. Global Warming and Wildearth Guardians sought relief from the EPA's (and greater government's) failures to adequately reduce greenhouse gas emissions which have increased 90% since 1970 (Environmental Protection Agency, n.d.). Ultimately, the courts dismissed the matter in 2013 for lack of subject matter jurisdiction, and the DC Circuit ruled it was a matter of state law. While seemingly disheartening, this unresolved case worked to fuel even more protest, demonstration, and legal change, demonstrating that climate change is more than a "trendy cause", but one that requires an inter-generational and inter-departmental coalition to be fruitful.

That same year, alongside 13 other youths, climate and hip-hop activist X filed *Martinez v. Colorado Oil and Gas Conservation Commission*, which claimed that the State of Colorado was negligent in its following of the Colorado Oil and Gas Conservation Act (Greenberg Traurig LLC, 2019). With a desire to halt fracking altogether in the state of Colorado, the lawsuit was denied the following year by Superior Court Judge Michael Scott. In the end, the priority was in balancing oil and gas development with public health. However, one notable result of the lawsuit has been the realization that youth-led legal action is not fantasy, but a reality that has always grown in the underbelly of the nation. For a more well-known example, we turn to the Colorado fracking lawsuit *Juliana et al. v. the United States et al.*

The 2015 case of *Juliana et al. v. the United States et al.* was filed by a group of 21 youth plaintiffs against the United States in violation of their constitutional right to life by neglecting to protect vulnerable communities from climate change and environmentally degrading practices (Our Children's Trust, n.d.). One of those plaintiffs was the previously-mentioned X. Represented by the non-profit Our Children's Trust, the plaintiffs sought to call out various executive branch officers, including former Presidents Donald Trump and Barack Obama, as well as various industry groups they asserted were perpetuating the climate crisis and irreparably harming the planet for future generations. Although previous litigation such as *American Power Electric Co. v. Connecticut*[24] offered a disheartening outlook, the plaintiffs remained strong, dismissal after dismissal, requesting appeal after appeal for what is a righteous example of change-making youth-led climate activism (American Electric Power Co., Inc. v. Connecticut, n.d.). While the case gained media attention in 2016 when US District Judge Ann Aiken[25] supported the plaintiffs' efforts, the decision was most recently repealed by the Court of Appeals for the Ninth Circuit in the winter of 2020 (Juliana et al. v. the United States et al., 2020). The same week the case was dismissed, Greta Thunberg's efforts were belittled and invalidated by the US Treasury Secretary Steve Mnuchin who claimed only a college degree entitled one to speak on energy and the climate crisis (Cummings, 2020). What can seem disheartening as one step forward results in three steps back, youth-led climate activism has undoubtedly led to tremendous positive impact. The key is remembering that every action causes a ripple effect and positively impacts the world around us, even if it is only protecting one tree, one beach, one person.

As will be mentioned in the "What Next? 5 Key Chapter Takeaways" section of this chapter, a requirement and true necessity moving forward is intergenerational support and championing. The climate crisis is not a burden to be shouldered by just one age group or generation but should be distributed amongst us all who have benefited and harmed our planet in one way or another. Instead of combatting and invalidating one another's thoughts and needs, government officials and youth activists alike must join forces and listen before refuting one another's points.

THE DIGITIZATION OF CLIMATE ACTIVISM

As we have seen, youth climate activists speak and act with their hearts, and their voices truly can be heard beyond the television or phone screen. Yet, that does not mean that digital presence and social reach are unimportant or unnecessary. As anyone that has a smartphone or Facebook account knows, social media and the online world can have an immense impact on the ways we speak, act, and even think. It requires little explanation to how and why digital movements thrive if we consider historical and modern examples and the boom in globalization, where social connection is facilitated through access to the internet, and the reality of network-led impact, according to the Theory of Network Society (Castells, 2000). We saw how, in the early 2010s, social networking helped fuel the Arab Spring across the Middle East (Emmanouilidou, 2020). And, most recently, we witnessed first-hand how Facebook and Twitter provided the tools for alt-right and neo-Nazi demonstrators to gather and cause irreparable harm during the Capitol Hill terrorist attack in January 2021[26] (Conger et al., 2021). While the Digital Age has brought about immense power for executing bigoted agendas, it also has given us the tools for community-building and social justice activism. For instance, the Black Lives Matter movement gained incredible expansion through the use of online social organizing[27] (Buchanan et al., 2020). A global organization dedicated to eradicating white supremacy and spearheaded by radical organizers Alicia Garza, Patrisse Cullors, and Opal Tometi, Black Lives Matter was created in 2013 in response to the acquittal of Trayvon Martin's murderer. Since 2013, and especially during the pandemic in 2020, digital platforms have allowed activists across the country and world to join the cause, especially through the facilitated spread of vital information on sites such as Facebook and the organization's own website. However, beyond the use of online groups and websites, digital activism has seen immense and unique power and reach through the use of hashtags (#).

Originally used as an organizational tool for grouping messages on Internet Relay Chat (IRC) in 1988, the hashtag tool wouldn't reach immense popularity until its use on the social media platform Twitter (Lips, 2018). Inspired by IRC, Twitter welcomed the hashtag to its toolbelt in 2007 as a way to facilitate the user experience on the site. And while the hashtag was adopted by numerous social networking sites such as Facebook, Google +, and Pinterest, it continues to be attributed to Twitter by many digital users. Months after being added to Twitter's functions, the hashtag gained popularity during the October 2007 wildfires in San Diego where users added #SanDiegoFire to their tweets to communicate real-time updates about the environmental disaster and coordinate rescue efforts[28] (Poulson, 2007).

Years later, in 2011, Plastic Free July began as an initiative to eradicate all plastic use and waste. Started by Rebecca Prince-Ruiz in Western Australia in conjunction with a small but mighty team, Plastic Free July bloomed as an international movement, sweeping across the globe and inspiring participants to change their daily habits. In 2020 alone, Plastic Free July had over 326 million participants who avoided 900 million kilograms of plastic waste by steering clear of, and finding alternatives to, single-use utensils, shopping bags, and more. However, this immense popularity is largely attributed to the use of social platforms such as Twitter through the use of #PlasticFreeJuly, which aided not only connecting participants to one another but also continuing campaign education efforts.[29]

Other viral hashtags surfaced as directed digital protests. For instance, the hashtag #StopSucking was pioneered by The Lonely Whale Foundation, an organization launched by actor Adrian Grenier and producer Lucy Sumner in December of 2015 that engages in global eco-focused initiatives. Their efforts led to the eventual eradication and banning of plastic straws in Seattle in July 2018 through their Strawless in Seattle campaign, making Seattle the largest metropolitan city to ban single-use plastic straws (Lee, 2017). That same year, The Lonely Whale, and specifically Adrian Grenier,[30] began the #StopSucking Twitter campaign in March of 2018 to encourage Starbucks to revisit its environmental commitments. Only months later, the multinational chain responded with a promise to exchange their single-use plastics for eco-friendly alternatives by 2020 (Jagannathan, 2018). As anyone who has visited a Starbucks in the last year would know, the chosen alternative to their impossible-to-recycle cups and green straws has been an easier-to-recycle sippy cup and compostable straws. While not the most ideal green solution, given that just over half of Americans have access to curb-side recycling,[31] it is a positive start (The Recycling Partnership, 2020). A more innovative solution could be requiring BYOC (bring your own cup) programs, offering large discounts for customers that bring reusables, or else offering a buy-back program for used cups and food wrappers. Since the Starbucks-specific #StopSucking online movement, the hashtag has remained exceptionally relevant, being used to promote ocean health and wildlife liberation, in conjunction with Earth Day or Plastic Free July, and numerous other environmental initiatives all seeking to eliminate single-use plastic straws around the globe, and using the power of online community-building and information sharing to garner attention and support.

Beyond eco-activism, hashtags have also supported the widespread popularity of gender and race-based movements such as #MeToo to broadcast and expose sexual harassment in the workplace and #BlackLivesMatter to raise awareness about police-related killings. The use of Twitter to campaign against police brutality peaked in May 2020 after the murder of Minneapolan George Floyd (Anderson et al., 2020). Just days after the murder, on May 27, 1 million tweets featured the hashtag #BlackLivesMatter. The following day, its use jumped to 8.8 million tweets, an exponential jump and marking the highest volume of the hashtag's use since the organization's commencement. In addition to using hashtags (#) and mentions (@), young activists have found platforms for their voices and their clamors for environmental justice on social networks such as Instagram, on podcasts, and through personal blogs.

Young digital activists have immense power at their disposal. Never before have youth been able to share their voices so readily and expansively than today, with dozens of popular social networks and billions of smartphone users ready to engage in the bite-sized and accessible offerings. Youth activist Leah Thomas (@greengirlleah), for instance, champions environmental intersectionality where she pushes for environmentalism to be seen as a racial issue, and vice versa. Her Instagram post from May 2020 featuring the phrase "Environmentalists for Black Lives Matter" in multi-colored font gained over 50,000 likes. Through her studies at Chapman College in Environmental Policy, she was able to garner the tools and support to be an environmental activist full-time, writing for various sites such as *Elle* and *Harper's Bazaar*, and gaining active followers for her organization Intersectional Environmentalist. Also in tune with her digital power, self-identifying Jew-Pina Kristy Drutman (@browngirl_green) manages the podcast, blog, and YouTube channel Brown Girl Green, where she bridges every-day environmentalism with broader themes such as racial identity and ableism. From across the ocean, Edinburgh-based and justice activist Mikaela Loach (@mikaelaloach) champions environmental justice in the United Kingdom through protest campaigns, eco blogging on WordPress, and educating via her podcast YIKES. As a medical student, Mikaela focuses on ethical living, refugee rights, and intersectional activism as a way to collectively unify and combat eco-destruction and promote sustainable living.

In the past few decades, the digital sphere has tremendously transformed the way we communicate with one another, and even the way we opine and protest. With the average American having 7.3 social media accounts on average, and 90% of Gen Z and millennials engaging actively on social media, the potential is incredible.[32] Plus, the amount of time users spend engaging on social media is steadily increasing. While a considerable cause for concern, it does mean that the potential for expanding one's digital activism reach is high as the average person uses social media for 2 hours and 7 minutes a day. Whether using an existing hashtag or creating a new one, collaborating on radical podcasts, or writing about coral reef health, digital activists can rest assured their content and reach is nearly certain, and not to be taken for granted.

CONCLUSION

Whether or not climate change has always been a part of your vocabulary or if you still find yourself struggling to define the 3Rs,[33] climate activism and discussions around climate change are only growing. As we have seen, many of the silent or neglected change-makers are youths, those who are continuously using their voices and passion to fuel their stance. From international change-makers such as Greta Thunberg and Xiuhtezcatl Martinez to digital movements such as #StopSucking, the landscape of what climate activism means is only broadening. We have known about climate change (formerly known as 'global warming') for decades, with environmental experts and scientists clamoring for the world to care. For decades we have seen the world awaken to this struggle, which has always been present but which has exacerbated over the past few decades as human-led destruction befalls our planet. With all of this information at our disposal, we are prepared and continuously learning and working to amend the damage. Learning from activism predecessors, climate activists of today and tomorrow can delve deeper into theoretical and practical understandings and solutions for our crisis. Whether it means using easily-accessible digital platforms, expanding our own knowledge of climate catastrophe into an intersectional one, or something else, we have the tools and resources at our disposal. We realize that we do not need to have advanced degrees to make a difference, we do not need a certain title to make a difference, and we do not need to look or speak a certain way to make a difference. The power to continue striving for a better planet and a better life for today and plenty of tomorrows is still within us.

WHAT NEXT? 5 KEY CHAPTER TAKEAWAYS

- **Education is key, especially our own education**. We learn more and more every single day, and not just within climate change discussions. It is important to remain open to learning and open to diverse and disruptive conversations, especially when they make us uncomfortable or are new to us. Acknowledging and embracing the reality that we are not experts is comforting, because it means we have so much to learn and so much opportunity for growth. Of course, it can be exhausting to try to keep up with what happens surrounding climate change, who the key change-makers are, and how to personally strive for impact, but we must carry ourselves forward and try. Whether you're a grade school teacher, climate change expert, or board member for a fracking company, you have the strength within you and responsibility to ensure climate change education does not end with you. Only then, when we all make an effort to use our voices, can we hope to create a better future for ourselves and for those around us.
- **Remember, you are not in it alone**. Being an activist, and especially a climate activist, can often make you feel alone. Sometimes it might feel like it is just you who cares about the world, but I assure you that is not true. As you have been able to see in this chapter and

throughout this handbook, there are countless others fighting the grand fight of saving our planet. However, your feelings of loneliness and hopelessness are not invalid in any way. Allow these feelings to remind you that your presence and support in our planet's recovery is well appreciated and see if you can at least imagine everyone else around the world that is doing the same thing. Maintaining a sustainable and long-lived life of activism requires replenishment, nourishment, and self-support, so remembering that you are not alone but in a fight amongst thousands, if not millions, is important.

- **The macro approach is just as important as the micro, and vice versa**. When we have discussions about climate change and activism, it can be easy to pigeonhole ourselves into a single perspective of what the causes and solutions are. This happens when we over-emphasize the importance of eliminating single-use plastics in our day-to-day lives but neglect the importance of curtailing their production in the first place. The same happens when we blame and criticize oil and gas companies for their dangerous practices that affect our waterways and wildlife when we ourselves drive gas-guzzling vehicles or refuse to use public transport. The macro problems and solutions are just as important as the micro ones. When we discuss climate change and how we can work to solve it, we must approach the issue holistically. One way is by engaging our communities and having open and honest discussions. Another is constantly remembering the importance of bridging the self, community, and system when approaching our activism. Only in this way can we realize the true depth of the issue which does not involve placing singular blame on one another, but on acknowledging our past collective faults and working together to compose potential and practical solutions.
- **Practice what you preach, and be inclusive**. As related to the above key takeaway, we must be examples of what we believe and request of the world. We serve as examples and as leaders for those around us, so it is crucial that we hold ourselves up to high expectations and standards when it comes to climate activism in our day-to-day lives. As students, social media influencers, or company owners, we must hold ourselves to higher standards when it comes to climate protection and intersectional climate activism. This also means engaging in cross-temporal and intergenerational activism with folks of all backgrounds. One trap we must be aware of is practicing exclusive activism where our hurt guides us to blame a particular group for the planet's suffering and thereby leads to us excluding those "blameworthy" individuals from making a difference alongside us. However, we are all different and do not always subscribe to the stereotypes of our identity groups. We know how faulty and damaging stereotypes can be anyways. As such, one of our priorities should be bridging social differences to ensure a holistic and in-depth form of activism that is truly intersectional and all-encompassing.
- **Be open to different forms of activism**. As we have seen in this chapter, activism looks like anything and everything, from holding picket signs to tweeting to holding celebration parties. As the digital age is only in its infancy, this activism umbrella will only diversify and broaden. As we continue to educate ourselves, learn from one another, and continue our activism practice, let us remember that we all engage in different ways. And, for the most part, no one way is better than another.

RESEARCH LIMITATIONS

This chapter on student and youth-led climate activism was fueled by my own life experiences and personal values. As a fallible human, I sought to present an accurate, up-to-date and holistic view of climate activism of the past decade. As a social media and digital nomad myself, I have had tremendous experience researching and learning about global happenings within climate activist spaces for the past decade of my life. A part of Generation Z, it is understandable that my approach would prioritize this generation of activists because it is the generation that I know intimately and relate to the most. Of course, this is limiting because the scope of who is and can be an activist transcends age-groups and generation categories. Given the scope of this chapter, however, approaching this work in that way would not have been possible. As such, there are plenty of other works that do an incredible job detailing the prowess and positive impact of climate activists throughout the movement's existence.

Moreover, in my attempt to be all-inclusive and intersectional in my approach to the events and individual activists I highlighted, I have attempted to achieve a balance in terms of racial, gender, sexual orientation, ability-based, and national representation, which was guided by my own self-directed approach and not external and objective criteria. The limitations here are, of course, which activists I was already familiar with, what connections I have already, as well as what activist movements and individuals interested me the most. Moving forward, these limitations could be mitigated through joint authorship or objective criteria for representation balance, for instance. It is also helpful for an author to explain who they are, which can aid readers to understand the author's potential biases in their writing.

ACKNOWLEDGEMENTS

The majority of the work written for this chapter was done in Smithville, Tennessee, which sits upon the traditional territory of ᏣᎳᎫᏪᏘᏱ Tsalaguwetiyi (East Cherokee), Shawandasse Tula (Shawanwaki/Shawnee), and S'atsoyaha (Yuchi) peoples. I am eternally grateful for those who have stewarded this space for thousands of years before me and for the ability to learn, grow, and feel safe enough in this land to write and contribute to the climate activist and academia space. This land acknowledgement serves as a reminder to myself and others that we are not in this alone.

NOTES

1.   This is not to say that wealthy individuals and donating groups should cease their giving, but it does mean that more is needed to ensure that nobody is neglected in this movement, left believing their actions are futile and unimportant. When it comes to in-kind donations, especially those in the thousands it is necessary and required, especially as more and more millionaires and billionaires arise from the sweat and tears of frontline individuals who are often young or else embody vulnerable identities. The wealth gap in the United States (and around the world) is nothing new, but this does require some responsibility while it is amended. One of the requirements is giving money to mitigate at least some of the damages done by the wealthier groups and individuals, who are more likely to overconsume, consume unintelligently and unsustainably, and perpetuate systemic racism and identity-based discrimination.

2. Some of the often forgotten greenhouse gasses, which also affect climate change include water vapor (H_2O), Methane (CH_4), Nitrous Oxide (N_2O), and Chlorofluorocarbons (CFCs).

3. Since the pre-industrial period, the average global temperature has increased by 1°C and is expected to increase by 0.2°C every decade. This has profound effects on the planet and its inhabitants, as many have noted over the past couple of years with increased violent natural disasters such as wildfires and tsunamis, increases in heat-related illnesses, increases in food shortages and droughts, and negatively affected waters and ocean life through coral reef acidification and impacted marine life reproductive habits. In October 2019, the Intergovernmental Panel on Climate Change (IPCC) released a Special Report on Global Warming which declared the planetary threshold to be 1.5°C which was also the target set by the Paris Agreement in 2015 and adopted by almost 200 countries to diminish the global impact of the climate crisis and global heating.

4. Originally, it was known that sea turtles had TDS and that the sex of their young was dependent on the temperature of the water. Most recently, this study found that there may be a greater number of fish and other marine species with TDS than previously believed, which "may compromise their viability by diminishing the number of females in response to even small increases in water temperatures". Since TDS accounts for greater numbers of males to be born at higher temperatures than females, this is likely to skew the sex ratio of adult fish and marine species which can then affect continued reproductive efforts and marine communities.

5. The Royal Society found numerous changes in silverside fish populations they were studying which were affected by overfishing practices. Some of the changes they found included changes in adult sizes, age maturation, productivity, and growth rate. Luckily, they also found that the observed changes in the fish populations could be reversible if the right conditions were met, although recovery times could differ in wildlife species versus harvested species.

6. In 2020, 6 in 10 Americans believed that the climate crisis posed a major threat to society, compared with 40% who believed that to be so in 2013.

7. For many agricultural workers, climate stability is key to crop yield and health. When severe weather patterns occur, such as droughts or soil acidification, this can affect the health of their crops and the stability with which they are cultivated. In fact, since 1960, the lowest agricultural yields occurred concurrently with climate crisis disasters such as droughts, floods, and early frosts.

8. Almost all urban areas (95%) at risk of higher climate change impact are in Asia and Africa, with megacities such as Lagos in Nigeria bearing the brunt of extreme weather vulnerabilities.

9. According to the report, it is possible to limit climate change and global heating through practices such as reducing CO_2 and other greenhouse gas emissions. However, it is also true that prior greenhouse gas emissions are irreversible, especially regarding ocean changes and sea levels.

10. According to Daniel Horton, an assistant professor of earth and planetary sciences at Northwestern University, "[Students] tend to arrive on campus with the knowledge that climate change is occurring ... and that it requires action." College campuses are increasingly equipping their students to not only educate themselves about key social and environmental issues around the world, but with the tools to learn how to really make a difference. From student councils to students willing to sit-in to protest fossil fuels on campus or intranet campaigns seeking support for cafeteria composting, the ability to have one's voice heard and lead to action is highly possible on university campuses. Additionally, more and more are incorporating environmental sustainability related coursework, reading, or entire departments into their school's existing study options. Loyola University Maryland, for instance, launched the first BBA in Sustainability Management in Maryland which combines responsible business with social and environmental activism.

11. By undertaking numerous emissions-reducing projects, Georgetown University reduced its carbon emissions by 20%. These projects included selected energy and electricity use reduction projects. The additional 50% in carbon emission reductions were attributable to the university's purchasing of Renewable Energy Credits.

12. The project began in 2013, inspired by a student initiative spearheaded by club Georgetown Energy originally proposed in 2011. It earned $250,000, leading to the eventual implementation of solar panels to student housing, which supported student wishes for the initiative with over 80% in favor of the project. Since 2020, six townhouses have been fashioned with panels, generating over 20,000 kWh per year or 27% of the total energy used by those townhouses. While a small endeavor,

the project can very well lead to additional campus-wide initiatives, as it has with initiatives like campus-wide recycling.

13. First celebrated on April 22, 1970, the first official Earth Day celebration was spearheaded by the University of Michigan in Ann Arbor where over 1,000 colleges and universities across the country and over 50,000 participants joined forces to educate themselves and the greater community on the climate crisis (HISTORY, 2009). Inspired by Rachel Carson's *Silent Spring*, the event was years in the making, inspired by the lofty goal of swaying the political climate to embrace climate activism. Since then, the annual celebration has garnered international support, celebrated by countries around the world and by activists seeking to make a positive difference.

14. This spectacular event, held in Trafalgar Square in November 2006, involved the communion of 25,000 individuals to promote political climate action. Known as one of the bigger student-led demonstrations, the Carnival of Climate Chaos forced ruling bodies in the UK to carefully consider environmental protection policies for the country, even influencing the Queen's speech the following week (BBC News, 2006).

15. This figure is from November 2019. Updated figures on edible food waste diverted to date because of the food digesters could not be found.

16. This is not to say that BLM's support on social media for the protests in Cuba in July 2021 were the best they could be, but they were representative of BLM's commitment to supporting causes beyond those directly or superficially connected to Black Lives Matter. This has also been the case for many other specific cause-based groups who have worked to incorporate identity into their activism practices. The point, however, is that there is intent and will to support and encourage universal liberation, regardless of the impact the support has on the targeted group, although that too should be considered high priority.

17. Here, I'm referring to the South African term "Ubuntu" which reflects the reality of humanity's interconnection and the complexity that unites us all. According to "ubuntu", it is impossible to champion for the cause of one and not for the cause of all, because another's suffering is also the suffering of oneself (Williams, 2018).

18. Fueled by the reality that lack of diversity entails lack of resources, New York City youth demanded equity in education access as well as in updating the cultural standards that dictate a school's makeup.

19. While most states in the US don't require schools to test lead levels in their water, the Flint crisis in Michigan began a national uproar led by educators, parents and students themselves demanding more transparency and care be taken for students and staff. As mentioned in the article, other DC-based schools had less fortunate results, no doubt related to the lack of financial resources within the school district. For instance, Sousa Middle School made the same demands as those made at Capitol Hill Montessori but the results weren't as stellar. While some water fountains gained filters, others were and continue to be completely shut off. Students were forced to drink from plastic water bottles, which is not only practically unsustainable but an environmental crisis in and of itself.

20. When mentioning the "savior complex" visible and alive in many social spaces, I mean the audacity in not only believing one has all the answers but that their answers are applicable to everyone. Going one step further, the "savior" might also believe that they can create customized or varied answers that work for different identity groups, even if they themselves are not a part of that group or affiliated with it in any meaningful way. An example could be me as a Mexican-American person believing I know the answer to caste discrimination in the Indian subcontinent. While I've experienced and even studied caste systems in Latin America, this does not make me an expert, and it especially does not make me an expert in a caste system I have never experienced and know little about.

21. This article explains the issues around common solutions to create an inclusive straw ban. Not only is every single person different, but disabilities also manifest in different ways where one person might find silicone straws to be their safe haven while another can only hydrate using a single-use plastic straw. The issue highlighted is that accountability is required and siloed thinking must be curbed. Only then can individuals realize that their impact is grand but that what works for them might not work for everyone else. Additionally, stopping at banning plastic straws is not enough, especially if the person berating a "no straw policy" refuses to use the bus, takes annual family trips

across the globe, and eats fish. There is little sympathy in hypocrisy, especially when all possible resources and knowledge are at one's disposal.

22. Not only is having the climate activist space predominantly "white and middle-class" an issue on diverse voices, but it also reflects the limited spread of interest and education as curious environmentalists (regardless of age) don't see themselves reflected in the spaces that interest them. When all of the "zero waste" YouTubers are middle-aged and wealthy white women, there is a certain space that is neglected. Beyond that, a huge part of the climate crisis is overconsumption. A 2017 study by the American Sociological Association found that black households spent (and consumed) less than white households, all else being constant. That is, there is a considerable difference, when all other factors are accounted for, in consumption habits in the US. While this study did not include additional races, this binary study does signify that white people are more likely to consume more. Paired with the fact that white people are also visibly more engaged, at least on social media, with the zero waste and climate movement. The problem here, which is beyond the scope of this chapter, is overconsumption and the question to start with is 'who is consuming the most?' and acknowledging that it goes beyond the individual and involves national cultural norms of overconsumption and entitlement common in the Global North.

23. In 2017, X was included on the "25 Under 25" list by *Rolling Stone* for his efforts in environmental and social activism, especially through his artistry with his album *Break Free* and book *We Rise*, which aim to incite action and support youth in their activist journeys.

24. *The American Power Electric Co. v. Connecticut*, argued in 2011, set the precedent that the courts were not appropriate decision-makers and rulers when it comes to determining appropriate pollution levels and climate regulation metrics, claiming only the Environmental Protection Agency (EPA) had that jurisdiction in setting emissions standards.

25. In 2016, US District Court of Oregon Judge Ann Aiken paved the way for progress with the case, stating that, "Exercising my 'reasoned judgment,' I have no doubt that the right to a climate system capable of sustaining human life is fundamental to a free and ordered society." Previously, several judges had passed and dismissed *Juliana et al. v. the United States et al.*, so Judge Aiken's support was monumental in its progress.

26. As beacons for cross-national social networking and connections, sites such as Facebook and Twitter have dealt with free speech, privacy, and safety issues for years. And while the giants have contended with their limited capabilities and rights to monitor and control, the Capitol Hill terrorist attack led to their banning of violence-clamoring former President Donald Trump.

27. While previous social activism movements have been wide-reaching, it was through the use of social media and online organizing that #BlackLivesMatter gained immense support and became what "may be the largest movement in U.S. history". By leveraging their support digitally, BLM has been able to raise funds through supporter-led fundraisers and continue with back protests and demonstrations in response to racial discrimination and white supremacy across the globe.

28. It was because of the immense efforts of San Diego residents Nate Ritter and Dan Tentler that communication about the San Diego fire began. The residents used their Twitter accounts to relay information in the moment about what they were witnessing from their homes. Since local and national media coverage was not enough, they decided to use Twitter as a blog of sorts. With the support of Chris Messina, co-founder of BarCamp and first user of the hashtag, Nate Ritter's tweets became more accessible with the now-added #SanDiegoFire at the end of each post.

29. While Plastic Free July is focused on changing habits in the month of July, you'll see participants and "eco-warriors" engaging with the hashtag and movement throughout the year (Plastic Free July, n.d.). To see some tweets using #PlasticFreeJuly, check out the hashtag repertoire https://twitter .com/hashtag/plasticfreejuly?f=live.

30. Adriene Grenier's first #StopSucking tweet called out Starbucks as a big business with enough wealth and reach to enact lasting positive change for ocean health. Later tweets that featured the hashtag spoke about big business green-washing and previously successful efforts for going plastic-free https://twitter.com/adriangrenier/status/976508086033747970?lang=en

31. According to The Recycling Partnership, only half of Americans have easy access to curbside recycling. This means that easily recyclable materials such as milk jugs and soda cans get discarded into the landfill where they emit harmful gasses and take decades (or even hundreds of years in the case of some plastics) to wither away. And because only half of Americans have access to curbside

recycling programs, only 32% of the 37.4 million tons of recyclable materials is being recycled, and 25.5 million tons is left to rot in a frozen state of nothingness in landfills.

32. Worldwide, the average number of accounts is 8.8, but given the information relating to generational use was exclusive to data on American users, I focused on the US-related information. In the US, 70% of the population engages in social media with use decreasing in older generations, but not dipping below 40% engagement at ages 65+. And while the focus on the section has been on Twitter, the highest user counts can be attributed to websites Facebook, YouTube, and WhatsApp. And while average global time spent on social media per day is 2 hours 24 minutes, I again focused on US statistics for continuity.

33. The 3Rs refer to "Reduce, Reuse, Recycle", which has recently expanded to the 5Rs of "Refuse, Reduce, Reuse, Repurpose, Recycle" and even the 7Rs which includes "Rethink" and "Rot" to promote conscious consumption and composting.

REFERENCES

American Electric Power Co., Inc. v. Connecticut. (n.d.). *Oyez*, fromhttps://www.oyez.org/cases/2010/10-174

Anderson, M., Barthel, M., Perrin, A., & Vogels, E. (2020, June 10). #BlackLivesMatter surges on Twitter after George Floyd's death. *Pew Research Center*. https://www.pewresearch.org/fact-tank/2020/06/10/blacklivesmatter-surges-on-twitter-after-george-floyds-death

Atewologun, D. (2018, August 28). Intersectionality theory and practice. *Oxford Research and Practice*. https://doi.org/10.1093/acrefore/9780190224851.013.48

BBC News. (2006, November 15). The Queen's Speech to Parliament. *BBC News*. http://news.bbc.co.uk/2/hi/uk_news/politics/6150274.stm

BBC News. (2020, January 14). Climate change: Where we are in seven charts and what you can do to help. *BBC News*. https://www.bbc.com/news/science-environment-46384067

BBC News. (2021, August 9). What is climate change? A really simple guide. *BBC News*. https://www.bbc.com/news/science-environment-24021772

Bon Appétit Management Company. (2019, August 20). *Study Finds College Students Waste 112 Pounds of Food Per School Year*. Bon Appétit Management Company. https://www.bamco.com/about/#panel-who-we-are

Buchanan, L., Bui, Q., & Patel, J. (2020, July 3). Black Lives Matter may be the largest movement in history. *The New York Times*. https://www.nytimes.com/interactive/2020/07/03/us/george-floyd-protests-crowd-size.html

Candid. (2019, September 4). Gates Foundation Commits $310 Million for Climate Adaptation Action. https://philanthropynewsdigest.org/news/gates-foundation-commits-310-million-for-climate-adaptation-action

Cardwell, N.T., Cummings, C., Kraft, M., & Berkenkamp, J. (2019, August). *Towards Cleaner Plates: A Study of Plate Waste in Food Service*. Retrieved from https://www.bamco.com/content/uploads/2019/08/Toward_Cleaner_Plates_WP_Aug20_2019_final.pdf

Castells, M. (2000). *The Rise of the Network Society: Economy, Society and Culture v.1: The Information Age: Economy, Society and Culture*. Wiley Blackwell Publishing.

Conger, K., Issac, M., & Frankl, S. (2021, January 6). Twitter and Facebook lock Trump's accounts after violence on Capitol Hill. *The New York Times*. https://www.nytimes.com/2021/01/06/technology/capitol-twitter-facebook-trump.html

Conover, D.O., Munch, S.B., & Arnott, S.A. (2009). Reversal of evolutionary downsizing caused by selective harvest of large fish. *Proceedings of the Royal Society B*, 276.http://doi.org/10.1098/rspb.2009.0003

Cummings, W. (2020, January 23). Treasury Secretary Steve Mnuchin tells climate change activist Greta Thunberg to get an economics degree. *USA Today*. https://www.usatoday.com/story/news/politics/2020/01/23/steve-mnuchin-tells-greta-thunberg-get-economics-degree/4551092002/

Danovich, T., & Godoy, M. (2018, July 11). Why people with disabilities want bans on plastic straws to be more flexible. *NPR*. https://www.npr.org/sections/thesalt/2018/07/11/627773979/why-people-with -disabilities-want-bans-on-plastic-straws-to-be-more-flexible

Education Data. (2021, August 7). *College Enrollment & Student Demographic Statistics*. EducationData. org. https://educationdata.org/college-enrollment-statistics

Ellison, K. (2012, May 9). An inconvenient lawsuit: Teenagers take global warming to the courts. *The Atlantic*. https://www.theatlantic.com/national/archive/2012/05/an-inconvenient-lawsuit-teenagers -take-global-warming-to-the-courts/256903/

Emmanouilidou, L. (2020, December 17). Arab uprising: What role did social media really play? *The World*. https://www.pri.org/stories/2020-12-17/arab-uprisings-what-role-did-social-media-really -play

Environmental Protection Agency. (2017, January 19). *Climate Impacts on Agriculture and Food Supply*. https://19january2017snapshot.epa.gov/climate-impacts/climate-impacts-agriculture-and -food-supply_.html

Environmental Protection Agency. (n.d.) *Global Greenhouse Gas Emissions Data*. https://www.epa.gov/ ghgemissions/global-greenhouse-gas-emissions-data

Fagan, M., & Poushter, J. (2020, April 13). Americans see spread of disease as top international threat, along with terrorism, nuclear weapons, cyberattacks. Pew Research Center. https://www.pewresearch .org/global/2020/04/13/americans-see-spread-of-disease-as-top-international-threat-along-with -terrorism-nuclear-weapons-cyberattacks/

Felipe-Gonzales, J. (2021, July 17). Black Lives Matter misses the point about Cuba. *The Atlantic*.https:// www.theatlantic.com/ideas/archive/2021/07/black-lives-matter-misses-point-about-cuba/619471/

Fossil Free Funds. (n.d.). *The Carbon Underground 200™*. https://fossilfreefunds.org/carbon -underground-200

Georgallis, P. (2017). The link between social movements and corporate social initiatives: toward a multi-level theory. *Journal of Business Ethics*, 142(4), 735–751. https://doi.org/10.1007/s10551 -016-3111-0

Georgetown University. (2013, April 11). *New Georgetown Solar Project Draws White House Attention*. https://www.georgetown.edu/news/new-georgetown-solar-project-draws-white-house-attention/

Golchin, R. (2021, April 21). Duke moves forward on sustainability but stops short of fossil fuel divestment. *The Chronicle*. https://www.dukechronicle.com/article/2021/04/duke-university-divestment -sustainability-acir-fossil-fuel

Greenberg Traurig LLC. (2019, January 22). Martinez v. Colorado Oil and Gas Conservation Commission Update. *Lexicology*. https://www.lexology.com/library/detail.aspx?g=5bbc2890-d98a -4264-bfc7-a979a4505710

Hanson, H. (2021, June 14). Greta Thunberg roasted world leaders at the G7 summit after their party pics went viral. *Narcity*. https://www.narcity.com/greta-thunberg-slammed-world-leaders-at-the-g7 -summit--heres-why

Hardt, M.J. (2016). *Sex in the Sea: Our Intimate Connection with Sex-Changing Fish, Romantic Lobsters, Kinky Squid, and other Salty Erotica of the Sea*. St. Martin's Press.

HISTORY. (2009, November 24). The first Earth Day. *A&E Television Networks*. https://www.history .com/this-day-in-history/the-first-earth-day

IPCC. (2021). *Climate Change 2021: The Physical Science Basis*. V. Masson-Delmotte, P. Zhai, A. Pirani, S.L. Connors, C. Péan, S. Berger, N. Caud, Y. Chen, L. Goldfarb, M.I. Gomis, M. Huang, K. Leitzell, E. Lonnoy, J.B.R. Matthews, T.K. Maycock, T. Waterfield, O. Yelekçi, R. Yu & B. Zhou (eds), Contribution of Working Group I to the Sixth Assessment Report of the Intergovernmental Panel on Climate Change. Cambridge University Press. https://www.ipcc.ch/report/ar6/wg1/downloads/ report/IPCC_AR6_WGI_Full_Report.pdf

Jagannathan, M. (2018, July 9). Starbucks will eliminate all plastic straws by 2020. *Market Watch*. https://www.marketwatch.com/story/starbucks-will-eliminate-all-plastic-straws-by-2020-2018-07-09 -12884232

Juliana et al. v. the United States et al. (2020). http://cdn.ca9.uscourts.gov/datastore/opinions/2020/01/ 17/18-36082.pdf

Klimaatadaptatie Groningen. (n.d.). *Kekashan Basu | Founder President of Green Hope Foundation.* https://klimaatadaptatiegroningen.nl/en/kehkashan-basu-or-founder-president-of-green-hope-foundation-or-canada

Kovacs, K. (2020, January 8). Climate change activism on college campuses. *Best Colleges.* https://www.bestcolleges.com/blog/how-to-stop-climate-change/

Lane, C. (2020, April 21). Celebrating 50 years of student environmental activism. *TopUniversities.* https://www.topuniversities.com/blog/celebrating-50-years-student-environmental-activism

Lee, J. (2017, September 8). The last straw? Seattle will say goodbye to plastic straws, utensils with upcoming ban. *The Seattle Times.* https://www.seattletimes.com/seattle-news/the-last-straw-seattle-will-say-goodbye-to-plastic-straws-utensils-with-upcoming-ban/

Lips, A. (2018, February 20). History of hashtags: How a symbol changes the way we search & share. *Social Media Week.* https://socialmediaweek.org/blog/2018/02/history-hashtags-symbol-changed-way-search-share/

McPherson, C. (2017, July 19). Environmental activist Xiuhtezcatl Martinez: A teen on the front lines. *Rolling Stone.* https://www.rollingstone.com/culture/culture-features/environmental-activist-xiuhtezcatl-martinez-a-teen-on-the-front-lines-197672/

Miller, R. (2015, April 9). Charging in progress: Georgetown's campus and global energy impact. *The Georgetown Voice.* https://georgetownvoice.com/2015/04/09/charging-in-progress-georgetowns-campus-and-global-energy-impact/

Nuñez, E., & Molloy, A. (2017, August 14). Schools fail lead tests while many states don't require testing at all. *News 21.* https://troubledwater.news21.com/schools-fail-lead-tests-while-many-states-dont-require-testing-at-all/

Ospina-Álvarez, N., & Piferrer, F. (2008). Temperature-dependent sex determination in fish revisited: Prevalence, a single sex ratio response pattern, and possible effects of climate change. *PLoS ONE,* 3(7). e2837. https://doi.org/10.1371/journal.pone.0002837

Our Children's Trust. (n.d.). Meet the youth plaintiffs. *Our Children's Trust.* https://www.ourchildrenstrust.org/federal-plaintiffs/

Plastic Free July. (n.d.). About us. *Plastic Free July.* https://www.plasticfreejuly.org/

Poulson, K. (2007, October 23). Firsthand reports from California wildfires pour through Twitter. *Wired.* https://www.wired.com/2007/10/firsthand-repor/

Richards, E. (2020, February 7). These activists are too young to vote in 2020 election, but climate change has them fed up. *USA Today.* https://www.usatoday.com/story/news/education/2020/02/07/black-history-month-climate-change-nyc-doe-gun-control-segregation/4648485002/

Roberts, K. (2021). Changing the world, one food waste at a time. *University of Delaware Research Magazine,* 8(2), ISSN 2150-5128. https://research.udel.edu/2020/12/01/changing-the-world/

Saint Vincent de Paul Baltimore. (n.d.). Everyone should have access to healthy food. *Saint Vincent de Paul Baltimore.* https://www.vincentbaltimore.org/what-we-do/hunger/

Shalom, F. (2021, May 17). Mayumi Sato awarded prestigious Gates Cambridge Scholarship. *McGill Reporter.* https://reporter.mcgill.ca/mayumi-sato-awarded-prestigious-gates-cambridge-scholarship/

Snyder, S. (2016, September 22). Penn to stay invested in fossil fuels. Why? Not a 'moral evil'. *The Philadelphia Inquirer.* https://www.inquirer.com/philly/blogs/campus_inq/Penn-to-stay-invested-in-fossil-fuels-Why-Not-a-moral-evil.html

Snyder, S., & Orso, A. (2019, December 23). A 'new wave' of activism on campus: Students are aggressively seeking their demands. *The Philadelphia Inquirer.* https://www.inquirer.com/education/protest-students-college-campus-fossil-fuels-speakers-fraternities-20191223.html

The Recycling Partnership. (2020). 2020 State of curbside recycling report. *The Recycling Partnership.* https://recyclingpartnership.org/wp-content/uploads/dlm_uploads/2020/02/2020-State-of-Curbside-Recycling.pdf

The University of Edinburgh. (2020, March 30). *Social responsibility and sustainability – Climate-positive investments.* The University of Edinburgh. https://www.ed.ac.uk/sustainability/what-we-do/responsible-investment/climate-investments

The University of Edinburgh. (2021, February 25). *Social responsibility and sustainability – Fossil fuel divestment.* The University of Edinburgh. https://www.ed.ac.uk/sustainability/what-we-do/responsible-investment/fossil-fuels

UN Environmental Program. (n.d.). *Worldwide Food Waste*. UNEP. https://www.unep.org/thinkeatsave/
    get-informed/worldwide-food-waste
UNFPA. (n.d.). *Youth Participation & Leadership*. United Nations Population Fund. https://www.unfpa
    .org/youth-participation-leadership
Wagner, K., & Kang, S. (2019, November 17). Fed up with the dump: The issue of food waste on campus.
    The Review. http://udreview.com/fed-up-with-the-dump-the-issue-of-food-waste-on-campus/
Williams, H.S. (2018, October 18). What is the spirit of Ubuntu? How can we have it in our lives? *Global
    Citizen*. https://www.globalcitizen.org/en/content/ubuntu-south-africa-together-nelson-mandela/
Xiuhtezcatl. (n.d.). https://xiuhtezcatl.com/

APPENDIX A: DEFINITION OF TERMS

- *Climate activist*: One involved in change-making within the environmental and climate change sphere, which can involve activism in the form of protests, demonstrations, petitions, online awareness campaigns, hashtag engagement, and more. Considering the changing landscape of activism in many social justice circles, climate activism has come to mean any and all forms of support, allyship, and direct campaigning for planet protection, and is meant to be inclusive.
- *Digitize*: The transformation of our day-to-day lives, information and communication, and several facets of our professional and personal lives into online forms which manifest through social media or other online engagement platforms.
- *Eco-anxiety*: Experiencing feelings of mental, emotional, and/or psychological distress due to issues concerning climate change. These feelings of anxiety and hopelessness can arise from the inundation of stressful and harrowing information about climate change issues, can be long-lasting, and can have a tremendous impact on one's mental health in the short and long term. In the context of this chapter, "eco-anxiety" is used to describe one of the impacts of climate change on youth, and especially on Generation Z, that is constantly engaged digitally and bombarded with global concerns and news stories about climate destruction and doom.
- *Fossil Fuel Divestment*: Removing or limiting investment in companies that support the mining and extraction of fossil fuels from the Earth given the tremendously negative impact on the planet and nearby communities. The intention is to reduce carbon emissions through engagement and substitution of energy sources to renewable ones.
- *Generation Y (Millennial)*: Individuals born between 1981 and 1996, distinguished from Generation Z by the lack of lifetime digital and online engagement characteristic of Generation Z. This generation, however, has generally been able to readily adapt to and learn how to use newer technological advancements and has been successful in incorporating digitization into their day-to-day lives which is not exclusive to their personal lives.
- *Generation Z*: Individuals born between 1997 and now, but mainly serves as a placeholder for the youth of today. While in the future, this term might refer to the youth of the most recent period, this chapter uses it to refer to the teens and 20-something individuals who, for the most part, live digitally and have known technological advancements such as the internet, smartphones, social media, and more throughout their lives. This generation is unique in its interactions with others and self as well as in the realities of digital impact on their lives in the form of activism rituals, mental health impacts, and general social communication and engagement practices.
- *Intersectional Activism*: A form of activism that is all-encompassing and inclusive of all social justice issues. The reality of intersectional activism is that everyone's identities are webbed, multifaceted, and nuanced. This requires activists to be aware of general and specific social issues that impact a variety of individuals all over the world and that touch on various parts of one's individual and collective identity. This form of activism is also in-depth and contemplative because it delves into issues beyond the superficial and connects social injustices for one group to injustices for other groups. This is the case, for instance, with environmental racism, gender-racial injustices, and more.

- *Social media*: Forms of online communication meant to promote digital connectivity and includes platforms such as Facebook, Instagram, Twitter, and YouTube.
- *Socioeconomic Status*: Interchangeable with SES and "class", this refers to the broad categorization based on individual or family income. In the context of this chapter, it is mainly used to refer to inequitable conditions faced by those with a lower SES who bear the brunt of having fewer resources and thus being more at risk of environmental discrimination and harm.
- *Student*: For the purposes and scope of this chapter, one who is in college, university, or K-12 schooling. The chapter will include students in the United States and around the world and, specifically, students who have engaged in climate activism.
- *Youth*: One who is under the age of 18. This chapter will deal with youth from the United States and beyond who are not in college or university but are assumed to be in primary or secondary school and who are engaged in climate activism.

10. Digital sustainability: tackling climate change with bits and bytes

Georg Reischauer and Lea Fuenfschilling

INTRODUCTION

Climate change is one of the biggest challenges of our times (Daddi et al., 2018; Etzion et al., 2017; Nyberg & Wright, 2022). More and more firms tackle this challenge with *sustainability management*, systematic firm-wide actions to advance a firms' sustainability (Delmas et al., 2019; George et al., 2015; Starik & Kanashiro, 2013). Recently, scholars have pointed towards the potential of leveraging various digital technologies for sustainability management (Frenken & Fuenfschilling, 2020; George & Schillebeeckx, 2021; George et al., 2020). Amongst the examples are big data analytics (Espinoza & Aronczyk, 2021; Etzion & Aragon-Correa, 2016), digital twins (Kulathinal et al., 2020), online communities to promote and develop sustainable products and services (Majchrzak & Malhotra, 2020; Porter et al., 2020; Vernay & Sebi, 2020), blockchain-based transparency (Bai et al., 2020; Upadhyay et al., 2021), and transaction platforms (e.g., car sharing or charging stations for electric vehicles) (Acquier et al., 2019; Frenken & Fuenfschilling, 2020; Frenken & Schor, 2017).

The growing body of literature that has been labeled *digital sustainability*[1] – advancing a firm's sustainable goals through the creative deployment of technologies that create, use, transmit, or source electronic data (George & Schillebeeckx, 2021; George et al., 2020) – presents a promising development. However, it is not yet fully clear how firms can leverage digital technologies as part of their sustainability management to tackle climate change. Specifically, our understanding is limited in two important respects. First, the functions that current digital technologies have from a sustainability management perspective remain unclear. For example, the blockchain technology can be used for contracting but also for transparency purposes. So far, however, there is no bigger picture of the role of current digital technologies in sustainability management and, more importantly, their potential for climate change. Second, we know too little about what organizational factors enable firms to benefit from these functions to scale their climate actions across levels (Andersen et al., 2021; Geels et al., 2016; Starik & Kanashiro, 2020; Zeiss et al., 2021).

The aim of this chapter is to provide an integrative picture and thereby advance our understanding of how a single firm can leverage digital technologies to tackle climate change across levels. We develop this picture in three steps. First, we argue that three levels are particularly relevant for sustainability management – the *single firm* (which is our focal unit of analysis throughout) *competitor and research organizations*, and *institutional actors*. In a second step, we identify key functions that current digital technologies provide – *(certified) measurement and information, motivation*, and *transaction* – and assess key promises and downsides with respect to their potential to tackle climate change. In a third step, we develop a *multi-level framework of digital sustainability enablers*. The framework details what organizational factors enable a firm to utilize the functions provided by digital technologies (i.e., (certified) measurement and information, motivation, and transaction) across levels (i.e., single firm, competitors and research organizations, as well as institutional actors). Throughout, examples from various industries are used. To ensure a focused discussion, we limit ourselves to examples and insights related to ecological sustainability that revolves around natural resources such as water, wood, or scarce materials. We thus do not further elaborate on the two other important sustainability forms, social and economic sustainability (Dyllick & Hockerts, 2002).

LEVELS RELEVANT FOR SUSTAINABILITY MANAGEMENT

The goal of sustainability management is to reduce a firm's negative ecological impacts imposed by existing production processes, procurement, supply chains, consumption, and disposal (Schaltegger et al., 2003). Following recent advances (Huang, 2019; Nyberg & Wright, 2022; Starik & Kanashiro, 2020), we propose three levels are particularly relevant for sustainability management: the single firm (which is our focal unit of analysis throughout this chapter), competitors and research organizations, as well as institutional actors. In what follows, we outline why each level is relevant for tackling climate change. See Figure 10.1 for a visualization. As this depiction shows, we do not argue for a nested or 'onion-ring' multi-level approach. While such conceptualizations of multiple levels are often intuitive, they tend to under-theorize the distinct logics and guiding principles of actors (Fuenfschilling, 2019; Fuenfschilling & Truffer, 2016).

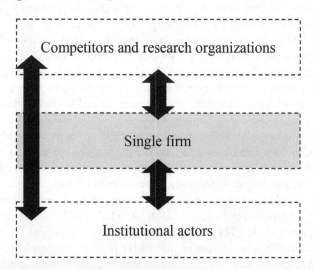

Figure 10.1   Main levels of sustainability management

The *single firm* is relevant as it is one key nucleus for collective climate change action. Defined as for-profit organizations and/or social enterprises that produce goods or services and that have a sustainability management system in place (Starik & Kanashiro, 2013), these actors connect and interact with both other collective actors (that we elaborate on later) and individual actors such as end consumer or interested citizen. The single firm is relevant for tackling climate change as it can be originator of "best practices" or technologies that increase ecological performance (Demirel & Kesidou, 2019; Wijen, 2014). For instance, a manufacturing firm redefines its production processes and reduces CO_2 emission with more eco-efficient technologies.

A further important level for sustainability management is *competitors*, i.e., for-profit organizations or social enterprises in the same industry as the focal firm, competing for the same customers. While classic approaches hardly considered competition as a distinct level relevant for sustainability management, recent advances suggest that cooperating with competitors can yield advantages for both a firm's economic and ecological performance (Manzhynski & Figge, 2020). Competing firms are relevant to tackling climate change for two reasons.

First, they are important when engaging in robust action (Etzion et al., 2017) that tackles climate change. When following this idea, firms embrace ambiguity (rather than striving for clarity), focus on short-term sustainability accomplishments (rather than long-term sustainability goals), and are satisfied with oblique development of its sustainable outputs (rather than linear progress). Analytically, robust actions have three levers: a participatory architecture that allows diverse actors to interact over time; multivocal inscriptions (or key terms) that can be interpreted in different ways by different audiences; and distributed experimentations to tackle a specific issue related to climate change, such as renewable energy. Consider the example of wind power. Competing firms may create a commitment by stakeholders from diverse domains (participatory architecture), which is likely to come with an eclectic mix of ideas to make wind energy work in a region (multivocal inscriptions) and the installment of prototypes of wind turbines based on a trial-and-error approach (distributed experimentation). The interplay of these tactics creates a sufficient feasibility of a certain type of renewable energy (Etzion et al., 2017). In several cases, especially in markets with fewer but larger firms, we witness that first movers create pressure for other firms to follow in the same direction. For instance, an energy group might decide to have a stronger focus on renewable emphasis after a main competitor did so (Reischauer, 2017).

A second reason is that competing firms of an industry together form a critical mass to scale sustainable technologies and/or promote sustainability standards on a larger scale (Devine-Wright et al., 2017; Landeta-Manzano et al., 2018; Reischauer, 2018). For example, the growing availability of public charging stations for electric vehicles with more standardized charging interfaces across carmakers promotes the electric vehicle technology more broadly, while allowing carmakers to design and market their cars independently.

Another important level for sustainability management is *research organizations*, understood as universities and/or private research organizations conducting research on technologies that advance the ecological performance of the firms implementing them. Research organizations are relevant as they often are the main source of new or improved sustainable technologies and diffuse insights into how to use and promote sustainable technologies (Hoppmann et al., 2020; Lozano, 2006). Consider the example of photovoltaics whose basic principles were identified at a university. Where research organizations also offer teaching, they play a crucial role in sensitizing and preparing future employees of firms (Lidgren et al., 2006). In some cases, we also see cooperation between research organizations and (competing) firms at one physical site and with a focus on driving a particular sustainable technology, as in the case of the WaterCampus Leeuwarden that focuses on water technologies. Such focused experimentations also allow regional socio-technical transitions (Fuenfschilling et al., 2019).

Finally, *institutional actors* are a key level for sustainability management. This broader category covers both, legally mandated actors – such as regional or federal governments and agencies (Ball et al., 2018), international organizations (e.g., UNO) (Valente & Oliver, 2018) – and international and/or national social movements, civil society, and geographically bounded communities (Hess, 2018; Vernay & Sebi, 2020). Institutional actors are relevant in at least three ways.

First, they play a key role in co-developing and/or implementing standards for sustainable technologies and guidelines for firms. These standards and guidelines have different forms, ranging from soft law over hard law to voluntary agreements (Manning & Reinecke, 2016; Schüßler et al., 2014). Examples on the global level include the Forest Stewardship Council, and the Global Reporting Initiative.

Second, especially for legally mandated actors, they are an important funding source to promote sustainable innovation (Brown & Hendry, 2009). Some countries have their own funding vehicles set in place. For example, the Federal Ministry for Climate Action, Environment, Energy, Mobility, Innovation and Technology in Austria set up the "Climate and Energy Fund" to fund research projects involving firms, research organizations, and, in some cases, civil society.

Third, institutional actors (especially geographically bounded communities) can be key to convince individual actors to adapt a sustainable technology (Vernay & Sebi, 2020). For example, homeowners who are considering installing digitally controlled solar photovoltaic systems on their homes have the opportunity to learn from their neighborhood school's or other local institutional actors building's solar installation, which can positively affect the homeowners' decision to install a photovoltaic system (Starik & Kanashiro, 2020).

FUNCTIONS OF DIGITAL TECHNOLOGIES AND THEIR ROLE IN TACKLING CLIMATE CHANGE

Informed by recent advances on how firms can leverage digital technologies (George & Schillebeeckx, 2021; George et al., 2020; Lember et al., 2019), we now identify the main functions provided by current digital technologies and assess their potential to tackle climate change. We argue that current digital technologies provide three key functions for sustainability management: (certified) measurement and information, motivation, and transaction. Table 10.1 summarizes this discussion. Table 10.2 provides a list with surveyed current digital technologies.

As we will show, a main drawback across functions inherent in digital technologies is a possible higher energy consumption, specifically of electricity. Energy-intensive technologies such as blockchain might ultimately cause a higher energy consumption as compared with not using that technology. However, with an advancement of approaches such as seawater cooling systems for data centers these disadvantages can be tackled (Mokhtari & Arabkoohsar, 2021).

The function of *(certified) measurement and information* denotes to (attesting and) quantifying input, throughputs, outcomes, and impact of current and/or future activities related to sustainability (George & Schillebeeckx, 2021; Upadhyay et al., 2021). The measurement or information is certified when a neutral technology, such as the blockchain technology (Upadhyay et al., 2021) or a distinct certification agency accounts for this function. In particular, the rise of sustainability standards and reporting requirements made this function a pivotal

Table 10.1   *Functions of digital technologies and their role in tackling climate change*

Function	(Certified) Measurement and information	Motivation	Transaction
Definition	(Attest and) Quantify input, throughputs, outcomes, and impact of current and/or future sustainability activities	Engage internal and external stakeholders to behave more sustainably	Offer and/or demand resources in a more efficient or effective way
Examples	• Crop yield forecasting (Paudel et al., 2021) • Tracking of supply chains (George et al., 2020)	• Gamified apps with energy points (George et al., 2020), app to display charging stations for electric vehicles	• Car sharing platform accessible via app • Platform for second-hand goods
Digital technologies/ phenomena based on digital technologies providing a function	• Remote sensors • Artificial intelligence/big data analytics • Digital twins • Blockchain	• Apps and information platforms • Global navigation satellite systems • Online communities • Artificial intelligence/ big data analytics	• Transaction platforms • Global navigation satellite systems • Blockchain
Key promises for tackling climate change	• Efficient (real-time) identification of harmful input, throughputs, outcomes, and impact • Awareness of exposure to climate risk • Higher transparency and credibility	• Low-threshold direct engagement to tackle climate changes • Large scale and/or real-time (co-)experimentations	• Higher efficiency • Low-threshold indirect engagement
Key downsides for tackling climate change	• Tackling symptoms, not root causes • For energy-intensive digital technologies (e.g., blockchain): High energy consumption	• Temporary behavior change • Data quality	• Rebound effects • Negative impact of shipping • For energy-intensive digital technologies (e.g., blockchain): High energy consumption

concern for sustainability management (Etzion et al., 2017; Nikolaou & Tsalis, 2013; Wijen, 2014). Examples include the forecasting of crop yield (Paudel et al., 2021) and the tracking of CO_2 submission of firms in a particular supply chain (George et al., 2020). Amongst the current digital technologies that provide these functions are remote sensors (George et al., 2020), artificial intelligence/ big data analytics (Vinuesa et al., 2020), digital twins (Kulathinal et al., 2020), and the blockchain technology (Bai et al., 2020; Upadhyay et al., 2021).

Leveraging these and other digital technologies for (certified) measurement and information is beneficial for climate change in at least two ways (Espinoza & Aronczyk, 2021; George & Schillebeeckx, 2021; Zeiss et al., 2021). First, doing so allows a quicker and more systematic identification of harmful input, throughputs, outcomes, and impact caused by a firm. Put differently, leveraging digital technologies is likely to increase the efficiency of assessing and improving negative impacts of a firm. Second, when measuring with the help of digital technologies, collective and individual actors can be made aware of their exposure to a specific climate risk, which in turn can prompt further responses. In particular, the interplay between numeric data and visualizations based on these data (e.g., heatmaps) can be more

Table 10.2   Surveyed digital technologies

Digital technology/phenomena based on digital technology	Definition
Artificial intelligence	Any software technology with at least one of the following capabilities: perception, including audio, visual, textual, and tactile (e.g., face recognition); decision-making (e.g., medical diagnosis systems), prediction (e.g., weather forecast); automatic knowledge extraction and pattern recognition from data (e.g., discovery of fake news circles in social media), interactive communication (e.g., social robots or chat bots); logical reasoning (e.g., theory development from premises) (Vinuesa et al., 2020)
Big data analytics	Analytics utilizing massive data sets, i.e., sets with large, more varied, and complex structure (Günther et al., 2017)
Block chain	Decentralized and fair share tracking system in which transactions are recorded and added in chronological order with the aim of creating permanent tracks free from possible modifications or tampering (Upadhyay et al., 2021)
Digital twins	Software that exposes users to a digital replication of the state and temporal evolution of a real-life object constrained by available observations and the laws of physics (Bauer et al., 2021)
Gamification	Implementation of game design elements in real-world contexts for non-gaming purposes (Sailer et al., 2017)
Information platform	Information channeling infrastructure that enables the categorization and search of relevant information and facilitates users' exchange of information and matching (Cennamo, 2021)
Online community	Group of users who partake actively in a certain digitally mediated service (Reischauer & Mair, 2018)
Transaction platform	Infrastructure to connect providers of resources with parties seeking these resources and to facilitate value-exchange transactions amongst them (Cennamo, 2021)

compelling than 'sheer' numbers. A current example on a global level is the Interactive Atlas of the Working Group 1 of the Intergovernmental Panel on Climate Change (IPCC). A third potential of (certified) measurement lies in the fact it that can increase transparency and credibility of a firm – this of course is only the case if data are made available to third parties, for example through a dashboard on the firm's website. An example is Water Disclosure Project (WDP) by the Carbon Disclosure Project (CDP) to create a database of corporate water usage information.

There are also downsides of (certified) measurement with regards to climate change. To start with, the emphasis on refining production processes may be only tackling symptoms and not getting towards the root causes of firm's negative impact. In other words, (certified) measurement may focus on system optimization instead of fundamental system change, thus impeding necessary sustainability transitions (Fuenfschilling, 2019). An example here is agriculture, where many digital solutions are assumed to help with sustainability issues such as crop yield (Rijswijk et al., 2021). However, scholars have also argued that a real sustainability shift would not lie in optimizing the current system, but instead transition from annual monocultures to perennial polycultures, which would solve many current sustainability issues in agriculture without relying on digitalization (Crews et al., 2018). Moreover, and especially for energy-intensive technologies such as blockchain, the energy consumption of systematically applying that technology may outweigh its benefits.

When utilizing digital technologies for *motivation*, a firm engages internal and external stakeholders to behave more sustainably (Lember et al., 2019). Examples include gamified apps where customers can earn energy points when proving they behaved more sustainably

(George et al., 2020), apps that display charging stations for electric vehicles, and gamified apps (coupled with virtual reality technologies) for employees on the shop floor that showcase potential benefits of sustainable behavior (e.g., better recycling of by-products and submission of ideas for sustainable innovation). An example at the global level is the 'Data for Climate Action' challenge by the 'UN Global Pulse', the UN Secretary-General's initiative on big data and AI for development, humanitarian action, and peace. In terms of digital technologies, this function is provided especially by apps installed on smartphones, artificial intelligence/ big data analytics, global navigation satellite systems, and online communities (Majchrzak & Malhotra, 2020; Porter et al., 2020; Vernay & Sebi, 2020),

Leveraging digital technologies for the purpose of *motivation* is beneficial to tackling climate change in at least two respects. First, as especially showcased with the example of gamified apps (Sailer et al., 2017), the threshold to motivate internal and external stakeholders to directly address climate change individually in a direct manner is quite low. Put differently, with relatively low efforts a large scale of individual and collective actors can be addressed. For example, individuals living close to the sea can provide observations regarding water quality based on simple rules to do so. The driving mechanism behind this is a playful competition. Second, digital technologies can enable large scale and/or real-time (co-)experimentations and thus to innovate quicker as compared with only innovating as a single firm.

However, using digital technologies to motivate can also have adverse effects on the quest to tackle climate change. One downside is rebound effects – an increase in energy efficiency does not necessarily lead to an equal decrease in energy demand due to changed customer behavior (Santarius & Soland, 2018). Another downside is temporary limited behavior change. While the threshold to engage is low, this may come with the potential issue that one also just as easily quits, meaning there is long-term behavior change. Moreover, as datasets are created by a large-scale input from individual actors, the quality of that data can be inadequate, and thus cannot be used for the decisions of the sustainability manager. Furthermore, this kind of gamification might only trigger motivation in a particular kind of individual and/or collective actor, while others still depend on more regulative or normative incentives and interventions for behavioral change. Moreover, a certain digital know-how is required to participate in these initiatives, which might constitute a hindering factor for some individual actors who are less familiar with technologies.

Another important function that digital technologies provides to sustainability management is *transaction* – to offer and/or demand resources in a more efficient or effective way, as compared with traditional (i.e., in-house) approaches (Lember et al., 2019). One example is the provision of a car sharing service where individual but also collective actors transact to get temporary access to a car (Gegenhuber et al., 2022; Reischauer & Mair, 2018). Amongst technologies that can be leveraged for that purpose are blockchain technology (Bai et al., 2020; Upadhyay et al., 2021), global navigation satellite systems, and transaction platforms, which are defined as two- or multi-sided matchmakers for sustainable goods or services (Acquier et al., 2019; Frenken & Schor, 2017; Frenken et al., 2020).

One beneficial effect of the transaction function is a higher efficiency in several ways. For instance, products and services are used and circulated more often, which reduces the need to buy new products and services. Moreover, as transaction platforms tend to streamline the process of buying a good or the right to temporary use of a resource, the resulting efficiency frees resources for other sustainability management tasks. A further beneficial effect is low-threshold and indirect engagement with climate change, especially for individual consumers. Consider the example of energy communities where property owners transact, often automatically, renewable energy produced by photovoltaic installations (Vernay & Sebi, 2020).

As with the other functions, there are some downsides when using digital technologies for the purpose of transaction. One downside is rebound effects. For example, when engaging in car sharing based on electric vehicles, one might increase the overall driving time. Second, and especially applicable for goods bought via transaction platforms, there can be negative ecological impact of shipping these goods. Third, and particularly applicable for energy-intensive digital technologies such as blockchain (Andersen et al., 2021), there might be again the issue that the energy consumption caused by applying the technology results in an overall higher energy consumption. In addition, scholars have also pointed to issues relating to justice and equality. This is especially relevant in regard to questions of ownership and property, which can be shared via platforms, therefore contributing to certain kinds of inequalities between the ones that own and the others. Furthermore, many new technologies have led to new relationships between firms, employees and customers that require new legal frameworks and/or present novel challenges in relation to power structures and built-in inequalities (Frenken & Fuenfschilling, 2020).

MULTI-LEVEL FRAMEWORK OF DIGITAL SUSTAINABILITY ENABLERS

Building on the above insights, we now develop a multi-level framework of digital sustainability enablers. In particular, for each level we describe organizational enablers (Hussain & Malik, 2020) that are particularly relevant to make digital sustainability work (George & Schillebeeckx, 2021; George et al., 2020; Lember et al., 2019). The resulting framework, which is summarized in Figure 10.2, details what organizational factors (middle of Figure 10.2) enable a firm to utilize the functions provided by digital technologies (vertical axis of Figure 10.2) across levels (horizontal axis of Figure 10.2).

Level / Function	Single firm	Competitors and research organizations	Institutional actors
(Certified) Measurement and information	Dynamic capabilities for digital technologies	Trustworthy intermediaries with digital presence	Standards to ensure data compatibility
Motivation		Alliance capabilities	Policy mixes for deploying digital technologies at a larger scale
Transaction	Modular products/ product service systems	Sustainable national/global platforms	

Figure 10.2   Multi-level framework of digital sustainability enablers

Single Firm

For the level of the single firm, we see two main enabling factors. First, and applicable to both functions, *(certified) measurement and information as well as motivation,* dynamic capabilities for digital technologies are key (Helfat & Raubitschek, 2018; Warner & Wäger, 2019). Defining a dynamic capability as a learned and pattern-based organizational process that enables firms to purposefully renew their resource, Helfat and Raubitschek (2018) argue that firms need three dynamic capabilities to effectively use digital technologies: innovation capabilities, environmental scanning capabilities, and integrative capabilities. Innovation capabilities focus on seizing and reconfiguring activities by supporting the development of new technologies. Consider the example of Uber, which developed prototypes for autonomous driving. Environmental scanning capabilities allow them to sense opportunities and threats. Another example is YouTube, which started out as dating platform. As the founders sensed that the video feature was key for users, they re-built the platform around the video feature. Finally, integrative capabilities are concerned with the introduction and modification of resources and other capabilities of a firm (such as innovation capabilities). Dynamic capabilities for digital technologies are enablers for the function's (certified) measurement and information as well as motivation as they push the firm towards stronger integration towards achieving these functions (Helfat & Raubitschek, 2018).

Second, when it comes to the *transaction* function at the level of the *single firm*, we consider modular products and services as key enablers. In general, modularity refers to the capacity of a system (such as a product like a car) to undergo changes within any of its subsystems (such as the engine of a car) without creating a ripple effect that hazards other subsystems (Tee et al., 2019). Modularity enables one to leverage the transaction-function as it allows offering one's product and services on several platforms. For instance, modularity allows a firm to offer its sustainable products or services on several platforms at once with very little cost.

Competitors and Research Organizations

Moving to the level of competitors and research organizations, we consider three enablers relevant. Regarding (certified) measurement and information, trustworthy intermediaries with digital presence are a particularly relevant enabler (Berkowitz, 2018; Reischauer et al., 2021; Valente & Oliver, 2018). One example is the Sustainable Development Solutions Network, which provides the interactive "Sustainable Development Report". Metaphorically speaking, these intermediaries are a multiplier of (certified) measurement and information and thereby enhance its impact.

An important enabler so that sustainability management can effectively exert the *motivation* function together with *competitors and research organizations* is the alliance capabilities for interacting competitors and research organizations. Alliance capabilities encompass learnt organizational activities to form, structure, and manage (a portfolio of) interorganizational relationships (Hoffmann et al., 2019). Doing so is highly relevant as being part of an alliance that is either based on trust or contracts (Hoffmann et al., 2019) provides important grounds to experiment and share knowledge more intensively and quicker in an open manner (Heimstädt & Reischauer, 2018). Consider the example of the Catena-X Automotive Network, a collaboration for secure and standardized data exchange in the automotive industry, including sustainability measures, launched in Germany. Founding members of the network include carmakers, software firms, tech companies, and research organizations.

Finally, turning to the function of *transaction*, we consider the presence of sustainable platforms with a national or global scope a key enabler for the level of competitors and research organizations (Frenken et al., 2020). Consider the example of fairbnb, a European vacation rental platform that gives back part of its revenues to support the projects of local communities. Such a platform allows firms – and, as in the example of fairbnb, also individual actors – to offer one's modular and sustainable products and services to a wider audience. In principle, a firm may also consider launching its own platform where it also sells its modular and sustainable products and services, albeit that this comes with considerable costs and risk of becoming institutionalized (Frenken et al., 2020; Mair & Reischauer, 2017).

Institutional Actors

Turning to the level of institutional actors, we deem two enablers as important for all three functions alike, i.e., *(certified) measurement and information, motivation, and transaction.* The first enabler is standards to ensure data compatibility (Teece, 2018). While the reporting of how a single firm and/or its supply chain impacts the natural environment is already a complex endeavor (Nikolaou & Tsalis, 2013), the complexity increases when it comes to accumulating data from various firms from various industries to provide data on the overall impact of an industry or region. One way to address these challenges is standards, our case for data compatibility. While the integration of digital technologies in other activities of a firm is helpful so that this aspect becomes a high-level priority at single firms, efforts of institutional actors – especially legally mandated ones – seem particularly relevant to foster harmonization across competitors, research organizations, and intuitional actors.

A second important enabler at the level of institutional actors are policy mixes for deploying digital technologies. Specifically, policies that neither favor particular sustainable technologies nor specific actors are a key driver of creating the grounds where diverse actors can engage in experimentation and thereby instill and drive sustainability transitions (Etzion et al., 2017; Köhler et al., 2019). A telling example is the High Tech Strategy 2025 developed by the German government that focuses on how to leverage digital technologies to foster sustainability, amongst other things.

DISCUSSION AND CONCLUSION

This paper joins debates on multi-level actions to tackle climate change in two ways. First, by developing a multi-level framework of digital sustainability enablers, it showcases how a firm and its sustainability management can engage in climate actions at multiple levels. In doing so, we follow the call by Starik and Kanashiro (2020) to generate insights on multi-level sustainability management that has a more holistic view. Second, by assessing the potential of digital technologies for tackling climate change and identifying functions for sustainability management across digital technologies, we add to insights on which tools can be leveraged for multi-level climate action. With this angle, we follow the vision of a "climate-proof management research" to create insights for theory and practice that mitigate the worst effects of climate change (Daddi et al., 2018; Nyberg & Wright, 2022) and thereby provide insights on "which new digital technologies may help to speed up sustainability transitions" (Andersen et al., 2021, p. 3).

This chapter is not without limitations. All of our suggestions assume that organizations "walk the talk" and actually perform what is reported to stakeholders, thus that they are not engaging in greenwashing or "box-checking" and compliance to standards as opposed to focusing on outcomes (Patala et al., 2017; Wijen, 2014). Moreover, to provide a focused discussion, we limited our examples and thinking to ecological sustainability. However, given the interrelatedness of ecological sustainability with economic sustainability and social sustainability (Dyllick & Hockerts, 2002) and the growing societal impact of digital technologies

(Andersen et al., 2021), further inquiries are needed to detail the role of digital technologies in the management of these sustainability forms.

The climate change is one of the most pressing challenges of our times. By elaborating on how digital technologies can be leveraged to tackle this challenge as part of sustainability management, we hope to inform and inspire scholars and practitioners on the path towards a more sustainable future.

NOTE

1. This view on digital sustainability focuses on digital technologies as a means to an end (advancing sustainable goals of a firm more broadly) and thus is not solely focused on making digital technologies more sustainable (e.g., data centers powered by renewable energy).

REFERENCES

Acquier, A., Carbone, V., & Massé, D. (2019). How to create value(s) in the sharing economy: Business models, scalability, and sustainability. *Technology Innovation Management Review, 9*(2).

Andersen, A. D., Frenken, K., Galaz, V., Kern, F., Klerkx, L., Mouthaan, M., Piscicelli, L., Schor, J. B., & Vaskelainen, T. (2021). On digitalization and sustainability transitions. *Environmental Innovation and Societal Transitions, 41*, 96–98.

Bai, C. A., Cordeiro, J., & Sarkis, J. (2020). Blockchain technology: Business, strategy, the environment, and sustainability. *Business Strategy and the Environment, 29*(1), 321–322.

Ball, C., Burt, G., De Vries, F., & MacEachern, E. (2018). How environmental protection agencies can promote eco-innovation: The prospect of voluntary reciprocal legitimacy. *Technological Forecasting and Social Change, 129*, 242–253.

Bauer, P., Stevens, B., & Hazeleger, W. (2021). A digital twin of earth for the green transition. *Nature Climate Change, 11*(2), 80–83.

Berkowitz, H. (2018). Meta-organizing firms' capabilities for sustainable innovation: A conceptual framework. *Journal of Cleaner Production, 175*, 420–430.

Brown, J., & Hendry, C. (2009). Public demonstration projects and field trials: Accelerating commercialisation of sustainable technology in solar photovoltaics. *Energy Policy, 37*(7), 2560–2573.

Cennamo, C. (2021). Competing in digital markets: A platform-based perspective. *Academy of Management Perspectives, 35*(2), 265–291.

Crews, T. E., Carton, W., & Olsson, L. (2018). Is the future of agriculture perennial? Imperatives and opportunities to reinvent agriculture by shifting from annual monocultures to perennial polycultures. *Global Sustainability, 1*, e11, Article e11.

Daddi, T., Todaro, N. M., De Giacomo, M. R., & Frey, M. (2018). A systematic review of the use of organization and management theories in climate change studies. *Business Strategy and the Environment, 27*(4), 456–474.

Delmas, M. A., Lyon, T. P., & Maxwell, J. W. (2019). Understanding the role of the corporation in sustainability transitions. *Organization & Environment, 32*(2), 87–97.

Demirel, P., & Kesidou, E. (2019). Sustainability-oriented capabilities for eco-innovation: Meeting the regulatory, technology, and market demands. *Business Strategy and the Environment, 28*(5), 847–857.

Devine-Wright, P., Batel, S., Aas, O., Sovacool, B., Labelle, M. C., & Ruud, A. (2017). A conceptual framework for understanding the social acceptance of energy infrastructure: Insights from energy storage. *Energy Policy, 107*, 27–31.

Dyllick, T., & Hockerts, K. (2002). Beyond the business case for corporate sustainability. *Business Strategy and the Environment, 11*(2), 130–141.

Espinoza, M. I., & Aronczyk, M. (2021). Big data for climate action or climate action for big data? *Big Data & Society, 8*(1), 2053951720982032.

Etzion, D., & Aragon-Correa, J. A. (2016). Big data, management, and sustainability: Strategic opportunities ahead. *Organization & Environment, 29*(2), 147–155.

Etzion, D., Gehman, J., Ferraro, F., & Avidan, M. (2017). Unleashing sustainability transformations through robust action. *Journal of Cleaner Production, 140*, 167–178.

Frenken, K., & Fuenfschilling, L. (2020). The rise of online platforms and the triumph of the corporation. *Sociologica, 14*(3), 101–113.

Frenken, K., & Schor, J. (2017). Putting the sharing economy into perspective. *Environmental Innovation and Societal Transitions, 23*, 3–10.

Frenken, K., Vaskelainen, T., Fünfschilling, L., & Piscicelli, L. (2020). An institutional logics perspective on the gig economy. *Research in the Sociology of Organizations, 66*, 83–105.

Fuenfschilling, L. (2019). An institutional perspective on sustainability transitions. In F. Boons & A. McMeekin (Eds), *Handbook of Sustainable Innovation* (pp. 219–236). Edward Elgar Publishing.

Fuenfschilling, L., & Truffer, B. (2016). The interplay of institutions, actors and technologies in socio-technical systems: An analysis of transformations in the Australian urban water sector. *Technological Forecasting and Social Change, 103*, 298–312.

Fuenfschilling, L., Frantzeskaki, N., & Coenen, L. (2019). Urban experimentation & sustainability transitions. *European Planning Studies, 27*(2), 219–228.

Geels, F. W., Kern, F., Fuchs, G., Hinderer, N., Kungl, G., Mylan, J., Neukirch, M., & Wassermann, S. (2016). The enactment of socio-technical transition pathways: A reformulated typology and a comparative multi-level analysis of the German and UK low-carbon electricity transitions (1990–2014). *Research Policy, 45*(4), 896–913.

Gegenhuber, T., Schuessler, E., Reischauer, G., & Thäter, L. (2022). Building collective institutional infrastructures for decent platform work: The development of a crowdwork agreement in Germany. *Research in the Sociology of Organizations, 79*, 43–68.

George, G., & Schillebeeckx, S. J. D. (2021). Digital sustainability and its implications for finance and climate change. *Macroeconomic Review*, forthcoming.

George, G., Merrill, R. K., & Schillebeeckx, S. J. D. (2020). Digital sustainability and entrepreneurship: How digital innovations are helping tackle climate change and sustainable development. *Entrepreneurship Theory and Practice, 45*(5), 999–1027.

George, G., Schillebeeckx, S. J. D., & Liak, T. L. (2015). The management of natural resources: an overview and research agenda. *Academy of Management Journal, 58*(6), 1595–1613.

Günther, W. A., Rezazade Mehrizi, M. H., Huysman, M., & Feldberg, F. (2017). Debating big data: A literature review on realizing value from big data. *Journal of Strategic Information Systems, 26*(3), 191–209.

Heimstädt, M., & Reischauer, G. (2018). Open(ing up) for the future: Practising open strategy and open innovation to cope with uncertainty. In H. Krämer & M. Wenzel (Eds), *How Organizations Manage the Future: Theoretical Perspectives and Empirical Insights* (pp. 113–131). Springer.

Helfat, C. E., & Raubitschek, R. S. (2018). Dynamic and integrative capabilities for profiting from innovation in digital platform-based ecosystems. *Research Policy, 47*(8), 1391–1399.

Hess, D. J. (2018). Energy democracy and social movements: A multi-coalition perspective on the politics of sustainability transitions. *Energy Research & Social Science, 40*, 177–189.

Hoffmann, W. H., Knoll, T., & Wörner, R. (2019). The organizational design of the alliance management system: A contingency perspective. In F. J. Contractor & J. J. Reuer (Eds), *Frontiers of Strategic Alliance Research: Negotiating, Structuring and Governing Partnerships* (pp. 216–234). Cambridge University Press.

Hoppmann, J., Anadon, L. D., & Narayanamurti, V. (2020). Why matter matters: How technology characterics shape the strategic framing of technologies. *Research Policy, 49*(1), 103882.

Huang, P. (2019). The verticality of policy mixes for sustainability transitions: A case study of solar water heating in China. *Research Policy, 48*(10).

Hussain, M., & Malik, M. (2020). Organizational enablers for circular economy in the context of sustainable supply chain management. *Journal of Cleaner Production, 256*, 120375.

Köhler, J., Geels, F. W., Kern, F., Markard, J., Onsongo, E., Wieczorek, A., Alkemade, F., Avelino, F., Bergek, A., Boons, F., Fünfschilling, L., Hess, D., Holtz, G., Hyysalo, S., Jenkins, K., Kivimaa, P., Martiskainen, M., McMeekin, A., Mühlemeier, M. S., Nykvist, B., Pel, B., Raven, R., Rohracher, H., Sandén, B., Schot, J., Sovacool, B., Turnheim, B., Welch, D., & Wells, P. (2019). An agenda for sustainability transitions research: State of the art and future directions. *Environmental Innovation and Societal Transitions, 31*, 1–32.

Kulathinal, R., Yoo, Y., & Kumar, S. (2020). The bits and bytes of biology: Digitalization fuels an emerging generative platform for biological innovation. In S. Nambisan, K. Lyytinen, & Y. Yoo (Eds), *Handbook of Digital Innovation* (pp. 253–265). Edward Elgar Publishing.

Landeta-Manzano, B., Arana-Landín, G., Calvo, P. M., & Heras-Saizarbitoria, I. (2018). Wind energy and local communities: A manufacturer's efforts to gain acceptance. *Energy Policy, 121*, 314–324.

Lember, V., Brandsen, T., & Tõnurist, P. (2019). The potential impacts of digital technologies on co-production and co-creation. *Public Management Review, 21*(11), 1665–1686.

Lidgren, A., Rodhe, H., & Huisingh, D. (2006). A systemic approach to incorporate sustainability into university courses and curricula. *Journal of Cleaner Production, 14*(9), 797–809.

Lozano, R. (2006). Incorporation and institutionalization of SD into universities: Breaking through barriers to change. *Journal of Cleaner Production, 14*(9), 787–796.

Mair, J., & Reischauer, G. (2017). Capturing the dynamics of the sharing economy: Institutional research on the plural forms and practices of sharing economy organizations. *Technological Forecasting and Social Change, 125*, 11–20.

Majchrzak, A., & Malhotra, A. (2020). *Unleashing the Crowd: Collaborative Solutions to Wicked Business and Societal Problems*. Palgrave Macmillan.

Manning, S., & Reinecke, J. (2016). A modular governance architecture in-the-making: How transnational standard-setters govern sustainability transitions. *Research Policy, 45*(3), 618–633.

Manzhynski, S., & Figge, F. (2020). Coopetition for sustainability: Between organizational benefit and societal good. *Business Strategy and the Environment, 29*(3), 827–837.

Mokhtari, R., & Arabkoohsar, A. (2021). Feasibility study and multi-objective optimization of seawater cooling systems for data centers: A case study of Caspian Sea. *Sustainable Energy Technologies and Assessments, 47*, 101528.

Nikolaou, I. E., & Tsalis, T. A. (2013). Development of a sustainable balanced scorecard framework. *Ecological Indicators, 34*, 76–86.

Nyberg, D., & Wright, C. (2022). Climate-proofing management research. *Academy of Management Perspectives, 36*(2), 713–728.

Patala, S., Korpivaara, I., Jalkala, A., Kuitunen, A., & Soppe, B. (2017). Legitimacy under institutional change: How incumbents appropriate clean rhetoric for dirty technologies. *Organization Studies*, 0170840617736938.

Paudel, D., Boogaard, H., de Wit, A., Janssen, S., Osinga, S., Pylianidis, C., & Athanasiadis, I. N. (2021). Machine learning for large-scale crop yield forecasting. *Agricultural Systems, 187*, 103016.

Porter, A. J., Tuertscher, P., & Huysman, M. (2020). Saving our oceans: Scaling the impact of robust action through crowdsourcing. *Journal of Management Studies, 57*(2), 246–286.

Reischauer, G. (2017). Geschichten, die Märkte für Erneuerbare Energien verändern: Ein relationaler Analyseansatz. In S. Giacovelli (Ed.), *Die Energiewende aus wirtschaftssoziologischer Sicht: Theoretische Konzepte und empirische Zugänge* (pp. 65–92). Springer VS.

Reischauer, G. (2018). Industry 4.0 as policy-driven discourse to institutionalize innovation systems in manufacturing. *Technological Forecasting & Social Change, 132*, 26–33.

Reischauer, G., & Mair, J. (2018). Platform organizing in the new digital economy: Revisiting online communities and strategic responses. *Research in the Sociology of Organizations, 57*, 113–135.

Reischauer, G., Güttel, W., & Schüßler, E. (2021). Aligning the design of intermediary organisations with the ecosystem. *Industry and Innovation, 28*(5), 594–619.

Rijswijk, K., Klerkx, L., Bacco, M., Bartolini, F., Bulten, E., Debruyne, L., Dessein, J., Scotti, I., & Brunori, G. (2021). Digital transformation of agriculture and rural areas: A socio-cyber-physical system framework to support responsibilisation. *Journal of Rural Studies, 85*, 79–90.

Sailer, M., Hense, J. U., Mayr, S. K., & Mandl, H. (2017). How gamification motivates: An experimental study of the effects of specific game design elements on psychological need satisfaction. *Computers in Human Behavior, 69*, 371–380.

Santarius, T., & Soland, M. (2018). How technological efficiency improvements change consumer preferences: Towards a psychological theory of rebound effects. *Ecological Economics, 146*, 414–424.

Schaltegger, S., Burritt, R., & Petersen, H. (2003). *An Introduction to Corporate Environmental Management: Striving for Sustainability*. Greenleaf.

Schüßler, E., Rüling, C.-C., & Wittneben, B. B. F. (2014). On melting summits: The limitations of field-configuring events as catalysts of change in transnational climate policy. *Academy of Management Journal, 57*(1), 140–171.

Starik, M., & Kanashiro, P. (2013). Toward a theory of sustainability management: Uncovering and integrating the nearly obvious. *Organization & Environment, 26*(1), 7–30.

Starik, M., & Kanashiro, P. (2020). Advancing a multi-level sustainability management theory. In D. M. Wasieleski & J. Weber (Eds), *Sustainability* (Vol. 4, pp. 17–42). Emerald.

Tee, R., Davies, A., & Whyte, J. (2019). Modular designs and integrating practices: Managing collaboration through coordination and cooperation. *Research Policy, 48*(1), 51–61.

Teece, D. J. (2018). Profiting from innovation in the digital economy: Enabling technologies, standards, and licensing models in the wireless world. *Research Policy, 47*(8), 1367–1387.

Upadhyay, A., Mukhuty, S., Kumar, V., & Kazancoglu, Y. (2021). Blockchain technology and the circular economy: Implications for sustainability and social responsibility. *Journal of Cleaner Production, 293*, 126130.

Valente, M., & Oliver, C. (2018). Meta-organization formation and sustainability in Sub-Saharan Africa. *Organization Science, 29*(4), 678–701.

Vernay, A.-L., & Sebi, C. (2020). Energy communities and their ecosystems: A comparison of France and the Netherlands. *Technological Forecasting and Social Change, 158*, 120123.

Vinuesa, R., Azizpour, H., Leite, I., Balaam, M., Dignum, V., Domisch, S., Felländer, A., Langhans, S. D., Tegmark, M., & Fuso Nerini, F. (2020). The role of artificial intelligence in achieving the sustainable development goals. *Nature Communications, 11*(1), 233.

Warner, K. S. R., & Wäger, M. (2019). Building dynamic capabilities for digital transformation: An ongoing process of strategic renewal. *Long Range Planning, 52*(3), 326–349.

Wijen, F. (2014). Means versus ends in opaque institutional fields: Trading off compliance and achievement in sustainability standard adoption. *Academy of Management Review, 39*(3), 302–323.

Zeiss, R., Ixmeier, A., Recker, J., & Kranz, J. (2021). Mobilising information systems scholarship for a circular economy: Review, synthesis, and directions for future research. *Information Systems Journal, 31*(1), 148–183.

PART III

MULTI-LEVEL CLIMATE ACTION PLACE AND PACE

11. Learning from city-level climate action planning

Bruce Paton

Climate action planning at the city level is one of the most immediate and powerful methods for responding to global climate change. Climate action by cities illustrates the potential for effective action at multiple levels in order to stop and reverse climate change.

This chapter focuses on learning from Sunnyvale, California, a medium-sized city in Silicon Valley. The insights are informed by the author's experience helping to shape the city's first and second climate action plan. It also draws on studies of climate action plans from leading US and European cities to put this city in context.

CITIES AS A FOCAL POINT FOR CLIMATE ACTION

In the absence of political consensus and policy action at the national level, climate action by cities has been a focal point for optimism and action in recent years (Hultman and Calhoun, 2018). In the absence of substantive progress by national governments cities have taken action to address the climate factors under their control.

Copenhagen, Denmark, for example, has set a goal to be the world's first carbon neutral city by 2025 (Copenhagen, 2020). Copenhagen has set aggressive goals for reduced carbon emissions from energy production and consumption, mobility, and city government operations. The city has also committed to aggressive retrofitting of existing oil-heated buildings.

Similarly, Stockholm, Sweden, has committed to a plan for a "fossil-free and climate positive" city by 2040 (Stockholms Stad, 2020). The city government has also committed to be "a fossil free organization by 2030". The city has set 2023 goals for reduced energy consumption, reduced greenhouse gas emissions from city operations, and a per capita limit on greenhouse gas emissions.

In the United States, a wide range of cities have adopted climate action plans. More than 600 cities have adopted climate action plans, including all of the ten largest cities (Markolf et al., 2018; Zero Energy Project, 2020). Roughly 127 million people, about 40% of the US population, live in cities with 50,000 or more residents. Only ten cities have populations above 1 million, but 310 cities are considered at least medium-sized cities, with populations of 100,000 or more. The large number of cities in the US contributes to both the opportunity for impact on climate change, and the complexity of mobilizing each city separately to act on its own challenges and opportunities.

New York City, the largest US city has adopted the OneNYC 2050 plan, committing to a "green new deal" (City of New York, 2019). The plan commits to creating sustainable transportation options "so that no New Yorker needs to rely on a car" (City of New York, 2022). The plan commits to 100% clean electricity by 2040, along with a wide range of other goals focused on building an inclusive economy, healthier lives, and equity and excellence in education.

In the state of California, more than 100 cities have adopted Climate Action Plans, in response to a state mandate. Los Angeles, California, has committed to 100% renewable energy by 2045, and committed to its own "Green New Deal" (City of Los Angeles, 2019). The plan focuses on 100% renewable energy by 2045, sustainable mobility, clean and healthy buildings, and specific targets for energy reduction in buildings.

San Jose, California, the tenth largest US city, has committed to becoming the "greenest city in the U.S.". The city has adopted a plan based on three pillars: (1) a sustainable and climate smart city; (2) a vibrant city of connected and focused growth; and (3) an economically inclusive city of opportunity. The city's plan includes nine strategies based on these three pillars focusing on land use, mobility, renewable energy, and efficient and affordable homes.

Despite the active engagement of many of the largest cities, State and Federal action on climate has lagged. As a direct and swift response to the US government's 2016 decision to withdraw from the Paris Agreement, former New York City Mayor Michael R. Bloomberg and then California Governor Jerry Brown, launched America's Pledge, an initiative to promote climate action leadership by US governors, mayors, and business leaders (Hultman and Calhoun, 2018).

The first report from this initiative estimated that actors representing more than half the US economy were actively engaged in fulfilling the Paris Agreement and had demonstrated their potential to drive decarbonization swiftly and effectively. The report presented a roadmap for ten Climate Action Strategies that are readily available for implementation by cities, states, businesses, and other actors. Table 11.1 shows the ten strategies cited in the report.

Table 11.1   Climate action strategies from the Bloomberg study (Hultman and Calhoun, 2018)

1. Double down on renewable energy targets
2. Accelerate the retirement of coal power
3. Encourage residential and commercial building efficiency retrofits
4. Electrify building energy use
5. Accelerate electric vehicle (EV) adoption
6. Phase down super-polluting hydrofluorocarbons (HFCs)
7. Stop methane leaks at the wellhead
8. Reduce methane leaks in cities
9. Develop regional strategies for carbon sequestration on natural and working lands
10. Form state coalitions for carbon pricing

Of the ten strategies identified in the study, at least five appear to be applicable for adoption at the city level. These include:

- #1: Double down on renewable energy targets
- #3: Encourage residential and commercial building efficiency retrofits
- #4: Electrify building energy use
- #5: Accelerate electric vehicle (EV) adoption
- #8: Reduce methane leaks in cities

The Bloomberg study (Hultman and Calhoun, 2018) concluded that current efforts by states, cities and businesses "are yielding significant results". These included 2017 GHG emissions rates at their lowest level in 25 years, and additions to renewable capacity sufficient to power 3 million homes. The report went on to identify a wide range of future actions to "go well beyond decarbonization commitments currently on the books". Many of the recommended actions are reflected in the city actions described later in this chapter.

More recent assessments of progress have reached less optimistic conclusions. A Brookings study (Markolf et al., 2018) raised questions about the efficacy of city pledges to reduce GHG emissions. The study asked:

> Are they working in the absence of binding national regulations? What kind of results are emerging? How far can city action go without bigger efforts at other levels, including federal?

The Brookings study also raised concerns about the effect of emissions from goods and services used by cities that the cities do not have control over. For example, emissions related to basic goods such as food or office supplies produced outside the city but consumed in the city would be outside the scope of current climate action plans.

The Brookings study's largest concern was that the plans currently in place will not be sufficient to limit warming to 1.5°C. This concern reflects two issues.

First, many cities have not yet prepared climate action plans. The study noted that "of the 100 most populous cities in the United States, only 45 have established greenhouse gas reduction targets and corresponding baseline GHG inventories". The study noted that the 45 large cities with climate action plans house roughly 40 million people (about 12% of the total US population). The study does add that over 600 local governments in the United States have developed Climate Action Plans that include emissions reduction targets and GHG inventories.

A second concern was that as of 2019, about two-thirds of cities (in the study of the 100 largest cities) were currently lagging their targeted emission levels. The report noted that, except in California, reduction targets set by cities are typically non-binding.

The 2021 Edition of the California Green Innovation Index (Next 10, 2021) expresses similar concerns. The Index warns that while California's economy is the greenest in the US, the state is not on track to meet its emissions reduction goals for 2030. The index reports that from 2018–2019, California reduced its GHG emissions by 1.6%. The study estimated that California would have to reduce emissions by 4.1% per year from 2019–2030 to achieve the 2050 goal of 50% reductions statewide against the baseline year.

The index did report progress on two key measures of transportation impact on GHGs. Both the total number of vehicles and the vehicle miles travelled decreased in 2019, and reduced further during 2020, the first year of the pandemic.

The index also documented a concern not typically addressed in city-level climate action plans. In 2020, wildfires became the second largest source of GHGs in California, behind only transportation. This trend indicates the growing connection between climate mitigation issues and climate adaptation concerns.

Together, these studies illustrate the range of opinions and evidence concerning the role of cities in addressing climate change. While the potential for leadership by cities is very strong, the absence of coordination at the Federal government level and the uneven adoption and implementation of climate action plans have limited the impact so far.

THE CALIFORNIA CONTEXT: SETTING THE STAGE FOR CITY LEVEL ACTION

The State of California has been active in responding to climate change for more than a decade. In 2006, the state legislature passed AB 32, one of the first state level programs to control greenhouse gas emissions and to address the effects of climate change. The bill set in motion creation of the state's cap and trade program for emissions and called for extensive coordination among state agencies to reduce emissions.

California developed an initial scoping plan to address climate change in 2008, followed by updates in 2013 and 2017. The 2017 plan calls for a 40% reduction in GHG emissions statewide by 2030 and an 80% reduction by 2050 (State of California, 2017). One significant requirement tied access to state grant funds for each city to adoption of a climate action plan.

Another action at the state level that has had significant impact on cities was the adoption of enabling legislation for Community Choice Aggregation (CCA) programs. CCAs are programs that take over decisions about the mix of electricity sources from the utilities that provide energy. A CCA purchases energy from the marketplace to meet local demands for clean energy. Typically, a CCA will offer a baseline option that offers a greener power mix than the local utility, but at a price comparable to the utility's rate. Many CCAs offer a 100% renewable (or at least non-fossil fuel) option at a price premium. At least ten US States have created enabling legislation for Community Choice Aggregation programs and at least seven more are considering adoption of similar programs (Lean Energy US, 2022).

Although California was not the first state to adopt CCAs, it has by far the most active programs as of 2022. More than 200 communities and more than 11 million customers in California are served by CCAs (Cal CCA, 2022). Table 11.2 illustrates the range of programs currently in place in California.

CLIMATE ACTION PLANNING IN SUNNYVALE, CALIFORNIA

The experience to date of Sunnyvale, California, in addressing climate change illustrates both the opportunities and challenges at the city level. Sunnyvale is considered a mid-sized city with a population of approximately 155,000 people. As of 2022, it is the 178th largest city in the US. Home to a wide range of computer and technology companies, Sunnyvale refers to itself as "the heart of Silicon Valley". The city sprang from a sleepy orchard community in the early 1960s to a sprawling hybrid of suburb and small city.

In response to a voluntary public–private initiative led by Sustainable Silicon Valley, Sunnyvale commissioned its first Greenhouse Gas (GHG) Inventory for city operations in 2007 (Melhus and Paton, 2012; Seto, 2008). The inventory documented that the energy-efficiency efforts of city operations had already reduced GHG emissions by 19% from the baseline. Based on the inventory, the City Council approved a target to reduce emissions by 20% below 1990 levels by 2010.

Led by an environmentally conscious mayor, the city created a Sustainability Commission in 2010. Among the charges for the new commission was the challenge to chart a path to address climate change for the city as a whole. Building on the work of a citizen working group chartered by the city, the Sustainability Commission recommended, and the City Council approved, the city's first Climate Action Plan in 2014 (City of Sunnyvale, Climate

Table 11.2   *California community choice aggregation programs*

CCA	Launched	Number of member cities and counties
Apple Valley Choice Energy	2017	1
Baldwin Park Resident Owned Utility District	2020	1
Butte Choice Energy	2021	2
Central Coast Community Energy	2018	26
CleanPowerSF	2016	1
Clean Energy Alliance	2021	3
Clean Power Alliance	2019	31
Desert Community Energy	2020	1
East Bay Community Energy	2018	12
King City Community Power	2018	1
Lancaster Choice Energy	2015	1
MCE	2010	34
Peninsula Clean Energy	2016	21
Pico Rivera Innovative Municipal Energy	2017	1
Pioneer Community Energy	2018	6
Pomona Choice Energy	2020	1
Rancho Mirage Energy Authority	2018	1
Redwood Coast Energy Authority	2017	8
San Diego Community Power	2021	5
San Jacinto Power	2018	1
San Jose Clean Energy	2019	1
Silicon Valley Clean Energy	2017	13
Solana Energy Alliance	2018	1
Sonoma Clean Power	2014	13
Valley Clean Energy	2018	3
Western Community Energy	2020	7

Action Plan, 2014). (The plan subsequently became known as CAP 1.0.) CAP 1.0 included an extensive list of action items for the city to address, ranging from installing LED street lights to transitioning the city's fleet of vehicles to electric vehicles as time and budget permitted.

One key recommendation of the first plan was creation of a Community Choice Aggregation (CCA) organization to take over decisions about the mix of electricity sources from the investor-owned utility, Pacific Gas & Electric (PG&E).

The second plan, called the Climate Action Playbook (City of Sunnyvale, CA, 2019a), defined a path to climate neutrality by 2050, with aggressive intermediate goals to reduce 2030 emissions by 54%. The second plan provided a much simpler framework to understand and communicate focused on six broad strategies, as shown in Table 11.3. These strategies align with four of the strategies in the Bloomberg study (renewable energy, building efficiency retrofits, electrifying buildings, accelerating EV adoption). In addition, they address a number of factors not highlighted in the Bloomberg study, such as resource efficiency.

The city's Climate Action Playbook addresses GHG emissions directly through four of these strategies – Promoting Clean Energy, Decarbonizing Buildings, Decarbonizing Transportation, and Managing Resources Sustainably. Dealing with these four categories varies significantly in the degree of complexity in both policy action and individual and organizational behavior change required.

Table 11.3   *Sunnyvale Climate Action Playbook strategies*

1.	Promoting clean energy
2.	Decarbonizing buildings
3.	Decarbonizing transportation – sustainable land use
4.	Managing resources sustainably
5.	Empowering our community
6.	Adapting to a changing climate

1. Promoting Clean Energy

The earliest major victory for the city focused on cleaning the source of electricity. The initial climate action plan called for creation of a CCA organization. Several council members worked with their counterparts in surrounding cities to build support for creating a regional CCA organization.

This enabled the city and its neighbors to shift electricity purchases from the investor-owned utility company producing natural gas and fossil fuel-powered electricity, to purchasing non-fossil fuel-powered electricity from a marketplace of producers. This change allowed the city to cut GHG emissions by nearly 25% in the first few years of the first climate action plan.

Silicon Valley Clean Energy (SVCE) was created in 2016, when 12 communities in Santa Clara County formed the Silicon Valley Clean Energy Authority. SVCE currently represents 13 cities in Santa Clara County (Silicon Valley Clean Energy, 2022). (San Jose, the largest city in the county chose to create its own CCA.) The enabling legislation for SVCE included a crucial provision that has contributed significantly to its success. Customers in the participating cities were automatically moved from the investor-owned utility, unless they specifically opted out. More than 97% of customers chose to remain in SVCE instead of opting to return to PG&E.

SVCE purchases power from independent operators and does not own any electricity production capacity of its own. In contrast to investor-owned utilities, SVCE does not have direct responsibility for amortizing the costs of large scale power plants and does not bear the risk of managing stranded assets. This structure provides them with considerable independence to purchase an electricity mix that can respond to declining costs of renewable energy production.

SVCE currently offers retail customers two broad options. All customers are automatically enrolled in the GreenStart program with electricity generated from "renewable sources such as wind, solar and carbon-free resources". SVCE describes this program as "carbon free, 50% renewable". This designation reflects the fact that this plan does include hydroelectricity, which is not considered renewable. SVCE has been able to offer energy in this plan at rates just below what customers would pay if they had stayed with the investor-owned utility.

Customers also have the option to opt in to the Green Prime program, which SVCE describes as "carbon free, 100% renewable". This portfolio, which includes wind, solar and geothermal energy and renewable energy purchased from the western grid, is available for a premium less than 1 cent per kilowatt hour (or about $5 per month per household) above the rate to purchase from the investor owned utility). PG&E continues to deliver electricity over existing power lines for SVCE and continues to manage billing for all customers in the city.

SVCE has become a major partner for participating cities and end customers. SVCE has become a major promoter of energy efficiency measures and administers programs to promote efficiencies that affect the next two priorities addressed in this chapter.

2. Decarbonizing Buildings

Emissions from buildings will be a long-term challenge in the battle to stop and then reverse climate change. A major recent victory was passage of a city "reach code" which required all new residential, commercial, and industrial building after January 1, 2021 to be all-electric. SVCE contributed significantly by developing and promoting a model city ordnance to enable reach codes. All but one of the cities participating in SVCE opted to adopt its own reach code. Significantly, the reach code passed in Sunnyvale with strong public support, and very little resistance from the building construction industry.

The city also chose to set an example in its new Civic Center building, which is currently under construction. When completed, the building will be LEED Platinum Certified, zero net energy and, in the city's estimation, the greenest city hall in the United States (Bourne, 2019). Figure 11.1 shows architects' rendering of the final building design.

Source: City of Sunnyvale, CA (2019b).

Figure 11.1   Sunnyvale, California's City Hall (under construction)

A more daunting challenge will be retrofitting existing buildings. A recent review of climate actions in the Silicon Valley region revealed that none of the cities had a plan to help existing buildings transition to all-electric operation. Hawken (2017, 2021) highlights the necessity to transition existing buildings and appliances from fossil fuels.

Griffith (2021) argues that the US will need to retire one fossil fuel-powered appliance or vehicle every second for the next 20 years to meet the goal of being effectively climate neutral by 2050. Neither Sunnyvale nor any of the cities in Santa Clara County currently has a concrete plan or stated intention to replace all existing fossil fuel-powered appliances in any time frame.

3. Decarbonizing Transportation – Sustainable Land Use

Following adoption of the CCA described above, and the resulting emissions reductions, transportation now accounts for 54% of direct emissions from the city. The second climate action plan includes a target to reduce vehicle miles travelled by 20% by 2030 and by 25% by 2050. The current plan includes broad strategies for achieving the goals, but nothing that could be described as a plan.

The city has participated in both educational and incentive programs to promote adoption of electric vehicles. The city has also taken steps to increase the supply of EV chargers. In particular, the "reach code" described above included requirements for new multifamily residential buildings and new commercial buildings to meet specific requirements to supply vehicle chargers.

However, the city's policy framework has no effective strategy to address the underlying problem of traffic congestion. Sunnyvale is one of many centers of employment and one of many residential centers in Silicon Valley. The entire region has been one of the most productive economies in the world, and as a result, has been a major net producer of jobs. Throughout the region, however, production of housing has not kept pace. The results have included high cost of housing, crowded highways, and major traffic delays.

Public discussion of the transportation goals in Sunnyvale has emphasized that city-level action will not be sufficient to achieve the goals. Because part of Silicon Valley lies on the San Francisco Peninsula, population growth has not been able to spread equally in all directions. The result has been a complex mosaic, characterized by a patchwork of low density, single family housing (a legacy of the rapid growth in the 1960s) along with growing numbers of multi-family housing units within the city.

However, the supply of jobs within Sunnyvale is much greater than the residential capacity. As a result, the Sunnyvale workforce commutes into the city from cities as far North as San Francisco, as far South as Gilroy (approximately a 1 hour drive from the South), from Santa Cruz county (on the Pacific Coast to the West) and to a very large and sprawling area to the East, referred to broadly as the East Bay. Figure 11.2 shows Silicon Valley and surrounding regions where Silicon Valley commutes begin or end.

The complexity of the problem is amplified by the structure of public transportation, which primarily serves North–South commuters, but does little to address East–West commutes. Addressing the needs of North–South travelers will require a focus on first-mile and last-mile solutions, increasing the convenience of commuting by public transportation. Solutions for East–West commuters will be more expensive, complex and time consuming to implement.

The past few years have brought growing recognition that the "transportation" problem is massively influenced by the limited supply of affordable housing. City officials acknowledge that addressing the transportation and housing challenges will require city action and effective coordination at the regional level.

While the city has a number of planning processes that affect transportation issues indirectly, there is currently no city department with responsibility or authority to plan for or address the underlying transportation problems. City level discussions on transportation currently default to two major modes. The city's Bicycle and Pedestrian Advisory Commission (BPAC) is responsible for advising the City Council on development of bicycle and other active transportation issues. The city's Planning Commission is responsible for decisions affecting traffic

Source: Wine and Vine Research (2022).

Figure 11.2   Silicon Valley and adjacent commuter destinations

congestion at specific intersections, and under new state rules for evaluating land use decisions for their impact on vehicle miles travelled.

There is no part of the city government with explicit or implicit responsibility for developing or administering any form of plan to address the city's part of the region's broad transportation problems. With no one in charge, it is difficult to envision a scenario that will effectively reduce the GHG emissions from the transportation needs resulting from the region's commuting patterns.

4. Managing Resources Sustainably

City action to reduce emissions from resource consumption has focused on recycling and waste diversion. In recent years, the city's solid waste programs have experienced significant challenges as the stream of plastic waste has seen modest increases, but the capacity to recycle materials (and recapture economic value) has plummeted. As a result, the city has a legal mandate to reach 90% diversion of waste from landfills by 2030, but no feasible path to achieve that goal.

One successful resource management program requires city residents to separate food scraps from other solid waste. The program significantly reduces landfill methane emissions caused by decomposition of organic wastes.

The challenges in achieving the waste reduction goals include two major issues. First, real progress to reduce plastic waste will require some combination of city level and state-level policy action. Second, the cities' Climate Action Plans focus on scope one and two emissions, masks the significant impact of scope three (indirect) emissions on the true climate impact of a city.

PROMOTING CITIZEN AND INDUSTRY ACTION

The progress demonstrated in Sunnyvale also illustrates the role of private citizens, technology companies, and commercial construction companies in accelerating change. Private citizens have acted in coordination to (1) demonstrate the feasibility of reducing household level emissions and (2) orchestrate public support for climate action. The city has also been heavily influenced by the presence of technology industry and construction industry leaders that have developed momentum for climate action.

Both private citizens and industry have helped accelerate climate action in the city. First, local households have demonstrated either partial or complete electrification of their homes and commutes. At the same time, local environmental groups have been effective at mobilizing citizens to support climate actions.

Technology companies and construction companies doing business in the city have also had significant impacts on the pace of progress toward climate neutrality. Construction of multiple LEED Platinum buildings and zero-net energy buildings has demonstrated the market attractiveness of energy efficient buildings, and neutralized resistance to more stringent building requirements.

DISCUSSION AND CONCLUSIONS

The experience of Sunnyvale illustrates both the strengths and limitations of city-level climate action planning. Table 11.4 highlights key effects from implementation of the Climate Action Plans. Acting on its own and in cooperation with neighboring cities, the city has been able to chart a path to climate neutrality by 2050 and make significant progress toward that goal. Leadership from households and businesses has demonstrated the feasibility of accelerated action to address climate change.

Table 11.4   Implementation of key Climate Action Plan strategies

Strategy	Milestones/impact
1. Promoting clean energy	Adoption of the CCA led to 98+% adoption. Reduced GHGs by nearly 25% in one year.
2. Decarbonizing buildings	Passed reach code requiring new construction to be all electric, beginning in 2021.
3. Decarbonizing transportation – sustainable land use	Active encouragement of EV purchases. Efforts to increase supply of chargers including in new multi-family residential buildings. Limited progress on strategies to reduce vehicle miles travelled.
4. Managing resources sustainably	Creation of food waste diversion program.

Implementation of the Climate Action Playbook and the Climate Action Plan that preceded it has led to steady progress toward the goal of 56% GHG reductions by 2030. The city reported 44% reduction versus the 1990 baseline as of 2020, and fully expects to meet the 56% reduction goal (City of Sunnyvale, Climate Action Scoreboard, 2022).

At the same time, the process has illuminated the need for more effective institutions to address problems that cross city boundaries. For example, transportation issues cannot be addressed effectively by a single city in the context of Silicon Valley because typical commutes do not begin and end in the same city. Unlike many other urban regions, commute patterns do not funnel traffic to a single large city center.

At a more complex level, Silicon Valley, like many other parts of California continues to develop a severe imbalance between the number of jobs created by a prosperous local economy and the supply of housing (both market rate and below-market rate) (Joint Venture Silicon Valley, 2022). Cites will not be able to address the GHG emissions from transportation until the region collectively addresses this jobs/housing imbalance.

The experience in Sunnyvale also illustrates the potential for more rapid change, if more effective action and a greater sense of urgency were evident at the state and Federal level. This city and others like it have accomplished considerable reductions in GHG emissions in the absence of Federal or state public policies that specifically limit emissions or provide direct economic incentives to do so. Table 11.5 summarizes key factors that have enabled or inhibited progress on climate action plan implementation.

The concerns expressed at the beginning of this study underline the urgency of acting at multiple levels. While many cities, including the one highlighted in this study have achieved impressive reductions, achieving the ambitious goals set for 2030 and 2050 will require more extensive coordination across levels of government and more effective cooperation among the sectors.

Table 11.5   Enablers and inhibitors of Climate Action Plan implementation

Strategy	Enablers	Inhibitors
1. Promoting clean energy	State-level enabling legislation for CCAs. Active engagement from city council.	Utility lobbying at state legislature to weaken CCA provisions.
2. Decarbonizing buildings	Stringent state building codes. Support from real estate industry for greener standards. Expertise and technical assistance provided by the CCA.	Lack of funds or incentives to retrofit existing buildings. Limited public knowledge of building retrofit options.
3. Decarbonizing transportation – sustainable land use	City Council, Planning Commission and city staff very supportive of green building requirements. Real Estate companies and local industries committed to green buildings.	Lack of accurate information about commute patterns. Fiscal pressures that emphasize job creation over creation of housing. Pandemic-related budget cuts delayed hiring of staff to focus on transportation.
4. Managing resources sustainably	Effective cooperation with waste management company to collect and sort materials.	Lack of recycling infrastructure.

Cities *have* accomplished significant reductions in greenhouse gas emissions, even with the absence of leadership at the Federal level. Progress has been particularly significant in greening the electricity supply, and in moving the great majority of new building construction to all-electric. But cities are not well equipped to address several key challenges. Table 11.6 highlights five key challenges.

Table 11.6   Key challenges in implementing climate action

Challenge	Need from other levels
Retrofitting existing buildings	Incentives to encourage residential commercial and industrial owners to retrofit.
Transportation (adoption of EVs)	Continuing incentives to promote adoption of EVs. Innovation by vehicle companies to make EVs affordable.
Transportation (reduction in vehicle miles travelled)	Cities lack the authority and resources to control vehicle miles travelled.
Resource consumption (recycling)	Increased recycling capacity. State or Federal limitations on the use of plastics.
Resource consumption (purchasing)	Leadership from private sector as well as state and Federal governments to influence city procurement policies.

First, the existing building stock will need to be retrofitted to eliminate natural gas appliances and inefficient electric appliances by 2040 in order to meet the 2050 GHG emissions goals. While a patchwork of incentives is in place to replace some existing appliances, such as refrigerators, few programs are currently in place to address the largest consumers of household fossil fuel consumption, such as water heaters, kitchen stoves and building heating and ventilation.

Second, cities in Silicon Valley have made individual efforts to encourage the adoption of EVs and to promote wider availability to chargers. The high price of EVs currently has limited the access of poor and middle-income families to EVs, continuing a wide range of equity issues. Continuation and expansion of existing incentives, along with private sector innovations will be needed to accelerate adoption of EVs.

Third, cities do not have structures or plans to address the underlying causes of transportation-related emissions. While a variety of regional coordination mechanisms exist, and capital-intensive mass transit projects are underway to address parts of the problems, neither specific cities nor the region as a whole have plausible plans to reduce vehicle miles travelled, which are responsible for transportation-related GHG emissions.

Fourth, a number of resource consumption issues fall outside the scope of existing city level climate planning efforts. For example, a number of cities, have recognized the significant climate impact from the production and use of plastic. Cities in the region, including Sunnyvale have implemented single use plastic bans, but they have largely focused on restaurants. Cities have neither the authority nor the market clout to influence major food production companies and other large-scale users of plastics to force significant reductions in the use of plastics.

Finally, cities are major consumers of vehicles, supplies and services. None of the cities in Silicon Valley currently has active programs to monitor and manage the climate impact from those purchases. In Silicon Valley, the potential for industry to chart a path for governments to follow on this issue is very high. Several Silicon Valley companies have significant programs in place to manage the sustainability of their supply chains. Governments at the city, county and state level can learn quite a bit from those efforts.

In summary, cities have been major innovators in the process of addressing climate change. As the US population continues to migrate to cities, cities will become increasingly important as a focal point for action to address climate change. The experience of one mid-sized city in Silicon Valley illustrates both the potential for cities to lead and the role that effective state and regional leadership can play in facilitating those efforts. It also illustrates the critical role that both industry and private citizens can play in promoting collective action at the city level.

At the same time, the major challenges that remain to be addressed underscore the critical need for effective cooperation among local, regional, state and Federal policymakers, and the enormous opportunity for more rapid and effective action if we have significant cooperation across multiple levels of public and private action.

REFERENCES

Bourne, J. (2019). Sunnyvale Civic Center moves forward. *The Silicon Valley Voice*, November 26, 2019. https://www.svvoice.com/sunnyvale-civic-center-moves-forward/ (accessed December 17, 2022).

Cal CCA (2022). Resources. https://cal-cca.org/resources/ (accessed December 17, 2022).

City of Los Angeles (2019). L.A.'s Green New Deal – Sustainable City Plan 2019, City of Los Angeles. Los Angeles, CA. https://plan.lamayor.org/sites/default/files/pLAn_2019_final.pdf (accessed December 17, 2022).

City of New York (2019). OneNYC – 2050 – Building a Strong and Fair City, Volume 1, April 2019. New York, NY: City of New York. https://onenyc.cityofnewyork.us/strategies/onenyc-2050/ (accessed December 17, 2022).

City of Sunnyvale, Climate Action Plan (2014). https://sunnyvale.ca.gov/civicax/filebank/blobdload.aspx?blobid=23736

City of Sunnyvale, CA (2019a). Climate Action Playbook. https://sunnyvaleclimateaction.org/playbook

City of Sunnyvale, CA (2019b). View of New Civic Center from Olive Avenue, [Photograph] from "Phase 1 Nears Construction", Sunnyvale, California, Horizon, Fall 2019, p. 3. https://www.sunnyvale.ca.gov/home/showpublisheddocument/192/637812511293270000

City of Sunnyvale, Climate Action Scoreboard (2022). https://sunnyvaleclimateaction.org/scoreboard

Copenhagen (2020). https://kk.sites.itera.dk/apps/kk_pub2/index.asp?mode=detalje&id=2062

Griffith, S. (2021). *Electrify: An Optimist's Playbook for Our Clean Energy Future.* Cambridge, MA: The MIT Press.

Hawken, P. (2017). *Drawdown.* New York, NY: Penguin.

Hawken, P. (2021). *Regeneration.* New York, NY: Penguin.

Hultman, N., and Calhoun, K. (2018). *Fulfilling America's Pledge – How States, Cities, and Businesses are Leading the United States to a Low-carbon Future.* New York: Bloomberg Philanthropies. https://www.bbhub.io/dotorg/sites/28/2018/09/Fulfilling-Americas-Pledge-2018.pdf.

Joint Venture Silicon Valley (2022). Silicon Valley Indicators. https://siliconvalleyindicators.org/ (accessed December 17, 2022).

Lean Energy US (2022). California. https://www.leanenergyus.org/california (accessed December 17, 2022).

Markolf, S. A., Azevedo, I. M. L., Muro, M., and Victor, D. G. (2018). Pledges and progress: steps toward greenhouse gas emissions reductions in the 100 largest cities across the United States. Brookings. https://www.brookings.edu/research/pledges-and-progress-steps-toward-greenhouse-gas-emissions-reductions-in-the-100-largest-cities-across-the-united-states/

Melhus, P., and Paton, B. (2012). The paradox of multi-stakeholder collaboration. Insights from sustainable Silicon Valley's regional CO$_2$ emissions reduction program. *Journal of Environmental Sustainability*, 2, 29–44.

Next 10 (2021). *California Green Innovation Index*, 13th edition. www.GreenInnovationIndex.org

Seto, B. (2008). *Addressing Climate Change Concerns at the Municipal Level: A Case Study on the City of Sunnyvale, California.* http://library.aesp.org/resources/Docuworks/file_display.cfm?id=350

Silicon Valley Clean Energy (2022). https://www.svcleanenergy.org/

State of California (2017). *California's 2017 Climate Change Scoping Plan.* https://ww2.arb.ca.gov/sites/default/files/classic/cc/scopingplan/scoping_plan_2017.pdf

Stockholms Stad (2020). *Climate Action Plan: A Fossil Free and Climate Positive Stockholm by 2040.* https://international.stockholm.se/city-development/the-eco-smart-city/

Wine and Vine Research (2022). [Image] California: Bay Area. https://www.wineandvinesearch.com/united_states/california/bay_area.php (accessed July 9, 2022).

Zero Energy Project (2020). Cities take the lead by building strong climate action plans. https://zeroenergyproject.com/2020/01/17/cities-take-the-lead-by-building-strong-climate-action-plans/ (accessed December 17, 2022).

12. Multi-level sustainability from the perspectives of a developing economy: a case study on climate resilient communities of Bangladesh

Sakib Mahmud

INTRODUCTION

Contemporary literature on sustainable management theory reveals that multi-level approaches under macro, meso, and micro levels or scopes are applied to deal with multiple sustainability issues to improve human health and overall well-being (Lemke & Bastini, 2020; Marsh, 2013; Mukhi & Quental, 2019; Rauschmayer et al., 2015; Starik & Kanashiro, 2020). This has become more prominent with the advent of climate-change induced developments, especially for developing countries that are considered highly vulnerable due to their geographic location (Eckstein et al., 2019; IPCC, 2018; Leah Filho et al., 2018; Stafford-Smith et al., 2017). For coastal communities in Bangladesh, which are exposed to various natural disasters, such as floods, riverbank erosions, drought, waterlogging, cyclones, and earthquakes, due to erratic changes in climate parameters, the level of risks and vulnerabilities is significantly higher compared with other low income and emerging countries (Banholzer et al., 2014; Kharin et al., 2007; Leah Filho et al., 2018). To minimize the negative impacts of climate change, *community-based adaptation* (CBA) involving multiple stakeholders is emerging as a promising local adaptation initiative that has the potential to empower people and strengthen community resilience (Kirkby et al., 2017; Shammin et al., 2022). Concurrently, representative stakeholders should correct for any *adaptation inequities* (Marino & Ribot, 2012; Sovacool & Linnér, 2016) that might arise due to differences in capacities of each community to undertake adaptation strategies at micro, meso, and macro levels. Furthermore, coordination failures among multiples stakeholders undertaking different CBA strategies can lead to *maladaptation*, a form of negative externality (Alston et al., 2014; Barnett & O'Neill, 2010; Magnan et al., 2016; Sovacool et al., 2015). Given such developments, the purpose of this chapter is to provide a brief sketch of locally-based multi-level sustainability initiatives to increase community-resilience against climate risks from the perspective of southern coastal areas of Bangladesh.

Climate Resilient Community-based Adaptation and Sustainability

Sustainability has often been conceived as relating to "meeting the needs of the present without compromising the well-being of future generations" (World Commission on Environment and Development & Brundtland, 1987). As climate change shifted the sustainability challenge from *conservation* to *adaptation* (Caniglia et al., 2017; Werners et al., 2013), the United Nation's Sustainable Development Goals (SDGs) represent more than 20 years of global endeavors to operationalize sustainability and sustainable development covering the realms of economic development, environmental responsibility, and social justice (United Nations, 2015). As shown in Figure 12.1, the SDGs provide a new framework to consider climate action within the multiple dimensions at multiple levels of sustainability (IPCC, 2018).

Source: United Nations (n.d.).

Figure 12.1   Sustainable Development Goals

Under the SDGs new framework, the IPCC stresses the need for far-reaching, multi-level, and cross-sectional climate mitigation strategies to be upscaled and accelerated with both incremental and transformational adaptation strategies (IPCC, 2018). Furthermore, the IPCC underlines that both incremental and transformational adaptation strategies would be required to effectively address future climate-related impacts (IPCC, 2018). For climate vulnerable coastal communities, the community-based initiatives are applied to a wide range of climate adaptation, such as:

- Disaster risk reduction (DRR) programs;
- Emergency preparedness;
- Flood/drought protection in sustainable agriculture;
- Water resource management;
- Food security; and,
- Resilient livelihood solutions.

According to Shammin et al. (2022, emphasis in original), contemporary studies on community-based adaptation (CBA) reveal that, "there is a push to *reconceptualize* CBA to become a flexible, learning process as part of a comprehensive toolbox of approaches for tackling climate change impacts and pursuing sustainable development." In fact, ground-breaking actions at the national, regional, and international levels are required to standardize local initiatives to ensure CBA can address multi-scalar and multifaceted challenges (Dolšak & Prakash, 2018; Shammin et al., 2022). Studies also reveal the importance to incorporate *monitoring and evaluation* tools and outcomes to facilitate the adaptation learning process for multiple stakeholders at multi-levels (Bahinipati & Patnaik, 2022; Mahmud et al., 2022; Shammin et al., 2022).

Community-based Adaptation (CBA) Classifications under Multi-level Sustainability

Considering the multi-level sustainability and the United Nations' 17 sustainable development goals, the community-based adaptation (CBA) activities for climate change in developing countries fall into six broad categories: (1) livelihood diversification; (2) infrastructure; (3) capacity building; (4) microfinance insurance; (5) ecosystem integrity, and (6) resource management (Shammin et al., 2022). Figure 12.2 illustrates the CBA categories for developing countries.

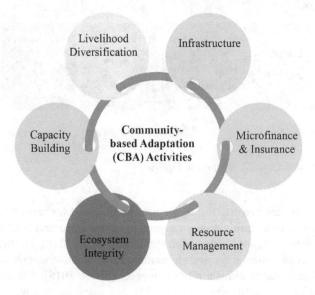

Figure 12.2   Classification of CBA activities

Categories of CBA Activities of Bangladesh Coastal Communities

Using the coastal areas of Bangladesh as a case study, Table 12.1 illustrates applications of the six categories of CBA. Starting with local and indigenous techniques for physical infra-structures to prevent damages to property, loss of agriculture crops, and loss of health from flooding due to severe storms, such as, cyclones,[1] Bangladesh coastal communities gradually increased their capacity to withstand storms and other natural disaster risks based on technical and financial support received from institutions, agencies and donors to transition towards new technologies, processes, and other products (Mahmud et al., 2022; Shammin et al., 2022).

Evidence also reveals community-based initiatives in Bangladesh coastal areas to restore ecosystem integrity and resource management through conservation of mangroves along the coast and development of natural erosion control bunds (IPCC, 2018; Shammin et al., 2022). At individual levels, coastal households seek support from different microfinance institutions (MFIs) to access microinsurance programs to reduce climate risks and from local communities to diversify their sources of income (Mahmud & Barbier, 2016; Mahmud et al., 2022; Shammin et al., 2022).

Table 12.1   *CBA activities in coastal communities of Bangladesh*

Sl. No.	CBA activity	Explanation of multi-sustainable activity	Global climate change induced natural disaster risks	Individual or multiple stakeholder participation	Examples from coastal Bangladesh
1.	*Infrastructure*	Local and indigenous techniques to build physical infrastructures	Prevent riverbank erosion; flooding from cyclones/ hurricanes/ excessive rainfall; reduce intrusion of saline water into the crop fields, etc.	Multiple	• Use of *cyclone shelters* that serve multi-purpose objectives such as saving human lives and livestock, and protect movable properties from damages • Use *bamboo-based structures* to prevent riverbank erosions
2.	*Capacity building*	Support from institutions, agencies, and donors to gradually enhance capacity to use new technologies and products	Reduce intrusion of saline water on agricultural land; lessen the severity of flooding from cyclones/ hurricanes/ excessive rainfall	Multiple	• Application of desalinization of water in coastal areas • Introduction of floating agriculture on a water hyacinth made in water-logged areas
3.	*Livelihood diversification*	Alternative income sources against livelihood activities based on seasonality and other long-term climatic conditions	Reduce the likelihood of loss of income and livelihood of people working in agriculture and other sectors affected by change of seasonality patterns due to climate change	Individual level through contracts	• Opting for rice variety that can withstand temporary flooding • Community-based initiatives that provide opportunities to diversify sources of income
4.	*Ecosystem integrity*	Multiple stakeholders in local communities working together to restore the integrity of nature with or without any formal institutional support	Prevent riverbank erosion; negative impacts of flooding and water-logging	Multiple	• Restoring tidal flooding of coastal rivers • Build natural protection of riverbanks and natural erosion control bunds • Reforestation of degraded Sundarban mangrove forest,[a] and other forest coverage along the coast

Sl. No.	CBA activity	Explanation of multi-sustainable activity	Global climate change induced natural disaster risks	Individual or multiple stakeholder participation	Examples from coastal Bangladesh
5.	*Microfinance and insurance*	Microfinance institutions (MFIs)b work with unbanked communities to access loans with capacity building goals	Lessen the severity of dealing with natural disaster risks, such as flooding, riverbank erosion	Individual level through contracts	• MFIs run microinsurance programs or provide loans with provisions for microinsurance programs to ensure borrowers are protected against different risks, such as, property damages, crop losses, and health risks against flood
6.	*Resource management*	Local community-based actions to protect lakes, rivers, and forests	Avoid or lessen the impacts of groundwater depletion; reduce the negative impacts of flooding from cyclones/ excessive rainfall	Multiple	• Conservation of mangroves to provide protection against cyclones and coastal flooding • Restoring forest lands to improve groundwater recharge

Note: [a] One of UNESCO's World Heritage Sites, the Sundarbans mangrove forest is the world's largest mangrove ecosystem (140,000 ha). It lies on the delta of the Ganges, Brahmaputra and Meghna rivers on the Bay of Bengal. [b] MFIs in Bangladesh include non-governmental organizations (NGOs), forest users' groups, fisheries' cooperatives, and farmers' organizations engaging in lending.
Source: Created by author following Mahmud & Barbier (2016), Mahmud et al. (2022) and Shammin et al. (2022).

Private Defensive Strategies as a Form of Adaptation among Bangladesh Coastal Communities

In conjunction with the community-based adaptations in coastal Bangladesh, Mahmud et al. (2022) and Mahmud and Barbier (2016) highlighted the importance of *private defensive strategies* of Bangladesh coastal households to mitigate and cope with risks from severe storms and other natural disaster events. Examples of private defensive strategies for adaptation by Bangladesh coastal households include converting a mud-built house to brick-built house, raising the height of the homestead, increasing the number of floors, repair of walls, installation of tube well for water, modernization of toilet, improvement of domestic animal sheds, ponds, and boundary of the house, raising the plinths, etc. Mahmud et al.'s (2022) study emphasized the influence of external and internal factors on a household's choice to participate in private storm protection actions. The factors are: (1) publicly sponsored climate-resilience programs, such as, embankments, cyclone/storm shelters, etc.; (2) access to a natural capital, such as, a mangrove forest; (3) access to financial and social capital; and (4) access to domestic and foreign remittances (Mahmud & Barbier, 2016; Mahmud et al., 2022).

Mahmud et al. (2022), for their case study, selected 600 households for a survey of 12 villages covering three coastal districts of Bangladesh that were exposed to the most recent severe storm events, Cyclone Sidr and Cyclone Roanu, which made landfall on 15 November 2007 and 23 May 2016, respectively. For the household survey, the authors employed a two-stage sampling method and structured questionnaires to conduct interviews. A pilot survey was conducted to improve the final version of the questionnaire. Figure 12.3 illustrates the case study area along with the tracks of Cyclone Sidr and Cyclone Roanu.

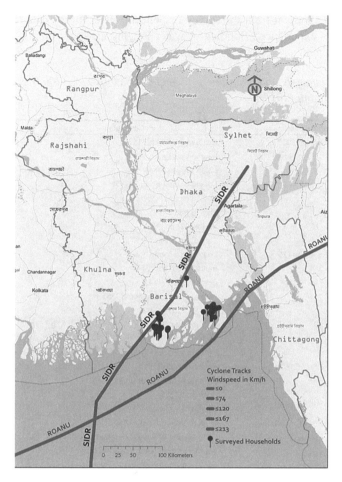

Figure 12.3   Study area along with the tracks of Cyclone Sidr and Cyclone Roanu

For private adaptation against major storm events, Mahmud et al.'s (2022) study shows that most of the households increased the number of floors (25%), sank new tube wells for water (24%), and improved their pond areas (12%) after Cyclone Sidr. The same adaptation strategies were applied post Cyclone Roanu. Survey results also reveal that income, savings, and donations were the major sources of funds for adaptation after these two major storm events. On perceptions of public (government-sponsored) adaptation measures implemented by the government, around 22% of the households think building embankments with stone and cement blocks is the most effective strategy, thus vindicating the involvement of multiple stakeholders' participation on dealing with multi-level sustainability issues due to climate-change induced natural disaster events.

Furthermore, Mahmud et al.'s (2022) findings show that the next most effective strategy is raising the height of the embankment (16.46%), one of the private adaptation initiatives, followed by building new cyclone shelters or expanding the existing ones (14%), raising floors or heights of the house (13.44%) and raising plinths (11.55%). Interestingly, other public adaptation measures, such as building clay embankment (9.15%) and afforestation (7.86%), did not get much approval from the survey respondents. The survey data show that 93.44% of the households experienced flooding or water logging affecting their houses. Table 12.2 summarizes the findings.

Table 12.2   *Damages and adaptation strategies: Cyclone Sidr (2007) and Cyclone Roanu (2016)*

Variable name	Description	Percentages (%)
Damages during Cyclone Sidr (2007)	Death in the family (157)	7.28
	Injury in the family (8)	0.37
	Loss of assets (385)	17.85
	Loss in domestic animals (589)	27.31
	Loss in crops (569)	26.38
	Loss in trees (447)	20.72
	No loss (2)	0.09
	Total frequencies (2157)	100
Damages during Cyclone Roanu (2016)	Death in the family (20)	1.72
	Injury in the family (3)	0.26
	Loss of assets (114)	9.78
	Loss in domestic animals (358)	30.70
	Loss in crops (300)	25.73
	Loss in trees (203)	17.41
	No loss (168)	14.41
	Total frequencies (1166)	100
Adaptation post-Cyclone Sidr (2007)	Repair of walls (39)	1.85
	Increase in number of floors (519)	24.67
	Brick wall (163)	7.75
	Tube well for water (514)	24.43
	Modernization of toilet (48)	2.28
	Improvement of domestic animal sheds (45)	2.14
	Improvement of pond areas (247)	11.74
	Improvement of boundary of the house (211)	10.03
	Others	15.11
	Total frequencies (2104)	100
Adaptation post-Cyclone Roanu (2016)	Repair of walls (21)	2.93
	Increase in number of floors (104)	14.53
	Brick wall (36)	5.03
	Tube well for water (256)	35.75
	Modernization of toilet (7)	0.98
	Improvement of domestic animal sheds (6)	0.84
	Improvement of pond areas (92)	12.85
	Improvement of boundary of the house (52)	7.26
	Others (142)	19.83
	Total frequencies (716)	100

Source   Mahmud et al. (2022).

Among the sources of funds to support private adaptation measures for home improvements post-Cyclone Sidr and post-Cyclone Roanu, Mahmud et al. (2022) found external finance through public and private donations to be the second most important source of funds followed by household savings. Table 12.3 sums up the findings.

Table 12.3   Sources of funds for adaptation

For adaptation after Cyclone Sidr (2007)	Percentage (%)	For adaptation after Cyclone Roanu (2016)	Percentage (%)
Savings	35.15	Savings	46.70
Loan	16.01	Loan	12.83
Donation	29.02	Donation	21.21
Help from friends/relatives	6.51	Help from friends/relatives	0.71
Sold land / asset	13.31	Sold land/ asset	18.54
Total frequencies ($N = 1334$)	100	Total frequencies ($N=561$)	100

The authors collected information on adaptation costs for the households based on their location to understand household investment on different adaptation initiatives under local context. As shown in Table 12.4, Mahmud et al. (2022) demonstrated that houses that are built outside the embankment (31.15% of the total households surveyed), spent Bangladesh Taka (BDT) 6169 more on average on adaptation costs compared with houses that are built inside the embankment. Their results also revealed that houses protected by the natural forest (11.94% of the total households surveyed) spent on average BDT 5272 less on adaptation costs than the houses that are not protected by the natural forest. Also, for households that are in lowland areas (33.45% of the total surveyed), average spending on adaptation costs is BDT 3227 more compared with households located in mid-and highland areas. Furthermore, the authors reported household perception on their homes being affected by tidal surge from a major cyclone event.

Table 12.4   Differences in adaptation costs based on household location

Location of the household	Average adaptation costs (in BDT)	Differences in adaptation costs (in BDT)	Comments
Protection from major storms due to being surrounded by natural forest			
House surrounded by forest	44915	5272***	Houses surrounded by forest spent
House not surrounded by forest	50187		BDT 5227 less
Protection from major storms due to located inside polder			
House located inside the polder	47497	6169***	Houses inside the polder spent BDT
House located outside the polder	53665		6169 less
Protection from major storms due to located on highland			
House located on the lowland	48814	3227*	Houses located on mid-and- highland
House located on the high land	45587		spent BDT 3227 less

Note: Independent samples t test with $N = 610$ observations. Statistically significant levels: ***1%, **5%, *10%.
Source: Mahmud et al. (2022).

Negative Externalities of Maladaptation and Soft Adaptation of Bangladesh Coastal Communities

Since most private adaptation strategies lead to private benefits, such as protection of health, less property damages, and other benefits from home improvements against cyclones, it is important to have coordination between private and public adaptation strategies to enhance the adaptive capacity of Bangladesh coastal communities. Contemporary literature on the politics of climate change adaptation, in fact, reveals the influence of a citizen–government dimension on the coproduction of soft adaptation through improvement in the social, technical, and organizational capacities of administrative and social systems against climate risks (Bovaird, 2007; Dolšak and Prakash, 2018; Parks et al., 1981). For any country with climate vulnerable coastal communities, like Bangladesh, it is imperative to introduce innovative and targeted policies to incentivize local communities to focus more on collective response as opposed to private adaptation strategies considering their local budget, resource capacity, and other constraints. In fact, collective action in response to the local context would allow coastal communities to meet the full potential of their community-based adaptation (CBA) programs. Conversely, communities might end up dealing with multiple negative repercussion effects of *coordination failure* arising from their failure to synthesize local private and public adaptation efforts.

Another type of negative externality that could arise from uncoordinated private adaptation strategies is *maladaptation*. Contemporary literature on the political economy of climate adaptation defines *maladaptation* as a result of an intentional adaptation policy or measure that directly increases the social, economic, and environmental vulnerabilities of the targeted population and/or other external actors of the community (Juhola et al., 2016; Magnan et al., 2016). For countries with climate vulnerable coastal communities, such as Bangladesh, *maladaptation* is the most likely outcome if private and public adaptation strategies are uncoordinated, and hence lead to negative spillover effects. A classic maladaptation example is the government sponsored seawalls and embankment projects. If these public sponsored storm and flood protection infrastructures are built to protect communities with substantial resources and/or political power, then such public programs are most likely to reduce the climate resilience of resource-poor and/or relatively weaker political power-based communities by directing the rising waters toward them. Hence, the maladapted public programs can strengthen and weaken climate resilience capacities of communities with different locations and other specific characteristics.

CONCLUSION

This chapter provides an overview of the multi-level local adaptation approaches under micro, meso, and macro levels from the perspectives of the developing economies. Using empirical evidence on community-based adaptation (CBA) and the private adaptation initiatives that are observed in southern coastal areas of Bangladesh, the chapter reveals that local CBA and private adaptation within the local institutional framework involves multiple stakeholders' participation to lessen the natural disaster risks (Mahmud & Barbier, 2016; Mahmud et al., 2022; Shammin et al., 2022; Sovacool et al., 2015). Furthermore, CBA initiatives involving multiple stakeholders are emerging as a promising platform to empower and strengthen local community's climate resilience (Kirkby et al., 2017; Mahmud et al., 2022; Shammin et al., 2022; Sovacool et al., 2015). However, lack of coordination on local adaptation efforts involving multiple stakeholders can lead to *adaptation inequities*. Such a situation can easily manifest due to coordination failures between citizens and governments on investments for soft adaptation infrastructure to strengthen technical, social, and organizational adaptive capacities of the local communities to deal with any climate-change induced stressors (Bovaird, 2007; Dolšak & Prakash, 2018). In addition, there is the possibility of dealing with the negative spillovers of *maladaptation* if public-sponsored hard infrastructure adaptation programs, such as embankments, seawalls, dams, etc., increase climate resilience for targeted communities but at the expense of weakening climate resilience of other vulnerable communities by directing the rising waters toward them. Therefore, it is imperative for governments and municipalities to coordinate their adaptation efforts with local CBAs to avoid any negative externalities that might arise from maladapted projects.

Using coastal areas of Bangladesh as a case study, findings reveal that local CBA initiatives fall under six categories. These are capacity building, diversification of income, infrastructure, ecosystem integrity, microfinance and microinsurance, and resource management. Local knowledge (experience) and indigenous techniques to build physical infrastructures are prominent in many coastal communities to reduce the risks from flooding, saline intrusion in crop fields, riverbank erosion, etc. Communities are also willing to seek assistance from local institutions as well as local and foreign agencies and donors for capacity building against natural disaster risks through knowledge sharing and new technology (or, process) adoption. Evidence also shows that local coastal communities work together for ecosystem integrity and resource management to mitigate the severity of health, property, and other losses against climate-induced disaster risks. Among other CBA initiatives, coastal households work as communities to access microloans that have provisions for microinsurance programs to lessen natural disaster risks. Although CBA initiatives involving multiple stakeholders enhance a community's adaptation capacities, there still exist potential trade-offs if the multi-level adaptation efforts are disjointed and uncoordinated. Without developing adequate assessment tools and adhering to best practices in project design and evaluation, CBA projects in the southern coastal areas of Bangladesh and other countries might be worsening adaptation inequities. Under such circumstances, private adaptation strategies become the only option for individual households, which may vary in their capacities to undertake these measures. Consequently, this could further worsen the adaptation inequalities since most communities usually have heterogeneous households with different socioeconomic and sociocultural characteristics.

In continuation of a private adaptation case study on Bangladesh southern coastal areas, Mahmud et al. (2022), from their field survey of 600 households, show that households save more in terms of housing improvement costs due to the protection that the Sundarban mangroves forest provide to them. This is higher than the households living outside the protection of the embankment and located away from mangroves and other forests. Likewise, the higher the home index value for households in terms of their homes' capacity to withstand storm and flood risks, the lower is the cost of home improvement after the major storm (or cyclone) event. The authors' findings also reveal that households with access to different forms of asset ownership have higher adaptation costs. Furthermore, a household that has access to external financing through private and public charities and donations invests more on cyclone-resistant home improvements. The authors did not find sufficient evidence from field survey data that remittances have a positive influence on household adaptation costs on home improvements.

Considering the significant presence of CBA initiatives and evidence of private adaptation strategies by the coastal households, the government needs to coordinate with the local communities, non-governmental organizations, and donor agencies to impart information, knowledge, and training on best practices in adaptation project design, implementation, and maintenance. If public adaptation projects, such as planting mangrove forests, hard adaptation infrastructures, etc., have greater potentials in saving lives and property compared with private adaptation efforts, then, appropriate policies should be introduced to incentivize local communities to focus more on collective response. For example, local communities can be encouraged to restore and maintain forests along the coastline as part of ecosystem integrity and resource management efforts through the creation of soft adaptation infrastructure that enhances the technical, organizational, individual, and social capacities of each community. Because of such a coordinated collective response, the government can make its climate-resilient programs – including post-disaster relief and rehabilitation programs – more effective.

To further the collective response for multi-level sustainability projects, governments can work with Microfinance Institutions (MFIs) to streamline and simplify regulations for financial institutions and NGOs, so that they can lend credit to households willing to invest in storm-resistant homes and other adaptation strategies. Local governments can also reserve development funds by forming public–private partnerships with key stakeholders of the communities to introduce efficient, equitable, and locally focused climate-resilient programs. Since responding to the local context through CBAs tends to produce local public goods, coordinated adaptation efforts, as such, suffer fewer collective action problems. Consequently, this puts socially heterogeneous communities in a better position to meet their sustainable development goals.

NOTES

1. According to the Hurricane Research Division of the National Oceanic and Atmospheric Administration (NOAA) (2019), a tropical cyclone is generally referred to as a *hurricane* in the Atlantic and the northeastern Pacific oceans; whereas, in the Indian and south Pacific oceans it is called a *cyclone*, and in the northwestern Pacific it is called a *typhoon* (Source: Hurricane Research Division, 2018, http://www.aoml.noaa.gov/hrd/).

REFERENCES

Alston, M., Whittenbury, K., Haynes, A., & Godden, N. (2014). Are climate challenges reinforcing child and forced marriage and dowry as adaptation strategies in the context of Bangladesh? *Women's Studies International Forum, 47*, 137–144

Bahinipati, C. S., & Patnaik, U. (2022). Climate change and human security in India evidence, opportunities, and challenges. In *Varying Dimensions of India's National Security* (pp. 197–213). Singapore: Springer.

Banholzer, S., Kossin, J., & Donner, S. (2014). The impact of climate change on natural disasters. In *Reducing disaster: Early warning systems for climate change* (pp. 21–49). Dordrecht: Springer. https://link.springer.com/book/10.1007/978-94-017-8598-3#toc

Barnett, J., & O'Neill, S. (2010). Maladaptation. *Global Environmental Change, 20*, 211–213.

Bovaird, T. (2007). Beyond engagement and participation: User and community coproduction of public services. *Public Administration Review, 67*(5), 846–860.

Caniglia, G., Schapke, N., Lang, D., Abson, D., Luederitz, C., Wiek, A., Laubichler, M., Gralla, F., & von Wehrden, H. (2017). Experiments and evidence in sustainability science: A typology. *Journal of Clean Production, 169*, 39–47.

Dolšak, N., & Prakash, A. (2018). The politics of climate change adaptation. *Annual Review of Environment and Resources, 43*, 317–341.

Eckstein, D., Künzel, V., Schäfer, L., & Winges, M. (2019). *Global Climate Risk Index 2020*. Bonn: Germanwatch.

Intergovernmental Panel on Climate Change. (2018). *Global warming of 1.5°C: An IPCC Special Report on the Impacts of Global Warming of 1.5°C above Pre-industrial Levels and Related Global Greenhouse Gas Emission Pathways, in the Context of Strengthening the Global Response to the Threat of Climate Change, Sustainable Development, and Efforts to Eradicate Poverty.* IPCC.

Juhola, S., Glaas, E., Linnér, B. O., & Neset, T. S. (2016). Redefining maladaptation. *Environmental Science & Policy, 55,* 135–140.

Kharin, V. V., Zwiers, F. W., Zhang, X., & Hegerl, G. C. (2007). Changes in temperature and precipitation extremes in the IPCC ensemble of global coupled model simulations. *Journal of Climate, 20*(8), 1419–1444.

Kirkby, P., Williams, C., & Huq, S. (2017). Community-based adaptation (CBA): Adding conceptual clarity to the approach, and establishing its principles and challenges. *Climate and Development, 10*(7).

Leal Filho, W., Modesto, F., Nagy, G. J., Saroar, M., Yannick Toamukum, N., & Ha'apio, M. (2018). Fostering coastal resilience to climate change vulnerability in Bangladesh, Brazil, Cameroon and Uruguay: A cross-country comparison. *Mitigation and Adaptation Strategies for Global Change, 23*(4), 579–602.

Lemke, C., & Bastini, K. (2020). Embracing multiple perspectives of sustainable development in a composite measure: The Multilevel Sustainable Development Index. *Journal of Cleaner Production, 246,* 118884.

Magnan, A. K., Schipper, E. L. F., Burkett, M., Bharwani, S., Burton, I., Eriksen, S., ... & Ziervogel, G. (2016). Addressing the risk of maladaptation to climate change. *Wiley Interdisciplinary Reviews: Climate Change, 7*(5), 646–665.

Mahmud, S., & Barbier, E. B. (2016). Are private defensive expenditures against storm damages affected by public programs and natural barriers? Evidence from the coastal areas of Bangladesh. *Environment and Development Economics, 21*(6), 767–788.

Mahmud, S., Enamul Haque, A. K., & Costa, K. D. (2022). Climate resiliency and location-specific learnings from coastal Bangladesh. In *Climate Change and Community Resilience* (pp. 309–321). Singapore: Springer.

Marino, E., & Ribot, J. (2012). Special issue introduction: adding insult to injury: Climate change and the inequities of climate intervention. *Global Environmental Change, 22*(2), 323–328.

Marsh, V. (2013) The link between health and sustainability. *Triple Pundit.* January 30. https://www.triplepundit.com/story/2013/link-between-health-and-sustainability/54646 (accessed March 26, 2019).

Mukhi, U., & Quental, C. (2019). Exploring the challenges and opportunities of the United Nations sustainable development goals: A dialogue between a climate scientist and management scholars. *Corporate Governance: The International Journal of Business in Society.*

National Oceanic and Atmospheric Administration (NOAA) (2019). What is a hurricane, typhoon, or tropical cyclone? Hurricane Research Division. Retrieved from: http://www.aoml.noaa.gov/hrd/

Parks, R. B., Baker, P. C., Kiser, L., Oakerson, R., Ostrom, E., Ostrom, V., ... & Wilson, R. (1981). Consumers as coproducers of public services: Some economic and institutional considerations. *Policy Studies Journal, 9*(7), 1001–1011.

Rauschmayer, F., Bauler, T., & Schäpke, N. (2015). Towards a thick understanding of sustainability transitions—Linking transition management, capabilities and social practices. *Ecological Economics, 109,* 211–221.

Shammin, M. R., Enamul Haque, A. K., & Faisal, I. M. (2022). A framework for climate resilient community-based adaptation. In A. K. E. Haque, P. Mukhopadhyay, M. Nepal, & M. R. Shammin (Eds.), *Climate Change and Community Resilience* (pp. 11–30). Singapore: Springer.

Sovacool, B. K., & Linnér, B. O. (2016). *The Political Economy of Climate Change Adaptation.* Springer.

Sovacool, B. K., Linnér, B. O., & Goodsite, M. E. (2015). The political economy of climate adaptation. *Nature Climate Change, 5,* 616–618.

Stafford-Smith, M., Griggs, D., Gaffney, O., Ullah, F., Reyers, B., Kanie, N., ... & O'Connell, D. (2017). Integration: The key to implementing the Sustainable Development Goals. *Sustainability Science, 12*(6), 911–919.

Starik, M., & Kanashiro, P. (2020). Advancing a multi-level sustainability management theory. In D. Wasieleski, & J. Weber (Eds.), *Business and Society 360 Part IV Sustainability*. Emerald Press. https://doi.org/10.1108/S2514-175920200000004003

United Nations (2015). Sustainable Development Goals. *SDGs Transform Our World, 2030*. United Nations General Assembly.

United Nations (n.d.). https://sdgs.un.org/goals. Last accessed February 18, 2022.

Werners, S., Pfenninger, S., Slobbe, E., Haasnoot, M., Kwakkel, J., & Swart, R. (2013). Thresholds, tipping and turning points for sustainability under climate change. *Current Opinion in Environmental Sustainability*, 5(3–4), 334–340.

World Commission on Environment and Development, & Brundtland, G. H. (1987). *Presentation of the Report of World Commission on Environment and Development to African and International and Non-governmental Organizations. June 7, 1987, Nairobi, Kenya*. World Commission on Environment and Development.

13. Multi-level climate action through circular supply chain management of ocean plastic

Andrea Neal, Michelaina Johnson and Megan Havrda

INTRODUCTION

Historically, we as a global community have often only looked at one piece of the problem at a time, such as the removal of plastic from the ocean. This type of siloed or linear problem solving usually does not take into account upstream and downstream possibilities and the impacts of plastic use and waste. Key metrics and data can be sidelined and frequently have not addressed human behavior or the economic or social sustainability of long-lasting solutions. Having a diverse, cross-disciplinary approach to designing and driving the Blue Economy could create positive, economically driven, multi-level climate action.

When looking at the world's most pressing environmental issues, including multi-decade plastic waste build up in the ocean, plus what enters the oceans annually, we need a holistic, circular understanding of the situation, the associated supply chains, and incentivizes to ignite solutions. By addressing supply chain gaps in the Circular Blue Economy, we can start and augment industries to not only address the immediate environmental problem of plastic pollution but also to generate new economic drivers.

These drivers can and will improve economic disparities through: job creation, education, awareness of the health impacts of plastic waste, tax incentivization, treaties, and policies being written now and via COP28, the 2022 United Nations 28th Climate Change Conference. Plastic affects the health of every living species on the planet. We can still turn the tide efficiently with accurate data and strong public–private relationships. With a healthy Blue Economy supply chain, we can create a monetary value for ocean plastic and design economic incentives to:

- remove plastic from the environment;
- upcycle and produce higher grade products from plastic waste;
- find alternatives to plastic for manufacturing and consumption;
- reduce plastic waste in the environment.

The world's plastic production has grown from two million metric tons (Mt) to a staggering 380 million metric tons (Mt) from 2005 to 2015 (Geyer et al. 2017). Globally, only 18% of non-fiber plastic was recycled in 2014 (Geyer et al. 2017). We often consider plastic inert. The reality is plastic is made from fossil fuels, plasticizers, and other additives (e.g., phthalate esters, heavy metals, bisphenols, poly- and perfluoroalkyl substances, catalyst remnants, dyes, flame retardants, UV stabilizers, antioxidants and antimicrobials), which make it a ubiquitous, multifaceted product.

When plastics are exposed to heat, UV irradiation, animal/microbial predation, weathering, and friction, they break down into increasingly smaller pieces (micro- and nano-sized plastic particles) and plasticizers, which can be very toxic endocrine-disrupting elements that leach into the environment, the food we eat, and our bodies – see Figure 13.1 (Gewert et al. 2015; Stubbins et al. 2021).

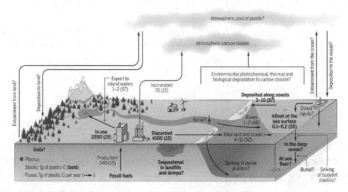

Source: MacLeod et al. (2021).

Figure 13.1   Mechanisms of ocean plastic degradation

International media frequently misportrays the socio-economic consequences of plastic waste. The constant negative spotlight on the size and pervasiveness of the issue has generated widespread apathy, discouraging people from understanding their individual ability to help remediate this global problem. When we apply circular multi-level climate action plans, we can transform massive problems into economic and business opportunities. Plastic waste offers a new material source that can be feedstock for numerous supply chains with diverse product applications.

By 2050, plastics are expected to reach production rates of more than 1100 Mt per year and claim 15% of the yearly greenhouse gas (GHG) emissions allotment (Zheng & Suh 2019). Plastics are a major part of global life-cycle GHG emissions. For conventional plastics, the GHG emissions per kg of polymer production are ~ 2.66 $kgCO_2e$ (cradle-to-resin) (Zheng & Suh 2019). Zheng and Suh (2019) calculated that the global life cycle GHG emissions of conventional plastics in 2015 were 1.7 Gt of CO_2-equivalent (CO_2e) and could grow to 6.5 $GtCO^2e$ by 2050 under the current trajectory (Zheng & Suh 2019).

Academic studies conclude that net-zero emission plastics can be achieved by utilizing existing commercialized technologies, such as recycling, carbon capture and biomass conversion systems (Meys et al. 2021). While these models are notable first steps, they don't take into consideration the entire supply chain, which includes 22 to 48 million metric tons per year of derelict plastic lost to the environment (MacLeod et al. 2021).

Since not all plastic feedstock is the same, additional thought needs to be placed on sources, evolving technologies, and GHG reduction benefits to the marketplace. These include cradle-to-cradle recycling, material recovery from the environment, advanced recycling (conversion) and its many forms of pyrolysis (high heat, low heat, microwave, nuclear, etc.) and fiber packaging to replace plastic. While academic breakthroughs are helping retool the $60+ billion plastic industry, there is a need for scalable pilots to show business cases and upgraded supply chains. By taking a holistic approach to the field and applying metrics that assess multiple aspects of the business and supply chain, we can optimize the industries' climate impact from the onset.

PROBLEM – PLASTIC WASTE

As of 2016, yearly estimates of global emissions of plastic waste to rivers, lakes, and oceans range from 9 to 23 million metric tons, with an additional 13 to 25 million metric tons lost annually in terrestrial environments (Borrelle et al. 2020; Lau et al. 2020; Meys et al. 2021). The social-environment–economic impacts of ocean plastic are complex. Ocean plastic impacts everything, including critical species loss, habitat destruction, "ghost fishing", invasive species impacts on fisheries and ecology, vessel strikes from ghost nets (re: damage/loss), impacts on oxygen production in waterways, tourism loss, human health, fierce weather surges, and most recently as an emergent component of the Earth's carbon cycle (Gewert et al. 2015; Stubbins et al. 2021).

Owing to the widespread impact of marine plastic waste on the economy, calculating the cost of destruction caused by abandoned, lost or discarded plastic (ALDP) is immensely difficult. NOAA estimates the Blue Economy in 2018 was responsible for $373 billion of U.S. GDP and 2.3 million jobs (Kelley et al. 2021). Despite these national advances, plastic waste continues to be produced and it finds its way into the ocean. For example, marine industries in the Asia-Pacific region are estimated to lose $1.16 billion per year due to marine litter (McIlgorm et al. 2011).

Every year, the amount of plastic in the environment increases and further degrades, causing additional proliferation into ecosystems, people, wildlife, and the carbon cycle (Stubbins et al. 2021) (Figure 13.2). Plastic meets the metrics of a "poorly reversible pollutant," both because emissions cannot be curtailed and because of its environmental persistence (MacLeod et al. 2021). MacLeod et al. (2021) introduced concerns of plastic pollution nearing an irreversible tipping point as plastic pollution accumulates to levels that exceed effect thresholds (Persson et al. 2013; MacLeod et al. 2014; Parsons et al. 2019; MacLeod et al. 2021).

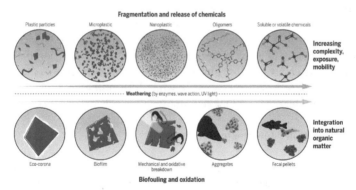

Source: C. Bickel, from Stubbins et al. (2021).

Figure 13.2   *The global plastic–carbon cycling system. Plastic-carbon values are calculated as 0.83 times plastic mass*

Solution – Support a Network of "Ocean Plastic Miners" through Fair Wages

Today more than 22 million people work as pickers globally and manage 30% to 80% of waste, depending on the region. Many plastic miners/pickers around the world are paid less than $1 per day to collect the misplaced waste of more economically advantaged people. Additional economic stressors are fishery collapse and strict regulations around fishing practices due to the global decline of our aquatic ecosystems and aquatic species. These environmental factors and concomitant regulations leave many skilled workers and infrastructure and equipment professionals out of work. By changing the current low-wage standard for ocean plastic miners to reflect the higher fishing industry wages, we can redirect this industry to include ocean plastic remediation.

Until recently few municipalities, states, and countries have recognized plastic miners' work as vital to their economies. However, good examples exist. The city of Pune in India created a paradigm shift around how waste pickers are treated and compensated for their indispensable labor by creating a local pickers' union, which formed a cooperative in 2008 in which all workers purchase shares and operate a door-to-door waste collection program. Thanks in part to the cooperative, "around 80 percent of Pune's citizens receive door-to-door waste pickup, including many of the city's previously unserviced slums" (Parsons et al. 2019).

Simultaneously, the pickers now receive a more livable wage and some benefits, notable union protections, and more respect for their labor (Parsons et al. 2019). Since 2008, waste pickers from around the world have formed the Global Alliance of Waste Pickers with groups in more than 28 countries representing mostly Asia, Latin America, and Africa. With the support of WIEGO, a global research-policy network, the Alliance of Waste Pickers has commenced, among several activities, raising awareness of the critical roles that pickers play in the supply chain management of waste, establishing and maintaining a cohesive, global network of pickers through consistent communications and conferences, and articulating the commitments of waste pickers to a more equitable, sustainable, and just world in the "Global Declaration of the 1st World Conference of Waste Pickers" (Gutberlet 2021).

One of the alliance's current initiatives involves integrating waste pickers as stakeholders into an emerging strategy called Extended Producer Responsibility (EPR), which is a set of environmental policies that make producers responsible for the impacts of their products over the course of their life cycle, including the post-consumer stage (Johannes et al. 2021). However, waste pickers still need better representation at the decision-making table. The Alliance of Waste Pickers asserts that pickers must play an active role in the creation of EPR initiatives by lending their first-hand expertise while EPR initiatives must expand the visibility, labor and social protections, and the decision-making role of pickers (Gutberlet 2021).

Solution – Supply Chain Management Support

Like the global fishing industry, marine plastic miners need support to maintain a steady supply chain that captures ocean plastic and upcycles it into usable resources, such as green energy and building materials. Many groups worldwide have started to specialize in ocean plastic cleanup. However, without a reliable supply chain to support the ocean plastic waste industry, much of the recovered material ends up in CO_2e-producing, end-of-life scenarios such as landfills and incinerators. Without municipal waste facilities, much waste goes back into the environment. Since recovery operations are often in locations without robust municipal trash and recycling facilities, recovered ocean plastic is often re-littered through the traditional "waste management techniques" of burying waste or disposing of it in waterways.

Thermoplastic wastes, such as polyethylene terephthalate (PET) bottles, are collected in urban areas close to industries. In rural areas, plastic collection rates are low due to scattered housing, low population density, poor social and economic conditions, low collection frequency and great distances from waste management facilities (Mihai & Grozavu 2019). In developing nations and remote rural regions, informal sectors take most of the responsibility for waste management (Johannes et al. 2021).

In high population density zones and areas close to industrial zones, there are existing market-based recyclable collection operations. This is not the case in remote and rural regions.

Johannes et al. (2021) identified six major issues with applying EPR to developing nations:

1. The high transportation cost of recyclable waste to a recycling facility.
2. Limited to no waste collection services in rural areas.
3. Limited facilities that accept difficult to recycle plastic waste.
4. Insufficient pollution control by the recycling industry.
5. Smuggled and unregistered products are a large part of the market, creating more free riding and orphaned products than registered producers' products.

Public/private partnerships for EPR projects can be designed to fit a region's needs and address the potential issues above. Waste management efforts need to be strengthened in areas where this service is currently absent. Building EPR programs in remote coastal regions and island nations, for instance, can create climate solutions for ocean plastic and municipal waste while building up the Blue Economy and improving communities' livelihood options.

Solution – Support for Critical Infrastructure:

Similar to the green energy sector, the ocean plastic waste management sector needs specialized equipment and infrastructural support. Ocean plastic comes into processing stations in various stages of degradation. This is due to the varying degrees of exposure to environments that degrade and foul different types of ocean plastic. The ocean plastic industry will require specialized infrastructure, including Ocean Plastic Material Recovery Facilities (OPMRFs), specialized sorting and cleaning equipment, boating/hauling vessels, transport trucks, and end-of-life conversion systems. OPMRFs are specialized sorting and management equipment and are distinct from land-based MRFs. OPMRFs are able to efficiently sort, clean, and find the next stage of life for this complex mixture of materials. For example, derelict fishing nets block up traditional cylindrical MRF grinders. These facilities need to be tailored to the regional ocean plastic recovery operations, the types of ocean plastic they remove (e.g., beach, coastal, open ocean, waterway), and end-of-life determined by regional supply chains. Financial support for these transitional efforts must invest in programs that recover as much marine plastic as possible. Other types of infrastructure include direct removal of waste plastic before it enters waterways and becomes ocean plastic.

Solution – Education and Certifications

Education plays a critical role in the transition from traditional building and energy development methods to greener and bluer operations. The same is true for the ocean plastic industry.

There are some organizations looking to develop blue maritime certifications and building protocols for marine health, such as Green Advantage, Green Marine, and General Society of Surveillance (SGS).

- *Green Advantage* is a non-profit organization that credentials personnel in green construction with a strong commitment to the three pillars of sustainability – physical, social, and economic environments. It currently offers three ANSI-accredited credentials for construction workers in green residential and commercial construction.
- *Green Marine* is a voluntary environmental certification program for the North American maritime industry that addresses key environmental issues through its 14 performance indicators. They focus on ship owners, ports, terminals, seaway corporations and shipyards based in Canada and the U.S.
- *SGS* is an international testing, inspection and certification company with over 96,000 employees that provide specialized solutions to make businesses faster, simpler and more efficient.

Industry-specific ocean plastic certifications are needed to help guide and unify the industry, supply chain, and workforce. Training and certifying ocean plastic miners and processors on how to safely remove, sort, clean, and convert ocean plastic from oceans, waterways, and coastlines prevent long-term damage to critical habitats and wildlife and develop long-term careers (Figure 13.3).

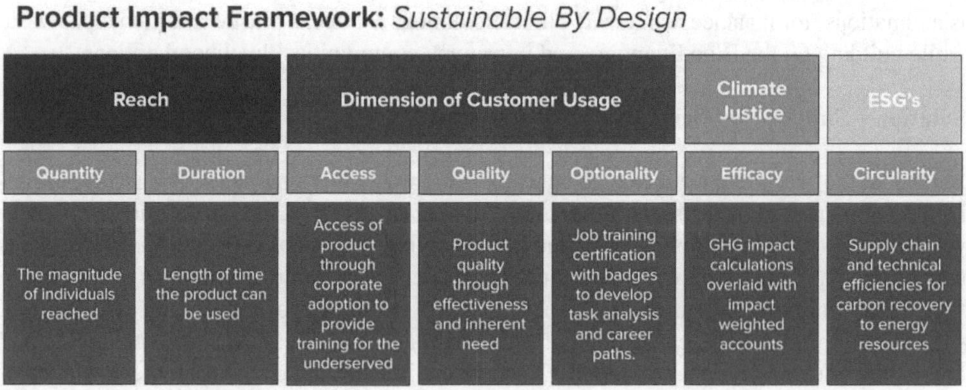

Product Impact Framework: *Sustainable By Design*

Reach		Dimension of Customer Usage			Climate Justice	ESG's
Quantity	Duration	Access	Quality	Optionality	Efficacy	Circularity
The magnitude of individuals reached	Length of time the product can be used	Access of product through corporate adoption to provide training for the underserved	Product quality through effectiveness and inherent need	Job training certification with badges to develop task analysis and career paths.	GHG impact calculations overlaid with impact weighted accounts	Supply chain and technical efficiencies for carbon recovery to energy resources

Figure 13.3   *From Green Advantage and Bring Back the Blue. Blue Energy ANSI – Accredited Certificate Development Program*

Solution – Job Development Initiatives

Job development initiatives in the ocean plastic supply chain can realize environmental justice goals for disadvantaged communities and address workforce development needs. For instance, Bring Back the Blue partners with organizations worldwide, including but not limited to:

- *Paso Pacifico*, a not-for-profit and official marine litter pick up partner for Ecuador and Nicaragua, which runs a successful Junior Ranger program. This program helps develop Blue Economy Jobs and training for at-risk youth populations in these countries.
- *Net Your Problem LLC* engages a variety of stakeholders and partners to create an economically viable pathway to recycle end-of-life fishing gear, improve waste management, contribute to the circular economy, and reduce energy use and greenhouse gas emissions related to virgin plastic production.
- *Ocean Voyages Institute* is a 501(c)3 non-profit organization founded in 1979. Since 2009, the non-profit has successfully carried out projects that detect and remove derelict nets from open ocean and coastal regions.
- *Ocean Sole Africa* is a social enterprise that positively impacts over 1,000 Kenyans through the collection of flip-flops and direct employment. It provides steady income to nearly 100 low-income Kenyans. Ten to fifteen percent of Ocean Soles' revenue goes to beach cleanups, vocational and educational programs, and conservation efforts.

Solution – Global Engagement

Globally, we are seeing new commitments from corporations and mandates from governmental agencies to reduce plastic waste. The UN Treaty on Plastic Pollution, spearheaded by the World Wildlife Fund (WWF), The Ellen MacArthur Foundation, and The Boston Consulting Group (BCG), has gained international attention from business, financial, and governmental sectors. The premise for the treaty is to establish a framework that will allow for the circular supply chain management of plastic pollution. Hundreds of major stakeholders from across the world have signed and committed to this call to action.

WWF and its partners in a 2020 report identified the following problems as preventing the circularity of plastic pollution (WWF et al. 2020):

- A lack of regulations, which would be required to scale.
- Most existing policies are misaligned with major problem drivers.
- Baseline data are lacking and hampering accurate impact assessments.
- Plastic pollution lacks a dedicated global agreement.

WWF and its partners further state that the UN Treaty on Plastic Pollution could create the enabling conditions to eliminate plastic leakage into the ocean (WWF et al. 2020). As we move forward, we should identify the key aspects that affect multi-level climate action based on impact and available solutions. For example, we can take a closer look at the manual removal of microplastics from the surface of the open ocean. In theory, this linear solution does its job: it removes microplastics from the surface of the ocean. However, if total impacts are accounted for, mechanical removal of microplastics from the ocean surface causes a lot of damage, which should be weighed against its positive impacts. These impact weights should include damage caused by removing associated phytoplankton species, the energy and carbon costs of large vessels that can manage these types of operations, product recovery value (if recovered for the next stage of life impact of that product/disposal method), fair wages, and gender and ethnic diversity, among others. Global engagement of private and public sector actions to reduce ocean plastic needs to take into account the circular supply chain management of waste. Removal and supply chain management of escaped plastic that has entered and is entering our aquatic and terrestrial ecosystems are major proponents of mitigating the long-term impacts of plastic on climate change.

A successful example of stakeholder engagement is the U.S. based non-profit Blue Frontier Campaign, which has a directory of over 1,400 Ocean Impact organizations and builds solution-oriented citizen engagement around ocean advocacy. One of the keys to its effectiveness is its "Hill Days" and biennial Blue Vision Summits. These events not only congregate a large constituency of stakeholders but also bring them together in large numbers to nationally advocate for ocean issues. These efforts have been key drivers of ocean policy. The process of how we bring thought leaders and academics before policymakers needs to be adjusted to develop the hand-in-hand working relationships required to create the positive change in ocean plastic and to meet our looming GHG reduction timelines.

PROBLEM – OCEAN PLASTIC A KEY DRIVER OF CLIMATE CHANGE

Plastic to date has been widely thought of as inert and immortal. Over the last decade, scientific studies have shown this is not the case. Plastic is a relatively new product with mass production for public use commencing in the mid-twentieth century. The scientific community is learning more and more about the material applications of plastic and its additives as well as their impacts on the environment and people. Old policies and equations are being re-evaluated with the current scientific understanding that plastics do break down. We also know that degradation of plastic in the environment is complex and contingent on a number of factors, which include plastic type, plasticizers, additives, buoyancy, charge and surface characteristics, and the environments they end up in. The scientific literature has also shown that plastic pollution directly and indirectly influences the global carbon cycle (Zheng & Suh 2019; Dees et al. 2020; MacLeod et al. 2021).

So what does this mean?

- *Direct*: 380 million metric tons (Mt) of fossil carbon are converted into plastic per year (Geyer et al. 2017; Dees et al. 2020) and degrade or are industrially converted (e.g., by incineration or landfilling) to carbon dioxide, methane, and other greenhouse gasses (Zheng & Suh 2019; MacLeod et al. 2021).
- *Indirect*: ocean plastic degradation and leaching phthalates impact dissolved organic carbon (DOC) concentrations, habitats and biochemical pathways of cyanobacteria and phytoplankton. Decreased populations of bacterial communities and disruptions to biochemical pathways, such as heterotrophic respiration (CO_2), methanogenesis (CH_4), denitrification (N_2O), photosynthetic capacity, genome-wide transcriptional changes, and growth lead to reduced carbon sequestration from the atmosphere (Tetu et al. 2019; Arp et al. 2021; MacLeod et al. 2021). The sinking, deposition and burial of fixed carbon in particulate organic matter to marine sediments is a key, long-term mechanism for sequestering

CO_2e from the atmosphere. Therefore, the balance between the regeneration of CO_2e and nutrients via remineralization versus burial in the seabed is one determinant of the effect of ocean plastic on climate change (Cavicchioli et al. 2019).

Solution – Direct Ocean Plastic Impacts on GHG Emissions

Diversion from landfill

Plastics in landfills break down and emit carbon and leach toxins, not only impacting global GHG emissions but polluting water and soil for decades with endocrine-disrupting chemicals. In 2018, nearly 27 million tons of plastics ended up in landfills in the United States (EPA-Online Jan 2021). In the U.S., carbon emissions from plastic incineration reached 5.9 million metric tons of carbon dioxide in 2015 and are predicted to reach 49 million metric tons by 2030 (Fahim et al. 2021). Over the past four decades, global plastic production has quadrupled (Stubbins et al. 2021). If this trend continues, the GHG emissions from plastics will reach 15% of the global carbon budget by 2050 (Eriksson & Finnveden 2009). In 2015, conventional (fossil fuel-based) plastics produced 1.8Gt CO_2e over their life cycle, excluding any carbon credits from recycling, which was 3.8% of the 47 $GtCO_2e$ emitted globally that year (Zheng & Suh 2019).

Reduce transport

Transport of waste to processing centers and landfills is a major contributor to maritime GHG emissions. Maritime decarbonization is one of the hardest sectors for which to implement solutions. While the impact varies from port to port, a majority of ports transport trash to municipal waste processing facilities.

Researchers are only beginning to understand the GHG emission impacts of transporting ocean plastic to landfills or conversion facilities. Sifakis and Tsoutsos (2020) stated that the key to net zero emissions from ports includes air quality, energy conservation and renewable energy systems, water pollution and quality, electrification/hybridization of equipment, noise pollution, waste management, smart energy management systems, and natural habitat quality preservation (Sifakis & Tsoutsos 2020).

Conversion of ocean plastic, plastic trash, and other waste into no-sulfur diesel, direct to energy grid resources, synfuels, and biofuels positively impacts five of these parameters. When other circular mitigation techniques are added to this, such as bioremediation and sorbents products converted to energy, all of the parameters can be met. While few studies have been done on ocean plastic and plastic waste conversion at ports, products created from this process can be used to reduce emissions from traditional fuels through mixing practices, powering port equipment and transport vehicles, fueling the regional energy grid, and hydrogen production.

Utilizing these fuels can significantly reduce SO_2 emissions. Large ports, such as the Port of Seattle in the U.S., produce almost 78,688 metric tons of CO_2e, with a 20% increase predicted by 2030 (Port of Seattle 2021). If we continue with business as usual, 15% of GHG emissions in 2050 will be from plastic going to landfills, and an additional 17% will come from maritime transport (Cames et al. 2015; MacLeod et al. 2021). The UN's International Maritime Organization (2020) reported that shipping represented about 2.89% of total anthropogenic carbon dioxide emissions in 2018. Maritime activities connect supply chains, markets, and geographies, with real impacts on ocean, human, atmospheric, and economic well-being. Around 90% of traded goods travel by sea (Narula 2014).

Trash is also transported from metropolises by boat to developing countries. Port vulnerabilities, international agreements, and GHG transport costs provide an economic incentive to place investments into port infrastructure to reduce transboundary transport of ocean plastic and plastic trash. Studies on ports are showing that there is a positive correlation between environmental, social, and economic issues when assessing port sustainability performance (Lim et al. 2019).

Onsite sorting, conversion, and distribution
With current legislation, such as the Basel Convention (effective on January 1, 2021), the export of plastic waste has been strictly limited, leaving the world with a huge plastic waste problem. By developing robust supply chain management for ocean plastic and plastic trash, we can generate solutions and customer bases closer to the sources and delivery points, thus making a large dent in our global GHG reductions. Proven and insurable conversion technologies exist that efficiently turn traditionally non-recyclable plastics into profitable products, such as diesel, avgas and building materials. By utilizing these technologies, we are able to make waste into wages, wealth, wearables, and energy.

Reducing single use plastic production
Less than 9% of plastics are recycled worldwide, with less than 1% of plastic recycled more than once (Geyer et al. 2017; Korley et al. 2021). Other downgraded CO_2e-generating disposal processes, such as incineration and landfills, account for approximately 80% of end-of-life scenarios for plastics. In 2015, approximately 12% of waste plastics were incinerated and 79% were accumulated in landfills or ecosystems around the world (Geyer et al. 2017; Korley et al. 2021).

Recently, advanced conversion has been added to the equation. Technological advances have made this process more efficient in the conversion of plastic to energy resources. Efficient industrial low temperature melt, microwave, and nuclear pyrolysis units are no longer things of the future. There are now several companies that make these units industrial sized. In fact, the plastic-to-fuel market is forecast to surpass U.S.$1.75 billion by 2028 with a compound annual growth rate of 28.8% (Acumen Research and Consulting 2021).

Technology revolution
The recycling and conversion industries are constantly evolving and improving. Multi-tech clean conversion pyrolysis facilities are optimal when dealing with ocean plastic due to the variety of inputs and ability to grow and adapt with industry changes as they become industrialized. For example, in 2019, a group from Purdue University developed a unit that used higher temperatures ranging from 380–500°C for up to five hours at a pressure of 23 megapascals (Chen et al. 2019). The high heat and pressure water system breaks down the plastic and converts it into oil with 91% conversion of polypropylene plastic into oil (current industrialized units are closer to 84% conversion). Other units are now efficiently converting plastic into hydrogen or direct input into energy grids (Aminu et al. 2020). Blockchain, AI, near and near-real time sensors, and other virtual technologies are being applied to MRFs to automate sorting, cleaning, sales, and processing. The speed at which the industry is evolving

means there are currently industrial options as well as newer technologies that can help generate a "best fit" facility for any site from remote to industrialized areas.

Solution – Indirect Ocean Plastic Impacts on GHG Emissions

Policy and data

Our knowledge of the impact of ocean plastics on the environment and people has been changing rapidly. We need to adjust policies and credits to reflect our greater understanding of plastic pollution in the ocean and other environments.

Incentivized removal of ocean plastic

Removal of ocean plastic before it degrades is a key part of reducing the harm of ocean plastics on the global carbon cycle. Programs that remove plastic from the ocean need support to maintain their socially and environmentally beneficial efforts. Government, corporate, and private backing helps to incentivize the creation of ocean plastic remediation programs in the public and private sectors. The support can and should be done in the form of plastic offsets, commerce, government prioritization and legislation, and philanthropy. Only a handful of operations are receiving appropriate financial support. This includes a holistic look at companies' and organizations' total impact, including GHG emissions, volume removal, environmental impact of removal process, gender and ethnic diversity, social, economic impact, and fair wages.

Value driven supply chain

Incentives are required to keep plastic in the supply chain and out of the environment. One of the issues with keeping plastic out of the environment is its low price point. There is little incentive for people to keep the pollutant from escaping into the environment. When products are made with circularity, supply chain and consumer behavior in mind, plastics are less likely to enter the environment and can instead be reused. For example, Sweden has a successful PANT system, in which consumers can visit deposit machines in supermarkets and recycle their old plastic bottles and cans in return for compensation that they can later spend at a market. In 2019, Swedes recycled 84% (1.8 billion) of purchased bottles and cans, not far below the government's recycling target of 90% (Sweden.se, online). Another notable example is Vermont's (USA) Beverage Container and Redemption Law ("the Bottle Bill"), which was developed to reduce litter and incentivize the cleanup of Vermont's roadsides. Under the law anyone can return a bottle or can to a retailer or redemption center to redeem the deposit (5–15 cents). The program has a 77% redemption rate (Vermont.gov, online; bottlebill.org, online).

PROBLEM – NOT ALL PLASTIC CREDITS ARE EQUAL

Due to mandates on plastic and carbon reduction and environmental commitments by governments and companies, climate action has merged with green capitalism to give rise to a new market direction called Climate Capitalism (Walenta 2020). Understanding climate risk impact has become a key tool and driver in auditing and showing the efficacy of Climate Capitalism to meet mandates and sustainability goals. Traditionally, tools such as climate risk assessments (CRAs) and science-based targets (SBTs) have been used for quantitative analysis. These assessments are linear and don't account for the full breadth of the plastic waste problem. The Harvard Business School has started to develop methods for a combined assessment called Impact-Weighted Accounts, which is a financial accounting method that reflects a company's financial, social, and environmental performance (Serafeim & Trinh 2020; Rouen & Serafeim 2021). As Rouen and Serafeim (2021, p. 20) stated, "According to the UN Sustainable Stock Exchanges, 44 exchanges around the world have released ESG disclosure guidance for their listed companies." Rouen and Serafeim (2021) point out that better accounting of our social and environmental impacts will help world leaders, executives, managers and investors to make better decisions and policies that will increase our ability to reduce our impact on climate change in a timely manner. Rouen and Serafeim (2021) have highlighted three areas that need attention to normalize impact-weighted accounts:

- *Regulatory organization that defines the scope of the environmental and social impacts.* This will help alleviate scope bias. In the ocean plastic space, this could be viewed as credits for ocean plastic removal vs. diverted ocean plastic removal.
- *Different impacts have different measurement bases.* This is an ongoing problem in accounting, but not addressing this gives rise to incomparable numbers across different impacts. This could be viewed as impacting costs on ecological regions such as coastline and estuaries vs. impacts on people who pick up ocean plastic (i.e., ocean plastic miners).
- *Accounting treatment that creates both stock and flow measures is needed.* Both of these weighted measurements are important for accountability and contracting purposes. Stock measurements become important for an impact-weighted balance sheet. Flow measurements become part of an impact-weighted income statement. Accounting for both is necessary so as to not develop negative environmental liability numbers that are counter-weighted by positive employment impacts.

The European Commission and regulatory agencies worldwide are defining the scope of sustainable finance. They are looking to develop green bond standards used to assess the environmental impact of economic activities. Rouen and Serafeim (2021, p. 24) state, "Missing vital impacts might positively or negatively bias the impacts" (Figure 13.4). This is especially true of the plastic offset industry. As the method development and certification of those methods are standardized for the open carbon offset market, the plastic offset market will follow suit.

These standardizations are just beginning in the plastic offset open marketplace. Companies such as Verra, a registry in the carbon offset space, and Bring Back The Blue, a plastic offset development company, are working on standardized method approaches. Not all plastic offsets are equal. In the plastic offset marketplace, many companies are selling offsets attached to "diverted ocean plastic," which is another name for coastal municipal recycling. These offsets should not have the same weighted value as plastic taken from and already impacting the ocean. Additionally, not all true ocean plastic offsets are equal. Coastal ocean plastic should not have the same value as open ocean plastic, and open ocean plastic should not have the same value as benthic ocean plastic. Methods-based approaches and weighted values of these should be the goal of the plastic offset community. In this accounting, these variables should be the basis of method valuation: location of removal, next stage of life and its complexities, transport type and distance to sorting and distribution, and life transition (i.e., recycling, incineration, landfill, conversion, economic impact, fair wage assessments, and gender and ethnic diversity).

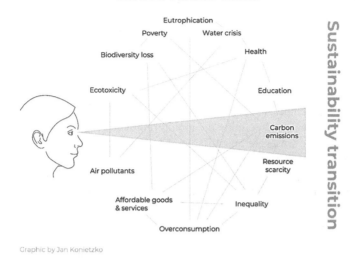

Figure courtesy of Jan Konietzko, PhD, Sustainability Advisor, Cognizant.

Figure 13.4   Carbon tunnel vision

Additional complexities arise in calculating all of these variables and their interconnection with CO_2e emissions and carbon offsets. Development of these market-based methods will be important for producing adequate valuations and driving circular economy practices for ocean plastic remediation and ocean plastic diversion practices. The plastic offset credit exchange should follow a course like the carbon offset industry, supported by an external compensation project(s) that generates a plastic-negative effect and follows certified methods verifying that impact. The creation of a market for plastic credits is crucial to generating demand for plastic waste and financial incentives to invest in the infrastructure and technology required to generate an ocean plastic circular climate solution.

Plastic credits offer compensation for the removal of a defined quantity of plastic from the environment for the proper disposal, recycling, reuse, or conversion of the material to another usable form. This system allows credit holders the right to offset the amount of plastic waste they generate, which includes the private sector, governments and individual consumers.

Solution(s) – Plastic Offset Credits – Carbon Offset Credits

Blockchain and data driven efficacy
Data are becoming a key driver in the valuation of credits. Recently, blockchain public, private and permission-based methods for data efficacy have gained popularity. Because of this decentralized system's minimum transaction costs, hacker resistant constructions, transparency, and auditability, most companies prefer blockchain technology (Khadke et al. 2021; Wong et al. 2021). Chidepatil et al. (2020) developed blockchain methodologies that can be applied to the waste management sector for plastic waste segregation and recycling processes (Chidepatil et al. 2020). Their methods address some of the core issues in plastic sorting and

the lack of reliable data about recycled plastics. They piloted how multi-sensor data fusion tools combined with artificial intelligence can help to segregate commingled plastic waste based on physicochemical parameters, such as color, polymer type, and density. When layered together, these tools help increase supply chain management efficiencies and GHG reductions.

Certified methods

Certified methods for standardized approaches on the open plastic market offset space will be key drivers in quantifying the value of a plastic offset project. Methodologies for developing an offset framework include establishing the project's baseline, identifying qualifying practice changes to reduce impact, and defining the monitoring requirements necessary to ensure that the reductions in plastic waste are quantifiable and verifiable (climeco.com, online). Methods development for ocean plastic will evolve as better data emerge on baselines and on the true impact of ocean plastic. In the carbon offset space, credible methodologies employ best practices based on the ISO 14064 standard, an International Standard for GHG Emissions Inventories and Verification. Due to the complexity of different kinds of environments and plastics that generate ecological impacts and breakdown parameters, more work on international standards needs to occur to generate a robust methods-compliant open plastic offset marketplace. To generate robust efficacy in (Plastic Offset) methods, there needs to be collaborative, transparent, and auditable efforts based on scientific integrity, conservativeness, and financial viability between projects and registries (climeco.org, online).

False advertising penalties

Greenwashing is a major problem in the plastic waste industry and comes in many forms, including misleading advertising and false reports of GHG reductions, product recyclability, and the amount of post-consumer material in products. Greenwashing occurs when a company intentionally misleads customers into thinking that their product production and/or services are environmentally friendly when they are actually harmful to the environment. A 2021 Survey by LendingTree found that of the 1,048 Americans surveyed, 55% said they were willing to spend more on sustainable and eco-friendly products, and 40% said they would boycott companies that weren't keen on going green. This trend toward eco-consciousness is more prevalent in Gen Z and Millennials, who are willing to boycott non-eco-products 58% and 50% of the time, respectively (lendingtree.com, online). With the growing market of 'eco-conscious' consumers wishing to be a part of the solution to reverse the plastic pollution crisis, advertisers are heavily incentivized to include green claims in their advertising, but they need guidance.

The lack of clear guidance from regulatory agencies means that there is a green light for companies to use vague language that can mislead consumers. ECOS and the Rethink Plastic alliance published a white paper study on the 'green' claims displayed on 82 different products containing plastics or plastic packaging based on an adaptation of the UNEP Fundamental Principles for providing product sustainability information (UNEP 2017; ecostandard.org, online).

They found that 75% of the companies' claims were self-made and not verified by independent third parties, 49% were potentially unclear to consumers as they did not provide sufficient information, 46% were irrelevant to addressing plastic pollution, and 26% lacked supporting evidence and were therefore considered unreliable (ecostandard.org, online). Some companies have great intentions and "trust" manufacturers who overstep claims, especially when it comes to the usability of ocean plastics in products.

Bluewashing is also a major problem. For instance, many companies are using "ocean diverted plastic" in products, advertising that their products are made from ocean plastic when they actually are not. However, ocean diverted plastic has never been in the ocean and can be readily incorporated like any recyclable materials since most has never been in the environment or has only been there for a short time. It is traditional municipal waste recycling under a deceptive name – ocean diverted plastic. In one illustrative incident, the CEO of Kevin Murphy, Laurent Misischi, made a very public apology when the company realized that their packaging was not being made from 100% ocean plastic as they had advertised and manufacturers had promised (Kevinmurphy.com, online). This type of corporate transparency and accountability should be applauded. While many companies in the marketplace turn a blind eye, Kevin Murphy addressed the issue head on. It is only with this type of corporate ethics that we can develop true sustainable solutions that go beyond marketing ploys.

The issue with ocean plastics is material integrity. At sea, ocean plastic is exposed to myriad environmental conditions and biota that intrinsically change the properties of that plastic and load them with other contaminants, including biota, salts, and other contaminants. Additionally, many ocean plastics are so weathered that it is hard to quickly identify the original polymer or product type. For these reasons, traditional recycling processes are not possible with most ocean plastics. Many products have to mix ocean plastic with virgin plastic or other recycled plastics to obtain the uniformity needed for products. These mixed plastics make it hard for the product to have a next stage of life except for incineration or landfilling. Advertising authorities are starting to realize this dilemma and crack down on false advertising. Lack of clear governmental rules and required third party validations of post-consumer and ocean plastic materials lead to a marketplace filled with blended plastic products (virgin, post-consumer and ocean plastic) that are advertised as 100% post-consumer or ocean plastic but do not meet these standards.

PROBLEM – OCEAN PLASTIC SUPPLY CHAIN

Supply chain issues can be thought of in three stages: (1) volume and types of products that are entering the environment and becoming ocean plastic; (2) feedstock supply chain associated with ocean plastic as it is removed from the environment; and (3) next stage of life for the ocean plastic after it is removed from the ocean.

These three stages need to be addressed to adequately develop a multi-level, climate-based supply chain solution to not only mitigate the waste but also create a profitable monetary stream from the 9 to 23 million metric tons per year entering our oceans and waterways (Borrelle et al. 2020; Lau et al. 2020; MacLeod et al. 2021). Island Nations, remote coastal communities and areas of economic disparity are often the hardest hit with the world's waste. Some of the explanations for these geographic disparities include lack of government supported municipal waste systems, minimal effective infrastructure to collect and recycle plastic waste, transportation costs, remoteness, low plastic literacy, regional storms that drive waste to coastlines, and cultural traditions and beliefs (Phelan et al. 2020).

The availability of fast-moving consumer goods and the rising standard of living are pushing plastic waste accumulation rates towards an irreversible tipping point (Geyer et al. 2017; MacLeod et al. 2021). The World Bank deems waste collection a critical step in managing waste. However, there is a large disparity in waste management by income level, with upper-middle and high-income countries providing nearly universal waste collection (The World Bank 2020).

- Low-income countries collect about 48% of waste in cities, but this proportion drops drastically to 26% outside of urban areas (The World Bank 2020).
- Sub-Saharan Africa collects about 44% of its waste (The World Bank 2020).
- Europe and Central Asia and North America collect at least 90% of their waste (The World Bank 2020).

However, the areas with the biggest problems are where the largest economic solutions lie. These supply chain opportunities need to be rethought, retooled, and given support so that regions and communities most impacted by ocean plastic can turn the low-value product into a high-value commodity that help to build economies while effectively managing plastic waste and ocean plastic that washes ashore. Some of the issues that arise when looking at adjusting current supply chain management protocols, infrastructure, and practices come from the current approaches for optimizing the industry. Studies and applied methods for supply chain efficiencies often include circular economy (CE) and sustainable supply chain management (SSCM), which to date have been separate disciplines (Schultz et al. 2021). The biggest gap when looking at plastic supply chains is the widespread distribution of plastics packaging, which typically is made from the least recyclable-marketable content (Figure 13.5, Table 13.1).

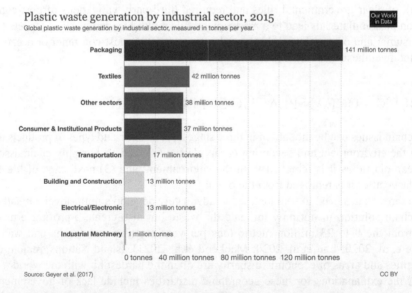

Source: From Hannah Ritchie and Max Roser (2018), Plastic pollution. Published online at OurWorldInData.org. Retrieved from: https://ourworldindata.org/plastic-pollution (Online Resource), (Geyer et al. 2017).

Figure 13.5   Generation of plastic waste by industry sector

Table 13.1   *Largest plastic waste producers*

Country	Plastic waste generation (tonnes)	% Plastic in solid waste	Income status	2016 Mismanaged plastic waste (tonnes)	% Mismanaged waste
United States	42,027,215	13.1	HIC	2,243,564	2.99
India	26,327,933	9.5	LMC	20,799,067	79.00
China	21,599,465	9.8	UMC	5,453,865	25.25
Brazil	10,675,989	13.5	UMC	2,691,344	25.21
Indonesia	9,128,000	14	LMC	5,522,440	60.50
Russian Federation	8,467,156	14.21	UMC	8,255,477	97.50
Germany	6,683,412	13	HIC	268,673	4.02
United Kingdom	6,471,650	20.2	HIC	295,884	4.57
Mexico	5,902,490	10.9	UMC	1,357,573	23.00
Japan	4,881,161	11	HIC	746,818	15.30
Thailand	4,796,494	17.59	UMC	2,985,818	62.25
Korea, Rep.	4,514,186	24.3	HIC	90,284	2.00
Italy	3,365,130	11.6	HIC	438,140	13.02
Egypt, Arab Rep.	3,037,675	13	LMC	2,718,719	89.50
France	2,929,042	9	HIC	59,167	2.02
Pakistan	2,731,768	9	LMC	1,966,873	72.00
Argentina	2,656,771	14.61	HIC	653,566	24.60
Algeria	2,092,007	16.9	UMC	41,840	2.00
Malaysia	2,058,501	15	UMC	409,127	19.88
Spain	1,832,533	9	HIC	36,651	2.00

Note: Data derived from Law et al. (2020). High income country (HIC), upper-middle income country (UMC), lower-middle income country (LMC), and low income country (LC).

The shift to single-use disposables has grown due to Covid-19, with an increasing supply of medical waste that needs special disposal. In Catalonia, Spain, and in China, there was an increase in medical waste (mostly plastic) of 350% and 370%, respectively, from 2019–2020 (Klemeš et al. 2020; Silva et al. 2021). Like many industries with expensive infrastructure, change is painfully slow. However, as we drive the industry forward, we also need to think about the impact of recovery solutions in which, like ocean plastic, not all recovery methods are synonymous. For example, energy recovery processes that involve incineration have significantly higher impact on GHG emissions than energy recovery through low impact advanced recycling such as microwave technologies.

An additional problem is the cost of infrastructure investments. Large-scale conversion projects with good efficiency ratings (50 tons per day or more conversion and 80% or greater efficiency) on average cost around U.S.$50 million. Waste management is labor-intensive and the cost of transportation, alone, is in the range of $20–$50 per ton (The World Bank 2020). For many low-income nations and remote islands that are hardest hit by plastic waste, the price tag for adequate infrastructure to divert plastic from landfill or incineration is staggering.

Many companies across the world are responding to the desire of their customers to "do better" by incorporating ocean plastics into their supply chain. Unfortunately, not all plastic is the same, and true ocean plastic presents many problems that land-based plastic does not. This includes material degradation. Microbes, sea life, salt, and ultraviolet irradiation all alter the surfaces of plastic in the ocean (Figure 13.6) (MacLeod et al. 2021). Only 2–5% of ocean plastic is either identifiable enough or has enough material integrity for traditional recycling. This means that many products are produced with mixed polymers, further degrading the opportunity for next life recycling.

In emerging economies, as discussed above, the material integrity and non-identifiable variety of ocean plastics are highly problematic in inserting ocean plastic into secure supply chains. Companies need uniformity, reliability, and large volumes of the materials used to manufacture their products. Unfortunately, the current traditional supply chain processes used for recycled materials don't fit ocean plastic well. The alternatives to traditional supply chain processes are a mixture of traditional and advanced recycling. As the industry of ocean plastic matures and new tools, advances, and technologies come to market, validation and metrics will be needed to show the efficacy and impact of these new supply chains methods.

Source: Imaging and analysis courtesy of Blue Ocean Sciences, LLC (Andrea Neal, PhD and Randall Mielke, PhD).

Figure 13.6   *Visualization of open ocean microbes hitching a ride on environmental pre-production resin pellets (PRPs): PRP 60 nm thin sections were stained with the Kanig uranyl-acetate technique and imaged with a FEI XL30 FEG ESEM using a STEM detector with an accelerating voltage of 20 kV. Samples from 2009 S/V Kaisei research cruise to the Subtropical Convergence Zone of the North Pacific Gyre, 3200 nautical miles from California Coast*

For larger scale, buoyant ocean plastics, such as derelict nets, there are enough data to justify a robust feedstock supply for ocean plastic supply chain development. In 2009, Macfadyen et al. (2009) estimated that 640,000 tons of fishing gear was lost, abandoned, or discarded per year. The European Union (EU) loses around 20% of its used fishing gear every year (approximately 11,000 tonnes) (Langedal et al. 2020). South Korea's marine debris buyback orchestrated by the Ministry of Land, Transport and Maritime Affairs collected 29,472 tons of plastic between 2004 and 2008 (Morishige 2010). These nets can cause economic damage to transport vessels. The Republic of Korea's Navy (ROKN) recorded that from January 2010 to December 2015 derelict fishing gear caused entanglement in 397.7 (± 37.5) naval vessels per year. The average amount of derelict fishing gear disentangled was 0.025 tons per ship and 10.0 (± 1.7) tons per year (Hong et al. 2017). When developing secure supply chains, it is important to note that for ocean plastic recovery, mega plastics (e.g., fishing nets) represent more than 46% of the total plastic load for the North Pacific Subtropical Gyre (Lebreton et al. 2018).

Solution – Plastic Entering the Ocean and Waterways

Producer responsibility overlaid with circular supply chain strategies is imperative to help stem the tide of ocean plastic pollution. Sustainable plastic usage would include mitigating the travel distance of materials to make products, using integrated AI-Sensor-Blockchain MRF methods, distance of delivery of products to customers, and designing products for reuse at end of life. Policies like those set forth in the 2018 European Strategy for Plastics in a Circular Economy and adopted into the Green New Deal (European Commission 2018, p. 65) are a good step in better design for product, manufacturing, delivery, and end of life. Through these commitments, all plastic packaging placed in the European market will be either reused or recycled in a cost-effective manner, and more than half of plastic waste generated in Europe will be recycled by 2030 (European Commission 2018).

This is a big step since the current amount of recycled plastic entering the EU value chain as raw material is just 6% of European plastic demand (European Commission 2018; Sheldon & Norton 2020). Supply chain product uniformity, especially packaging, is important to increase the recycling capacity of ocean plastic. Uniformity is a big component of the successful transition of plastic waste into upcycled plastic products and advanced conversion recycling. Supply chains developed around ocean plastic derelict nets have shown us the path towards effective supply chains of recycled ocean plastic content due to the uniformity of the resource. ECONYL is one such example. Their supply chain includes regenerated nylon made by Aquafil. Every 10,000 tons of ECONYL raw materials produced saves 70,000 barrels of crude oil and 65,100 tonnes of CO_2 equivalent emissions (econyl.com, online). Their supply chain strength comes in the form of uniform feedstock from fishing nets. This type of model becomes more repeatable with different product types when more commitments for uniformity and recyclability of plastic product production are made.

Solution – Ocean Plastic Supply Chain Development

A robust workforce of plastic miners is important for removing plastic from the ocean. Currently, derelict nets are the easiest product around which to develop supply chains. These nets are also the most prevalent and largest ocean plastic pollutant found in near-surface interfaces in the ocean. Larger plastics, such as derelict nets, comprise 92% of the plastic found on the surface of the North Pacific Subtropical Gyre (Chen et al. 2018). Recovery of ocean plastic is easiest from coastal areas and surface layers of water bodies.

Ocean Voyages Institute (OVI) is considered one of the world's leaders in effective at-sea cleanups. In 2019 and 2020, the organization removed 434,000 pounds of ghostnets and mixed commercial and consumer plastic (Figure 13.7). OVI also has a proprietary program that determines the exact locations of the targeted derelict nets they remove from the North Pacific Subtropical Convergence Zone, which utilizes satellite beacons attached to large ghost nets to track the nets.

They recover these tagged nets with sailing cargo ships to reduce their impact on GHG emissions that would occur from similar ocean salvaged motorized vessels. By targeting net removal, OVI removes high impact debris that damages aquatic species and vessels and prevents some derelict nets from ending up on reefs and shorelines. An analysis of 870 gillnets found many were derelict for years. Most were recovered from northern Puget Sound and high-relief rocky habitats. Documented marine organisms included 31,278 invertebrates (76 species), 1036 fishes (22 species), 514 birds (16 species), and 23 mammals (four species); 56% of invertebrates, and 93% of fish. All birds and mammals were dead when recovered (Good 2010). Removal of derelict nets reduces hazards to vessels at sea, prevents migration of invasive species in critical habitats and fisheries, and helps prevent death to critical and endangered species, such as seabirds, the Hawaiian monk seal, green sea turtles, whales and other sea life.

Source: Andrea Neal, PhD.

Figure 13.7   *Derelict net from S/V Kaisei research cruise to the Subtropical Convergence Zone of the North Pacific Gyre, 3400 nautical miles from California Coast*

Plastic debris has been estimated to cause more than U.S.$13 billion in economic damage to marine ecosystems each year and is now widely recognized as a serious threat to the marine environment (Avio et al. 2017). Recovering derelict nets from open oceans has a greater operational expense and risk, the rewards and gains in this supply chain model justify it. For example, each derelict net can weigh 2–6 tons of a consistent material, often nylon, which if priced as fish on the open marketplace, would be valued at ≈ U.S.$3,000–U.S.$18,000 per ton depending on product and grade.

Supply chains of coastal ocean plastics have other operational logistics to consider. Women-owned and operated enterprise Ocean Sole Africa, based in Nairobi, Kenya, is a social enterprise that has upcycled flip-flops found along the beaches and waterways in Kenya since 2013 and supports over 100 employees. Currently, Ocean Sole Africa operates its art workshop in Nairobi and picks up 5–10 tons of ocean plastic from Kenyan beaches weekly. Approximately 1 ton of this comes from flip-flops that they turn into art and sell worldwide. Another quarter to half a ton per week is utilized in mosquito nets and building products. This leaves 80–90% of the trash they remove without a home, with the main destination being land-fill. The available feedstock supply is immense for Kenya, where 37,000 tons of plastic leak into the ocean every year (Paruta 2020). Kenya produces approximately 465,000 tons per year of mismanaged waste (Paruta 2020). In Kenya, 73% of all plastic waste is uncollected. Eight percent is collected for recycling, and 19% is disposed of in unsanitary landfills or dumpsites (Paruta 2020).

Bring Back the Blue is working with Ocean Sole Africa to develop a robust materials recovery facility, supply chain and plastic offset plan (specifically for Ocean Plastic) to expand Ocean Sole's operations from one coastal region to 536 km of Kenya's Indian Ocean coastline, generating steady jobs, supporting the local communities, upcycling plastic to building materials that can be used locally, and helping generate a robust Blue Economy for Kenya. These efforts will generate a business case for long-term sustainable jobs supported by a secure ocean plastic supply chain, generating a blue circular economy that provides a higher standard of living for at-risk demographics.

Solution – Regional Supply Chain Development

While these efforts are logistically easier and less risky than open ocean remediation of larger ocean plastics, such as derelict nets, they are more complex due to the variety and variable degrees of degradation of the recovered ocean plastic. This type of supply chain operation needs a more robust material recovery sorting facility than traditional recycling supply chains or open ocean derelict net supply chains. Regional supply chains need to be considered when developing methods. Each region has its own needs, political climate, regional management of resources, religions, community groups, and businesses. Supply chains must be assessed for their feasibility as well as their GHG emission, economic, and social impacts. Third party validated methods, combined with public facing blockchain technology, are recommended for tracking and tracing all impact metrics from removal to product production.

As we develop regional supply chains, we should not only consider the potential increase of ocean plastic feedstock but also where a majority of plastics exports are shipped from and where their destinations lie. Three countries – the United States, Japan and Germany – were responsible for almost one-third of plastic waste exports between 1988 and 2020 (Environmental Investigation Agency 2021). China imported the most plastic waste worldwide between 2010 and 2020 with 65% of imports (Environmental Investigation Agency 2021). For decades, this collect–sort–export model dominated the plastic waste sector until China put the brakes on the global system in 2018. That year, China issued the "National Sword" policy, banning the importation of most international plastics and other materials out of concern for the nation's environmental and public health and their recycling facilities' capacity (Environmental Investigation Agency 2021).

Following the ban, predominantly exporting countries started sending their waste to mostly low-income countries, namely in Eastern Europe and Southeast Asia, as well as quickly filling up their landfills and incinerators, contributing further to greenhouse gas emissions. Those countries then became overwhelmed and placed their own limits on waste imports, forcing the entire globe to reckon with how we deal with our refuse. New amendments to the Basel Convention became effective on January 1, 2021, which strictly limits what plastic waste can be exported. These amendments were signed by 187 countries, not including the U.S. Despite this, some states within the U.S., including California (Quinn 2021), have passed laws that help to comply with the international community's objectives to reduce the export of plastic waste and obligate exporters to focus on internally processing their refuse rather than externalizing it.

Several factors incentivized the movement of plastic across borders and oceans, including low contamination standards, cheap labor costs, high demand for recycled materials, and favorable rates for filling up cargo vessels that would have otherwise returned to China vacant. Doing business as usual is not possible anymore and governmental policies and commitments are wisely pushing us to do better with our supply chain models. Simply put, when we produce products closer to the customer to meet demands, we significantly reduce our GHG impacts. With that in mind, both due to regulatory goals and global demands and goals for GHG reductions, the new ocean plastic supply chain logistics model should allow for localized collection, production, and delivery to customers. These efforts should be supported through offsets, government incentivizations and customers, who are demanding quicker turnaround and delivery times of their products.

Solution – Blue Economy Jobs

Port and opportunity zone action steps can help to improve people's quality of life through employment opportunities, education for employees and locals, and enhanced social stability of areas surrounding ports (Narula, 2014). Near-port populations are usually low-income communities and communities of color, highlighting further the links between ports as emblematic of the trend in the U.S. that such groups unfairly face higher rates of health and access concerns related to pollution from major industrial activities (U.S. EPA 2020).

However, a trifecta of shared interests – infrastructure, regulatory jurisdictions, local governments and climate-related risks – obligate ports to find ways to work with near-port communities in the creation of long-term sustainability and investment strategies. The U.S. EPA cited multiple legal stipulations, including the National Environmental Policy Act (NEPA) and the federal Executive Order 12898, as a means to instigate ports to engage with near-port communities. The U.S. EPA put forward multiple federally-created tools for stakeholder engagement. Port professionals are principally concerned with efficiency, especially energy efficiency, because constant fuel consumption undergirds all port operations (Sifakis & Tsoutsos 2020).

A new blue circular industry can help to provide solutions to ports' challenges by providing well-paying jobs, fostering a healthier marine environment, and generating clean energy production through onsite conversion of ocean plastic to energy. By addressing the gaps in the circular supply chain, Blue Economy industries can be incubated and existing ones augmented. These industries not only address the gravity of plastic pollution and GHG but also generate new economic drivers. These drivers can and will improve economic disparities through job creation, education, STEM-related vocations, and regional health impacts. BBTB plans with this initiative to collaborate with Opportunity Zone leaders and organizations to understand, and together address, the needs of each community to provide local, long-term, well-paid jobs.

Solution – Circular Product Development

Current plastic value chains follow mostly linear models, with 90% of plastic feedstocks coming from fossil origin (oil and gas) and 4–8% of the world's oil production used to make plastics (about half of this is used as material feedstock and half as fuel/energy for the production process) (World Economic Forum 2016). The majority of plastic production goes into products with a short lifespan, such as packaging. In particular, plastic packaging is almost exclusively made for single use and landfill disposal or incineration. Today, 95% of plastic packaging material value, or U.S.$80–120 billion annually, is lost to the economy after a short first use (World Economic Forum 2016). In the supply chain world of plastics, uniformity is king. A more uniform and steady supply of feedstock allows for a constant and profitable next stage of life for product manufacturing or conversion. Conversion technologies that efficiently turn traditionally non-recyclable plastics into profitable products, such as diesel, avgas and building materials, work best with uniform and reliable feedstock.

Through the generation of a uniform feedstock, we are able to keep plastics out of landfills while generating profit and usable goods from ocean plastics. Plastic credits can provide the necessary financial backing for the generation of a robust ocean plastic supply chain that supports the removal of ocean plastic from the ocean, coasts and waterways and diverts plastics from landfills, specifically those deemed necessitating consent for transboundary movements by The Basel Convention.

Third party validated methods and certifications for an industrialized ocean plastic supply chain are needed to develop a robust workforce and auditable product. This process is similar to the incentivizations from governments and through carbon offset methods to provide subsidies for carbon capture/removal projects to make them competitive in the marketplace.

CONCLUDING REMARKS

Social, economic, and environmental issues are intrinsically interconnected. The true efficacy of measuring the impact of multi-level climate change solutions should take into account the circular impact of social, economic, and environmental issues. We now know that plastic and its constituents are impacting everything from global carbon cycling systems to biological functions such as reproduction. By 2050, plastics are expected to reach production rates of more than 1100 million metric tons per year, of which 22 to 48 million metric tons per year will end up in the environment (Macleod et al. 2021).

In tandem with this environmental threat is a disturbing social and economic injustice. For decades, communities of economic disparity have borne the adverse effects of pollution, including ocean plastic pollution. A recent UN report confirmed that plastic pollution disproportionately and severely impacts marginalized groups. The clean energy revolution can and must lift up all communities.

Toward that end, there are now industrialized, state-of-the-art, plastic-to-clean energy technologies in the works that need trained and credentialed workers. For example, Waste-to-Energy infrastructure projects in areas of disparity offer a four-fold win for:

1. Unemployed and underemployed workers – good paying, meaningful employment and career advancement in a burgeoning industry.
2. Disadvantaged communities – more employed residents, economic stimulation, reduced pollution, locally produced clean energy.
3. Employers – trained and credentialed workers available to do important work, tax incentivization and investment opportunities.
4. Environment – cleaner oceans, beaches and ports, better habitat for flora and fauna, and clean, locally-produced energy.

The bottom line is we have a problem that needs proactive multi-level climate action to generate immediate solutions. Through the business case studies and research that address the gaps in the circular ocean plastic supply chain, we can augment these new Blue Economy industries. These initiatives not only address the immediate environmental problem of plastic pollution but also generate new economic drivers. These drivers can and will improve: economic disparities through job creation, coastal and ocean ecosystem health, environmental education, health of communities impacted by plastic waste, and creation and implementation of policy in several nations, international treaties, and COP26 commitments.

REFERENCES

Acumen Research and Consulting. (2021). *Plastic to Fuel - Global Market and Forecast Till 2028.* Acumen Research and Consulting.

Aminu, I., Nahil, M. A., & Williams, P. T. (2020). Hydrogen from waste plastics by two-stage pyrolysis/low-temperature plasma catalytic processing. *Energy & Fuels*, 34(9), 11679–11689.

Arp, H. P. H., Kühnel, D., Rummel, C., MacLeod, M., Potthoff, A., Reichelt, S., ... & Jahnke, A. (2021). Weathering plastics as a planetary boundary threat: Exposure, fate, and hazards. *Environmental Science & Technology*, 55(11), 7246–7255.

Avio, C. G., Gorbi, S., & Regoli, F. (2017). Plastics and microplastics in the oceans: From emerging pollutants to emerged threat. *Marine Environmental Research*, 128, 2–11.

Borrelle, S. B., Ringma, J., Law, K. L., Monnahan, C. C., Lebreton, L., McGivern, A., ... & Rochman, C. M. (2020). Predicted growth in plastic waste exceeds efforts to mitigate plastic pollution. *Science*, 369(6510), 1515–1518.

bottlebill.org (online). https://www.bottlebill.org/index.php/current-and-proposed-laws/usa/vermont

Cames, M., Graichen, J., Siemons, A., & Cook, V. (2015). Emission reduction targets for international aviation and shipping. Policy Department A: Economic and Scientific Policy, European Parliament, B-1047 Brussels.

Cavicchioli, R., Ripple, W. J., Timmis, K. N., Azam, F., Bakken, L. R., Baylis, M., ... & Webster, N. S. (2019). Scientists' warning to humanity: Microorganisms and climate change. *Nature Reviews Microbiology*, 17(9), 569–586.

Chen, W. T., Jin, K., & Linda Wang, N. H. (2019). Use of supercritical water for the liquefaction of polypropylene into oil. *ACS Sustainable Chemistry & Engineering*, 7(4), 3749–3758.

Chen, Q., Reisser, J., Cunsolo, S., Kwadijk, C., Kotterman, M., Proietti, M., ... & Koelmans, A. A. (2018). Pollutants in plastics within the north Pacific subtropical gyre. *Environmental Science & Technology*, 52(2), 446–456.

Chidepatil, A., Bindra, P., Kulkarni, D., Qazi, M., Kshirsagar, M., & Sankaran, K. (2020). From trash to cash: How blockchain and multi-sensor-driven artificial intelligence can transform circular economy of plastic waste? *Administrative Sciences*, 10(2), 23.

climeco.com (online). https://climeco.com/creating-carbon-offsets-it-starts-with-a-methodology/

Dees, J. P., Ateia, M., & Sanchez, D. L. (2020). Microplastics and their degradation products in surface waters: A missing piece of the global carbon cycle puzzle. *ACS ES&T Water*, 1(2), 214–216.

econyl.com (online). https://www.econyl.com/e-books

ecostandard.org (online). https://ecostandard.org/wp-content/uploads/2021/07/ECOS-RPa-REPORT -Too-Good-To-Be-True.pdf

Environmental Investigation Agency. (2021). *The Truth Behind Trash: The Scale and Impact of the International Trade in Plastic Waste*. https://rethinkplasticalliance.eu/wp-content/uploads/2021/09/ EIA_UK_Plastic_Waste_Trade_Report.pdf

EPA Online. (2021). "Plastics: Material-specific data," EPA, 5 January. [(Online]).

Eriksson, O., & Finnveden, G. (2009). Plastic waste as a fuel-CO_2-neutral or not? *Energy & Environmental Science*, 2(9), 907–914.

European Commission. (2018). Communication from the Commission to the European Parliament, the Council, the European Economic and Social Committee and the Committee of the Regions. Brussels.

Fahim, I., Mohsen, O., & ElKayaly, D. (2021). Production of fuel from plastic waste: A feasible business. *Polymers*, 13(6), 915.

Gewert, B., Plassmann, M. M., & MacLeod, M. (2015). Pathways for degradation of plastic polymers floating in the marine environment. *Environmental Science: Processes & Impacts*, 17(9), 1513-1521.

Geyer, R., Jambeck, J. R., & Law, K. L. (2017). Production, use, and fate of all plastics ever made. *Science Advances*, 3(7), e1700782

Good, T. P., June, J. A., Etnier, M. A., & Broadhurst, G. (2010). Derelict fishing nets in Puget Sound and the Northwest Straits: Patterns and threats to marine fauna. *Marine Pollution Bulletin*, 60(1), 39–50.

Gutberlet, J. (2021). Grassroots waste picker organizations addressing the UN sustainable development goals. *World Development*, 138, 105195.

Hong, S., Lee, J., & Lim, S. (2017). Navigational threats by derelict fishing gear to navy ships in the Korean seas. *Marine Pollution Bulletin*, 119(2), 100–105.

International Maritime Organization. (2020). *Fourth IMO Greenhouse Gas Study 2020*. IMO.

Johannes, H. P., Kojima, M., Iwasaki, F., & Edita, E. P. (2021). Applying the extended producer responsibility towards plastic waste in Asian developing countries for reducing marine plastic debris. *Waste Management & Research*, 39(5), 690–702.

Kelley, E., Digiantonio, G., Renta, I., Newcomb, L., Matlock, G., Bayler, E., ... & Wielgus, J. (2021). *2020 NOAA Science Report*. NOAA.

Kevinmurphy.com (online). https://kevinmurphy.com.au/choices-we-make/ocean-waste-plastic/ ?location=usa

Khadke, S., Gupta, P., Rachakunta, S., Mahata, C., Dawn, S., Sharma, M., ... & Dalapati, G. K. (2021). Efficient plastic recycling and remolding circular economy using the technology of trust–blockchain. *Sustainability*, 13(16), 9142.

Klemeš, J. J., Van Fan, Y., Tan, R. R., & Jiang, P. (2020). Minimising the present and future plastic waste, energy and environmental footprints related to COVID-19. *Renewable and Sustainable Energy Reviews*, 127, 109883.

Korley, L. T., Epps III, T. H., Helms, B. A., & Ryan, A. J. (2021). Toward polymer upcycling—adding value and tackling circularity. *Science*, 373(6550), 66–69.

Langedal, G., Aarbakke, B., Larsen, F., & Stadig, C. (2020). *Clean Nordic Oceans Main Report–A Network to Reduce Marine Litter and Ghost Fishing*. Nordic Council of Ministers.

Lau, W. W., Shiran, Y., Bailey, R. M., Cook, E., Stuchtey, M. R., Koskella, J., ... & Palardy, J. E. (2020). Evaluating scenarios toward zero plastic pollution. *Science*, 369(6510), 1455–1461.

Law, K. L., Starr, N., Siegler, T. R., Jambeck, J. R., Mallos, N. J., & Leonard, G. H. (2020). The United States' contribution of plastic waste to land and ocean. *Science Advances*, 6(44), eabd0288.

Lebreton, L., Slat, B., Ferrari, F., Sainte-Rose, B., Aitken, J., Marthouse, R., ... & Reisser, J. (2018). Evidence that the Great Pacific Garbage Patch is rapidly accumulating plastic. *Scientific Reports*, 8(1), 1–15.

lendingtree.com   (online).   https://www.lendingtree.com/credit-cards/study/consumers-would-spend -more-on-eco-friendly-products/

Lim, S., Pettit, S., Abouarghoub, W., & Beresford, A. (2019). Port sustainability and performance: A systematic literature review. *Transportation Research Part D: Transport and Environment*, 72, 47–64.

Macfadyen, G., Huntington, T., & Cappell, R. (2009). Abandoned, lost or otherwise discarded fishing gear. *UNEP Regional Seas Reports and Studies*, No. 185; FAO Fisheries and Aquaculture Technical Paper, No. 523. Rome, UNEP/FAO, 1–115. https://www.fao.org/3/i0620e/i0620e.pdf

MacLeod, M., Arp, H. P. H., Tekman, M. B., & Jahnke, A. (2021). The global threat from plastic pollution. *Science*, 373(6550), 61–65.

MacLeod, M., Breitholtz, M., Cousins, I. T., Wit, C. A. D., Persson, L. M., Rudén, C., & McLachlan, M. S. (2014). Identifying chemicals that are planetary boundary threats. *Environmental Science & Technology*, 48(19), 11057–11063.

McIlgorm, A., Campbell, H. F., & Rule, M. J. (2011). The economic cost and control of marine debris damage in the Asia-Pacific region. *Ocean & Coastal Management*, 54(9), 643–651.

Meys, R., Kätelhön, A., Bachmann, M., Winter, B., Zibunas, C., Suh, S., & Bardow, A. (2021). Achieving net-zero greenhouse gas emission plastics by a circular carbon economy. *Science*, 374(6563), 71–76.

Mihai, F. C., & Grozavu, A. (2019). Role of waste collection efficiency in providing a cleaner rural environment. *Sustainability*, 11(23), 6855.

Morishige, C. (2010). Marine Debris Prevention Projects and Activities in the Republic of Korea and United States. A compilation of project summary reports. NOAA technical memorandum NOS-OR&R 36.

Narula, K. (2014). Emerging trends in the shipping industry–transitioning towards sustainability. *Maritime Affairs: Journal of the National Maritime Foundation of India*, 10(1), 113–138.

Parsons, S., Maassen, A., & Galvin, M. (2019) Urban transformations: In Pune, India, waste pickers go from trash to treasure. wri.org.

Paruta, P. (2020). *National Guidance for Plastic Pollution Hotspotting and Shaping Action. Final Report for Kenya 2020*. United Nations Environment Programme.

Persson, L. M., Breitholtz, M., Cousins, I. T., de Wit, C. A., MacLeod, M., & McLachlan, M. S. (2013). Confronting unknown planetary boundary threats from chemical pollution. *Environmental Science & Technology*, 47(22), 12619–12622.

Phelan, A., Ross, H., Setianto, N. A., Fielding, K., & Pradipta, L. (2020). Ocean plastic crisis—Mental models of plastic pollution from remote Indonesian coastal communities. *PloS One*, 15(7), e0236149.

Port of Seattle (March 2021). *Draft – Charting the Course to Zero: Port of Seattle's Maritime Climate and Air Action Plan*. Port of Seattle.

Quinn, M. (2021). California governor signs full slate of circular economy bills. *Waste Dive*. 6 October 2021.   https://www.wastedive.com/news/california-legislature-recycling-organics-newsom-plastic/ 606531/?fbclid=IwAR2-H0NDXNBe5cWEFPIQZ3Uv0VfYGBY27WKsU4vQvyJPl9MLmiKnzE _Kwwg

Ritchie H., & Roser, M. (2018). Plastic pollution. Published online at OurWorldInData.org.

Rouen, E., & Serafeim, G. (2021). Impact-weighted financial accounts: A paradigm shift. *CESifo Forum*, 22(3), 20–25. München: ifo Institut-Leibniz-Institut für Wirtschaftsforschung an der Universität München.

Schultz, F. C., Everding, S., & Pies, I. (2021). Circular supply chain governance: A qualitative-empirical study of the European polyurethane industry to facilitate functional circular supply chain management. *Journal of Cleaner Production*, 317, 128445.

Serafeim, G., & Trinh, K. (2020). A framework for product impact-weighted accounts. Impact-Weighted Accounts Research Report. *Harvard Business School Accounting & Management Unit Working Paper* (20-076).

Sheldon, R. A., & Norton, M. (2020). Green chemistry and the plastic pollution challenge: Towards a circular economy. *Green Chemistry*, 22(19), 6310–6322.

Sifakis, N., & Tsoutsos, T. (2020). Planning zero-emissions ports through the nearly zero energy port concept. *Journal of Cleaner Production*, 125448.

Silva, A. L. P., Prata, J. C., Walker, T. R., Duarte, A. C., Ouyang, W., Barcelò, D., & Rocha-Santos, T. (2021). Increased plastic pollution due to COVID-19 pandemic: Challenges and recommendations. *Chemical Engineering Journal*, 405, 126683.

Stubbins, A., Law, K. L., Muñoz, S. E., Bianchi, T. S., & Zhu, L. (2021). Plastics in the Earth system. *Science*, 373(6550), 51–55.

sweden.se (online). https://sweden.se/climate/sustainability/recycling-and-beyond

Tetu, S. G., Sarker, I., Schrameyer, V., Pickford, R., Elbourne, L. D., Moore, L. R., & Paulsen, I. T. (2019). Plastic leachates impair growth and oxygen production in Prochlorococcus, the ocean's most abundant photosynthetic bacteria. *Communications Biology*, 2(1), 1–9.

The World Bank (2020). Trends in solid waste management. https://datatopics.worldbank.org/what-a-waste/trends_in_solid_waste_management.html (accessed April 21, 2020).

UNEP (2017). Guidelines for providing product sustainability information: Global guidance on making effective environmental, social and economic claims, to empower and enable consumer choice. *UN Environment*.

U.S. Environmental Protection Agency Office of Transportation and Air Quality (2020). *Environmental Justice Primer for Ports: The Good Neighbor Guide to Building Partnerships and Social Equity with Communities*. Report No. EPA-420-B-20-007, 2020. https://www.epa.gov/community-port-collaboration/environmental-justice-primer-ports

vermont.gov (online). https://dec.vermont.gov/waste-management/solid/product-stewardship/bottle-bill

Walenta, J. (2020). Climate risk assessments and science-based targets: A review of emerging private sector climate action tools. *Wiley Interdisciplinary Reviews: Climate Change*, 11(2), e628.

Wong, S., Yeung, J. K. W., Lau, Y. Y., & So, J. (2021). Technical sustainability of cloud-based blockchain integrated with machine learning for supply chain management. *Sustainability*, 13(15), 8270.

World Economic Forum (2016). *The New Plastics Economy Rethinking the Future of Plastics*. World Economic Forum.

WWF, the Ellen MacArthur Foundation and BCG (2020). The business case for a UN treaty on plastic pollution. https://www.plasticpollutiontreaty.org/UN_treaty_plastic_poll_report.pdf

Zheng, J., & Suh, S. (2019). Strategies to reduce the global carbon footprint of plastics. *Nature Climate Change*, 9(5), 374–378.

14. The climate sprint: an agile process for catalytic collaboration towards a just transition
Dennis West and Jimmy Jia

INTRODUCTION

Climate action faces the challenge of scaling up collaborations at multiple levels while each organization operates at different speeds in achieving net zero global carbon emissions by 2050 (Race to Zero Campaign, 2021; Slawinski and Bansal, 2015). Previous work on climate action focused on the *scope* of systems change in terms of top-down governance and harder-to-abate sectors (Slawinski et al., 2017; Starik and Kanashiro, 2020; Starik and Rands, 1995). Drawing more attention to the *pace* of climate action would help us understand better the non-linear processes that may amplify across multiple levels (Greenwood and Hinings, 1996; Plowman et al., 2007). In this chapter, we rebalance these approaches by addressing the question of how organizations can develop tools and processes that guide the pace as well as scope of climate action across multiple levels.

Over the following three sections, we develop a new approach – the Climate Sprint Model – to experiment, evaluate, and generate tools and processes for catalytic collaboration in the climate action field (Figures 14.1 and 14.2 below): first, we draw on organization theory and the practitioner literature to connect the 'Decisive Seven' (D7) framework on catalytic collaboration for systems change (Besharov et al., 2021) with an agile product development method known as 'Scrum' (Schwaber and Beedle, 2002). Second, we use the Climate Sprint model to analyze a real-world example of multi-level climate action at the intersection of cleantech innovation and climate justice that involves different system roles and corporate functions. In the spirit of 'engaged scholarship' (Hoffman, 2021; Van de Ven, 2007), we conclude the chapter by identifying further opportunities for academic research and professional leadership.

CATALYTIC COLLABORATION

Climate action faces a dual problem of collaboration: accelerating climate action while ensuring equity (Robinson, 2018). The just transition demonstrates a fundamental tension between cleantech innovation and climate justice faced by states, businesses, social movements and other NGOs: speeding up cleantech innovation may counter-intuitively involve actions that temporarily slow down the process to secure climate justice (e.g. broader public participation in open policy forums). Vice versa, slowing down on one level may enable actors to speed up on another level. For example, joint projects between scientific researchers (long time cycles) and industry experts (short time cycles) can create much needed knowledge transfer. Recent interdisciplinary research on climate mitigation and adaptation is concerned with the impacts of different temperature scenarios and the policies needed for climate-resilient development across net-zero pathways (IPCC, 2021). The IPCC recognized the importance of cross-sector partnerships (D.7, IPCC, 2018) which has recently received attention in organizational studies (Ansari et al., 2019; Klitsie et al., 2018). Economic and social transformations need to be significantly accelerated and increased; however, distributed action across multiple levels poses a challenge to effective collaboration (Hale, 2016; Victor et al., 2019). For example, Senator Joe Manchin in 2021, while representing the State of West Virginia, was able to hold up the green infrastructure bill from passing at the US Federal level. Similarly, in Switzerland, rural and suburban levels voted overwhelmingly against federal carbon legislation in a 2021 referendum.

Table 14.1   The Decisive Seven (D7) roles

	Role	Key objectives	Examples
Highlighting	Shakers	Raise public awareness and advocate for action	Climate justice advocates and activist groups
	Analysts	Generate scientific evidence	Climate scientists and science editors in media organizations
Orchestrating	Playmakers	Provide financial support for diverse forms of climate action	Foundations with focus on climate justice and/or cleantech
	Weavers	Convene organizations across sectors to shape public and corporate policy	UNFCCC high-level champions and policy advisors
	Frameworkers	Develop accountability systems for goals, standards and pathways	Carbon accounting and impact measurement experts
Operationalizing	Pioneers	Develop and deliver climate solutions	Industry representatives and cleantech start-up founders
	First Aiders	Deliver services to directly address climate-related emergencies	Climate justice law firms and humanitarian crisis response teams

Catalytic collaboration involves three reinforcing feedback-loops and organizations specialized in one of these catalytic activities and, depending on the context of the specific project, may assume secondary roles as well. The D7 framework (see Table 14.1) for catalytic collaboration is built around key systems-level activities (Besharov et al., 2021): highlighting (creating awareness and providing evidence); orchestrating (convening actors and allocating resources); and operationalizing (developing and implementing solutions). These three systems-level activities consist of seven organizational roles: Shakers (raising public awareness), Analysts (generating scientific evidence), Playmakers (providing financial support), Weavers (convening organizations across sectors), Frameworkers (developing accountability systems for goals, standards and pathways), Pioneers (developing and delivering climate solutions), and First Aiders (delivering real-time services to addressing climate-related emergencies). Although the goals overlap, focusing only on the differences can create silos and, in turn, weaken collaboration across multiple levels.

THE CLIMATE SPRINT

One way collaborative efforts across the levels of the individual, organizations, communities, and nation states can be sustained is through establishing organizational routines (George et al., 2016). Under certain conditions, routines can generate innovation (Chesbrough et al., 2006; Deken et al., 2016) and one prominent example studied by organization scholars is agile software development (Goh and Pentland, 2019; Mahringer et al., 2019; Rost et al., 2020). Agile is a project management philosophy that originated in software development (Beck et al., 2001; Hobbs and Petit, 2017; Von Hippel, 2006). Scrum is a common implementation of agile project development, a grounds-up approach beyond 'staff' and 'line' functions that stresses self-organization of teams to achieve a common outcome. One critical advantage is that software development can continue even if the customer modifies the goals as the project progresses (Schwaber and Sutherland, 2017). Scrum is responsive to constant change during the development cycle. Under traditional waterfall project management, a project is planned out in advance and teams are assigned to tasks based on the plan. However, customer needs might change during the buildout. To incorporate these changes, the plan would need to be re-visited, teams re-allocated, timelines re-evaluated, potentially causing lengthy delays (Flewelling, 2018).

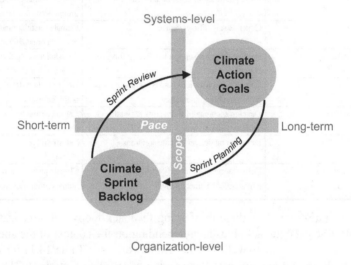

Figure 14.1   The Climate Sprint Model across multiple levels

As depicted in Figure 14.1, we propose adopting the "Scrum technique," developed by the software industry to manage the pace and scope of climate action. Climate goals often shift, much like changes in customer needs. The requisite teams and skills to be assembled will change as well. This makes it challenging to use a waterfall project planning technique to tackle climate change. While the Scrum process itself has many nested feedback loops for communication conceived for collaboration at the level of cross-functional teams, its techniques can synchronize the timescale of change among organizations who are working at different levels and paces in a given social, economic, technological, and physical system. We will first introduce the literature on the Scrum technique and then apply its key elements to multi-level climate action.

With Scrum, the emphasis is on collaborating with customers in a responsive manner such that changes can be incorporated without affecting the larger development effort (Bott and Mesmer, 2020). Self-forming teams are given autonomy to decide how to solve the problem at hand. Rather than plan everything out in advance, Scrum fosters a trial-and-error learning through rapid feedback, frequent group discussions, cross-pollination and multi-disciplinary teams (Flewelling, 2018).

Scrum and agile have since been adopted into many fields beyond software development, such as systems engineering (Bott and Mesmer, 2020), executive management (Davidson and Klemme, 2016), organizations (Levine and Prietula, 2014) and pedagogy (Bettio et al., 2013). It is best used in applications where managers need the flexibility to make best guesses based on present information and adjust plans on the fly. In the climate action field, new analysis and insights continuously shift state-of-the-art approaches. Partnerships developed a decade prior to agile collaboration practices may no longer be relevant as new understandings develop (e.g. carbon capture, carbon offsetting, fusion technology). The Scrum methodology may be a good tool in this instance to help coordinate catalytic change as we learn, shift, and adapt.

The climate field shares similar challenges to those in the software industry has had to overcome. Climate actions are so long in duration that societal needs would have shifted during the decades of implementation. Climate actions serve the worldwide population as its "customer" or beneficiaries, and customer needs differ by their geography, demographic, among other attributes. Climate teams constantly shift, as priorities change, new organizations formed, and new partnerships created.

The Scrum Process

Scrum is a cyclical process that can be understood as four phases (1) processes to generate an ideal of the intended result; (2) processes to break down large problems into addressable components; (3) processes to manage the execution of mutually agreed upon tasks; and (4) a feedback process that adjusts progress and learns from previous successes and failures.

The first step is to generate the goals of the project, formulated as a user story and done in a Sprint Planning Meeting. The user story tells what needs to be done, such as the functionality, not *how* it needs to be done, leaving it open to the software developers to determine processes and steps to achieve it. User stories are a way of communicating requirements among stakeholders, including the users of a product, the managers of the product's development, the business developers who are selling the product, and so on. The user story can be seen as a mediating instrument, communicating in the vernacular what can be understood by multiple stakeholders. As such, user stories are central to the software development process.

A common user story template is, "As a [person], I would like to [some action] so that I get [some value]" (Flewelling, 2018). An example of a climate-related user story in the built environment can be: "As a real estate owner, I would like to retrofit my building so that it does not become non-compliant with energy performance standards." This specific user story contains further questions that require detailed answers, such as: how inefficient is the current equipment, what is the value of the building, or how much is the owner willing to spend on the retrofit? The user story implies a group of stakeholders involved – finance, mechanics, engineers, investors, to name a few.

Sometimes, a single story is comprised of many functional outcomes. These large groups of functionalities are referred to as *epics*. Step 2 is to take epics and break them down into more manageable stories for incremental improvements (Flewelling, 2018). This also happens in the Sprint Planning Meeting. The process includes workshops and stakeholder engagement exercises where a multitude of actors can collaborate. For example, a smaller user story within the previous epic could be, "As a real estate owner, I would like to replace my boiler so that it is less likely to fail unexpectedly."

Sometimes, one wants to create a larger epic to capture additional possible outcomes behind a user story. Consider this modification: "As a real estate owner, I would like to reduce the carbon footprint of my property portfolio." Rather than framing the problem around non-compliance of energy standards, this epic reframes the goal into reducing the carbon footprint, thereby including the management of water, air, materials, and other environmental resources.

The collection of user stories for a project is known as a *product backlog*.

Once a user story is small enough, it can be broken down into *tasks*. Tasks are discrete and ideally can be accomplished within a single day. Example tasks for the story of replacing a boiler might be:

- Write a Request for Proposal (RFP)
- Email the RFP to the contractor database
- Create a technical specification document of what's needed
- Convene a meeting to select the quote
  - Book a room for a selection meeting
  - Check calendars of the CFO, Director of Facilities, Project Manager
- And so on.

After generating a list of tasks, Step 3 is to manage their execution. A *Sprint* is a pre-determined amount of time, commonly two weeks to one month, where tasks are completed. The final outcome of the Sprint Planning Meeting is to set the incremental goal of the Sprint. Tasks to be done within the Sprint are added to a Sprint Backlog. During the sprint, no changes are allowed to be made that would endanger the goal of the sprint (Schwaber and Sutherland, 2017). Sprints are focused on making specific, incremental improvements to the larger project.

Built into the Scrum process are many feedback loops (Step 4). On a daily basis, teams have a *Daily Scrum Meeting*, commonly a 15-minute meeting where each member of the team reports daily goals and yesterday's accomplishments. This allows the team to communicate any needs for real-time adjustments before executing tasks. At the end of a sprint, there is a *Sprint Review Meeting*, an informal gathering to solicit feedback on the sprint, encourage collaboration, and revise the product backlog, user stories, and epics based on new learnings. The customer may also provide feedback on what was accomplished and can give new direction, if necessary. The review meeting informs the next Sprint Planning Meeting and the creation of the next Sprint Backlog. In this manner, Scrum can deliver incremental functionality while being responsive to changing needs and requirements. Further, the Scrum team can learn from each other, improving each subsequent sprint.

Sprint Planning Meetings are where Steps 1, 2, and 3 occur. Near the beginning of the project, these planning meetings can be long meetings and workshops to help set the agenda of the epics (Step 1) and prioritize stories (Step 2) among stakeholders. As the project progresses, the meetings will likely become shorter, epics and stories will change less frequently, and the team will learn how to work together more fluidly.

Scrum also has well-defined team roles. The *Owner* is an individual who holds the vision for the product. The owner's role is to prioritize the backlog and give feedback on the new functionality. The owner does not perform any work, only provides feedback and prioritizations. The *Team* is a group of individuals who are doing the work. Teams should be cross-functional such that the team has enough skills to do the job. Example software development teams might include website, database, algorithms, design, user experience, and testers among other expertise and skills. The team also self-organizes and decides on how to best deliver on the tasks. The *Scrum Master* makes sure that the team adheres to the Scrum process. They ensure communication amongst team members by facilitating the meetings (daily Scrum, planning and review meetings). As a coach, they help the owner and team maximize value from the process and remove impediments. The Scrum Master is a unique role – it cannot be held by the owner nor by a member of the team. The Scrum Master also does not perform any of the technical work.

To summarize, the owner determines the priorities, the team breaks down epics into stories into tasks and executes the sprints, and the Scrum Master ensures discipline in adherence to the process.

The Climate Sprint Model

The Climate Sprint Model adds two Scrum roles, the *Climate Solutions Owner* and the *Climate Scrum Master*, to operationalize the existing D7 organizational roles. This helps to hold the space for organizations and each of their individual participants or teams to form joint development teams and collaborate across different levels.

The Climate Solutions Owner is typically a highly experienced and connected actor who selects the priorities across sectors that are previously agreed in high-level policy forums and state or non-state entities with the legitimacy to make strategic decisions on net zero targets and corresponding climate-resilient development pathways.

We have seen industries convene before to coordinate multi-level innovation processes across organizations. In 1965, Gordon Moore, the co-founder of Intel, observed that the number of transistors on a computer chip doubles every year. In 1971, the International Technology Roadmap for Semiconductors (ITRS), as a consortium of industry experts, developed multi-year research and development plans in order to maintain the industry's development in line with Moore's Law. This included collaboration with the entire chip manufacturing supply chain, from materials manufacturers to quality assurance technologies. Analogously, actors in the climate action field moved to formulate roadmaps, e.g. following a "Carbon Law" (Exponential Roadmap, 2020). On an international level, the Race to Zero campaign and the Marrakech Partnership are working towards sector-based collaborations whereby leaders innovate and progress within specific "swim lanes" (UNFCCC, 2021). However, it is unclear at this point how industry sectors and geographic regions effectively pursue net zero targets if the challenges of collaboration across multiple levels are left unaddressed.

The Climate Scrum Master is independent from the Climate Solutions Owner and the D7 roles, ideally appointed from the team of agile development experts of a cross-sector partnership organization. The key responsibility is to ensure the process of the Climate Sprint Model.

In the initial stage, three fundamental rules must be observed:

1. Every D7 role needs to be represented in each development team.
2. The Climate Solutions Owner is determined based on the key objective.
3. The Scrum Master role cannot be held by any organization holding a D7 role or the role of the Climate Solutions Owner.

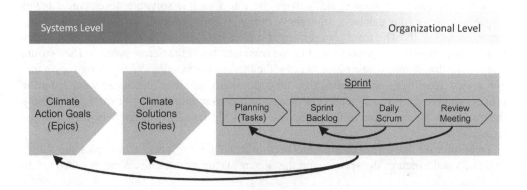

Figure 14.2   The multi-level processes of the Climate Sprint Model

BOX 14.1 ROLES IN THE CLIMATE SPRINT MODEL

*   *Climate Solution Owner*: Responsible for setting the priorities for the Climate Solutions in a problem space specified by the Climate Action Goals.
*   *Scrum Master*: Responsible for ensuring that the sprint process is followed, and the moderation of the team meetings and feedback loops.
*   *Team Members*: D7 members who contribute specialist expertise representing the organizations that fulfil the D7 roles described in Table 14.1.

The organizations appoint their set of participants based on the expertise and resources needed. The Climate Solutions Owner sets the priorities linked to the long-term net zero pathways of a given geographic region, industry sector, or other area of climate action (*outcome responsibility*). In areas with high consensus about the policy goals across stakeholder groups, the discrete tasks are identified using the agile development technique by the D7 participants. These tasks enter the Climate Backlog. It is important to note that D7 and scrum roles are not tightly bound, and that any organization can take on the agile roles.

Every Climate Sprint is geared towards completing the tasks within the Climate Backlog. Following the Scrum analogy, the Climate Sprint provides processes:

1. To generate an ideal of the intended result – the net zero targets.
2. To break down large problems – long-term climate resilient development pathways – into addressable components that sectors and levels can address within the sprint timeframe.
3. To manage the coordinated execution of mutually agreed upon tasks that require multiple disciplines, skill sets, and access to different stakeholder groups.
4. A feedback process that adjusts progress and learns from successes and failures of those organizations implementing on-the-ground solutions.

BOX 14.2 ELEMENTS OF THE CLIMATE SPRINT MODEL

- *Climate Sprint*: A pre-determined amount of time where tasks are completed. The authors suggest three to six month cycles, proportionate to the overall timeline.
- *Climate Action Goals*: Epics that describe the totality of climate tasks that can be done.
- *Climate Solutions*: A collection of user stories for a given project epic.
- *Climate Sprint Backlog*: A list of tasks to be completed in a sprint that makes progress towards climate solutions.
- *Weekly Scrum*: A one-hour meeting where each D7 organization reports prior week's accomplishments and communicates subsequent week's goals.
- *Climate Planning Meeting*: A meeting amongst stakeholders where the owners prioritize epics and stories and the teams of D7 players break down actions into tasks and assign them to the sprint.
- *Climate Sprint Review Meeting*: Feedback process at the end of each sprint to reflect, share best practices, and adjust current progress to net zero pathways.

As shown in Figure 14.2, the process of the Climate Sprint Model is structured into two phases. The Sprint itself operates on the organizational level in small and diverse teams to complete the tasks within a given time period. Note that the duration of the Sprint is always defined relative to the net zero pathway, its overall and interim targets and phases. The notion of a 3- to 6-month sprint may not be intuitive, but it is proportionate to 30-, 50-year or even longer planning horizons. No matter how long the duration, the Climate Sprint must retain the key characteristic of a limited and achievable set of tasks within an active Sprint, followed by a reflective Sprint Review phase. Through those two phases, the Scrum Master makes sure that all D7 organizations are moving in the same direction towards completion of the tasks (*process responsibility*).

The Climate Sprint Review Meeting is a retrospective of the most recent sprint, providing feedback from the organizational level to the systems-level and, thus, includes a broader set of players that are facilitated through the D7 roles. The information learned will inform the next Sprint Planning Meeting, where changes in the long-term pathways or net zero goals must be reflected and updated in the user stories of the Climate Solutions, which are broken further down into policy, industry, and product development tasks for the specific Climate Sprint at hand. The Climate Solutions Owners are important intermediaries between the organizational level and the systems-level and require significant support and legitimacy to fulfill their role successfully.

The Climate Sprint model offers multiple advantages. At its core is the routinization of innovation processes through structured information flows between the solution space – the level of organizations – and the problem space – the systems level. The Climate Solution Owner sets priorities based on systemic needs while the team members provide feedback on the organizational level based on what actions worked. Importantly, the feedback provides a mechanism for the inclusion of voices who are not commonly involved on the systemic level. On-the-ground realities of diversity, equity and inclusion can be fed into systemic planning on a real-time basis, and epics and user stories can be updated from new learning experiences. As a consequence, the Climate Sprint is a tool for collective experimentation and sense-making under high uncertainty and complexity (Weick, 1993).

The success of this model relies on the adherence to the process which may not suit every organizational culture and industry setting. Significant investment in terms of time and training needs to go into the interdisciplinary, cross-sectoral teams (von Hippel, 2005; Von Hippel and Van Krogh, 2003). Alignment and "growing" into the different roles across different organizational boundaries remain a constant struggle which cannot be solved by the Climate Sprint model alone but requires buy-in and regular settlement of higher-level issues at the top leadership level of organizations. One needs to fully acknowledge the "organized anarchy" of organizational choice wherever the window of opportunity for solutions and problems is narrow amidst dynamic interaction, colliding preferences, technological uncertainty (Cohen et al., 1972). Consequently, where resources for learning and development are scarce, the Climate Sprint model is unlikely to reach its full potential.

Finally, Climate Sprints are useful at tackling wicked problems in a dynamic uncertain world that evolves into new "adjacent possibles" (Longo et al., 2012). The specification of the solution and the problem may change depending on where the organization is intervening in the system (Meadows, 1999). It is important to continuously assess the goals and developments on the systems and the organizational level to decide if, when, and how the Climate Sprint model can be useful. However, from using the feedback loops of the Climate Sprint, the holders of solutions and problems can increase the likelihood of success through rapid recombination.

To conclude, every stakeholder within the D7 framework has a different role, expertise, network, and set of values and incentives. However, if the groups were able to self-organize under a Climate Solution Owner and a Climate Scrum Master, the teams may be able to improve collaboration (yet still work within their own expertise and swim lanes). The Climate Sprint Model enables regular communication to the stakeholder groups such that incremental improvements can be made consistently and converge on an outcome on a net zero pathway.

Applying the Climate Sprint Model: The CleanTech Alliance

The CleanTech Alliance (CTA), headquartered in Seattle, WA, is a trade organization with over 1000 members across ten US states and three Canadian provinces. Early on, the CTA has operated beyond Washington State through regional partnerships in the Cascadia region with Oregon and with British Columbia in Canada. The complexity arises from contested policy arenas, uncertain technology contexts, and complex institutional environments. Recent evidence of the tension of climate justice and cleantech innovation is demonstrated by the difficult negotiations around passing the Infrastructure Investment and Jobs Act in the US (US Congress, 15 November 2021, Pub.L. 117–58).

Overall, the CTA exhibits a broad set of events from innovation showcases to leadership summits and breakfast series. The organization has an advocacy workstream and commercialization programs. The commercialization workstream includes incubators, accelerators, pitch events, product launch labs and a program for acquisition. CTA's office also acts as a switchboard for events of their members and partners, with more or less self-organized activities.

Recently, the CTA won a Washington State grant to create an innovation cluster for the built environment. Its role is to convene the products, services, production, operations, maintenance, and related infrastructure progress to help develop the economy while staying in line with the State's climate goals. The organizations involved in CTA are across diverse industries, from fusion power startups to mechanical contractors. CTA is therefore an ideal organization to analyze via the Climate Sprint Model – it is seeking to create regional economic opportunities from climate innovation and action. We held several conversations with key people involved and reviewed internal documents and the public websites. We mapped the D7 and scrum roles onto the different actors involved and then provide an example for the Climate Sprint process that could be combined with the organization's existing efforts, as depicted in Table 14.2. We demonstrate where gaps may be in convening stakeholders for collaborations.

Table 14.2   Climate Sprint roles in the Cleantech Alliance

		Role	Examples from CTA Board Members
Scrum Roles		Climate solutions owner	WA Department of Commerce, following the State Energy Strategy
		Scrum Master	CleanTech Alliance
Highlighting		Shakers	Environmental justice movements (Climate Solutions)
		Analysts	Research institutions (Pacific Northwest National Laboratory, Idaho National Laboratory, University of Washington, Washington State University)
Orchestrating		Playmakers	Clean Energy Fund of WA State
		Weavers	Oregon BEST, NEBC, Climate Solutions, Canadian Counsel
		Frameworkers	Department of Ecology, Department of Insurance, Department of Natural Resources
Operationalizing		Pioneers	Entrepreneurs (AR Solar, BetaHatch, Omidian, Helion Energy)
		First Aiders	Contractors (McKinstry, University Mechanical) and utilities (Puget Sound Energy, Avista, SnoPUD)

Sources: https://www.cleantechalliance.org/about/board-of-directors/; last accessed 8 December 2021.

From a role perspective, many of the existing CTA board members already play at least one D7 role across different industry arenas (policy, research, advocacy, etc.) related to clean-tech and climate change. Their individual and corporate membership as well as partners are embedded in international, national, and sub-national networks. However, member organizations are unevenly distributed across the D7 framework. For example, CTA is predominantly driven by organizations specializing in the D7 roles of Pioneers (e.g. first to market ideas and technologies) and Weavers (e.g. consultants, advisors, experts). The CTA has taken some steps to create new links. For example, the CTA has dedicated a "Justice, Equity, Diversity & Inclusion Committee" to link up to the environmental justice movement. An important feature of the CTA is the involvement of several universities and national laboratories, which play an Analyst role by publishing peer-review papers, thought leadership white papers and analyses of energy policies.

The CTA members are unevenly distributed across the pace of change they can make, and the speed of service delivery required from them. For example, First Aiders need to respond immediately to problems. This can be mechanical contractors, who are called upon to fix faulty equipment, often only when it breaks, and utilities, who need to maintain power 24/7. However, there is a lack of consultants and experts, as Weavers, who participate in updating the building and energy codes that often takes years, if not decades. Our analysis also shows several opportunities for collaborations across multiple levels that function at different paces. For example, fusion companies, such as CTFusion and Helion, are Pioneers and innovate at a rapid pace on the future of electric power. Meanwhile, electric utilities, such as Avista, Puget Sound Energy, and SnoPUD, as First Aiders, operationalize the delivery of power and are very slow to innovate.

The analysis also highlights how goals can shift. In 2012, the state published its second energy strategy, focusing on energy transformations via efficient and coordinated transportation, energy efficiency, and diversifying energy supply through distributed energy (State of Washington, 2012). In 2021, the goal was an equitable transition to a clean energy future (State of Washington, 2020). The shift in goals requires a reorganization of the energy and cleantech sectors in terms of resources, priorities, and investments. We categorize the State of Washington as the Climate Solutions Owner as the state prioritizes funding activities based on the energy strategy.

CTA is an archetypical organization to implement a Climate Sprint Model. Climate change goals for Washington State will continue to shift as the state adopts to climate change. CTA membership already has a central role across multiple industry sectors and already has structured collaboration processes. However, there is no collaboration with a specific rhythm of work to synchronize the pace of regional climate action. Their central position in the cleantech innovation field would make them good candidates to mediate the pace of change amongst members. The first step would be to categorize their membership and spheres of influence by D7 organizational team members. This would identify stakeholders who are missing and underrepresented. The second step would be to identify a Climate Solutions Owner that can set priorities for climate action in the region. After that, the CTA could take up the role of Scrum Master, facilitate the creation of Climate Action Goals, and guide Climate Sprints to make to make incremental improvements.

CONCLUSION

This chapter has drawn attention to the problem of *pace* in climate action that complements the more widely recognized challenges of the *scope* of change. We argue that the acceleration and scale of economic and social transformation needed to reach net zero emissions by 2050 requires a different approach to collaboration that borrows from the techniques of agile development. We developed the Climate Sprint Model as a process-oriented and theoretically grounded guide to experiment, evaluate, and generate tools and processes for catalytic collaboration across timescales in the climate action field. The Climate Sprint Model is relevant for policymakers, industry leaders, and social movements seeking to accelerate climate action while ensuring consistency and inclusiveness.

Further research into the *pace* of climate action could improve our understanding of why climate negotiations fail due to misalignment of different levels of climate action and how to address these shortcomings. If the Decisive Decade until 2030 is understood as a ten-year programming phase of a 30- to 50-year roadmap to net zero, then interim targets and phases could be aligned with long-term pathways. The Climate Sprint Model can facilitate cross-sector collaboration in different ways. The model can be used for allocating organizational roles, evaluation of progress and continuous learning on the partnership-level. Furthermore, attending to the various cycles of change in industry sectors and geographic regions with different climate risk and historical emissions profiles, provides further opportunities to overcome blockages on different levels to steer a complex transformation and to keep global temperature rise well below 2, if not 1.5 degrees.

REFERENCES

Ansari, S., Furnari, S., Gray, B., McDonnell, M. H., & Purdy, J. M. (2019, July). Cross-sector partnerships for social innovation: Challenges and enabling conditions. *Academy of Management
Proceedings*, 2019(1), 14635. Briarcliff Manor, NY 10510: Academy of Management.

Beck, K., Beedle, M., Van Bennekum, A., Cockburn, A., Cunningham, W., Fowler, M., ... & Thomas,
D. (2001). *The Agile Manifesto*.

Besharov, M., Joshi, R., Vaara, E., & West, D. (2021). *The Decisive Decade: Organising Climate Action
– Catalytic Collaboration for Systems Change*. University of Oxford, Saïd Business School, and the
Mission 2020 Campaign.

Bettio, R. W. D., Pereira, D. A., Martins, R. X., & Heimfarth, T. (2013). The experience of using
the scrum process in the production of learning objects for blended learning. *Informatics in
Education*, 12(1), 29–41.

Bott, M., & Mesmer, B. (2020). An analysis of theories supporting agile scrum and the use of scrum in
systems engineering. *Engineering Management Journal*, 32(2), 76–85.

Chesbrough, H., Vanhaverbeke, W., & West, J. (2006). *Open Innovation: Researching a New Paradigm*.
Oxford University Press.

Cohen, M. D., March, J. G., & Olsen, J. P. (1972). A garbage can model of organizational choice.
Administrative Science Quarterly, 1–25.

Davidson, A., & Klemme, L. (2016). Why a CEO should think like a Scrum Master. *Strategy &
Leadership*.

Deken, F., Carlile, P. R., Berends, H., & Lauche, K. (2016). Generating novelty through interdependent
routines: A process model of routine work. *Organization Science*, 27(3), 659–677.

Exponential   Roadmap   (2020),   https://exponentialroadmap.org/wp-content/uploads/2020/03/
ExponentialRoadmap_1.5.1_216x279_08_AW_Download_Singles_Small.pdf, accessed 8 December
2021.

Flewelling, P. (2018). *The Agile Developer's Handbook: Get More Value from Your Software
Development: Get the Best Out of the Agile Methodology*. Packt Publishing Ltd.

George, G., Howard-Grenville, J., Joshi, A., & Tihanyi, L. (2016). Understanding and tackling societal
grand challenges through management research. *Academy of Management Journal*, 59(6), 1880–1895.

Goh, K. T., & Pentland, B. T. (2019). From actions to paths to patterning: Toward a dynamic theory of
patterning in routines. *Academy of Management Journal*, 62, 1901–1929.

Greenwood, R., & Hinings, C. R. (1996). Understanding radical organizational change: Bringing
together the old and the new institutionalism. *Academy of Management Review*, 21(4), 1022–1054.

Hale, T. (2016). "All hands on deck": The Paris agreement and nonstate climate action. *Global
Environmental Politics*, 16(3), 12–22.

Hobbs, B., & Petit, Y. (2017). Agile methods on large projects in large organizations. *Project
Management Journal*, 48(3), 3–19.

Hoffman, A. J. (2021). *The Engaged Scholar: Expanding the Impact of Academic Research in Today's
World*. Stanford University Press.

IPCC (2018). Summary for policymakers. In V. Masson-Delmotte, P. Zhai, H.-O. Pörtner, D. Roberts,
J. Skea, P. R. Shukla, A. Pirani, W. Moufouma-Okia, C. Péan, R. Pidcock, S. Connors, J. B. R.
Matthews, Y. Chen, X. Zhou, M. I. Gomis, E. Lonnoy, T. Maycock, M. Tignor, & T. Waterfield
(eds), *Global Warming of 1.5°C. An IPCC Special Report on the Impacts of Global Warming of 1.5°C
Above Pre-industrial Levels and Related Global Greenhouse Gas Emission Pathways, in the Context
of Strengthening the Global Response to the Threat of Climate Change, Sustainable Development,
and Efforts to Eradicate Poverty*. Geneva, Switzerland: World Meteorological Organization, 32 pp.

IPCC (2021). Summary for policymakers. In V. Masson-Delmotte, P. Zhai, A. Pirani, S. L. Connors, C.
Péan, S. Berger, N. Caud, Y. Chen, L. Goldfarb, M. I. Gomis, M. Huang, K. Leitzell, E. Lonnoy, J.
B. R. Matthews, T. K. Maycock, T. Waterfield, O. Yelekçi, R. Yu, & B. Zhou (eds), *Climate Change
2021: The Physical Science Basis. Contribution of Working Group I to the Sixth Assessment Report
of the Intergovernmental Panel on Climate Change*. Cambridge, UK and New York, NY, USA:
Cambridge University Press, pp. 3–32. doi:10.1017/9781009157896.001.

Klitsie, E. J., Ansari, S., & Volberda, H. W. (2018). Maintenance of cross-sector partnerships: The role
of frames in sustained collaboration. *Journal of Business Ethics*, 150(2), 401–423.

Levine, S. S., & Prietula, M. J. (2014). Open collaboration for innovation: Principles and performance. *Organization Science*, 25(5), 1414–1433.

Longo, G., Montévil, M., & Kauffman, S. (2012, July). No entailing laws, but enablement in the evolution of the biosphere. In *Proceedings of the 14th Annual Conference Companion on Genetic and Evolutionary Computation* (pp. 1379–1392).

Mahringer, C. A., Dittrich, K., & Renzl, B. E. (2019, July). Interdependent routines and innovation processes – an ethnographic study of Scrum teams. *Academy of Management Proceedings*, 2019(1), 11891. Briarcliff Manor, NY 10510: Academy of Management.

Meadows, D. H. (1999). Leverage points: Places to intervene in a system, https://donellameadows.org/archives/leverage-points-places-to-intervene-in-a-system/, accessed 20 March 2022.

Plowman, D. A., Baker, L. T., Beck, T. E., Kulkarni, M., Solansky, S. T., & Travis, D. V. (2007). Radical change accidentally: The emergence and amplification of small change. *Academy of Management Journal*, 50(3), 515–543.

Race to Zero Campaign (2021). Transforming our systems together: A global challenge to accelerate sector breakthroughs for COP26 – and beyond. UNFCCC, UN Climate Change Conference UK 2021, COP 25, Marrakesh Partnership. https://racetozero.unfccc.int/wp-content/uploads/2021/02/Race-to-Zero-Breakthroughs-Transforming-Our-Systems-Together.pdf

Robinson, M. (2018). *Climate Justice: Hope, Resilience, and the Fight for a Sustainable Future*. Bloomsbury Publishing USA.

Rost, M., Peter, M., Mahringer, C., and Renzl, B. (2020). Rollen-Anforderungen zur Zusammenarbeit in Scrum Teams. *Austrian Management Review*, 10, 36–46.

Schwaber, K., & Beedle, M. (2002). *Agile Software Development with Scrum* (Vol. 1). Upper Saddle River: Prentice Hall.

Schwaber, K., & Sutherland, J. (2017). The Scrum Guide™ The Definitive Guide to SCRUM: The Rules of the Game. Retrieved from https://scrumguides.org/index.html.

Slawinski, N., & Bansal, P. (2015). Short on time: Intertemporal tensions in business sustainability. *Organization Science*, 26(2), 531–549.

Slawinski, N., Pinkse, J., Busch, T., & Banerjee, S. B. (2017). The role of short-termism and uncertainty avoidance in organizational inaction on climate change: A multi-level framework. *Business and Society*, 56(2), 253–282.

Starik, M., & Kanashiro, P. (2020). Advancing a multi-level sustainability management theory. In Wasieleski, D. & Weber, J. (eds), *Business and Society 360 Part IV Sustainability*. Emerald Press. https://doi.org/10.1108/S2514-175920200000004003

Starik, M., & Rands, G. P. (1995). Weaving an integrated web: Multilevel and multisystem perspectives of ecologically sustainable organizations. *Academy of Management Review*, 20(4), 908–935.

State of Washington (2012). *2012 Washington State Energy Strategy: With Forecasts 2012–2035*.

State of Washington (2020). *Washington 2021 State Energy Strategy: Transitioning to an Equitable Clean Energy Future*.

UNFCCC (2021). Climate Action Pathways, https://unfccc.int/climate-action/marrakech-partnership/reporting-and-tracking/climate_action_pathways, accessed 8 December 2012.

Van de Ven, A. H. (2007). *Engaged Scholarship: A Guide for Organizational and Social Research*. Oxford University Press on Demand.

Victor, D. G., Geels, F. W., & Sharpe, S. (2019). *Accelerating the Low Carbon Transition. The Case for Stronger, More Targeted and Coordinated International Action*. Brookings Institution. Available online at: https://www.brookings.edu/wp-content/uploads/2019/12/Coordinatedactionreport.pdf, accessed 8 December 2021.

von Hippel, E. (2005). Open source software projects as user innovation networks. In J. Feller, B. Fitzgerald, S. A. Hissam, & K. R. Lakhani (eds), *Perspectives on Free and Open Source Software*. Cambridge, MA: MIT Press, 267–278.

Von Hippel, E. (2006). *Democratizing Innovation*. MIT Press, p. 216.

Von Hippel, E., & Van Krogh, G. (2003). Open source software and the 'private-collective' innovation model: Issues for organization science. *Organization Science*, 14(2), 209–223.

Weick, K. E. (1993). The collapse of sensemaking in organizations: The Mann Gulch disaster. *Administrative Science Quarterly*, 628–652.

PART IV

MULTI-LEVEL CLIMATE ACTION ECONOMICS AND FINANCE

15. An emerging multi-level approach to climate action in the US banking sector

Amy K. Townsend

INTRODUCTION

The US banking sector is working to mitigate and adapt to climate change. This is a relatively recent occurrence resulting from several drivers, including growing stakeholder calls for climate and environmental accountability, climate action progress by peer banks and other financial institutions (FIs)[1] in the US and abroad, a presidential administration committed to climate action, an evolving federal regulatory environment, and pressure to step up governmental and corporate commitments at the 26th UN Climate Change Conference of the Parties held in Glasgow. These and other drivers are converging to form a multi-level approach to reducing the negative climate impacts in the banking sector in the US and abroad. Banks, federal government agencies, and relatively new non-governmental banking organizations created to address anthropogenic climate change are heavily affecting the direction and timing of climate action by US banks. This chapter outlines the multi-level climate response emerging in and around the US banking sector.

RISK, CLIMATE CHANGE, AND THE US BANKING SECTOR

Much of the US banking industry's approach to climate change revolves around risk, which is defined by the International Organization for Standardization as "the effect of uncertainty on objectives." Using this definition, risk is not necessarily negative; it simply stems from uncertainty. The effect of this uncertainty can be a negative or positive departure from what was anticipated. As a result, risk can make planning around climate change more difficult because meeting one's goals is not guaranteed. In the US banking sector, risks are inherent in changing weather patterns, extreme weather events, the collapse of industries in some regions (e.g., agriculture, fisheries), disruptions in the food supply, perturbations in supply chains, the collective transition to renewable energy, populations' access to fresh water and sufficient nutritious food, and more.

In March 2021, the Board of Governors of the Federal Reserve System published a report titled "Climate Change and Financial Stability" (Brunetti et al. 2021). In it, the authors explained that "climate change refers to changes in the usual conditions of nature of the Earth's oceans, fresh water, and atmosphere" and includes effects such as storms of increased intensity and frequency, increased ocean acidity, and more (Ibid.). Figure 15.1 illustrates the relationships among climate change-related risks, human economic activity, and risks to financial systems.

The authors indicate that climate-related financial or economic risks could increase vulnerabilities to the financial system through such activities as a rapid repricing of large asset classes,

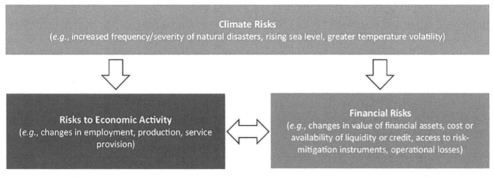

Source: Brunetti et al. (2021).

Figure 15.1 *Relationships among climate risks, risks to economic activity, and financial risks*

loss to levered financial intermediaries, and disrupted function of the financial markets. Such climate change-driven effects are addressed by the Federal Reserve's framework for monitoring financial stability in two ways: (1) as shocks to the financial system, and (2) as financial system vulnerabilities that could transmit or worsen shocks.

Figure 15.2 and Table 15.1 illustrate ways in which climate-related risks create vulnerabilities in the US financial system. Figure 15.2 provides examples of several climate-related risks; as these risks increase in frequency and severity, they are expected to have different features that increase financial system vulnerabilities. For example, acute climate hazards, such as the repeating occurrence of intense hurricanes over the same region, could impact financial risks and models and create vulnerabilities in asset valuations.

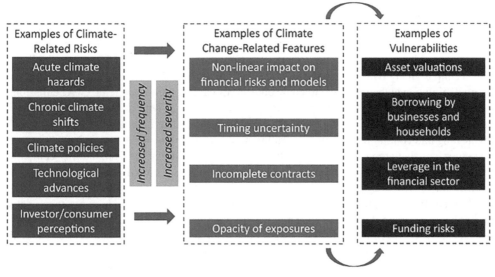

Source: Brunetti et al. (2021).

Figure 15.2 *Examples of climate-related risks, climate change-related features, and vulnerabilities*

Table 15.1 provides examples of risks to climate, economy, finance, and financial stability in the real estate and insurance sectors. Following the example provided above, the increased incidence of intense hurricanes over the same region can affect both the real estate and insurance industries. This can occur through flooding and devaluation of coastal parcels and destination areas, disruption to the local economy, the need for higher insurance rates to cover the cost of more buildings being damaged or destroyed, and greater uninsured losses.

Table 15.1   Four climate-related risk types affecting the real estate & insurance industries

	Climate risks	Economic risks	Financial risks	Financial stability risks
Real Estate	Rising sea levels, frequency of storm surges	Increased inundation of coastal parcels	Decreased value of coastal real estate	Abrupt repricing of mortgage lending markets
Insurance	More frequent and severe hurricanes, wildfires, etc.	Greater disruption to local economic activity	Pressure for higher rates, lower supply of insurance and reinsurance	Greater uninsured losses, spillover effects

Source: Brunetti et al. (2021).

In its report, the Federal Reserve indicated the need to better understand financial risks and financial stability risks related to climate change. It also reported the need to undertake a more thorough analysis of the ways in which climate change-related risk might create hidden vulnerabilities in the US financial sector to facilitate better monitoring of the relationship between financial stability and climate change.

US BANKS

Several US banks have committed to reduce their greenhouse gas (GHG) emissions. One of the most profound ways to accomplish this is by focusing on "financed emissions." Financed emissions are those GHG emissions that come from the activities undertaken by bank clients. For example, many banks provide loans to client companies that are involved in oil and gas or coal mining, which are known to contribute significantly to anthropogenic GHG emissions.

As Figure 15.3 illustrates, there are three types of financed emissions – scope 1, scope 2, and scope 3. Scope 1 emissions are those GHG emissions that a company produces directly by heating and cooling its facilities, operating its vehicles, and so forth. Scope 2 emissions are the emissions that are produced indirectly via the energy it purchases from another company. Scope 3 emissions are all emissions for which a company is indirectly responsible across its entire value chain.

Tackling financed emissions is important because, on average, the GHG emissions related to bank underwriting, loans, and investments are over 700 times greater than the bank's own emissions (PwC 2022). Several US banks have announced their financed emissions goals for scope 1, scope 2, and scope 3 activities. Bank of America, Citi, Goldman Sachs, HSBC, JPMorgan Chase & Co., and Morgan Stanley established GHG emissions reductions in the energy and power sectors. For example, by 2030, Bank of America announced that it will reduce its auto manufacturing clients' financed emissions by 44% gCO_2e/km (scopes 1 and 2,

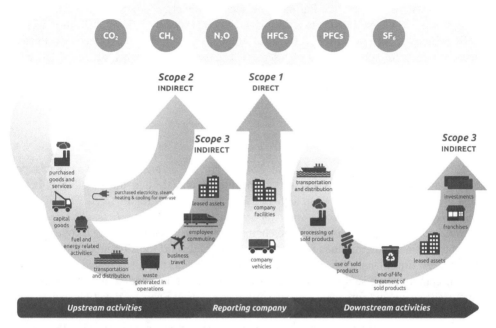

Source: GHG Protocol (2013, p. 6).

Figure 15.3   *Examples of scope 1, scope 2, and scope 3 emissions*

end use scope 3), energy clients' financed emissions by 42% gCO_2e/MJ (scope 1 and scope 2 emissions) and intensity by 29% gCO_2/MJ (end use scope 3 carbon emissions), and power generation clients' carbon emissions intensity by 70% $kgCO_2/MWh$. HSBC committed to reduce its scope 1, 2, and 3 emissions by 34% in the energy sector and its scope 1 emissions in the power sector. Meanwhile, Morgan Stanley committed to reduce its GHG scope 1, 2, and 3 emissions by 29% in the energy sector, 58% in the power sector, and 35% in the auto sector.

Most banks are using the Net Zero Emissions by 2050 (NZE2050) global scenario in their target setting efforts. Created by the International Energy Agency, the NZE2050 scenario is intended to provide a "narrow but achievable pathway" to net zero carbon dioxide emissions by 2050 for the global energy sector to limit the increase in global temperature to 1.5° Celsius in alignment with the Paris Agreement.

In addition to scope 1–3 activities, there are many other efforts that US banks have undertaken to reduce their negative impacts on climate change. Below is just a sample of some banks' commitments and activities.

Bank of America

In 2019, Bank of America achieved its goals of 100% renewable electricity and carbon neutrality for its operations (Bank of America 2022a). In 2021, the bank committed to spend $1 trillion by 2030 toward sustainable business activities that include more efficient transportation, construction, energy, and agriculture as part of a broader $1.5 trillion sustainable finance commitment. As mentioned above, in April 2022, Bank of America announced its 2030 financed emissions targets focusing on three sectors – energy, power generation, and auto manufacturing. The bank intends to reduce its GHG emissions by 75% by 2030 from its 2010 baseline (Bank of America 2022b). By 2024, the bank anticipates setting net zero financed emissions targets for additional industry sectors. The bank plans to reach net zero GHG emissions for all of its activities by 2050. The bank has also created goals for its operations and supply chains, such as committing to using sustainable aviation fuel for 20% or more of its total annual commercial and corporate jet fuel use.

Citi

In December 2020, Citigroup released its *Finance for a Climate-Resilient Future II* report, which assessed the company's impact on the global climate and the possible effects of global climate change on the company. In 2021, it released a report titled *Task Force on Climate-related Financial Disclosures Report 2021: Citi's Approach to Climate Change and Net Zero*. That report committed the company to net zero emissions for its operations by 2030 and for financed emissions by 2050. In its efforts toward transitioning to a low-carbon economy, the firm plans to spend $500 billion by 2030. Citi has also created a Global ESG Council, comprised of senior managers, to oversee ESG goals and activities; added to its Climate Risk team; and formed a Natural Resources & Clean Energy Transition team to assist its power, energy, and chemicals clients in their transition toward net zero emissions. The company has committed to a $500 billion environmental finance goal, which will fund and facilitate solutions for renewable energy, energy efficiency, a circular economy, clean tech, green buildings, sustainable transportation, water quality and conservation, and sustainable agriculture and land use.

Goldman Sachs

In 2020, Goldman Sachs created a framework around climate and inclusive growth and announced its intent to spend $750 billion by 2030 on related investing, financing, and advisory services. The firm created a Sustainable Finance Group to direct its sustainability efforts across the entire firm; it then developed sustainability councils within each of its businesses led by a senior leader within the firm. In February 2021, Goldman Sachs issued its first sustainability bond. The firm has created new tools to help clients decarbonize their portfolios, invested in a large renewable energy developer in India, and built one of the largest solar commercial/industrial businesses. Goldman Sachs was also the first US bank to disclose under the Sustainability Accounting Standards Board (SASB) standards.

HSBC

HSBC plans to be net zero by 2030 for its own operations and supply chain. The company has committed to reducing its clients' financed emissions to net zero by 2050 in the oil and gas and power and utilities sectors. The bank will reduce its fossil fuels financing to what is needed to limit the global temperature increase to 1.5° Celsius and is phasing out thermal coal financing. It will continue working with clients that are actively engaged in the transition to cleaner energy and that employ good industry practices around ESG issues. The company plans to finance and invest between US$750 billion and US$1 trillion in its transition to net zero.

In 2022, the bank plans to review and update its financing and investment policies as they relate to its goal of achieving net zero GHG emissions by 2050. This will include revisiting its financing and investments in oil and gas, methane emissions, and environmentally key areas, such as the Amazon, Arctic, and UNESCO World Heritage sites. The bank expects to publish financed emissions targets for capital markets activities in the fourth quarter of 2022 after the Partnership for Carbon Accounting Financials (PCAF) publishes its accounting standard for capital markets. In 2023, the bank plans to publish a Climate Transition Plan to communicate its climate strategy, science-based targets for 2030 and 2050, and how its net zero plan will be integrated in its policies, procedures, governance, and strategy.

JPMorgan Chase & Co.

Since 2016, JPMorgan Chase has facilitated and funded almost US$210 billion in green initiatives. In April 2021, the firm announced its intention to spend US$2.5 trillion over 10 years (2021 through 2030) on activities related to climate and sustainable development. This commitment aligns with the company's strategy as it relates to the Paris Agreement. The firm is providing some of its clients with access to sustainability-related financing, research, and advice, particularly in the areas of renewable energy, sustainable finance, agriculture and food technology, and efficiency technology. It also committed to spend some of those funds tackling inequality by promoting social and economic development in advance of the United Nations Sustainable Development Goals. Finally, it intends to advance economic inclusion that focuses on small business financing, home lending, education, healthcare, and affordable housing in developed markets.

Morgan Stanley

In 2018, Morgan Stanley made a commitment to source all of its global operations and business travel energy needs from renewable energy by 2022. It enabled the construction of two wind farms that provide much of that renewable energy and also plans to spend US$250 billion by 2030 to fund low-carbon solutions. In addition, the company plans to become carbon neutral in all of its financed emissions by 2050. Morgan Stanley is one of 17 global financial firms that uses the Paris Agreement Capital Transition Assessment to measure how well climate scenarios are aligned with financial portfolios. This will indicate how well the bank's financial portfolios align with the Paris Agreement goals.

In November 2021, Morgan Stanley released a report titled *Methodology for Morgan Stanley's 2030 Interim Financed Emissions Targets on the Path to Net-Zero*. The report recognized the need for a multi-level collaboration on climate change involving civil society, government, and business. In its report, Morgan Stanley states that it will use its net-zero commitment as its "north star" and will integrate climate throughout its business activities and risk management. The firm's 2030 commitments include carbon dioxide emission reductions in three sectors – auto manufacturing (35%), energy (29%), and power (58%) (Morgan Stanley 2021). The firm asserts, "Our goal at Morgan Stanley is to help develop a new approach to financing GHG-intensive sectors that contributes to achieving a zero-carbon global economy by mid-century" (Morgan Stanley 2021, p. 4).

PNC Bank

PNC Bank has also undertaken efforts to enhance its environmental sustainability and reduce its negative impacts on climate. It met its 2020 energy, carbon emissions, and water use goals early – in 2017 – and intends to reduce its carbon emissions and energy use by 75% and water use by 50% by 2035. By 2025, the company plans to be 100% reliant on renewable energy.

FEDERAL GOVERNMENT

Local, state, and federal governments can pass climate change-related laws, become signatories to international climate change-related agreements, and pressure regulatory agencies to create mandatory regulations. Some of the most recent federal activities are mentioned below.

Executive Order on Climate-related Financial Risk

On May 20, 2021, President Joseph Biden issued the Executive Order on Climate-related Financial Risk, which instructed federal entities to create and report on sustainability strategies. In an attempt to mitigate risks to consumers, homeowners, businesses, workers, the federal government, and the US financial system, federal agencies were asked to identify the nation's climate change-induced economic vulnerabilities and develop appropriate policies to address those vulnerabilities. While not an enforceable law, this broad, cross-government executive order established climate change mitigation activities and adaptation strategies as a federal priority and laid the foundation for future policy. It also requires the Department of Labor to reconsider two rules published in late 2020 that limited investment and shareholder decisions to pecuniary factors without concern for environment, social, and governance (ESG) factors.

This executive order also called for a report from the Financial Stability Oversight Council (FSOC), which is chaired by Treasury Secretary Janet Yellen and led by the heads of federal government agencies. The purpose of this report, described below, is "assessing, in a detailed and comprehensive manner, the climate-related financial risk" facing the US economy (Pedersen and Lang 2021).

Bills

Environmental bills introduced under the Biden administration that relate to the US banking industry include but are not limited to the following:

• The Addressing Climate Financial Risk Act of 2021 (HR 1549): Introduced on March 3, 2021, to establish the Advisory Committee on Climate Risk on the Financial Stability Oversight Council.
• The Sustainable Investment Policies Act of 2021 (HR 3605): Introduced on May 28, 2021, to update the Investment Advisers Act of 1940 by facilitating the disclosure and transparency of large asset managers' sustainable investment policies.

- The Climate Change Financial Risk Act of 2021 (HR 3571): Introduced on May 28, 2021, to require the Federal Reserve System's Board of Governance, in cooperation with other federal agency heads, to create and conduct climate change-related financial risk analyses.
- The Retirees Sustainable Investment Opportunities Act (HR 3604): Introduced on May 28, 2021, to amend the Employee Retirement Income Security Act of 1974 by allowing retirement plans to disclose sustainable investment policies.

New Roles and Personnel

The Biden administration created new climate-related roles, including a Special Presidential Envoy for Climate (John Kerry), Department of Treasury Climate Counselor (John Morton), and Securities and Exchange Commission (SEC) Climate Counsel (Mika Morse). It also appointed Darrin Benhart as Office of the Comptroller of the Currency (OCC) Climate Change Risk Officer and Acting Chairman for the CFTC. In addition, the OCC joined the international Network of Central Banks and Supervisors for Greening the Financial System.

Regulatory Agencies

Federal and state regulatory agencies can create new requirements to which banks must adhere, and US federal regulatory agencies have begun to respond to the call to address anthropogenic climate change. Some examples are provided below.

US Federal Reserve

The US Federal Reserve was created in 1913 by the Federal Reserve Act following several financial panics. Its purpose is to maintain full employment and stable prices via monetary policy and bank regulation. With regard to climate change, the US Federal Reserve will have to consider the risk exposure that lenders face in addressing (a) climate impacts (e.g., storms, fires, relocation, ecosystem loss), (b) climate change mitigation and adaptation activities (e.g., reforestation, carbon capture), (c) and a shift from working with high carbon-emitting industries to cleaner industries and infrastructure (e.g., transition from fossil fuels to renewable energy).

According to Lael Brainard, a US Federal Reserve Governor, natural disasters driven by extreme weather in the nation's Midwest and West over the past five years have cost US\$630 billon (Fernholz 2021). Given the likelihood that we will increasingly experience local, regional, and global climate disruptions and shocks that can derail both employment and price stability, the US Federal Reserve will be challenged to navigate the road to decarbonizing the US economy. Financial institutions will be subject to scenario analysis by the central bank. The nature of climate change-related shocks makes it unlike other shocks to the financial system because climate change is ongoing and cumulative with increasingly frequent and increasingly severe shocks expected over time.

In order to address both known and hidden climate risks in the financial system, the US Federal Reserve created a Supervision Climate Committee (SCC) to facilitate the agency's capacity to assess the financial risks associated with climate change. The SCC's work to ensure the stability of US FIs represents one pillar of the Federal Reserve's framework for addressing climate-related financial and economic consequences and is considered a micro-prudential approach. This approach considers how traditional channels such as legal, market, operational, credit, and reputational risks affect the stability of individual companies.

On March 23, 2021, the Federal Reserve's Board of Governors reported the establishment of a new Financial Stability Climate Committee (FSCC). This committee intends to create a program to assess and address risks related to climate change and financial stability. It will provide a new stress test around climate disruption for US financial institutions. This represents a second core pillar and a macroprudential approach to climate that considers how climate change could affect stability across the financial system. Work will be done in coordination with the Financial Stability Oversight Council and its member agencies. The Federal Reserve also co-chairs the Basel Committee on Banking Supervision's Task Force of Climate-Related Financial Risks, which is tasked with ensuring global financial security and stability.

Despite these efforts, the Federal Reserve's response to climate change-related risks has trailed that of other central banks (Fernholz 2021; Saphir and Dunsmuir 2021). For example, the European Central Bank (ECB) and Bank of England have already released plans around transitioning to a cleaner economy. Both the ECB and Chinese government have developed green bond programs to buy debt that funds renewable energy and other greener projects as part of the transition away from climate-unfriendly activities.

Despite the United States' role as one of the largest emitters of greenhouse gases and the threat that the effects of climate change pose to the stability of the US financial system, the Federal Reserve sees these policies as outside its narrow mandate to maintain financial and economic stability (Saphir and Dunsmuir 2021). Analysts suggest that this should not be controversial and that addressing climate change is well within the Federal Reserve's purview.

The Federal Reserve was the last signatory to the Network for Greening the Financial System. This late arrival to address the threat of climate change is seen by some as a risk given that the lack of timely monetary policy could result in a US financial system vulnerable to the effects of climate change and climate shocks. This could result in negative consequences not only for the US economy but also for the global financial system.

Federal Deposit Insurance Corporation (FDIC)
The Federal Deposit Insurance Corporation (FDIC) is an independent US government agency that was established in 1933 by the Banking Act. Its function is to provide insurance coverage for bank deposits as a means of creating financial stability in the event of bank failure. (There is a corollary agency, the National Credit Union Administration, which insures customer deposits in credit unions.)

The FDIC provides regulatory oversight of banks in order to reduce their risk of failure. Thus, it is responsible not only for insuring bank deposits but also for setting monetary policy and overseeing large US bank holding companies. Given that climate change has the potential to cause significant shocks to the US financial system, it would be reasonable for the FDIC to provide guidelines around how banks might respond to anthropogenic climate change.

Although the FDIC has existing guidelines for banks to establish environmental risk programs, it has only recently become substantively involved in climate change as a member of FSOC.

Financial Stability Oversight Council (FSOC)
FSOC was created by the Dodd-Frank Act to conduct the following activities:

- Monitor the financial services marketplace in order to identify potential threats to US financial stability.
- Monitor financial regulatory proposals and developments.
- Make recommendations in such areas that will enhance the integrity, efficiency, competitiveness, and stability of US financial markets.
- Facilitate information sharing and coordination among Council member agencies and other federal and state agencies.
- Recommend to the Council member agencies general supervisory priorities and principles that emerge from discussions among the member agencies.
- Identify gaps in regulation that could pose risks to US financial stability (FSOC 2021, p. 1).

FSOC released its *Report on Climate-Related Financial Risk* on October 21, 2021. It names climate change as an emerging threat to US financial stability and provides 30 recommendations that FSOC members can implement to improve resiliency of the US financial system. These recommendations fall under the following four areas: (1) build capacity and expand efforts to tackle climate-related financial risk, (2) fill data and methodological gaps that pertain to climate change, (3) increase public climate-related disclosures, and (4) assess and mitigate risks that could harm US financial system stability.

The report indicated that assessing US financial stability as it relates to climate change involves the following four steps:

1. Define climate change risks and their potential impacts on the US financial sector.
2. Quantify the impacts of climate risk on US economic activity.
3. Evaluate the connections between financial risks and economic impacts, which can include effects upon market, liquidity, credit, and so forth.
4. Assess US financial stability.

The report described two categories of financial risk related to climate change. They are (1) physical risks (harm to people and property from acute and chronic climate events or phenomena), and (2) transition risks (stresses to sectors and institutions from changes in technologies, policy, or consumer/business sentiment). Additionally, the report announced the creation of two committees – the staff-level Climate-related Financial Risk Committee, which identifies priorities and coordinates among FSOC members, and the Climate-related Financial Risk Advisory Committee, which gathers information and analysis on risks pertaining to climate change.

It is worth noting that FDIC Chairman Jelena McWilliams abstained from approving FSOC's Report on Climate-Related Risk released in October 2021.

Office of Comptroller of the Currency (OCC)
The Office of Comptroller of the Currency (OCC) regulates the biggest US bank subsidiaries. After the fallout of a few events that threatened to destabilize the financial markets – namely, the savings and loan crisis and the Great Recession of 2008 and beyond – the OCC implemented robust guidelines and heightened standards around risk in the banking sector (Forrester et al.

2021). The established standards require banks with FDIC insured deposits to be structured so that authority and responsibility for monitoring adherence to company policies is clear. These banks must have effective risk management and timely reporting in place and comply with all applicable laws. In addition, clear procedures should govern asset management.

The OCC published its standards around increased oversight of larger federally chartered banks in 2014. These heightened standards require the larger banks to implement a risk governance framework that is overseen by the board of directors. This risk governance framework must comprise at least the eight risk areas, known as stripes, defined by the OCC.

Acting Comptroller of the Currency, Michael J. Hsu, stated that he has "prioritized the need to incorporate climate change into risk management frameworks to address the safety and soundness of the federal banking system" (Kelly 2021). Hsu suggested that the boards of large banks need to begin asking their management teams the five questions shown below (Ibid.); the OCC provided additional guidance for ongoing risk management around each question (Hsu 2021).

1. What is our overall exposure to climate change?

   Hsu suggested that banks answer this question by creating the ability to plan for various scenarios around the many varied climate change outcomes. He indicated that this might be akin to the Comprehensive Capital Analysis and Review (CCAR) stress tests that are already required of large banks by the US Federal Reserve. Essentially, the Federal Reserve develops CCAR scenarios ranging in severity and requires banks to respond to how they would attend to each scenario. This helps to uncover weaknesses in the large banks and identifies areas where financial instability lies.

   With regard to climate, the OCC indicated that bank management will need to report both qualitative and quantitative metrics to the board. Management will also "develop a framework, a risk taxonomy, metrics, data, scenarios, and a strong understanding of the first- and second-order impacts that physical and transition risks may have on the bank's portfolio" (Forrester et al. 2021). Hsu stated, "Boards should push senior management hard to develop scenario analyses, both top down and bottom up, as doing scenario analysis well takes time. But time is running out" (Kelly 2021). The Network for Greening the Financial System has developed several scenarios that could be used in banks' climate risk planning.

2. Which counterparties, sectors, or locales warrant our heightened attention and focus?

   Two types of risk should be considered – physical and transitional. Physical risks are those associated with climate change and could include events such as fire, drought, storms, flooding, and so on. Transitional risks are those associated with the transition away from climate damaging activities (e.g., burning fossil fuels) toward more climate neutral or beneficial ones (e.g., relying on renewable energy). Once-lucrative markets can become non-lucrative, and bank clients that are heavily invested in dying industries might be considerably devalued with stranded assets on their balance sheets. As a result of physical and/or transitional climate risks, some borrowers might become less creditworthy, and banks will need to integrate this analysis into their management of climate risks.

3. How exposed are we to a carbon tax?

   Hsu indicates that as challenging as transition risks – such as a carbon tax – are to identify and quantify, banks must begin their analysis somewhere. A scenario in which a carbon tax is adopted immediately could serve as a good place to begin. A carbon tax would be placed on products and services that emit greenhouse gases, such as carbon dioxide. The more emissions are associated with a product or service, the higher the tax. Although the immediate adoption of a carbon tax is unlikely in the US, it represents an example that could be useful in scenario planning by helping a bank to identify its areas of greatest exposure, risk, and correlated positions. This exercise would inspire the development of processes, data, and calculations that can lead to more robust transition risk measurement practices overall.

4. How vulnerable are our data centers and other critical services to extreme weather?
   Financial Industry Regulatory Authority (FINRA) rules already require large banks with broker–dealer subsidiaries to have disaster recovery and business continuity plans in place to prepare for pandemics, severe storms, and other potentially disruptive events. These plans should incorporate possibly disruptive climate change scenarios as well.

5. What can we do to position ourselves to seize opportunities from climate change?
   Just as climate change will render some industries unfavorable, others will become preferred. Industries and companies that address climate change or mitigate its negative impacts can provide financial opportunities for banks and investors. Furthermore, banks that do business with companies with strong climate risk management plans in place might be more sustainable over the longer term. Finally, climate is a cross-sectional/cross-organizational subject. Banks will need to find a robust way to respond to climate threats and prepare for climate opportunities throughout the organization, which might make identifying accountable individuals and governance a challenge.

Hsu indicated that large banks' management teams should be prepared to answer these questions over the next 12 months and that they need to begin factoring climate risk into their risk management calculations.

On November 8, 2021, the OCC announced its intent to publish high-level framework guidance for big US banks around how to manage climate risk (Pedersen 2021). This framework guidance, which would apply to lenders with more than US$100 billion in assets, was released on December 16, 2021, as a set of draft principles with a public comment period that ended on February 14, 2022. These principles are intended to support banks' efforts in managing financial risk around climate and to establish a high-level framework for financial risk management; they would affect such areas as governance, credit, liquidity, and risk management.

Commodities Futures Trading Commission (CFTC)
The CFTC created a Climate Risk Unit to ensure that new products related to climate or ESG fairly facilitate capital allocation, price discovery, market transparency, and hedging. On September 9, 2020, the CFTC's Climate-Related Market Risk Subcommittee released its *Report on Managing Climate Risk in the US Financial System*. The report indicated that climate change is a threat to the US financial system's stability and its ability to sustain the US economy. Even under upbeat emissions reduction forecasts, the world will continue to have to deal with the effects of some degree of climate change.

As a result, US and world financial markets might face disruptions via disorderly price adjustments, the inability of markets/market participants to adapt to rapid policy changes, changing consumer preferences, and/or evolving technology. A stressed financial system might be less able to provide credit or access to insurance and other financial products (e.g., hedging instruments). Regulators are limited by what they do not know, such as how varying types of climate threats might interact. For example, physical and transition risks might combine to increase system vulnerabilities of an already strained financial system that is struggling to recover from a pandemic. The report urges US financial regulators to move quickly and with care to address the emerging threats posed by climate change to the US financial system.

Securities and Exchange Commission (SEC) recommendations on ESG disclosures
The SEC has been one of the most proactive financial regulators in working to assess the potential impacts of climate change on the US financial system. In 2021, SEC Chair Gary Gensler indicated that the SEC would improve its climate-related disclosure for publicly traded companies, including the United States' biggest banks. Following a public comment period, the SEC will issue recommendations around ESG disclosures.

The SEC Chair also directed the Division of Corporation Finance to examine climate-related disclosures found in public company filings. In 2010, the SEC provided guidance to public companies around climate-change-related disclosure requirements. SEC staff have been directed to review how well public companies followed the 2010 guidance and determine how the market is handling risks related to climate change.

Joint efforts
The Federal Reserve, Federal Deposit Insurance Corporation (FDIC), and Office of the Comptroller of the Currency (OCC) have signaled to US banks the need for both qualitative and quantitative actions around managing climate change risk. There are several governmental regulatory bodies working together on responses to climate change within the US financial services industry. For example, in 2010, the Financial Stability Oversight Council (FSOC) was founded by top US financial and banking regulators working to identify and respond to systemic risks that face the insurance, banking, securities, and derivatives industries. As mentioned previously, in 2021, FSOC released its *Report on Climate-Related Financial Risk*. The report provides more than 30 recommendations to "support the ongoing and urgent whole-of-government effort to address climate change, and help the financial system support an orderly, economy-wide transition toward the goal of net-zero emissions" (FSOC 2021).

For the first time, FSOC recognized climate change as an emerging threat to the stability of the US financial system. The economy is already being harmed by climate-related events, which are expected to worsen over time. The report recognized that US financial regulators have much work ahead in their responses to climate-related risk and that this work will require significant FSOC member coordination. A few key recommendations are shown below.

- *Building capacity and expanding efforts to address climate-related financial risks*: Council members should prioritize internal investments in "staffing, training, expertise, data, analytic and modeling methodologies, and monitoring" and increase public communication of climate-related efforts.
- *Filling climate-related data and methodological gaps*: Council members should identify and ensure that consistent, reliable data are used in assessing climate risks and "develop consistent data standards, definitions, and relevant metrics" that address data gaps and issues.
- *Enhancing public climate-related disclosures*: Council members should review and update their public disclosure requirements to encourage comparability, consistency, and useful information around climate-related opportunities and threats.

- *Assessing and mitigating climate-related risks to financial stability*: Council members should employ scenario analysis in analyzing financial risks related to climate and use scenarios that have already been developed, such as those by the Network of Central Banks and Supervisors for Greening the Financial System (NGFS) and the Financial Stability Board (FSOC 2021). The Network of Central Banks and Supervisors for Greening the Financial System was founded in 2017 as a means to address climate-related threats to the financial system. The coalition develops policy recommendations for its 90 members, which include regulatory agencies and central banks. It released several climate change-related scenarios in 2021 that can be used by FIs in their climate risk management plans.

Meanwhile, in December 2020, at a Center for American Progress webinar, four Federal financial regulators called for cooperation between US and international regulators in the effort to mitigate the negative impacts of climate change. The regulators were Lael Brainard (Federal Reserve Governor), Allison Herron Lee (Securities and Exchange Commission Commissioner), Martin Gruenberg (FDIC Director), and Rostin Behnam (Commodity Futures Trading Commission Commissioner). The four indicated that US financial agencies are behind their global counterparts in their response to addressing climate-related risk and need to become proactive. Gruenberg stated, "International leadership by the United States will be essential if we are to make global progress on climate change, including its financial stability risks. We are behind the curve and we have a lot of ground to make up" (FDIC 2020).

For the Federal Reserve's part, it has hired climate scientists, and staff are working with FEMA and NOAA on climate risks. Brainard suggested that long-term climate scenario analysis allows for flexible responses to various situations in different time frames and can be a helpful tool that differs from the short-term focus of bank stress tests in ensuring sufficient capital (Knutson 2020). Conversely, the type of modeling used to assess credit risks tends to be backward looking and could be incompatible with the realities of present and future climate effects.

The SEC Commissioner emphasized the need for collaboration on risk around climate change and for standardized public company disclosures on climate change activities. Lee suggested requiring financial advisors to disclose how they address investor requests for climate change in their investment portfolios. Further, Lee stressed that all credit rating agencies must be transparent with regard to how they will integrate climate concerns into their rankings, how they weight various factors, and that their models are consistent.

The CFTC Commissioner, who sponsored the agency's Climate-Related Risk Subcommittee, stated that the needed structures are already in place for federal financial regulators to make climate change rules. In September, the Subcommittee issued a report titled *Managing Climate Risk in the US Financial System*, which stated that increasing weather events threaten the United States' financial system and its ability to sustain long-term economic growth. The report included 53 recommendations on managing climate risk, the most important of which, according to its authors, is to create an effective price on carbon that is consistent with the Paris Agreement and is implemented across the entire economy.

Non-Governmental Organizations (NGOs)

NGOs are helping FIs with their climate change mitigation and adaptation work and using their influence to affect policy. As the risks and costs associated with anthropogenic climate change become more apparent and stakeholder pressure becomes greater, many of the nation's largest banks have joined forces with one or more industry organizations committed to reducing greenhouse gas (GHG) emissions. The main climate change-related industry organizations are the Partnership for Carbon Accounting Financials (PCAF) and Net Zero Banking Alliance (NZBA).

Partnership for Carbon Accounting Financials (PCAF)
The Partnership for Carbon Accounting Financials (PCAF) is a consortium of 252 financial institutions (as of April 14, 2022). It was founded by Dutch financial institutions in 2015, made to include North American institutions in 2018, and scaled up globally in 2019. Sixteen PCAF members volunteered to create the PCAF Core Team to develop the Global GHG Accounting and Reporting Standard (the Standard) (PCAF 2020), including Amalgamated Bank, Bank of America, Boston Common Asset Management, and Morgan Stanley. PCAF sought feedback for the Standard from several stakeholder types, including financial institutions, NGOs, corporations, and others. FI members headquartered in the US (as of March 2022) are shown in Table 15.2.

Table 15.2   Financial institution membership in PCAF

Financial institution	Category	Total financial assets (in million $US, including lending and investments)	Status	Date joined	Date of first disclosure	Date of most recent disclosure
Amalgamated Bank	Commercial bank	16,507	Disclosed	March 2019	April 2021	April 2021
Angel Oaks Capital, LCC	Asset owner/ managers	22,400	Committed	November 2021	–	–
Bank of America	Commercial bank	2,434,079	Committed	July 2020	–	–
Beneficial State Bank	Commercial bank	1,011	Disclosed	March 2019	June 2021	June 2021
BlackRock	Asset owner/ managers	9,007,411	Disclosed	May 2021	January 2022	January 2022
Boston Common Asset Management	Asset owner/ managers	2,700	Committed	March 2019	–	–
Citi	Investment bank	1,951,158	Disclosed	August 2020	January 2022	January 2022
Clearwater Credit Union	Commercial Bank	524	Disclosed	March 2019	January 2022	January 2022
Climate First Bank	Commercial Bank	124	Committed	January 2022	–	–
Coastal Enterprises, Inc. (CEI)	Development bank	107	Committed	September 2019	–	–
Comerica, Inc.	Commercial Bank	114,700	Committed	August 2020	–	–
EIG Global Energy Partners	Asset owner/ managers	21,900	Disclosed	December 2020	September 2021	September 2021

Financial institution	Category	Total financial assets (in million $US, including lending and investments)	Status	Date joined	Date of first disclosure	Date of most recent disclosure
Fifth Third Bank	Commercial Bank	205,000	Committed	March 2021	–	–
Hannon Armstrong	Commercial Bank	6,200	Committed	September 2020	–	–
Huntington National Bank	Commercial Bank	175,000	Committed	February 2022	–	–
Kitsap Bank	Commercial Bank	15,000	Committed	January 2022	–	–
Liberty Mutual Insurance	Insurance	94,000	Committed	August 2021	–	–
Morgan Stanley	Investment bank	947,795	Committed	July 2020	–	–
Natural Capital Investment Fund, Inc.	Development bank	60	Committed	June 2021	–	–
New Hampshire Community Loan Fund	Development bank	145	Committed	January 2022	–	–
PNC Financial Services	Commercial Bank	791,000	Committed	April 2021	–	–
Raise Green, Inc.	Asset owner/ managers	3	Committed	June 2021	–	–
Regions Financial Corporation	Commercial Bank	163,000	Committed	January 2022	–	–
Self-Help Credit Union and Ventures Fund	Commercial Bank	2,700	Committed	September 2019	–	–
SLC Management	Asset owner/ managers	149,000	Committed	February 2022	–	–
Sunrise Banks	Commercial Bank	1,132	Committed	March 2019	–	–
Truist Financial Corporation	Commercial Bank	522,000	Committed	October 2021	–	–
US Bank	Commercial Bank	841,000	Committed	November 2021	–	–
Verity Credit Union	Commercial Bank	587	Committed	March 2019	–	–
Vermont Community Loan Fund	Development Bank	43	Disclosed	December 2019	December 2020	December 2020
VSECU	Commercial Bank	1,118	Committed	March 2019	–	–

Source: PCAF (2022)

The Standard helps FIs analyze and disclose the greenhouse gas (GHG) emissions that result from their loans and investments (financed emissions). All financed emissions disclosures are to be aligned with the Standard. These financed emissions can be disclosed for any financial accounting period using GHG accounting methods. This is the first globally accepted standard for measuring and disclosing financed emissions across the following six asset classes:

1. Listed equity and corporate bonds
2. Business loans and unlisted equity
3. Project finance
4. Commercial real estate
5. Mortgages
6. Motor vehicle loans

Measuring financed emissions by asset class is important in enabling FIs to accurately disclose GHG emission exposure as well as climate change-related risks. It also allows FIs to establish baseline emissions for the purpose of target setting in accord with the Paris Agreement.

According to PCAF, using the Standard is an FI's first step toward aligning with the Paris Agreement. It is followed by target setting and strategy development, both of which involve scenario analysis, then taking action. This is an iterative process in that each step informs the others.

Net Zero Banking Alliance (NZBA)
On April 21, 2021, 43 founding banks and the Prince of Wales' Sustainable Markets Initiative Financial Services Taskforce launched the Net-Zero Banking Alliance (NZBA). Since that time, additional members have joined. As of April 14, 2022, there were 108 member banks from 40 countries representing 38% of global banking assets valued at US$68 trillion. US-headquartered members are shown in Table 15.3.

Table 15.3   NZBA members headquartered in the US and commitment dates

NZBA members headquartered in the US	Date signed
Amalgamated Bank	April 2021
Bank of America	April 2021
Blue Ridge Bank	December 2021
Citi	April 2021
Climate First Bank	December 2021
JPMorgan Chase	October 2021
Morgan Stanley	April 2021
The Goldman Sachs Group, Inc.	October 2021
Wells Fargo & Company	October 2021

Member banks of this body, convened by the United Nations Environment Programme Finance Initiative, intend to share peer information and strategies for decarbonization. NZBA provides a framework and operational guidelines for its members. NZBA members have committed to ensuring that their investment and lending portfolios create net-zero emissions by 2050. The signatory banks will also create an intermediate target by 2030 or sooner.

NZBA Commitment Statement

The CEO of any bank wishing to be a member must first sign the NZBA Commitment Statement, which states that the signatory bank will undertake the following:

- "**Transition** the operational and attributable GHG emissions from their lending and investment portfolios to align with pathways to net-zero by 2050 or sooner.
- **Within 18 months** of joining, set 2030 targets (or sooner) and a 2050 target, with intermediary targets to be set every 5 years from 2030 onwards.
- **Banks' first 2030 targets** will focus on priority sectors where the bank can have the most significant impact, i.e. the most GHG-intensive sectors within their portfolios, with further sector targets to be set within 36 months.
- **Annually publish** absolute emissions and emissions intensity in line with best practice and within a year of setting targets, disclose progress against a board-level reviewed transition strategy setting out proposed actions and climate-related sectoral policies.
- **Take a robust approach** to the role of offsets in transition plans." (UNEPFI 2021)

Member banks are also required to use a set of guidelines based on the bank-led United Nations Environment Programme's Financial Institution Guidelines for Climate Target Setting for Banks. The guidelines are based on the following four target setting principles:

1. "Banks shall set and publicly disclose long-term and intermediate targets to support meeting the temperature goals of the Paris Agreement.
2. Banks shall establish an emissions baseline and annually measure and report the emissions profile of their lending portfolios and investment activities.
3. Banks shall use widely accepted science-based decarbonisation scenarios to set both long-term and intermediate targets that are aligned with the temperature goals of the Paris Agreement.
4. Banks shall regularly review targets to ensure consistency with current climate science." (UNEPFI 2021)

OPPORTUNITIES FOR IMPROVEMENT

Despite the rapid progress made in the US banking sector over the past few years, it remains to be seen whether today's commitments go far enough or fast enough to meet the Paris Agreement goals. In April 2022, the United Nations Intergovernmental Panel on Climate Change released a report stating that the world will become uninhabitable if does not rapidly change its energy policies (United Nations 2022). Signatories of the 2015 Paris Agreement voluntarily agreed to take actions to limit the planet's global warming to 1.5° Celsius; yet, the UN report indicated that the world is on track to increase planetary warming by more than twice that amount.

Below are three recommendations for improving the US banking sector's chance of meeting the 1.5° Celsius goal outlined in the Paris Agreement.

1. *Meet Climate Goals Sooner*: At this juncture, the most beneficial thing that the US banking industry can do is to implement their GHG emissions reduction goals far ahead of the 2030 and 2050 deadlines outlined by some banks. Given how quickly the negative

effects of climate change have occurred, it would be prudent and, perhaps, necessary for the US banking system and its customers to speed its GHG emissions reduction targets significantly.

2. *Set Absolute Goals, Not Relative Ones*: Many of the banks setting GHG emissions reduction targets in their financed emissions are using relative improvements rather than absolute ones. Citigroup is the only major US bank that has set a goal of reducing its absolute GHG emissions by 2030; Bank of America, Goldman Sachs, JPMorgan Chase, and Morgan Stanley's GHG emissions reduction targets are all based in relative terms. Wells Fargo has not committed to being net zero by 2030.

3. *Approach Climate and Sustainability Holistically*: If US banks want to reduce or eliminate their GHG emissions, they can focus on all aspects of their companies – their missions, operations, employees/contractors, facilities and sites, and products and services. These are described below.

   - *Mission*: The bank's commitment to reduce its negative impacts on climate change and the larger, more encompassing issue of sustainability can be incorporated into the company's mission statement or a separate environmental statement in order to ensure that it is always a priority and key driver behind bank decisions.

   - *Employees/contractors*: Company employees and contractors should be trained to recognize and address risks to climate or environmental sustainability on the job. They can also find ways to reduce resource use and waste. Whenever feasible, banks can provide telecommuting options to their employees in order to reduce the GHG emissions associated with commuting.

   - *Operations*: Company operations include a broad array of activities, such as accounting, cafeteria, corporate investing, daycare/childcare, hiring, marketing, printing and graphics, procurement, recycling, stakeholder relations, and supply chains. One example of creating more climate-friendly operations is by investing company profits in environmentally sustainable companies and providing that option to employees via their 401(k) or retirement programs.

   - *Facilities and Sites*: Company facilities, whether leased or owned, can be designed, built, and maintained using sustainable building principles, including energy efficiency and renewable power. Companies can be responsible for the sustainable use/environmental impact on their sites. Sites include the places where facilities are located (type 1), places that supply the company with its natural resources (type 2), and the places that are affected by the company's activities, products, and services over time (type 3), including airsheds and watersheds.

   - *Products and Services*: Finally, the company can consider sustainability, including its climate impacts, over the entire life cycle of all of its products and services (Townsend 2009; Townsend and Heine 2012).

SUMMARY

Several US banks have committed to net zero financed emissions by 2050 and have developed additional goals to reduce their own carbon emissions. Because climate change is broad in scope and will increasingly affect everyone from individual householders to governments, businesses, and non-governmental organizations, our response to it must be equally broad in scope. A multi-level approach is needed to address the growing magnitude, frequency, and severity of climate events and systemic shocks. It would rely on many different entities, including governments (federal, state, and local), businesses, non-governmental organizations (NGOs), individuals, and other stakeholders. Such a multi-level approach has begun to occur within and around the heavily regulated US banking sector.

For example, the Biden administration is implementing a cross-governmental approach to mitigating threats posed by climate change while attempting to support the transition to a cleaner, more climate-neutral industry. Federal agencies that oversee and regulate the US banking industry are realizing that anthropogenic climate change-related risk is a threat to the stability of the US financial system and are beginning to act accordingly by developing guidelines and standards for the banks to follow. Meanwhile, the nation's banks are being encouraged to enact climate scenario risk planning as a means of addressing the very real threat of climate shocks that grow in size, intensity, severity, and frequency.

Non-governmental industry organizations are working with their members – be they banks or other financial institutions – to develop standardized approaches to calculating financed emissions, scenario planning for risk management, and providing transparent reporting mechanisms by which all banks can be assessed for their ability to withstand worsening effects of climate change and climate shocks. Finally, banks are working internally, with their peers, and with their clients and other stakeholders to identify threats, opportunities, and hidden risks associated with climate change. Although not discussed in this chapter, it is worth noting that shareholders, customers, investors, and other stakeholders can use their votes, money, and voices to influence FI's climate change-related activities. Only an integrated, multi-level approach to anthropogenic climate change will provide the broad-based and multi-scaled response needed to reduce the negative climate impacts of the US banking sector.

The US banking sector has taken some initial and substantial steps in reducing its GHG emissions by focusing on financed emissions and some other activities. However, there are further opportunities for improvement by abbreviating the zero GHG emissions timelines, shifting from relative to absolute GHG emissions reductions, and focusing on all parts of the business, including the mission, employees and contractors, operations, facilities and sites, and products and services.

NOTE

1. Financial institutions include commercial banks, development banks, investment banks, promotional banks, financial services groups, insurance companies, asset owner/managers, and export credit agencies.

REFERENCES

Bank of America (2022a). *Approach to Zero.* https://about.bankofamerica.com/content/dam/about/pdfs/approach-to-zero-2022.pdf (accessed May 27, 2022).

Bank of America (2022b). Bank of America announces 2030 financing activity targets as part of net zero commitment. https://newsroom.bankofamerica.com/content/newsroom/press-releases/2022/04/bank-of-america-announces-2030-financing-activity-targets-as-par.html (accessed April 13, 2022).

Brunetti, C., Dennis, B., Gates, D., Hancock, D., Ignell, D., Kiser, E. K., Kotta, G., Kovner, A., Rosen, R. J., and Tabor, N. K. (2021). *Climate Change and Financial Stability.* Board of Governors of the

Federal Reserve System. https://www.federalreserve.gov/econres/notes/feds-notes/climate-change
-and-financial-stability-20210319.htm (accessed March 19, 2022).

Commodities Futures Trading Commission (2020). *Managing Climate Risk in the US Financial System: Report of the Climate-Related Market Risk Subcommittee*. Market Risk Advisory Committee of the US Commodity Futures Trading Commission. https://www.cftc.gov/sites/default/files/2020-09/9 -9-20%20Report%20of%20the%20Subcommittee%20on%20Climate-Related%20Market%20Risk %20-%20Managing%20Climate%20Risk%20in%20the%20US%20Financial%20System%20for %20posting.pdf (accessed March 19, 2022).

FDIC (2020). Remarks by Martin J. Gruenberg, Member, FDIC Board of Directors, The Financial Stability Risks of Climate Change at the Center for American Progress. December 18, 2020. https:// www.fdic.gov/news/speeches/2020/spdec1820.html (accessed November 15, 2021).

Fernholz, T. (2021). This is how the Federal Reserve will confront climate change. https://www .msn.com/en-us/money/markets/this-is-how-the-federal-reserve-will-confront-climate-change/ar -AAQeGbd?ocid=uxbndlbing (accessed November 15, 2021).

Forrester, J. P., Webster, M. S., Taft, J. P., and Bisanz, M. (2021). *Initial Climate Change Risk Management Expectations Issued by US OCC*. Available online https://www.mayerbrown.com/ en/perspectives-events/publications/2021/11/initial-climate-change-risk-management-expectations -issued-by-us-occ (accessed November 15, 2021).

FSOC (2021). *FACT SHEET: The Financial Stability Oversight Council's Response to Climate-Related Financial Risk*. Available online https://home.treasury.gov/system/files/136/FACT-SHEET-The -Financial-Stability-Oversight-Councils-Response-to-Climate-Related-Financial-Risk.pdf (accessed November 15, 2021).

Greenhouse Gas Protocol, World Resources Institute, WBCSD (2013). *Technical Guidance for Calculating Scope 3 Emissions*. Available online https://www.ghgprotocol.org/sites/default/files/ ghgp/standards/Scope3_Calculation_Guidance_0.pdf (accessed March 19, 2022).

Hsu, M. J. (2021). Five climate questions every bank board should ask. Available online https://www .occ.gov/news-issuances/speeches/2021/pub-speech-2021-116.pdf (accessed November 15, 2021).

Kelly, M. (2021). OCC nudges banks on climate change – radical compliance. November 10, 2021. Available online https://www.radicalcompliance.com/2021/11/10/occ-nudges-banks-on-climate -change/ (accessed November 15, 2021).

Knutson, T. (2020). Federal financial regulators call for cooperation to address climate change. *Forbes*. December 18, 2020. Available online https://www.forbes.com/sites/tedknutson/2020/12/18/federal -financial-regulators-call-for-cooperation-to-address-climate-change/?sh=42cb08da2e31 (accessed November 15, 2021).

Morgan Stanley (2021). *Methodology for Morgan Stanley's 2030 Interim Financed Emissions Targets on the Path to Net-Zero*. Available online https://www.morganstanley.com/content/dam/msdotcom/ about-us/netzero/Morgan-Stanley-Net-Zero-Target-Methodology.pdf (accessed February 3, 2023).

PCAF (2020). *The Global GHG Accounting & Reporting Standard for the Financial Industry Executive Summary*. https://carbonaccountingfinancials.com/files/downloads/PCAF-Global-GHG-Standard -exec-summary.PDF (accessed November 14, 2021).

PCAF (2022). *Financial Institutions Taking Action*. https://carbonaccountingfinancials.com/financial -institutions-taking-action (accessed March 20, 2022).

Pedersen, B. (2021). Big-bank climate risk guidance coming by year-end: OCC chief. *American Banker*. November 3, 2021. https://www.americanbanker.com/news/big-bank-climate-risk-guidance-coming -by-year-end-occ-chief (accessed November 15, 2021).

Pedersen, B., and Lang, H. (2021). Will FDIC, OCC follow Fed into global climate group? *American Banker*. May 18, 2021. https://www.americanbanker.com/news/will-fdic-occ-follow-fed-into-global -climate-group (accessed November 15, 2021).

PwC (2022). Financial institutions are pledging to lower carbon footprints: Here's what you need to know about financed emissions. Available online https://www.pwc.com/us/en/services/esg/library/ financed-emissions.html#:~:text=What%20are%20financed%20emissions%3F%20In%20current %20carbon%20accounting,Scope%203%20Category%2015%20emissions%2C%20or%20financed %20emissions (accessed March 20, 2022).

Saphir, A., and Dunsmuir, L. (2021). The US Federal Reserve's take on greening the economy: That's not our job. November 1, 2021. Available online https://finance.yahoo.com/news/u-federal-reserves

-greening-economy-050622676.html?guccounter=1&guce_referrer=aHR0cHM6Ly93d3cuYm
luZy5jb20v&guce_referrer_sig=AQAAAMz8w89ngCfCFKvw2RQ88y19dGF26cJHPjjqG6D
FlkYSDrTDgkgCeIvXuyIEtibeVeexJ21B8kBGBdfp9RMU5tiEgPZlJ6nBm9ZdNXCpdYEig
-tqD9XSy2-O08Fj-xxs8-yw8sYAQdkFn4OEmhE17oE03suc0wubXIZOajhpu6e4 (accessed November
15, 2021).

Townsend, A. K. (2009). *Business Ecology*. Atglen, PA: Schiffer Publishing.

Townsend, A. K., and Heine, G. (2012). *Green Business Development Training Manual*. Developed for
the US Department of Health and Human Services.

United Nations (2022). *UN Climate Report: It's 'Now or Never' to Limit Global Warming to 1.5
Degrees*. Available online https://news.un.org/en/story/2022/04/1115452 (accessed April 13, 2022).

United Nations Environment Programme Finance Initiative (UNEPFI) (2021). *Net Zero Banking
Alliance – United Nations Environment Programme – Finance Initiative*. Available online https://
www.unepfi.org/net-zero-banking/ (accessed November 15, 2021).

16. Harnessing the power of investors to drive climate innovation

Gabrielle J. Evans

As the Earth's environment further disintegrates because of society's dependency on fossil fuels, and the negative impacts of such disintegration are further witnessed on both a physical and financial level, corporate sustainability and sustainable investing have become folded into the intricate fabric of the world economy. These environmentally focused investment approaches have not only become accepted, but also popular and praised over time as both a morally and financially sound strategy to managing and investing assets. The continuity and reinforcement of such strategies will be vital to the development of a greener world. An effective tool at reinforcing this behavior for those who are already participating – and, more importantly, motivating those who have not yet implemented this mindset or strategy – is an investment-focused tax incentive. As such, this chapter will propose a new and novel tax incentive, which will be referred to as the "Green Tax Incentive," to codify the encouragement of individual and institutional investment in companies that contribute to a greener world or otherwise combat the effects of climate change.

Because the stock market is a widely used wealth building tool for both the companies listed and also the investors participating, the Green Tax Incentive will target this financial platform as a means to fund climate-focused companies, thereby driving climate-innovative technologies. Specifically, this tax incentive will target the capital gains tax.

The successful execution of the Green Tax Incentive will depend on multi-level participation from various economic, political, institutional, and individual actors. The collaboration of such actors will be discussed in this contribution. Moreover, the incentive's impact on these actors and society at large will be explored, as well as its limitations as a policy tool.

BACKGROUND ON SUSTAINABLE INVESTING

Although this chapter will focus solely on the environmental component of sustainability, it is important to recognize the full definition of corporate sustainability. Corporate sustainability can be defined as "an integrated, systemic approach by business that builds, rather than erodes or destroys, economic, social, human and natural capital" (Visser quoted in Landrum, 2017, p. 3). Sustainable investing is similar but involves individual or institutional investors, rather than business leaders, and is defined by the Forum for Sustainable and Responsible Investment (US SIF) as "an investment discipline that considers environmental, social and corporate governance (ESG) criteria to generate long-term competitive financial returns and positive societal impact" ("Sustainable Investing Basics", 2021).

Overall, the commitment to corporate sustainability and sustainable investing has been trending upward. For instance, when the UN-backed Principles for Responsible Investment (PRI) invited investment companies to sign a document representing their commitment to considering ESG-related factors in investment decisions, just 63 companies signed (Eccles and Klimenko, 2019). Twelve years later, in 2018, that number grew to 1,715 and represented $81.7 trillion in assets under management (Eccles and Klimenko, 2019). Even more poignant, the US SIF reported that, by the end of 2019, one out of every three dollars under professional management in the United States was managed according to sustainable investing strategies ("Sustainable Investing Basics", 2021).

While there are many approaches to sustainable investing, Alhoj et al. (2012) categorize the seven common strategies in the European Social Investment Forum, briefly outlined below. These strategies are often used in combination with one another based on an investor's values, level of diligence or management, and market savviness, amongst other factors.

1. Negative or exclusionary screening
    Investors avoid deploying their capital into industries deemed unethical or contrary to one's values; common examples include weapons or tobacco.
2. Norms-based screening
    Investors only deploy their capital into companies that adhere to a set of international standards, such as those defined in the Ten Principles of the UN Global Compact.
3. Best-in-class approach
    Investors deploy their capital into companies with strong ESG performance.
4. Sustainability-themed investing
    Investors commit their capital to one or more sustainability-focused themes, such as an environmental or social focus, with environmental themes being the most common; examples of categories within this theme are renewable energy and ecological conservation, amongst others.
5. ESG integration in financial analysis
    Investors or asset managers systematically include ESG-related "…risks and opportunities into traditional financial analysis and investment decisions based on a systematic process," which weighs and attempts to quantify the impact of ESG factors on a company's future financial performance.
6. Sustainability engagement and voting
    Investors actively engage with companies on ESG performance, by way of voting, to influence outcomes, also known as active ownership.
7. Impact investing
    Investors deploy capital in ESG-positive companies, but with a less passive approach than the other methodologies listed, with the expectation of generating social and environmental impact and a positive financial return; examples include social business/entrepreneurship and microfinance (i.e., the offering of financial services to those who would traditionally lack access due to systemic inequality).

Since these approaches to sustainable investing are not mutually exclusive, investors could use any number of the above methodologies to screen, research, and analyze sustainable companies or funds. Prudent investors will use multiple strategies simultaneously to maximize financial return and reduce risk while ensuring that they are investing in companies that align with their values.

A crucial component to understanding why someone would participate in the Green Tax Incentive, which is outlined in the next section, is to first explore why investors participate in sustainable investing in the first place. Generally, one may engage in such an investment strategy with the following principles in mind: personal beliefs or morals, financial returns, or long-term focus. Any one or combination of these motivations can influence investors to participate in sustainable investing. A brief description of each motivation is outlined below.

Personal Beliefs or Morals

Many grapple with their personal contribution to exacerbating climate change, based on their daily habits and actions and how these may emit greenhouse gases. This trend towards personal responsibility is exemplified by the many personal carbon footprint calculators that can be found online, which are used to estimate a particular household's carbon dioxide emissions after receiving the user's input on their day-to-day activities. Tools like these place a level of responsibility on individuals to change their behaviors and adopt more sustainable habits. Sometimes these guilt-inducing exercises are effective at doing so, and other times not. Those who do feel morally compelled to make a positive change, and also have the financial means to do so, may choose to adopt a sustainable investing strategy. As such, many environmentally-conscious investors are adopting a sustainable investment strategy to make the world, as they see it, a better place while also taking a personal stance on climate change.

Financial Returns

Investors are becoming increasingly aware that their money would be best served, and also preserved, if placed in companies or industries that are ESG-committed, as they are best poised to perform well in a warming world. This awareness has been quantified in numerous reports and studies, an example of which can be found in a study conducted by the Harvard Business School, which reported that companies committed to ESG-related causes in the 1990s, measured by a number of criteria, outperformed the control group over the next 18 years (Eccles and Klimenko, 2019). Another study conducted in 2017 by Nordea Equity Research reaffirms this phenomenon by reporting that from 2012 to 2015, companies with the highest ESG ratings outperformed their lowest-rating counterparts by as much as 40% (Eccles and Klimenko, 2019). More generally, Eccles and Klimenko (2019) cited a study performed by Bank of America Merrill Lynch in 2018, which concluded that firms with higher ESG performance tended to be higher-quality stocks with less volatility and were also less likely to go bankrupt. Therefore, there is ample evidence to suggest that sustainable investing is a financially wise strategy, which has motivated many investors to adopt the strategy.

Long-term Commitment

This particular motivation to participate in sustainable investing is related to the financial returns motivation but is more nuanced. To explain: in general, investors and financial managers are realizing that if they are to be truly committed to a long-term investment strategy, some of which have an actual fiduciary responsibility to do so, then they must also factor climate change into their strategy, since this issue is and will continue to be increasingly relevant as the science predicts. Sustainable investing is therefore a vital component to a long-term investment strategy.

The foundation of the Green Tax Incentive is based upon the notion that the investors already participating in sustainable investing for one or more of the above reasons will reaffirm their commitment to it, and that those who are not already participating in this type of investing will be motivated to start, in response to the Green Tax Incentive's decreased tax burden on sustainable investments; the end result being an increased amount of capital deployed in climate-focused companies. Moreover, if investor behavior or society in general progresses as it should regarding climate change and the commitment to decelerating it, both because of societal norms/pressures and also as a result of the Green Tax Incentive, then sustainable investing may become synonymous with investing in general, as all companies would then be performing on an ESG-basis. This is an overarching goal of the Green Tax Incentive – to elevate investors' behavior to the point at which it is no longer needed.

TAX INCENTIVE PROPOSAL

Although sustainable investing has become increasingly popular, the climate is still on a dire warming trajectory. Therefore, companies that are at the helm of confronting climate change require additional support and funding to further their missions and develop more innovative approaches to curbing climate change.

The stock market is a powerful crowdsourcing tool that raises money for the listed company, establishes its market value, holds management accountable to a continued growth strategy, and provides transparency to investors. In the context of climate change, the stock market is an untapped vehicle with the potential to drive the desperately needed innovations in the climate space. As such, harnessing the power of the stock market to help the environment and those companies which protect it is the main objective of the proposed Green Tax Incentive.

A tax incentive can be defined as "fiscal measures used by governments to attract investment domestically and internationally in certain key sectors of the economy" (Bolnick quoted in Munongo et al., 2017, p. 152). If deployed properly, tax incentives have the potential to drive the advancement of green technologies by encouraging targeted investments in this area. These policy tools can come in many forms, such as tax credits or subsidies, but the Green Tax Incentive will target the capital gains tax rate specifically.

A capital gain is the profit made on the sale of an asset (asset price at the time of sale minus asset price at the time of purchase = capital gain), which is currently taxed at a lower rate than ordinary income. Capital gains can be further delineated as short- or long-term, with each being taxed at a different rate. Short-term capital gains are incurred if the asset is held for a year or less, and any holding period longer than that would signify a long-term capital gain. To encourage a longer holding period and discourage short-term or speculative investing, the IRS imposes a lower tax rate on long-term capital gains and vice-versa.

Just as a lower long-term capital gain rate was imposed to encourage a longer holding period on investments, the Green Tax Incentive would encourage investors' behavior as well, but regarding which stocks they purchase rather than solely the length of time that they are held. Specifically, the Green Tax Incentive would lower the long-term capital gains rate on investments made in public companies qualified as "sustainability-purposed," defined below, thereby aiming to attract investors and raise capital for these environmentally focused businesses. In essence, the taxes triggered at the time of sale of a "sustainability-purposed" stock would be lower than its non-qualifying counterpart. To connect the proposed incentive to one of the common sustainable investment strategies outlined in the previous section, the Green Tax Incentive would encourage sustainability-themed investing, particularly relating to the environmental theme, at the very least, and investors could then tailor their strategy by layering in additional approaches.

Table 16.1 is a potential tax rate table under the Green Tax Incentive, based on the 2021 rates imposed by the IRS of the United States.

Table 16.1   Tax rate table

Income	Short-term capital gains tax rate	Long-term capital gains tax rate	Green tax incentive *long-term* capital gains tax rate
Up to $9,525	10%	0%	0% (no change)
$9,526 to $38,600	12%	0%	0% (no change)
$38,601 to $38,700	12%	15%	11.25%
$38,701 to $82,500	22%	15%	11.25%
$82,501 to $157,500	24%	15%	11.25%
$157,501 to $200,000	32%	15%	11.25%
$200,001 to $425,800	35%	15%	11.25%
$425,801to $500,000	35%	20%	15%
$500,001 and over	37%	20%	15%

Source: IRS.gov.

The table applies a 25% reduction in tax burden under the Green Tax Incentive compared with the typical long-term capital gains rate. For illustrative purposes, here is an example of the tax savings earned on investments that would qualify under the Green Tax Incentive:

> An investor purchases $150,000 worth of "sustainability-purposed" stocks (i.e., stocks of companies that qualify for the Green Tax Incentive).
> They hold the stocks in a non-retirement brokerage account for 5 years, at which point they decide to sell them for $250,000, representing growth of $100,000. This is the investor's only income for the year.
> Since the investment was held longer than a year, this investor's tax burden would be $11,250 under the Green Tax Incentive, constituting $3,750 in tax savings compared with the typical long-term capital gains tax rate. These savings become very meaningful as the investment value increases.

Note that this table is just an example of the tax rates that could be applied under the Green Tax Incentive. Economists and policymakers would have to contemplate the most effective tax rate to promote participation in the Green Tax Incentive while also retaining an appropriate tax base. Also note that the above table does not contemplate a change to short-term capital gains tax rates under the Green Tax Incentive. While this could be explored, the Green Tax Incentive strives to encourage long-term, sustained investment so it is not being contemplated in this setting.

Also note that the Green Tax Incentive could apply the decreased tax rate on qualified companies' stocks starting either (1) from the time the incentive is first implemented (for instance, assume that an individual had initially invested in a green economy company in 2010 and the Green Tax Incentive was enacted in 2022, and the investor then decides to sell this stock in 2025, they would pay the full capital gains tax on gains earned from 2010 to 2022, but receive the special rate on gains earned from 2022 through 2025), or (2) at the time of sale, regardless of when the qualified investment was first purchased. The former possibility could promote fairness and encourage initial participation in the incentive, but the latter would reward investors who had the foresight to adopt a sustainable investment strategy earlier, prior to knowing that they would reap the benefits of a lower capital gains tax rate. However, from an implementation perspective, the first option might be preferred because it has a higher likelihood of adoption and acceptance by lawmakers, as they stand to lose a large amount of potential tax revenue with the alternative option. For the purposes of this chapter and to increase the likelihood of implementation, the Green Tax Incentive will apply option 1, but further discussion surrounding this topic ought to be had to determine the best overall approach for all parties impacted.

Qualified Companies

To grant a proposed tax incentive to investors, lawmakers must decide exactly which types of companies would qualify as eligible investments for the incentive program, thereby earning their investors the right to a lower capital gains tax rate at the time of sale. As such, the Green Tax Incentive will only apply to those companies dedicated to improving, and whose operations inherently improve, the state of the environment and altering the trajectory of climate change. To be explicit, this chapter will refer to these companies as "green economy companies."

The industries that contribute most to the changing climate are energy, transportation, food, and agriculture (Ritchie and Roser, 2020). As such, the companies that are operating as a direct foil to the status quo of these industries would be the ideal candidates of the Green Tax Incentive. Examples of these green economy companies include alternative or clean energy companies (solar, wind, hydropower, etc.), sustainable ag-tech companies, alternative-fuel vehicle manufacturers (electric cars, scooters, etc.), or sustainable food companies (alternative meats, companies that create technology to reduce food waste, etc.).

Companies that are solely involved in corporate "greening" activities would not be eligible for the Green Tax Incentive. For instance, if McDonald's replaced all single-use plastic with recyclable material going forward, or even if the company chose to build nuclear power plants (assuming the law permitted) to source all of its energy more efficiently, thereby cutting its carbon footprint, it would still not qualify as a green economy company. This is because the fast-food chain's operations would not be inherently dedicated to sustainability or the betterment of the environment. However, if McDonald's decided to shutter all restaurants (assuming they were corporately held) and instead operate as a sustainable agriculture company, developing and utilizing innovative precision farming techniques to optimize its planting time and minimize its water use, thereby becoming a sustainable food vendor to restaurants and other food retailers, it could then qualify as a green economy company and its investors would benefit from the Green Tax Incentive.

The distinction outlined in the above scenario ought to limit companies' temptation to greenwash (i.e., the utilization of manipulative tactics to falsely portray a company as environmentally friendly) in an attempt to qualify for the Green Tax Incentive. While a different policy could and ought to target companies such as McDonald's to participate in corporate greening activities, because they are also a crucial component to creating a more sustainable economy, the Green Tax Incentive will have a narrower focus. This will increase the incentive's chance of success since tax incentives could be more effective when narrowly focused and minimally used (James, 2013).

Weak Versus Strong Sustainability – To What Degree of Sustainability does the Green Tax Incentive Embody

Companies and countries have adopted varying degrees of sustainability that guide and reflect their values, and also direct their actions. As such, sustainability can be mapped along a spectrum, both on a micro-level (company-specific perspective) and a macro-level (higher-level perspective of a government or society). These models have been synthesized into one, unified model in a literature review performed by Landrum (2017, pp. 13–16), which categorizes the micro- and macro-level models in stages, outlined below for discussion purposes:

Non-participatory: This would include climate deniers and ignorers.

Stage 1: Very weak sustainability or Compliance: Characterized by "defensive" or regulated activities that are "externally forced."

Stage 2: Weak sustainability or Business-centered: A "proactive" stance on sustainability that is driven by self-serving purposes to remain competitive.

Stage 3: Intermediate sustainability or Systemic: In this stage, businesses adopt an ESG-mindset and are operated for the good of humanity, "…but there continues to be an increased growth, production, and consumption orientation with limited integration of environmental or ecological science."

Stage 4: Strong sustainability or Regenerative: Does not pursue growth and "adopts practices to repair the damage of the industrial consumer economy."

Stage 5: Very Strong or Coevolutionary: Acts in tandem with nature and is "…reminiscent of lifestyles of indigenous cultures…" that did not seek to "…control, manage, or manipulate the environment."

When analyzing the above stages of sustainability in relation to the Green Tax Incentive, one can conclude that the policy would be categorized, at best, as Stage 3 or Systemic sustainability. This is because the Green Tax Incentive would target capital gains earned in the stock market, and participation in this marketplace is predisposed upon the notion that, on average, it will grow and grant participants returns that outpace inflation. As such, the Green Tax Incentive seeks to capitalize on investors' pursuit of monetary growth or gain. This is not to say that the Green Tax Incentive, because it is not the embodiment of Stage 5-level sustainability, should not be imposed. The stock market has been around for many years with no indication of dismantlement any time soon. Therefore, it is important to continue leveraging current financial and societal paradigms, such as the stock market, to promote environmental good while also working towards a more sustainable future – which this incentive aims to do. Nonetheless, this solution is founded on a financial system that, because it is predisposed upon the current economic model of continued growth and consumption, is not inherently the most sustainable.

The companies eligible for the Green Tax Incentive would straddle both the Systemic and Regenerative stages of sustainability, since green economy companies would be committed to practices that "repair the damage of the industrial consumer economy" but also seek growth as a participant in the public stock market.

Positive or Negative Reinforcement over Punishment

The Green Tax Incentive would not include measures to punish behaviors antithetical to the ones in which the incentive is promoting. In other words, the Green Tax Incentive would not call for an increased tax burden on investments made in "unsustainable" or "anti-green economy companies," such as gas or coal companies. Instead, this tax incentive would be focused on rewarding positive, sustainability-related behaviors rather than punishing non-sustainable investing. The reason for such a distinction is the lack of impact that a puni-tive provision to the Green Tax Incentive would have on reducing emissions. Moreover, the potential negative psychological component of including a punishment in this policy could be detrimental to its effectiveness.

Environmental advocate Bill Gates, who wrote How to Avoid a Climate Disaster, has professed that "…divestment, to date, probably has reduced about zero tons of emissions. It's not… [as if] you've capital-starved [the] people making steel and gasoline" (Gates quoted in Ross, 2019). This is because the demand for heavy emitting industries such as steel and gas-oline will still exist even if investments are divested from these industries. Gates suggests to instead invest in "…ventures working on innovations to cut greenhouse gases" (Ross, 2019), which the Green Tax Incentive would promote.

Furthermore, psychological and neuroscientific studies have shown that positive or negative reinforcement is more effective at motivating action than positive or negative punishment (Guitart-Masip et al., 2014). There is also evidence that when faced with potential punishment, human action is often inhibited altogether due to what is known as the "freeze" response (Sharot, 2017). Understanding these mechanisms of human behavior can help policymakers develop the most effective policies for motivating or deterring behavior. It is not unreasonable to assume that some investors, especially individual investors who tend to be less sophisticated than their institutional counterparts, would choose not to participate in the tax incentive alto-gether when faced with potential punishment. As such, since the overriding priority of this tax incentive is to motivate people to act – namely, invest – then the Green Tax Incentive should avoid punitive provisions, at least to start. A periodic analysis of the incentive's effectiveness should be analyzed to revisit the issue and determine if such measures ought to be imposed.

IDEAS FOR IMPLEMENTATION AND MULTI-LEVEL ACTION

Collaboration and cooperation amongst individuals, private and public companies, govern-ments, and other market actors will be crucial to the effective enactment of the Green Tax Incentive. This proposed incentive is therefore dependent upon multi-level action and partic-ipation. This section will first offer potential methods for categorically determining whether a company qualifies as "green-economy" and thus grants its investors eligibility to participate in the Green Tax Incentive; next, it will discuss some ideas for multi-level participation.

How to Determine Qualified Companies

- *Sector classification*
  When a company is first listed on a stock exchange (i.e., it goes public), its shares are categorized under a certain sector which describe the company's core activities. Therefore,

a new "Sustainability" sector category could be created for the Green Tax Incentive's purposes. The company's investment bank (the entity that handles the company's IPO) would detail the sustainable nature of the enterprise's core operations and list its shares under the "Sustainability" sector. Stocks listed under this sector would then be eligible for the capital gains tax break. Note that this implementation strategy would require participation from trading platforms such as TD Ameritrade or Robinhood to recognize this new sector classification and apply it to the appropriate companies so that investors can easily discern which companies fall under this new sector.

For pre-existing public companies, management would have to file a claim with the SEC requesting that its company's shares be categorized under the "Sustainability" sector, thus signaling to its investors that their shares would qualify for special tax treatment under the Green Tax Incentive.

- *Rating system and SEC reporting*
  The mission of the Securities & Exchange Commission (SEC) is to "protect investors, maintain fair, orderly, and efficient markets, and facilitate capital formation" ("The Role of the SEC"). To this end, companies are required to report their financials and other metrics to the SEC. To effectively implement the Green Tax Incentive, the SEC could develop specific criteria for rating companies' environmental sustainability levels (and potentially social and governance performance as well) and require public companies to track and submit particular metrics based off of this rating system. From there, the rating system could establish a specific threshold that must be met to make a company eligible for the Green Tax Incentive. This would revolutionize sustainable investing by standardizing the system by which companies report their ESG-related activities, educating investors and making this type of information easily accessible to everyone.

- *Private sector and SEC integration*
  Rather than solely utilizing the SEC to establish guidelines for sustainability reporting and a rating system to analyze and categorize companies based on these reporting metrics, the government could enlist the help of the private sector to partially outsource these administrative duties. Currently, the system for reporting or grading a company's ESG performance is in its nascency, but there are organizations out there attempting to standardize these metrics, such as the Impact Management Project. The SEC could contract with this organization to assist in establishing these standards and developing a rating system to score companies on ESG performance.

  The SEC could also require the accounting firms that provide assurance services to public companies' financial performance to also provide assurance relating to ESG performance. One or both methods would take part of the pressure and costs off of the SEC and put them onto private companies and the green economy companies themselves.

- *Special ETF/sustainability index*
  This method would most likely require the cooperation from the private sector as well, as past indexes have been established by corporations, not governmental agencies. Nonetheless, this method would involve establishing an index (e.g., the S&P 500) that tracks sustainable companies. As such, the investors of companies listed under this newly created index would be eligible for the capital gains tax incentive.

- *New stock exchange*
  This method might be viewed as the most ambitious of the three, and would again require private sector collaboration with government. It would involve creating an entirely new

stock exchange that would become the default platform for trading green economy stocks. It should be noted that this idea is not all that unique – a group of Silicon Valley entrepreneurs recently unveiled a new stock exchange, coined the Long-Term Stock Exchange (LTSE), designed to promote a long-term focus on investing and operating public companies, rather than the short-term focus that has dominated the traditional stock exchanges such as the New York Stock Exchange (NYSE) and the Nasdaq Stock Market (Nasdaq) (Schleifer, 2019). Therefore, it is possible that the same could be done but with a different goal in mind, such as spurring investment in sustainable companies.

- *New investment vehicle*
This method is more focused on the tax collection component of the Green Tax Incentive. To explain, once it is determined that a company reaches the sustainability threshold to grant its investors the tax incentive, there must be a system in place to then apply this lower tax rate to the appropriate investors' capital gains. This could be done by adding lines to tax return forms for taxpayers to fill out if they are eligible for the Green Tax Incentive, or the federal government could create an entirely new investment vehicle, such as a 401(k) or Roth IRA, in which investors could hold their green economy companies. This new investment vehicle would then signal to the government/IRS that a different tax rate ought to be applied to these assets when an investor sells shares within it, making the process more seamless.

Multi-level Participation

As this chapter has already alluded, the Green Tax Incentive will only reach its full potential if individuals, governmental institutions, private companies, and the sustainable companies themselves come together to harmonize their efforts to both participate in and implement this policy effectively. Individual and institutional investors must participate in the incentive; governments must codify the incentive into law and establish reporting systems; private companies must fill the gaps that the government cannot meet on its own; sustainable companies must commit themselves to new reporting guidelines; and the list goes on.

For this proposal to be passed into law, one could argue that it should first garner the support of the media and everyday investors. To drive this support, the Green Tax Incentive must reach a larger audience. This could be accomplished through journalistic approaches and even social media. Once public support is generated, lawmakers and federal agencies would be much more driven to act on behalf of their constituents or popular opinion. Moreover, if this public support were to be further legitimized by the endorsement of the financial service industry, specifically those at the forefront of the SRI/ESG movement, and environmental not-for-profits, the case for implementation would become even stronger. These endorsements could be made by these firms and organizations by publishing articles that discuss and potentially expand upon, or even revise, this proposal. Essentially, any attention or publicity that these entities generate for the Green Tax Incentive may help the cause. Furthermore, lobbyists, on behalf of the financial service industry, could also play a big part in promoting and advocating for this proposal and codifying it into law. The financial service industry, or more specifically, the firms that bundle sustainable stocks together and sell them as "sustainable" funds, would have much to gain from the Green Tax Incentive if it were implemented, as the policy has the potential to increase the popularity of – and ultimate investment in – these environmental fund categories. The top players in this industry may thus be incentivized to utilize lobbyists to drive implementation forward.

Not only will these actors have to harmonize their efforts to achieve what this chapter is proposing, but other seemingly unrelated participants will have to contribute as well. One example of such a participant is teachers. An important component to motivating investor behavior and promoting participation in the Green Tax Incentive is education. Oftentimes, when a tax incentive is released by the government, many individuals have not been apprised of the new measure and therefore do not participate. Essentially, no one has notified them of the new incentive program, or, if they have, has not explained it to them in a digestible and actionable manner. It is therefore up to teachers, either individually or together with the school systems at large, to establish courses on financial literacy, at least at the high school level, and require that students take these courses in order to graduate. These financial literacy programs should specifically include education as it relates to the stock market and retirement preparation. It is relatively well known, at least anecdotally, that many individuals do not have a solid understanding of the stock market and are intimidated by it. The Green Tax Incentive will need participation from all types of people, so establishing this type of education is critical not only to its success as an incentive program, but also to the success of everyday individuals.

EXPLORING THE POTENTIAL EFFECTS OF THE GREEN TAX INCENTIVE

Potential or Intended Positive Effects

The primary purpose of the Green Tax Incentive is to promote investment in environmentally focused companies, assisting in their development and driving innovation that will abate the deteriorating climate. As such, the incentive intends to spur economic growth and encourage risk taking in this subsector of the economy. The logic here is that any rational investor would be more willing to invest in a company deemed "risky" (i.e., is experimenting in new technology or is a smaller, less established firm without much of a track record) if they knew that their rewards (capital gains) would be taxed at a lower rate, thus providing them with an even higher return than average if the company does succeed. This type of investment environment would nourish these innovative companies that may otherwise never had the chance to bring their product or service to the market due to capital deprivation.

Furthermore, federal tax incentives have been a driving force behind the growth of renewable energy over the past decade (Bhattacharyya, 2020), and the Green Tax Incentive could further catalyze this growth. One example of tax incentives' effectiveness is outlined in a report by Rhodium Group on the potential effects of the Clean Energy for America Act. According to the report, the tax incentives included in the proposed Clean Energy for America Act could potentially transform the power sector, cut air pollution by 84% in five years, reduce carbon dioxide levels by 76% below 2006 levels in just a decade, and lead to the creation of 600,000 jobs every year over the next ten years, amongst other positive environmental and social impacts (Larsen et al., 2021). The Green Tax Incentive has the potential to expand upon current or future policies such as the one just described, working in tandem with these policies to make the net result even more impactful. For instance, because the Green Tax Incentive aims to provide more capital to environmentally focused businesses by attracting investors, these companies would have more funds to allow them to take advantage of other tax incentives, such as the ones proposed in the Clean Energy for America Act.

The Green Tax Incentive not only has the potential to compound the positive impacts of other policies, but it also has the potential to counteract the negative effects that certain policies may have on the investing environment. As has been proposed by progressive lawmakers, capital gains tax rates may be raised on the wealthiest individuals. While this would produce additional tax revenue for federal governments, it could nonetheless negatively impact investors' behavior.

According to an analysis performed by Goldman Sachs based on data from the Federal Reserve, the wealthiest Americans hold between one and one and a half trillion dollars in capital gains made on stocks, accounting for about 3% of the entire US stock market (Choe, 2021). If faced with an increased tax bill on capital gains, there is concern that these investors and any others impacted by the hike in tax rates could sell off their stocks before the new rate is imposed (Choe, 2021), shaving value off the stock market for all investors, including working-class Americans who invest in 401(k) plans. However, the Green Tax Incentive could mitigate this potential impact by providing a more tax-sheltered outlet for tax-concerned investors. While many might criticize the ultra-wealthy's tax avoidance schemes such as the one just described, these high net-worth individuals will continue to participate in these types of sophisticated tax avoidance maneuvers regardless, so why not give them an environmentally positive and productive outlet to do so while also avoiding a sell-off?

The Green Tax Incentive could also add jobs to the economy, at least within the industries the incentive impacts. A jobs report released in 2020 found that nearly 600,000 jobs were lost in environmentally sustainable industries such as renewable energy, energy efficiency, clean vehicle, and grid and storage companies due to the pandemic (Jordan, 2020). Tax incentives such as the Green Tax Incentive have the potential to create short-term revitalization of these industries by producing more investment in these types of companies, thus promoting job creation. Moreover, the Green Tax Incentive could assist in long-term job creation in these industries and those related to them by the same token; if companies are better capitalized, they will, in turn, be in a more favorable position to retain and hire employees.

Lastly, but not exhaustively, another positive and intended impact of the Green Tax Incentive would be the promotion of individual participation in the fight against climate change. The Green Tax Incentive would provide an outlet for everyday individuals to assist in preserving the environment, some of which may have not otherwise participated in the stock market due to personal values or hesitation to participate in a financial market in which they are not familiar or educated.

Potential Negative Effects and how to Counteract

If adopted, the following potential negative effects of the Green Tax Incentive should be considered and addressed by policymakers.

It is possible that this particular tax incentive, since it would only apply to stock market participants, would disproportionately benefit the wealthy. While the Green Tax Incentive would not aim to inherently benefit wealthy individuals and is intended to promote participation across the socioeconomic spectrum, stock market participation rates are higher amongst wealthier individuals, as is evidenced by data released by Pew Research in 2020. According to the data collected, just 52% of US families have invested in the stock market and 88% of these families have a household income above $100,000 (Parker and Fry, 2020). While the definition of the term "wealthy" is somewhat subjective, a household income of $100,000 is meaningfully above the US median of about $68,000 (US Census Bureau, 2020). Regardless, stock market participation is only available to families with some degree of discretionary income, which places a barrier of entry on participation in the Green Tax Incentive, thereby only directly benefiting financially secure households.

The only way to truly counteract this paradigm is to lift the standard of living in the US, which requires multilateral action on behalf of the US government and private institutions. However, one discrete policy measure that could directly impact stock market participation, and thus provide access to the Green Tax Incentive, relates to financial literacy. If state governments mandated financial literacy courses in secondary schools, as previously discussed, students might become more comfortable investing in the stock market and would also be more likely to achieve financial security. In sum, if equal opportunities existed for all income and racial backgrounds, and financial literacy were a cornerstone of early education, then access to a tax benefit such as the Green Tax Incentive would expand to most Americans. Moreover, even if the Green Tax Incentive does disproportionately favor the wealthy, this unintended consequence will put the wealthiest families' money to good use for the benefit of the environment and society at large, thereby lifting everyone up, at least indirectly.

Since the Green Tax Incentive would decrease the long-term capital gains tax rate on qualified investments, it would have a direct negative impact on tax revenue generated by the government, which is another consequence of the policy. Most tax incentives will result in revenue loss to the government, and one type of such revenue loss can be attributed to changed behavior on behalf of businesses in an effort to receive the tax incentive, creating lost revenue from abandoned projects (Easson and Zolt, 2002). The goal of the Green Tax Incentive, however, is to generate beneficial outcomes that outweigh the negative monetary impact on the federal government.

Furthermore, tax incentives tend to reduce investment in non-participatory countries and non-qualified sectors of the economy (Munongo et al., 2017). If the Green Tax Incentive only applied to investments in qualified US companies, then investments in green economy companies headquartered in other countries may suffer. However, this could be counteracted if foreign governments enact their own version of the Green Tax Incentive, which would elevate the Green Tax Incentive's overall impact on the world economy and environment. Therefore, this type of incentive should be adopted by foreign governments to unite and deploy the full power of the world stock market into driving investments in green economy companies. As for potentially decreasing investment in non-qualified sectors of the economy, that is a fair trade-off to encourage investment in companies that will help create a greener, more sustainable economy and world at large.

The Green Tax Incentive might also disproportionately favor large, well-established companies, such as Tesla or similar large-cap companies. While Tesla is an environmentally innovative company and would traditionally qualify for the Green Tax Incentive under the definition of a green economy company, the Green Tax Incentive is more intended to provide capital to companies that may not otherwise be capable of securing it. To counteract this effect, one may consider applying the Green Tax Incentive to qualified companies only when they first go public. Companies that are just entering the IPO phase of their business lifespans are typically smaller than their well-entrenched predecessors (i.e., those companies with shares already listed on a stock exchange), and therefore more in need of capital since the primary purpose of going public is to raise money.

However, if the tax incentive were only applicable to qualified IPOs, this would reduce the overall impact of the incentive as it would limit its scope. Also, in an effort to qualify its shares for the Green Tax Incentive, this IPO provision may encourage companies to go public before they are ready, and their stock prices may become artificially inflated as a result. This artificial inflation could be caused by investors who purchase green economy stocks solely to receive the tax benefit without having performed any analysis on the company beforehand, thereby driving the price of the stock up based on non-related, speculative factors as opposed to the company's inherent financial value.

Therefore, the Green Tax Incentive ought to apply to companies at all stages of their life cycles, not just the IPO stage, which might help reduce speculative investing. Instead, policy-makers could consider limiting the Green Tax Incentive to companies with market capitalizations under a certain amount, preventing incumbent companies such as Tesla from being the sole beneficiaries of the tax incentive.

Expanding the Green Tax Incentive to Include More Broadly Sustainable Companies

This proposal has set forth a narrow set of criteria for qualifying an investment under the Green Tax Incentive. One reason for this approach is to promote pointed investment in environmentally purposed companies that may otherwise lack the opportunity to raise the necessary capital for the research and development of their innovative, climate-solution-driven product or service. If the Green Tax Incentive were expanded, investors would be less motivated to purchase the stock from a lesser-known company's IPO and more motivated to purchase stocks of incumbent environmental companies, which may not drive the necessary change and action that the world needs.

Another reason for the narrow criteria is to prevent investor confusion and simplify the qualification system. To elaborate, if the Green Tax Incentive were expanded to include companies that are not environmentally purposed per se, but participate in environmentally sustainable business practices, the threshold for qualification becomes much more blurred and complicated. For instance, take the McDonald's example from previous sections: if McDonald's were to source 100% of its energy from solar or wind power and eliminate all plastic use, but continue to sell animal products and source them from unsustainable, mass farming operations, would its investors still qualify for the Green Tax Incentive? Or suppose that McDonald's underwent this same transformation and the company also decided to source its animal products from sustainable farms, would it now qualify? One may say that it should, but maybe not at the full 25% tax rate reduction since the company is still selling animal products, which are still problematic in terms of causing climate change. As one can see, a company's particular situation can become be so nuanced that it may be difficult to determine qualification. Given the Green Tax Incentive's novelty, starting with a clearer "guidebook" or set of standards might be wise to decrease the chances of investor confusion and increase the chances of investor participation and overall success.

However, this is not to say that this expanded version of the Green Tax Incentive should not be explored further and potentially implemented after a qualification system is more maturely developed. If sustainability reporting tools became more sophisticated, or a country's government were to mandate that public companies include sustainability metrics in their reporting, the qualification process may become manageable; it would just be a matter of assigning scores to companies for their sustainability practices, as discussed previously in the Rating System and SEC Reporting section of this chapter.

Ultimately, an expanded version of the Green Tax Incentive is the goal, as it has a much greater potential of influencing a broad change in company behaviors, but it could take a lot more time to solidify. Therefore, it is recommended that the Green Tax Incentive be limited, at first, to environmentally purposed companies to expedite the implementation process.

CONSIDERATIONS AND LIMITATIONS

While the Green Tax Incentive has the potential to harness the power of investors to drive climate innovation, there are obvious limitations to its effectiveness, some of which are outlined below.

- The incentive will require plenty of logistical effort to enact and the establishment of strict guidelines to prevent potential pitfalls.
- Although the Green Tax Incentive may motivate other countries to implement their own versions, it is not guaranteed, and therefore, might be limited in its impact.
- As previously mentioned, the tax incentive represents Stage 3 or intermediate sustainability, and one could argue that society should be moving towards Stage 4 or Stage 5 of sustainability if there is any hope ameliorating the worst impacts of climate change.
- The Green Tax Incentive alone, even at its best, will not solve the climate crisis that the world faces. It is only a piece in solving the climate change puzzle.
- Guidelines for what qualifies as a sustainable company are currently vague. The reporting system and categorization of what makes a company environmentally sustainable would have to vastly improve, become more sophisticated, and integrate within the current financial system. This would obviously be a big undertaking, but, as discussed, could be worth the effort.
- Even with the suggestions outlined above regarding implementation, the Green Tax Incentive will require more SEC resources and thus result in considerable costs to the government.
- This proposal makes general judgement calls as to what form the tax incentive should take on, but any number of variations of the tax incentive would be better than nothing.
- Lastly and probably most importantly, the Green Tax Incentive proposed in this chapter only considers public companies and does not address private companies. While the Green Tax Incentive could be extended to private companies as well, the management of such an incentive would be much more laborious, as private companies are not currently required to report earnings or activities to the SEC. Therefore, another mechanism or governing body would have to assume responsibility for the management of such a program, and private companies may not willingly participate in it.

CONCLUSION

The world cannot afford to avoid the climate disaster it faces any longer. This proposed tax incentive offers a potential targeted solution to a pervasive and deeply set problem – the economy's dependency on fossil fuels and the harmful emissions that result from this dependency and other human-related activities. The Green Tax Incentive aims instead to fuel investment in companies that will lead the charge in fighting climate change. At best, the incentive will succeed in this goal, while at worst, the incentive will create burdensome costs to the government with limited reward. Having said that, some Congress or Parliament members may claim that we cannot afford to implement this tax incentive, but one could argue that we cannot afford not to try. If the Green Tax Incentive is a success, it will be a true embodiment of what multi-level action and participation can accomplish.

REFERENCES

Alhoj, E., Blanc, D., Barby, C., Christopher, R., Cozic, A., Dittrich, S., ... Vogele, G. (2012). *European SRI Study 2012*, Eurosif A.I.S.B.L., 2012. https://www.eurosif.org/wp-content/uploads/2014/05/eurosif-sri-study_low-res-v1.1.pdf.

Bhattacharyya, B. (2020). *Renewable Energy Tax Credits: The Case for Refundability*, Center for American Progress, 28 May 2020. https://www.americanprogress.org/article/renewable-energy-tax-credits-case-refundability/.

Choe, S. (2021). Explainer: Capital gains tax hike targets wealthy investors. *AP NEWS*, Associated Press, 28 April. https://apnews.com/article/personal-taxes-business-51d52c89505becbd62c6a03469d5a9bc.

Easson, A., and Zolt, E. (2002). Tax Incentives. Washington: World Bank Institute.

Eccles, R.G., and Klimenko, S. (2019). The Investor Revolution. Shareholders are getting serious about sustainability. *Harvard Business Review*, May–June, 106–116.

Guitart-Masip, M., Duzel, E., Dolan, R., and Dayan, P. (2014). Action versus valence in decision making. Trends in Cognitive Sciences, 18(4), 194–202, ISSN 1364-6613. https://doi.org/10.1016/j.tics.2014.01.003 or https://www.sciencedirect.com/science/article/pii/S1364661314000205.

James, S. (2013). Effectiveness of tax and non-tax incentives and investments: Evidence and policy implications, 1 September. https://ssrn.com/abstract=2401905 or http://dx.doi.org/10.2139/ssrn.2401905.

Jordan, P. (2020). *Clean Energy Employment Initial Impacts from the COVID-19 Economic Crisis, April 2020*. Carlsbad, CA: BW Research Partnership. https://e2.org/reports/clean-jobs-covid-economic-crisis-april-2020/.

Klimenko, S., and Eccles, R. G. (2020). Shareholders are getting serious about sustainability. *Harvard Business Review*, 24 November. https://hbr.org/2019/05/the-investor-revolution.

Landrum, N. E. (2017). Stages of corporate sustainability: Integrating the strong sustainability worldview. Organization & Environment, 31(4), 287–313. doi:10.1177/1086026617717456.

Larsen, J., King, B., Kolus, H., and Herndon, W. (2021). *Pathways to Build Back Better: Investing in 100% Clean Electricity*. Rhodium Group, LLC, 7 October. https://rhg.com/research/build-back-better-clean-electricity/.

Munongo, S., Akanbi, O., and Robinson, Z. (2017). Do tax incentives matter for investment? A literature review. Business and Economic Horizons, 13, 152–168. 10.15208/beh.2017.12.

Parker, K., and Fry, R. (2020). *More than Half of U.S. Households Have Some Investment in the Stock Market*. Pew Research Center, 27 July. https://www.pewresearch.org/fact-tank/2020/03/25/more-than-half-of-u-s-households-have-some-investment-in-the-stock-market/.

Ritchie, H., and Roser, M. (2020). CO_2 *and Greenhouse Gas Emissions*. Published online at OurWorldInData.org. https://ourworldindata.org/co2-and-other-greenhouse-gas-emissions.

Ross, A. (2019). Tackling climate change – an investor's guide. *Financial Times*, 20 September 2019. https://www.ft.com/content/fa7a4400-d940-11e9-8f9b-77216ebe1f17.

Schleifer, T. (2019). America's newest stock exchange wants to fix one of capitalism's fundamental challenges. Vox, May 22. https://www.vox.com/recode/2019/5/22/18629621/long-term-stock-exchange-explainer-capitalism-quarterly-earnings.

Sharot, T. (2017). What motivates employees more: Rewards or punishments? *Harvard Business Review*. https://hbr.org/2017/09/what-motivates-employees-more-rewards-or-punishments.

"Sustainable Investing Basics" (2021). *The Forum for Sustainable and Responsible Investment*, Naylor Association Management Software. https://www.ussif.org/sribasics.

"The Role of the SEC". *The Role of the SEC | Investor.gov*, US Securities and Exchange Commission. https://www.investor.gov/introduction-investing/investing-basics/role-sec.

US Census Bureau (2020). *Income and Poverty in the United States: 2020*. Census.gov, US Department of Commerce, 18 October. https://www.census.gov/library/publications/2021/demo/p60-273.html.

17. Culture, education, and sustainability: a systemic approach

Madhavi Venkatesan

INTRODUCTION

The relationship between the present speed of climate change and human activity was addressed in absolute language by the Intergovernmental Panel on Climate Change (IPCC) (2021) in its sixth assessment report. The simple statement provided in the report's introduction under the header *The Current State of the Climate* declared, "It is unequivocal that human influence has warmed the atmosphere, ocean, and land. Widespread and rapid changes in the atmosphere, ocean, cryosphere, and biosphere have occurred" (Intergovernmental Panel on Climate Change, 2021). This recent human attribution to climate change provides not a wake-up call but validation that action is needed and needed immediately. Given the increase in research, discussion, promotion of behavioral change, and activism over the past 30 years, there is reason for optimism that large-scale mobilization is possible; however, this requires widespread effort.

The human relationship with the environment is rooted in the social and symbiotic construction of culture, where culture is defined as the social institutions and norms that identify a group. The "social" aspect is determined by power dynamics and legitimacy of specific individuals and groups and may or may not be rooted in self-interest, while the "symbiotic" is based on the relationship between the group and the environment that a given society inhabits. The symbiotic aspect of culture provides an initial understanding of "if" and "how" specific cultures and their societies incorporate stewardship responsibilities and seek to live sustainably, where sustainability is defined as the intertemporal balancing of human needs against the needs of other species and the ecosystem. To this end, historically cultural norms have been framed by religion and or spiritual practice and reflect the human role and purpose on the planet (Samuels, 1987; Wagner-Tsukamoto, 2017; Mgaloblishvili, 2018). In turn, observed if not referenced as such, economic systems are typically outcomes of cultural norms and reflect human behavior relative to a specific environment. The challenge in the current period is in understanding the economic systems that operated in individual cultures, as this has been obscured with the global imposition of a single economic framework in the 1940s.

With the adoption of the Gross Domestic Product (GDP), a market-based, production-oriented, and resource intensive indicator, economic progress is not defined to explicitly include symbiosis with the environment. Rather, expenditure on final goods and services in each period is the target. Further, the implicit presumption of human dominance of the environment permeates human activity given the indicator's focus (Bradley, 2020). Interestingly, it is the perception of the environment as a resource that arguably defines the human impact on our planet and has prompted global activity that is inconsistent with sustainability.

Of significance is that our current GDP-focused economic system aligns and reflects a Christian orientation to the Earth, a domination of the Earth centered on human gratification and consistent with the religious orientation of the invading peoples that provided the foundation for the US. According to White Jr. (1967) Christianity succeeded in substituting pagan animism with a culture of individualism and anthropocentrism, amplified by domination over nature. As conveyed in the Bible's book of Genesis, man is regarded as the special being of God's creation. He is assigned the task of controlling nature, the Earth's resources, and all living creatures. In this manner, the paradox of Christianity is consenting limitless use of resources, along with the interpretive license of dominion.

In the present period, there are but a few societies that have maintained a cultural identity independent of a GDP measurement. These groups are primarily comprised of Indigenous communities and are scattered over the globe. However, their exclusive status has only exacerbated their vulnerability, by not providing them with the economic status to ensure their independence. These societies are unfortunately increasingly threatened with their own extinction as their informal property rights are marginalized and the land they inhabit is developed for market-based production (Altman, 2009). Their inability to establish complete autonomy related to their own activities, highlights the relationship between aggression and domination, providing the opportunity to explicitly address that the market mechanism is not a reflection of human evolution but rather an outcome of the relationship between competition and cooperation. Both reflect cultural norms; the former promotes individualism and the latter collectivism. Arguably, collectivism fosters empathy and is aligned with social and environmental sustainability (Janardhanan et al., 2020; MacNeill, 2020). However, in the United States (US) active marketing has promoted the perception that collectivism is inconsistent with human nature along with the view that competition promotes superior outcomes (Ball, 2001). Indeed, even the government has promoted the need for competition as "fundamental to a thriving and fair economy" (Boushey and Knudsen, 2021). Although these comments were made to promote understanding of the exploitive outcomes related to market consolidation, they are short-sighted from the perspective that they only focus on the potential income benefits and do not highlight that competition must also be integrated with social welfare, so that externalities and exploitation are explicitly not acceptable for measured, market-based gains to be realized. Competition without conscience does not promote equity but may harm it. The evidence of this is observable in many aspects of modern secular society where the assumptions of human and firm behavior are readily both apparent and likely attributable to the endogenization of economic theory: self-gratification and profit-seeking. The requisite for empathy is also a sentiment espoused by Adam Smith (1759) in *The Theory of Moral Sentiments*, his first book, which also provides context for the much cited, but little read *The Wealth of Nations*, Smith's second book (Sen, 1994).

Adam Smith was a moral philosopher and has been labeled as the founder of modern economics. His contribution was not to the mathematization of the discipline, which can be largely attributed to the 20th century, rather it was in fostering an understanding of human behavior and the inclusion of conscience in decision-making. In reading his books it is also obvious that he had a normative perspective of how society should behave. These attributes differ significantly from present-day economics where theory is employed independent of context, and the discipline in its attempt to be categorized as a science has distanced itself from normative assessment and instead relied on mathematics to appear objective. However, the use of mathematical methods obscures, not eliminates subjectivity and normative judgement, in that equations implicitly include perceptions and beliefs, and data similarly incorporates bias.

This chapter addresses the relationship between economics and culture, the role of culture in environmental protection and climate change, and the need to address environmental stewardship with stakeholder engagement, inclusive of regulatory channels (macro), grassroots educational campaigns (micro-level), and institutional action (meso-level) to facilitate climate action. The discussion centers on the importance of widespread economic literacy education to address the cultural norms promoted by GDP. Economic literacy, it is argued, enables individuals to understand how assumptions of economic behavior have been normalized into society, and can similarly be augmented. Further, economic literacy provides the connection between assumptions and measures of economic activity. The discussion concludes with a case study highlighting the significance of economic literacy in promoting collective climate action.

CULTURE AND ECONOMIC MEASUREMENT

To a large extent, the perceived relationship between human systems and environmental systems affects the level of resource use and environmental augmentation. Culture, in the form of religion and spiritual beliefs, can be asserted to have contributed to the perception of stewardship relative to human needs and wants. Further, culture was the basis of economic activity and the constraints on specific actions. Where religion and or spiritual practice has legitimized human domination, a human footprint would be expected, compared with religion and or spiritual practice that aligned human activity with a responsibility for stewardship or constrained development for other reasons such as direct control or religious beliefs (Armstrong, 1994; Chung and Duchrow, 2013; Bradley, 2020; Yackel-Juleen, 2021).

Our current society in the US builds on the systems established at settlement and it is evident that the perception of the environment as a resource dominates economic thought (Kawashima and Tone, 1983). It is embedded within our discussion of the production possibilities frontier (PPF) and our policy interest in ensuring that we seek to maximize production subject to resource constraints at any given point in time. In the case of production, this conforms to policy – monetary and fiscal – that seeks to maintain or establish the economy at its peak in business cycle terms or at its potential relative to the GDP measure. In the US this is most evident in the dual mandate of the Federal Reserve. "The monetary policy goals of the Federal Reserve are to foster economic conditions that achieve both stable prices and maximum sustainable employment" (Federal Reserve Bank of Chicago, 2020), conditions that are consistent with an economy attaining its potential GDP.

The underlying and guiding assumption of production and consumption decisions is premised on the belief that individuals in an economy have insatiable desires to consume and are only constrained by income. Alongside, the theory of the firm, legitimized by Milton Friedman (1970), is that the purpose of business is profit not social responsibility. This assumption is reflected in the PPF when efficiency is defined as any production combination found on the PPF line (Figure 17.1). On this line, the economy is maximizing production relative to resource constraints.

To the extent that the allocation of resources at a given point in time considers intergenerational equity and threshold extraction rates consistent with the prevention of resource depletion, and enables repopulation for renewable resources, the trade-off decisions may or may not be consistent with sustainable resource utilization. Further, to the extent that a society is taught or maintains the social norm of satiation of needs relative to that of wants, the efficient

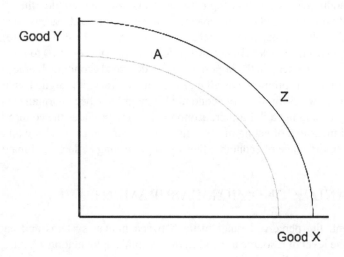

Source: Author.

Figure 17.1   Production possibilities frontier

allocation of resources may not embody the maximum production related to the resources available from a long-term perspective.

In Figure 17.1, the PPF line labeled Z represents a society for which insatiable wants have been embedded into the culture and the PPF represents the maximum production possible in an economy given resource availability at a given point in time. This society must rely on the identification of new resources and technology to enable future consumption or an outward shift of the PPF over time. On the other hand, the society depicted as operating on PPF A, while having the ability to attain PPF Z, would be inconsistent with full resource utilization. Society A, though representing a society that is guided by the cultural value of intergenerational equity and the satiation of needs relative to the balance of environmental and social sustainability, would be inefficient based on prevailing economic theory. The Z economy would consider A to represent an inefficient use of resources if some resources were left idle. Further, the country operating at A would not be attaining its potential GDP and, as a result, would appear to be a weaker economy on a GDP hierarchy.

GDP is a measure of production capacity within a nation's domestic borders and what it essentially captures is the total value of goods and services sold at a specific point in time. In the US, consumption expenditures account for more than two-thirds of GDP. Because prices change routinely, the value of GDP is found in its growth rate period to period using a base year price and, in comparison, at a point in time to another country's GDP values, or growth rate. This comparative evaluation has become a proxy for the economic strength of a country. But as an aggregate measure, GDP does not capture the changes in quality of life, or standard of living, or even income distribution. These are significant limitations that were noted by developers of the indicator.

ECONOMIC GROWTH AND CLIMATE IMPACTS

The most significant environmental impact attributed to economic growth has been the increased speed in climate change due to fossil fuel-based energy production as well as the growth in energy dependence in both direct consumer use and in the production of consumer goods. However, there is a distinction in the use of energy. Developed countries' use of energy is significantly higher than that of developing countries, with the US (see Figure 17.2) being the cumulatively highest contributor to greenhouse gas emissions (Ge, Friedrich and Damassa, 2014). Evidence suggests that profitability parameters on the part of businesses promote a circumvention of regulatory restrictions on the production and responsibility for externalities, leading to production shifting to developing countries where regulations may be limited and the focus on GDP growth may result in the trade-off between environmental and social protection to growth in production capacity (Coscieme et al., 2020).

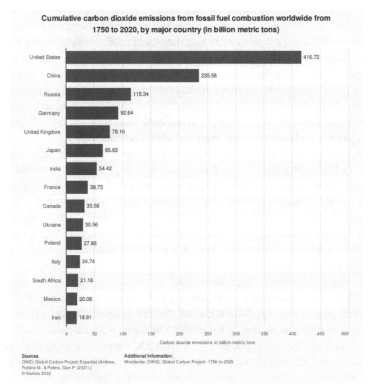

Source: OWID (2021).

Figure 17.2 *Cumulative CO_2 emissions*

Economic growth has been achieved using resources and the advancement of technology, where the latter has promoted more efficient use of resources. However, growth has not been without adverse consequences to the environment. Atmospheric greenhouse gas emissions are one of several externalized impacts related to the coupling of economic growth with environmental exploitation and degradation. Sustainable development challenges the present context of growth by relying on a decoupling of economic growth rates and environmental impacts. Decoupling is defined by the OECD as "breaking the link between 'environmental bads' and 'economic goods'" (Organisation for Economic Co-operation and Development, OECD, 2002, p. 4). Decoupling would yield a lower rate of increase in environmental degradation relative to economic growth (e.g., GDP):

> Decoupling may be either absolute or relative [...] Absolute decoupling is said to occur when the environmentally relevant variable is stable or decreasing while the economic driving force is growing. Decoupling is said to be relative when the growth rate of the environmentally relevant variable is positive, but less than the growth rate of the economic variable. (OECD, 2002, p. 4)

Given the strength of consumer expenditures in developed countries' GDP, transformation to sustainable development may be catalyzed through education – economic literacy – that promotes a shift in consumption value orientation to include a responsibility for the holistic impact of a given consumption choice – a conscience-based framework. The result could potentially lead to internalization of externalized costs of production to ensure sustainable use of environmental resources as well as labor. In essence, if consumers had the information to make a rational choice – to be the rational economic agents that the pricing model of economics assumes but that social frameworks and institutions do not universally foster or develop – consumers would be better empowered to exercise the power inherent in consumption decisions. To the extent that cultural norms are consistent with stewardship, consumer behavior would then implicitly include environmental and social responsibility.

For example, there is no market price for air; it is assumed to be free, more importantly it is also required for life. Correspondingly, it is a costless component of the production process; waste has been released into the atmosphere for years. If there had been a cultural norm that prevented the release of airborne waste that was embedded in demand, the pollution that has collected in the atmosphere for the past 300 years could have been averted simply by the social recognition of its impact relative to the benefits resulting from its creation. As simple as it may sound, consumers could have promoted the welfare of the atmosphere through their collective demand that air quality be preserved.

The moral values embedded and communicated within demand and supply determine the way a need or want is attained. The implicit morality, simply stated, is assessed as the net benefit on an aggregate basis, which means that the benefit to a few can be justified if it exceeds the costs to even the many. To the extent that there is no discussion of the values and behavioral factors assumed and reflected in demand and supply – arguably, implicit values – the values and the subsequent behaviors become endogenous to the economic system. Explicit awareness of present behavioral assumptions inclusive of the "unlimited wants" of consumers, the profit maximization motivations of producers to meet investor returns, and the understated resource depletion resulting from externalized or understated costs offer the potential to modify active and embedded behavior.

Consumption choices are based on demand and supply of a good and are identified with satisfying a need or a want. The impact of consumption decisions can be significant when there is asymmetry of information; fundamentally, there is a relationship between economic and environmental outcomes and consumption choices. Purchases affect labor and environmental resource use. However, most purchase decisions are made through a market mechanism, where the consumer is not aware of the entire production process and waste is not a factor in the consumption decision. This limitation in information transparency often creates a discon-nect between the social and environmental justice sensitivities of a consumer and the realities of their consumption choice in enabling and maintaining the values that they espouse.

ECONOMIC LITERACY AND INTERNALIZING EXTERNALITIES

Equilibrium, the point at which demand, and supply are equal (see Figure 17.3) is assumed to yield a market outcome where resources are efficiently allocated; neither demand nor supply can be made better off without making the other worse off. The price at which the quantity demanded equals the quantity supplied is therefore expected to embody the cost associated with production, including return to the supplier and the benefit of consumption of the good or service. However, production and consumption are not limited to the transactional nature of exchange of the final good at the determined market price. In the process of production and consumption, there are costs that are not factored that impact the well-being of the economy at large and these are referenced as externalities. In essence, externalities arise when an individ-ual or firm engages in activities that influence the well-being of others and where no compen-sation is provided in exchange for the imposition. The lack of inclusion of externalities in the cost assessment or consumption expense of a particular good, leads to the undervaluing of that good and potential for both over-consumption and heightened waste. From the PPF perspec-tive, since prices are a signal of resource use, underpricing may lead to higher consumption, fostering overuse beyond natural regeneration rates and ultimately unsustainable outcomes, as most readily apparent in the speed of climate change.

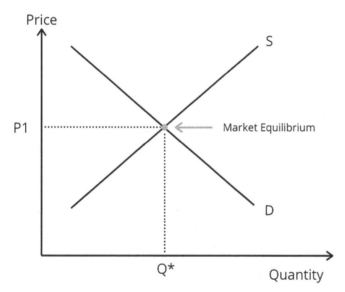

Source: Author.

Figure 17.3   *Market equilibrium*

Each step in a product's lifecycle may have costs that are not captured in price because firms have no incentive to include costs that they do not need to regulatorily address. Their focus is profit maximization (investor returns) and individuals presently are assumed to be incentivized to maximize consumption subject to an income constraint – the lower the prices the more of their insatiable desire to consume can be fulfilled. Lifecycle assessment enables evaluation of a process from the stance of an impartial bystander and given the pre-existing moral responsibility of the observer, offers the opportunity to internalize externalities in production and consumption that are contributors to environmental and social justice, attributes of sustainability.

Typically, externalities are characterized as negative, signifying that the externality yields an adverse outcome. These externalities are referenced as being negative externalities. However, there is a potential that a positive outcome could be generated, leading to a positive externality. In the discussion of externalities, it is often assumed that market participants perceive the externalities generated by their actions as acceptable due to their focus on the immediate gratification of their needs. For the producer, this equates to externalizing the cost of the disposal of waste products into waterways and the air, where no cost is directly borne to adversely impact profits, but arguably intertemporal costs can be assessed that may impact the enjoyment and longevity of multiple life forms and generations of human life. For the consumer, the externality can be evaluated in the indifference to waste creation at the point of the consumption decision or even the externalities associated with the production of the good or service being purchased, the supply chain. In the case of the former, the cost of the disposal of packaging material is typically marginal to zero, relatively negligible, but disposal creates a negative externality in the landfill, incinerator, or recycling plant that could have been avoided with a thoughtful exercise of demand. At present, the type of internalizing of externalities that has occurred has been limited to quantifying the externality to an overt cost. However, to the extent that the costs may remain understated, and the market mechanism is not cognizant and focused on the elimination of the externality-based cost but rather the minimization of overall costs, this process has yielded suboptimal outcomes. For example, assume that a firm produces ambient pollution because of the incineration of waste. If a governmental regulatory body institutes a fee or cost for pollution, effectively charging the firm for the ability to pollute the air, the producer can delegate responsibility for environmental stewardship to the price of pollution. Additionally, depending on the demand for the service offered, the producer may not only be able to transfer the costs now associated with polluting activity to the consumer, but may also be able to maintain the pollution level. The more the consumer needs the good, also referred to as being inelastic – limited price sensitivity – the more of the fee can be transferred. Assuming that the good is a necessity, the consumer will be inelastic to the change in price and maintain the need-based quantity of the good. In this example, the negative externality related to internalizing the cost has not changed. Instead, only the responsibility of pollution has been transferred to a cost, revenue to the regulating body has been generated, and the consumer has suffered erosion in her overall disposable income and purchasing power. The impact of the latter outcome may be an unexpected contractionary phenomenon to GDP as less money will be available for other consumption expenditures. Fundamentally, the consumer has continued to maintain demand because the complete impact of the externality being created by their consumption is not understood. Even in the case of inelastic demand, consumer awareness can promote regulatory intervention that yields a change in the product provided.

Externalities are defined as a type of market failure based on the premise that optimal social outcomes result from individual economic agents acting in self-interest. However, if instead of being a market failure, externalities could be evaluated to assess and develop an optimizing strategy between individual interests and enhanced social outcomes, externalities could be internalized within the market model as a preference. Perhaps externalities only indicate a lack of holistic awareness on the part of the consumer and producer or a cultural bias toward immediate gratification. These characteristics can be potentially modified through education. Optimal and universally acceptable strategies could then be adopted to promote sustainability. The success of this internalization strategy relies on the development of the educated rational economic agent as a consumer. If consumers are aware of the responsibility inherent in their consumption and are aware of the environmental and social impact of production processes, consumer demand can create the coalescing framework to augment preference to exhibit demand for sustainably produced products. The augmentation in demand does not allow for the opportunity of delegation of responsibility of pollution capacity to a cost or, alternatively, the incorporation within a cost minimization framework. As a result, the change in preference and subsequent modification in demand promotes the development of market outcomes that are environmentally and socially optimal from the position of what is supplied. From the perspective of the present discussion, economic literacy can be a tool in facilitating climate action.

MULTI-LEVEL STAKEHOLDER ENGAGEMENT: CLIMATE ACTION FOR SUSTAINABILITY

Given that the culture of expenditure as formed through a GDP-focused economic framework has affected stakeholders differently, depending on variations in demographic characteristics (e.g. age, sex, family status, education level, income, occupation, and race), religious and spiritual beliefs, length of residency and citizenship status, as well as other characteristics, education related to economic processes and the relationship between consumption-production and externalities may not be sufficient to foster common behavioral change related to environmental protection. Evidence suggests that even with consumers who identify as environmentally sensitive, cognitive dissonance, habit, access, and other limitations are related to the visibility of a value-action gap, where beliefs are not mimicked in actual behavior (Venkatesan et al., 2021).

Realistically, reducing information asymmetries to promote decision-making consistent with conscience and empathy is therefore necessary but not sufficient. Where education may be insufficient, stakeholder engagement recognizes the cognitive barriers created because of historical educational inequity, social norms, and other barriers observable in the value-action gap. Stakeholder engagement fundamentally requires education and information dissemination that is congruous with endogenized perceptions of "what's in it for me" and other manifestations of individualized decision-making prevalent because of prevailing and economic framework related cultural norms, along with other incentives that affect individual behavior, which may include a predisposition to community welfare. Simply stated, stakeholder engagement, recognizes that individuals and groups within society may be motivated by different objectives. In implementation, therefore, the process requires communication strategies that recognize the variation in incentives and incorporate these in fostering a common outcome that is beneficial to the whole.

The stakeholder engagement process identifies stakeholders in relation to their proximity to both the effect on the change being implemented as well as the impact of the targeted change to them. The structure, as provided in Figure 17.4, follows a multi-dimensional simultaneous process where change is being addressed at the micro (individual), meso (community), and macro (multi-community) levels based on the incentives that determine the operation of each level and alignment of these to a common outcome. From the perspective of environmental stewardship, these levels are increasingly apparent in the present US context both with respect to activism within each as well as the limited to lack of alignment across and within each strata.

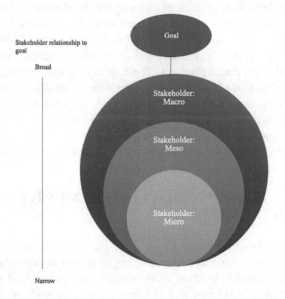

Source: Venkatesan et al. (2020).

Figure 17.4   Micro, meso, and macro levels of stakeholder engagement

On a micro level, grassroots activism has increased discussion on environmental degradation and sustainability (The Goldman Environmental Prize, 2021). However, a lack of common perception on the definition of sustainability as well as the approach to the environment (e.g., anthropocentric, ecosystem-centric) has yielded inconsistent outcomes. On a meso level, variations in perception of institutional purpose, for example in the business sector, have yielded to greenwashing, making it challenging to discern whether sustainable practices are operationalized, or sustainability is just a new form of marketing (River, 2021). Looking at the macro level, the prioritization of the environment is affected by the focus on economic growth, which due to resource utilization inherently affects resource utilization rates and can be argued as incompatible with achieving sustainability. This latter attribute also affects the legitimacy of profit-maximization and individual gratification without constraint other than income, effectively providing a common thread among stakeholder categories. From this perspective the measurement and framework of the economy offers an opportunity for alignment of incentives, providing a justification for both facilitating economic literacy across stakeholders and modification of economic evaluation to a sustainability aligned indicator, in lieu of GDP

(Fleurbaey, 2009). The actual process of engagement could follow that of Venkatesan et al. (2020) as provided in Table 17.1.

The multi-level stakeholder process incorporates the value of the process itself as opposed to the goal orientation of present engagement processes. The inclusion of continuous improvement in the stakeholder engagement process effectively reinforces the significance of the process of engagement and recognizes the dynamic aspect of engagement. From this perspective it can also be noted that stakeholder engagement for climate action is both educationally transformative and culturally transformative. To the extent that stakeholders understand the implication of GDP-focused economic policies on cultural norms, there is an opportunity to modify and align cultural norms with conscience-based decision-making that considers environmental parameters. In turn, by redefining societally acceptable behavioral standards with respect to the environment, inclusive of other species, there is the potential to establish an economic framework that aligns to these norms (dos Santos et al., 2017). So, instead of an economic framework determining economic activity, economic agents define the economic framework by engaging in activities that align to their values. Culture is defined by environmental understanding and defines the economic system to align to these sentiments and perceptions.

Table 17.1   Principles of stakeholder engagement

Identify the goal
Determine stakeholders and stratify stakeholders based on their relationship to the goal
Determine stakeholder incentives
Determine the appropriate communication channel for each stakeholder and map the relationship between stakeholders; use this mapping to develop a communication nomenclature that assures the broadest reach
Develop messaging strategies that align each stakeholder's incentive to the identified goal
Communicate the goal across stakeholders using education to promote the alignment of stakeholder interests with the goal
Facilitate communication across stakeholders to ensure that there is alignment across stakeholders with respect to a common goal
As the goal is being disseminated, assess stakeholders for ideas and suggestions, providing flexibility to augment the engagement process and the goal as new information surfaces
Maintain communication channels and facilitation of communication between groups even after the goal is reached to ensure continuous improvement and the long-term viability of the intention of the initial goal

Source: Venkatesan et al. (2020).

Specific to climate action, multi-level stakeholder engagement is a necessity. The American perception of climate change is characterized best as a range and is impacted by political perspective, social media, and availability of information as promoted by news outlets. These channels, along with others, limit information and critical engagement. For example, "in 2007, 71% of Americans believed burning fossil fuels would affect the climate. This share fell to 51% in 2009, and 44% in 2011" (Furlow and Braun, 2021). The IPCC report likely affected the 2007 perception, while later years highlight the effect of climate denier communications (Samantray and Pin, 2019).

Since 2011, the Paris Agreement and the subsequent Trump Administration's pro-growth stance in lieu of emissions reduction, fostered increased awareness of man-made climate change (Roberts, 2018, para. 8). In 2016, Pew Research noted that the influence of political alignment was most significant when comparing the far opposite ends of the spectrum:

> The stakes in climate debates seem particularly high to liberal Democrats because they are especially likely to believe that climate change will bring harms to the environment. Among this group, about six-in-ten say climate change will very likely bring more droughts, storms that are more severe, harm to animals and to plant life, and damage to shorelines from rising sea levels. By contrast, no more than about two-in-ten conservative Republicans consider any of these potential harms to be "very likely"; about half say each is either "not too" or "not at all" likely to occur. (Pew Research, 2016, para. 11)

As of 2021, according to a study from The Associated Press–NORC Center for Public Affairs Research and the Energy Policy Institute at the University of Chicago, there are stronger commonalities across party lines specific to the need for climate action. Although "more Democrats, 89 percent, are likely to agree that climate change is happening, than similarly minded Republican counterparts, 57 percent" (Knickmeyer et al., 2021, para. 15).

The challenge, correlation, and causation of the partisan divide lies not only in variations in inter-party-political biases but also in the increasing selection bias related to information dissemination. Further, the rise in social media, and media in general, has limited exposure to variety in viewpoints, promoting self-reinforcement of opinion and increased polarization in communication (Gladston and Wing, 2019). All these attributes provide the rationale for stakeholder engagement and the need for tailored communication strategies aligned to the incentives of stakeholder groups. The use of stakeholder engagement is commonplace in marketing but far less so in the realm of civic action where, arguably, it is the desire to avoid risk, an intangible, compared with garnering profit or material gratification, that is the focus. For this reason, stakeholder engagement for social change typically starts at the local level as the micro stage and moves upward as traction increases across local systems.

GRASSROOTS CLIMATE ACTION: CASE STUDY

Grassroots movements begin with the identification of an issue by an individual and they grow because of individual communication. Typically, a formation of a small group of individuals follows and a plan of action and goal are developed. All individuals involved are volunteers, although there may be a leader, and the motivation for involvement is in addressing a common issue. Given the size of the group relative to the issue, both intra-group and external communication are vital. Specific to the latter, because resources are limited to those donated by group members, media (i.e., newspapers, local television, radio), especially social media (i.e., Facebook, Instagram, Twitter) is a primary vehicle for marketing. The focus of communications is education to promote broader public interest in the issue, as well as perception of the group's influence and representation within its community.

As public interest and support in their goal increase, grassroots movements embody the democratic process. They promote collective action (Loh, 2003; Poulos, 2015). In the United States there have been numerous examples of grassroots activism, from the abolition of slavery to women's suffrage, to the fight for universal civil rights. These movements have also included more localized actions, such as Love Canal and the protection of the Grand Canyon. On a global level, the most well-known grassroots movement was started by Greta Thunberg in 2018. At that time, Greta, a 15-year-old schoolgirl, began her school strike for climate. Although her strike began alone, she was eventually joined by others and inspired a global mobilization to address Climate Change, #Fridays4Future (Fridays for Future, 2020). All these grassroots actions identified a failure to protect or provide acceptable standards as identified by an individual and/or the community that was affected. Further, all, ultimately, through the use of communication and media, created widespread awareness. Awareness, led to knowledge that inspired the interest of the collective whole to support the change, as demonstrated in the action of the government, which is, arguably, in a democratic system the reflection of society (Freudenberg and Steinsapir, 1991; Ferguson and Hirt, 2018).

In 2019, Sustainable Practices, a non-profit established in Barnstable County (Cape Cod) Massachusetts, initiated a plastic bottle ban campaign across the 15 towns that comprise the county. The sections that follow provide a foundation in the issue that initiated the movement, the use of economic literacy, and the process of engaging community stakeholders: consumer, businesses, and municipal government. The discussion provides a framework for grassroots action in promoting climate action, starting at the individual (micro), to the town (meso), and ultimately, the county (macro).

In recognition of the significance of education and aligned to the Principles of Stakeholder Engagement in Table 17.1, Sustainable Practices, initiated from the start of its efforts an education-focused outreach plan that addressed the variety of communication channels and interests among its stakeholders. The plan included social media: Facebook, Instagram and Twitter, websites; and grew to incorporate educational programming: podcasts, dedicated webpages, and routine public lectures with and without co-sponsors. The topics addressed economic literacy and common misconceptions in a reader-accessible format and highlighted the qualitative costs of single-use plastic bottle consumption across the product's life cycle: production, consumption, and disposal, as depicted in Figure 17.5.

Source: Sustainable Practices (2020).

Figure 17.5   *Life cycle of a plastic bottle*

In addressing the life cycle of single-use plastic bottles, the communication strategy actively addressed specific and overall product concerns, thereby allowing a targeting to specific stakeholder interests, concerns, and education needs. An example of stakeholder communications is provided in Table 17.2.

Table 17.2   Stakeholder communications: life cycle assessment of single-use plastic

Production: *What is the impact of plastic production on the climate?*

Oil and natural gas are the major raw materials used to manufacture plastics; these non-renewable resources are associated with adverse effects to the environment and human health (American Chemistry Council, 2019). An estimated 200,000 barrels of oil are used daily as either a direct or indirect input in the production of plastic packaging for the United States alone. The impact of single-use plastic bottles is significant.

With approximately 480 billion plastic bottles consumed in 2018 with an average size of 1 liter this means that the CO_2 footprint was between 67 billion and 192 billion kg of CO_2 per year. That is the equivalent of
• Driving 248 to 710 billion kilometers by car or the annual CO_2 output of about 5 to 74 million cars.
• The entire yearly CO_2 footprint of a nation like Greece (72 billion kg) or the Netherlands (175 billion kg) in 2017.
• Up to one third of the entire aviation industry (543 billion kg) (Tapp Water, 2019).

Emissions from plastics production and incineration could account for 56 gigatons of carbon between now and 2050. That's 56 billion tons, or almost 50 times the annual emissions of all of the coal power plants in the US (National Public Radio, 2019).

Consumption: *What are the impacts of single-use plastic on human health?*

From a human health perspective, plastic has the potential to leach the chemicals that comprise it into the food and beverages it holds. The most well-known of these chemicals is bisphenol-A (BPA), which was first used as a synthetic estrogen in the 1930s. During the plastic manufacturing process, not all BPA gets locked into chemical bonds; as a result, non-bonded, residual BPA can work itself free, especially when the plastic is heated, whether it's a baby bottle in the dishwasher, a food container in the microwave, or a test tube being sterilized in an autoclave. Bao et al. (2020) found a relationship between higher BPA ingestion and higher risk of death. In recent years, dozens of scientists around the globe have linked BPA to myriad health effects in rodents: mammary and prostate cancer, genital defects in males, early onset of puberty in females, obesity and even behavior problems such as attention-deficit hyperactivity disorder (Hinterthuer, 2008). Additional research is being conducted with respect to the connection between synthetic estrogens found in plastic and their impact on "the risks of heart attack, obesity and changes in the cardiovascular system" (Borrell, 2010).

Other chemicals in plastic, phthalates, are often used as softeners for PVC plastic, to make plastic more flexible. But phthalates have been found to be harmful to human health. Bis(2-ethylhexyl) phthalate (DEHP), Benzyl butyl phthalate (BBP), Dibutyl phthalate (DBP), and Diisobutyl phthalate (DIBP) are classified as endocrine disruptors that are toxic to reproduction, which means that they may damage fertility or the unborn child (European Chemicals Agency (ECHA), n.d.). Both BPAs and phthalates are found in plastic containers available on the market today.

New research is being conducted on the health impacts of single-use plastic in medical procedures. Specifically, phthalate chemicals that are used in medical devices have been associated with "alterations in autonomic regulation, heart rate variability, and cardiovascular reactivity" (Jaimes, 2017). Researchers caution that plastic use is not without an impact and may affect a patient's ability to recover from medical processes (American Heart Association News, 2019).

Disposal: *Isn't litter the problem and can't recycling help?*

Recycling was never, and is still not, the solution. This is because plastic comes in many different varieties, requiring each plastic to be recycled by a different process. There are also serious environmental, and human health impacts related to recycling. Recycling is not emissions free and emissions from plastic are toxic to both human and environmental health (Ecology Center, n.d.). Additionally, since the chemical structure of plastic degrades with recycling, virgin plastic is still needed to create a new single-use plastic bottle from recycled plastic. Further and for this reason, recycling is a downstream consumer-oriented activity; since more waste occurs in the production process, recycling is not sufficient to mitigate overall plastic waste (Monroe, 2014). Interestingly, the plastics industry itself has promoted plastic recyclability, "while continuing to promote the consumption of single-use plastics" (The Berkeley Ecology Center, 1996). Recycling, just like litter reduction activities, places the burden on the end consumer to eliminate waste but does not offer a solution to the plastic waste problem (Plumer, 2006). Both recycling and anti-litter programs promote an unsustainable production level at the cost of consumer and environmental health; the rationale, to promote profit.

Banning: *Won't this affect businesses and access to water?*

The question assumes that there are no costs associated with the sale of plastic bottles, but there are. Many communities are paying for the removal of plastic. The value of sorted plastic is dependent on the market for recycling. When manufacturing virgin plastic is cheaper, used plastic becomes an expense and plastic can get landfilled or burned instead. Outside this market cost are the human health care costs associated with the leaching of chemicals from plastic bottles and the environmental costs of the ingestion of plastic by land and sea animals. In humans, consumed plastic leachate is associated with endocrine disruption, fertility issues, ADHD, obesity, autoimmune disease, and cardiovascular disease; for animals, ingestion often results in death due to gastrointestinal blockage. Perhaps even more overlooked is the cost of greenhouse gas impacts related to the production of plastic. Plastic is expected to have a greater greenhouse gas footprint than the current coal industry by 2030 based on present consumption levels.

Should a product be sold, for which the revenue generated is subsidized by taxpayer dollars and the long-term health and well-being of human life, non-human life, and the Earth itself?

Sustainable Practices' educational outreach efforts have benefited from increased global action and reporting on the adverse impact of single-use plastic consumption. However, the connection between plastics and climate change has been slower in dissemination than issues of plastic litter. Despite the launch of the *Fossils, Plastics, & Petrochemical Feedstocks* report in 2017 by the Center for International Environmental Law, where the relationship between plastic and petrochemical companies was clearly stated and the prediction made that plastics would account for 20% of oil consumption by 2050, the composition of plastic and its production-based environmental risks remain largely unknown and undiscussed by the public (Center for International Environmental Law, 2017, pp. 5–6).

According to a study conducted by Genomatica, "Consumers are unaware that many products they use daily, from plastics to personal care products to gasoline, are made from crude oil" (Genomatica, 2019, para. 8); specific to plastic bottles, 44% did not know that petroleum was the source for the product. The limited understanding of where products come from alongside an interest in promoting sustainability provided an opportunity to connect individual behavior with climate action. However, variations in interest required active stakeholder engagement. For example, in 2021, the Pew Research Center reported that observable variations existed across the US population with respect to climate action and these could be attributed to age and even race, with those most likely to face climate impacts, the younger generation and economically vulnerable groups, most focused on the need for credible intervention (Funk, 2021). For Sustainable Practices, the urgency and legitimacy for climate action through plastic reduction was further legitimized by the August 2021 report from the IPCC and the connection between plastics and climate change reported by Beyond Plastics, which noted the expectation of the climate impact attributable to the petroleum industry will exceed coal by 2030 (Beyond Plastics, 2021, p. 7).

For its own localized engagement, the organization used newspapers: letters to the editor and opinion columns, as well as interviews; radio: local public radio and commercial stations; education opportunities: public libraries, public schools, churches, town events, and forums; and fundraisers. The communication channels promoted the same message but in language and venues that appealed to different constituents. All these channels culminated in mobilization for regulatory action while facilitating public awareness of the relationships between plastic production and greenhouse gases.

Sustainable Practices' outreach centered on fostering climate action specific to individual behavior change. The drafting and filing of by-laws in each town for town voting on banning single-use plastic water bottles then engaged an even wider audience. At each town meeting the organization was able to relay the climate and human health impact of present and expected future growth in plastic consumption, highlighting that as energy was going green, the risk that the carbon footprint may not decline was increasing with continued use of single-use plastic products.

With each passage across the 15 towns that comprise Cape Cod, the organization was able to take individual action to a collective county-wide level. By continuing the action town by town, the organization was also able to maintain communication with its increasing number of followers. This latter attribute aligns with the final principle of stakeholder engagement noted in Table 17.1. It has also promoted further and direct action on the climate by establishing the first county-wide effort.

FINAL COMMENTS

This chapter has provided a model for change that centers on education but also highlights the need for individual awareness of the significance of economic frameworks in both influencing and reinforcing cultural norms. The discussion provides an overview and methodology for stakeholder engagement that relies on a process-driven approach that incorporates continuous improvement. The most significant attribute of the discussion is the reliance on economic literacy as a tool for change. The limitation of this method is that there is a high cost of communicating with all stakeholders, and the ability of establishing alignment to a common outcome focused on sustainability may be challenged by the entrenchment of the social indicators of GDP (i.e., self-gratification and profit-maximization) on the part of some economic agents.

The benefit of the discussion, however, is the focus on the relationship between GDP and culture and the simplicity related to changing an economic measure relative to the holistic impact that this action creates. At the present time, there is discussion in regulatory and academic circles about the need to re-evaluate economic purpose. The move from a GDP indicator has already been implemented by a few countries, with New Zealand being the most recent. The modification in measure has resulted in the use of measures of well-being, happiness, and environmental protection to determine economic status. Additionally, given that these attributes are related to not just individual existence but the experience of an individual within a society, they are also aligned with fostering collectivism (Bahadur et al., 2013). Given that trust and collectivism are highly correlated, and trust is an indicator of resilience, the speed of climate change activity may be better addressed (i.e., mitigation, adaptation) by those communities that are culturally aligned and economically supported in being a collective (Ntontis et al., 2020). In other words, climate action is a first step, catalyzing community is a necessity.

REFERENCES

Altman, J. (2009). Contestations over development. In J. Altman & D. Martin (eds), *Power, Culture, Economy: Indigenous Australians and Mining* (Vol. 30, pp. 1–16). ANU Press. http://www.jstor.org/stable/j.ctt24h9wx.9.

American Chemistry Council. (2019). Plastics 101. https://plastics.americanchemistry.com/Plastics-101/.

American Heart Association News. (2019). Chemical widely used in medical plastic alters heart function in lab tests. https://www.heart.org/en/news/2019/07/31/chemical-widely-used-in-medical-plastic-alters-heart-function-in-lab-tests.

Armstrong, K. (1994). *A History of God: The 4000-year Quest of Judaism, Christianity and Islam*. New York, New York: Ballantine Books.

Bahadur, A.V., Ibrahim, M. & Tanner, T. (2013). Characterising resilience: Unpacking the concept for tackling climate change and development. *Climate and Development*, 5(1), 5565. https://doi.org/10.1080/17565529.2012.762334.

Ball, R. (2001). Individualism, collectivism, and economic development. *The Annals of the American Academy of Political and Social Science*, 573, 57–84. http://www.jstor.org/stable/1049015.

Bao, W., Liu, B., Rong, S., Dai, S.Y., Trasande, L. & Lehmler, H. (2020). Association between Bisphenol A exposure and risk of all-cause and cause-specific mortality in US adults. *JAMAOpen*, 3(8), e2011620.

Beyond Plastics. (2021). The new coal: Plastics & climate change. https://static1.squarespace.com/static/5eda91260bbb7e7a4bf528d8/t/616ef29221985319611a64e0/1634661022294/REPORT_The_New-Coal_Plastics_and_Climate-Change_10-21-2021.pdf.

Borrell, B. (2010). Bisphenol A link to heart disease confirmed. https://www.nature.com/news/2010/100113/full/news.2010.7.html.

Boushey, H. & Knudsen, H. (2021, July 9). *The Importance of Competition for the American Economy*. The White House. https://www.whitehouse.gov/cea/written-materials/2021/07/09/the-importance-of-competition-for-the-american-economy/.

Bradley, A.R. (2020). Biblical stewardship and economic progress. In T. Akram & S. Rashid (eds), *Faith, Finance, and Economy*. Cham: Palgrave Macmillan. https://doi.org/10.1007/978-3-030-38784-6_3.

Center for International Environmental Law. (2017). *Fossils, Plastics, & Petrochemical Feedstocks*. https://www.ciel.org/wp-content/uploads/2017/09/Fueling-Plastics-Fossils-Plastics-Petrochemical-Feedstocks.pdf.

Chung, P.S. & Duchrow, U. (2013). Epilogue: A theology of God's life and emancipation from greed and dominion. In *Church and Ethical Responsibility in the Midst of World Economy: Greed, Dominion, and Justice* (1st ed., pp. 265–280). The Lutterworth Press. https://doi.org/10.2307/j.ctt1cgfbzc.18.

Coscieme, L., Mortensen, L.F., Anderson, S., Ward, J., Donohue, I. & Sutton, P.C. (2020). Going beyond Gross Domestic Product as an indicator to bring coherence to the Sustainable Development Goals. *Journal of Cleaner Production*, 248, 286–296. https://www.sciencedirect.com/science/article/pii/S0959652619341022.

dos Santos Gaspar, J., Marques, A.C. & Fuinhas, J.A. (2017). The traditional energy-growth nexus: A comparison between sustainable development and economic growth approaches. *Ecological Indicators*, 75, 286–296. https://www.sciencedirect.com/science/article/pii/S1470160X16307531.

ECHA. (n.d.). Chemicals in plastic products. https://chemicalsinourlife.echa.europa.eu/chemicals-in-plastic-products

Ecology Center. (n.d.). PTF environmental impacts. https://ecologycenter.org/plastics/ptf/report3/

Federal Reserve Bank of Chicago. (2020, October 20). The Federal Reserve's Dual Mandate. https://www.chicagofed.org/research/dual-mandate/dual-mandate#:~:text=What%20is%20the%20dual%20mandate,longer%2Drun%20goals%20and%20strategies.

Ferguson, C. & Hirt, P. (2018). Power to the people: Grassroots advocacy for environmental protection and democratic governance. In C. Miller & J. Crane (eds), *The Nature of Hope: Grassroots Organizing, Environmental Justice, and Political Change* (pp. 52–76). Louisville, Colorado: University Press of Colorado.

Fleurbaey, M. (2009). Beyond GDP: The quest for a measure of social welfare. *Journal of Economic Literature*, 47(4), 1029–1075. http://www.jstor.org/stable/40651532.

Freudenberg, N. & Steinsapir, C. (1991). Not in our backyards: The grassroots environmental movement. *Society & Natural Resources*, 4(3), 235–245.

Friedman, M. (1970). A Friedman doctrine – the social responsibility of business is to increase its profits. *New York Times*. https://www.nytimes.com/1970/09/13/archives/a-friedman-doctrine-the-social-responsibility-of-business-is-to.html.

Fridays for Future. (2020). https://fridaysforfuture.org/what-we-do/who-we-are/.

Funk, C. (2021, May 26). Key findings: How Americans' attitudes about climate change differ by generation, party and other factors. Pew Research Center. Retrieved from https://www.pewresearch.org/fact-tank/2021/05/26/key-findings-how-americans-attitudes-about-climate-change-differ-by-generation-party-and-other-factors/.

Furlow, J. & Braun, M. (2021). America's polarized politics of climate change. *Intereconomics*, 2021(6). https://www.intereconomics.eu/contents/year/2021/number/6/article/america-s-polarized-politics-of-climate-change.html.

Ge, M., Friedrich, J. & Damassa, T. (2014). 6 graphs explain world top 10 emitters. http://www.wri.org/blog/2014/11/6-graphsexplain-world%E2%80%99s-top-10-emitters.

Genomatica. (2019). Consumers agree: It's too hard to be sustainable. https://www.genomatica.com/consumers-surprised-everyday-products-made-from-crude-oil/.

Gladston, I. & Wing, T. (2019). *Social Media and Public Polarization over Climate Change in the United States*. Climate Institute. https://climate.org/wp-content/uploads/2019/08/Social-Media-and-Public-Polarization-over-Climate-Change.pdf

Hinterthuer, A. (2008). Safety dance over plastic. *Scientific American*, 299(3), 108–111.

Intergovernmental Panel on Climate Change. (2021). Summary for policymakers. In V. MassonDelmotte, P. Zhai, A. Pirani, S.L. Connors, C. Péan, S. Berger, N. Caud, Y. Chen, L. Goldfarb, M.I. Gomis, M. Huang, K. Leitzell, E. Lonnoy, J.B.R. Matthews, T.K. Maycock, T. Waterfield, O. Yelekçi, R. Yu & B. Zhou (eds), *Climate Change 2021: The Physical Science Basis. Contribution of Working Group I to the Sixth Assessment Report of the Intergovernmental Panel on Climate Change*. Cambridge University Press. https://www.ipcc.ch/report/ar6/wg1/downloads/report/IPCC_AR6_WGI_SPM.pdf.

Jaimes III, R., Swiercz, A., Sherman, M., Muselimyan, N., Marvar, P.J. & Posnack, N.G. (2017). Plastics and cardiovascular health: Phthalates may disrupt heart rate variability and cardiovascular reactivity. *American Journal of Physiology, Heart and Circulatory Physiology*, 313(5).

Janardhanan, N., Nishioka, S. & Zusman, E. (2020). *Eco-resurgence for Asia: Invoking Indigenous Knowledge and Philosophy to Shape Economic Recovery and Sustainable Living*. Institute for Global Environmental Strategies. http://www.jstor.org/stable/resrep29011.

Kawashima, Y. & Tone, R. (1983). Environmental policy in early America: A survey of colonial statutes. *Journal of Forest History*, 27(4), 168–179. https://doi.org/10.2307/4004898.

Knickmeyer, E., Swanaon, E. & Ellgren, N. (2021, October 26). Majority in US concerned about climate: AP-NORC/EPIC poll. AP News. https://apnews.com/article/climate-joe-biden-science-environment-and-nature-only-on-ap-1e48e3315d2e0b618ccaa4a8d466e057.

Loh, P. (2003). We must all be accountable in a grassroots movement. *Race, Poverty and the Environment*, 10(1), 28–28.

MacNeill, T. (2020). Indigenous sustainable development. In *Indigenous Cultures and Sustainable Development in Latin America*. Cham: Palgrave Macmillan. https://doi.org/10.1007/978-3-030-37023-7_11.

Mgaloblishvili, A. (2018). Beyond neoclassical economics: The impact of religion on the Economic disparity between Georgia and Estonia. *Baltic Journal of European Studies Tallinn University of Technology*, 8(2). doi: 10.1515/bjes-2018-0014.

Monroe, L. (2014). Tailoring product stewardship and extended producer responsibility to prevent marine plastic pollution. *Tulane Environmental Law Journal*, 27(2), 219–236.

National Public Radio. (2019). Plastic has a carbon footprint but that isn't the whole story, all things considered. https://www.npr.org/2019/07/09/735848489/plastic-has-a-big-carbon-footprint-but-that-isnt-the-whole-story.

Ntontis, E., Drury, J., Amlôt, R., Rubin, G.J. & Williams, R. (2020). What lies beyond social capital? The role of social psychology in building community resilience to climate change. *Traumatology*, 26(3), 253–265. https://doi.org/10.1037/trm0000221.

OECD. (2002, May 16). Sustainable development. Indicators to measure decoupling of environmental pressure from economic growth. https://www.oecd.org/officialdocuments/publicdisplaydocumentpdf/?doclanguage=en&cote=sg/sd(2002)1/final.

OECD. (2021, December 1). Environmental considerations in competition enforcement. https://one.oecd.org/document/DAF/COMP(2021)4/en/pdf.

OWID. (2021, December 1). Cumulative carbon dioxide emissions from fossil fuel combustion worldwide from 1750 to 2020, by major country (in billion metric tons) [Graph]. In *Statista*. Retrieved December 19, 2022. https://www-statista-com.ezproxy.neu.edu/statistics/1007454/cumulative-co2-emissions-worldwide-by-country/.

Pew Research. (2016, October 4). The politics of climate. https://www.pewresearch.org/science/2016/10/04/the-politics-of-climate/.

Plumer, B. (2006). The origins of anti-litter campaigns. https://www.motherjones.com/politics/2006/05/origins-anti-litter-campaigns/.

Poulos, H. (2015). How do grassroots environmental protests incite innovation? In C. Hager & M. Haddad (eds), *Nimby is Beautiful: Cases of Local Activism and Environmental Innovation Around the World* (pp. 15–32). New York, New York: Berghahn Books.

River, B. (2021, April 29). The Increasing Dangers of Corporate Greenwashing in the Era of Sustainability. *Forbes*. https://www.forbes.com/sites/beauriver/2021/04/29/the-increasing-dangers-of-corporate-greenwashing-in-the-era-of-sustainability/?sh=1d8b92814a32.

Roberts, T. (2018). One year since Trump's withdrawal from the Paris climate agreement. *Brookings*. https://www.brookings.edu/blog/planetpolicy/2018/06/01/one-year-since-trumps-withdrawal-from-the-paris-climate-agreement/

Samantray, A. & Pin, P. (2019). Credibility of climate change denial in social media. *Palgrave Communications*, 5(127). https://doi.org/10.1057/s41599-019-0344-4.

Samuels, W.J. (1987). Religion and economics: An historical perspective. *The Centennial Review*, 31(1), 47–57. http://www.jstor.org/stable/23740635.

Sen, A.K. (1994). *Economic Wealth and Moral Sentiments*. Zurich: Bank Hoffman.

Smith, A. (1759). *The Theory of Moral Sentiments*. London: Printed for A. Millar, and A. Kincaid and J. Bell, in Edinburgh.

Sustainable Practices. (2020). Life cycle of a plastic bottle. https://sustainablepracticesltd.org/bottle-ban.

Tapp Water. (2019). What is the carbon footprint of bottled water? https://tappwater.co/us/carbon-footprint-bottled-water/.

The Berkeley Ecology Center. (1996). The seven myths of "recycled" plastic. *Earth Island Journal*, 11(4), 26–26.

The Goldman Environmental Prize. (2021, September 21). How grassroots environmental activism has changed the course of history. https://www.goldmanprize.org/blog/grassroots-environmental-activism/.

Venkatesan, M., Dreyfuss-Wells, F., Nair, A., Pedersen, A. & Prasad, V. (2021). Evaluating conscious consumption: A discussion of a survey development process. *Sustainability*, 13. https://doi.org/10.3390/su13063339.

Venkatesan, M., Erickson, J. & Carmichael, C. (2020). The rationale and principles for engagement in an ecological economy. In R. Costanza, J. Erickson, J. Farley & I. Kubisewski (eds), *Sustainable Wellbeing Futures: A Research and Action Agenda for Ecological Economics*, 300–314. Cheltenham, UK and Northampton, MA, USA.

Wagner-Tsukamoto, S.A. (2017). The cities of Genesis: Religion, economics and the rise of modernity. *Textual Cultures*, 11(1/2), 206–245. https://www.jstor.org/stable/26662797.

White, Jr., L. (1967). The historical roots of our ecological crisis. *Science*, 155, 1203–1207.

Yackel-Juleen, M.L. (2021). "And god saw that it was good": Biblical and theological connections. In *Everyone Must Eat: Food, Sustainability, and Ministry* (Vol. 9, pp. 73–108). 1517 Media. https://doi.org/10.2307/j.ctvcb5b3t.6.

Index